VAh, Oct. 1998

Trade and Investment in China

The Chinese economy is one of the most important in the world. It has a tremendous growth rate and is the scene of massive foreign investment. China is under close scrutiny both as a market that could provide massive returns to investors and because of its potential to become the most powerful economy in Asia.

This new study examines the economic relationship between China and Europe, its importance and how it is likely to evolve. The book is divided into three parts; the first covering the flow of trade, direct investment and technology transfer. The second presents case studies of manufacturing and service industries – automobiles, toys, watches, telecommunications, banking and insurance – where the bilateral relationship is particularly strong. The third assesses the strengths and weaknesses of the current relationship, and speculates about its future prospects.

The trade relationship between Europe and China is being re-evaluated by both sides and this book is a valuable contribution to that process. Sino-European relations are of great contemporary and future interest not only to Europe and China, but also to commentators, competitors and governments in the United States, Japan and elsewhere in Asia.

Roger Strange is Senior Lecturer in Economics, The Management Centre, King's College London. **Jim Slater** is Director of the Graduate Centre of the Birmingham Business School. **Limin Wang** is Lecturer in Economics, The Management Centre, King's College London.

Routledge Studies in the Growth Economies of Asia

1. **The changing capital markets of East Asia**
   Edited by Ky Cao
2. **Financial reform in China**
   Edited by On Kit Tam
3. **Women and industrialization in Asia**
   Edited by Susan Horton
4. **Japan's trade policy**
   Action or reaction?
   Yumiko Mikanagi
5. **The Japanese election system**
   Three analytical perspectives
   Junichiro Wada
6. **The economics of the latecomers**
   Catching-up, technology transfer and institutions in Germany, Japan and South Korea
   Jang-Sup Shin
7. **Industrialization in Malaysia**
   Import substitution and infant industry performance
   Rokiah Alavi
8. **Economic development in twentieth-century East Asia**
   The international context
   Edited by Aiko Ikeo
9. **The politics of economic development in Indonesia**
   Contending perspectives
   Edited by Ian Chalmers and Vedi Hadiz
10. **Studies in the economic history of the Pacific Rim**
    Edited by Sally M. Miller, A.J.H. Latham and Dennis O. Flynn
11. **Workers and the state in new order Indonesia**
    Vedi R. Hadiz
12. **The Japanese foreign exchange market**
    Beate Reszat
13. **Exchange rate policies in emerging Asian countries**
    Edited by Stefan Collignon, Jean Pisani-Ferry and Yung Chul Park
14. **Chinese firms and technology in the reform era**
    Yizheng Shi
15. **Japanese views on economic development**
    Diverse paths to the market
    Kenichi Ohno and Izumi Ohno
16. **Technological capabilities and export success in Asia**
    Edited by Dieter Ernst Tom Ganiatsos and Lynn Mytelka
17. **Trade and investment in China**
    The European experience
    Edited by Roger Strange, Jim Slater and Limin Wang
18. **Technology and innovation in Japan**
    Policy and management for the 21st century
    Edited by Martin Hemmert and Christian Oberländer
19. **Trade policy issues in Asian development**
    Prema-chandra Athukorala
20. **Economic integration in the Asia Pacific region**
    Ippei Yamazawa

Trade and Investment in China
The European experience

Edited by Roger Strange, Jim Slater and Limin Wang

London and New York

First published 1998 by Routledge
11 New Fetter Lane, London EC4P 4EE

Simultaneously published in the USA and Canada
by Routledge
29 West 35th Street, New York, NY 10001

In editorial matter and selection, © 1998 Roger Strange, Jim
Slater and Limin Wang, in individual contributions, © 1998
the contributors

Typeset in Times by Pure Tech India Ltd, Pondicherry
Printed and bound in Great Britain by Biddles Ltd,
Guildford and Kings Lynn

All rights reserved. No part of this book may be reprinted or
reproduced or utilised in any form or by any electronic,
mechanical, or other means, now known or hereafter invented,
including photocopying and recording, or in any information
storage or retrieval system, without permission in writing from
the publishers.

British Library Cataloguing in Publication Data
A catalogue record for this book is available from the British Library

Library of Congress Cataloguing in Publication Data

Strange, Roger.
Trade and investment in China : the European experience / Roger
Strange, Jim Slater, and Limin Wang.
p.   cm. – (Growth economies of Asia)
Includes bibliographical references and index.
1. China–Commerce–Europe.   2. Europe–Commerce–China.
3. Investments, European–China.   I. Slater, Jim, 1947–   .
II. Wang, Limin, 1963–   . III. Title. IV. Series: Growth
economics of Asia series.
HF3838.E8S77   1998
382′.095104–dc21   97-43912
CIP

ISBN 0-415-18267-0

Contents

List of figures	vii
List of tables	viii
Notes on contributors	xii
Abbreviations	xvi

Introduction   1

1   Trade and investment in China   7
      Roger Strange

Section I
The trade and investment environment

2   Foreign trade and investment: policy reforms in China in the mid-1990s   45
      M. John Foster

3   EU trade policy towards China   59
      Roger Strange

4   Regionalism in Asia and its impact on Sino-European trade   81
      Richard Pomfret

5   Europe's role in the transfer of technology to China   98
      Paul Whitla and Howard Davies

6   The technology intensiveness of China's trade with the European Union   114
      Jian Chen, Roger Strange and Limin Wang

Section II
Industry studies

7   European involvement in the automotive industry in China   131
      Gordon Robinson and Ian Stones

vi Contents

8   Kids' stuff: the organisation and politics of the China–EU
    trade in toys   147
    Jim Newton and Lai-hing Tse

9   The persistence of key capabilities in flexible production
    networks: the watch industry in Switzerland and Hong
    Kong/China   166
    Howard Davies

10 European multinational strategy in telecommunications
    services in China   188
    Jeremy Clegg, Syed Kamall and Wai-Shau Mary Leung

11 The choice of market-servicing mode for European banks
    in China   207
    Peter Chi-Ming Fu

12 The insurance industry in China: the experience of
    European, US and Japanese firms   228
    Xiaohong Wu and Roger Strange

Section III
Future prospects and conclusions

13 Outward investment from China   269
    Jim Slater

14 Conclusions: an assessment of the strengths of the
    current and the future economic relationships between
    China and Europe   284
    Jim Slater

Appendices

Appendix A   291
Appendix B   294
Appendix C   296

Index   302

Figures

8.1	Levels of hierarchy in the commodity chain of the toy trade between the European Union and China	155
11.1	A schematic representation of entry choice factors	214
12.1	Underwriting and trading ratios of PICC, 1980–94	239
12.2	Underwriting ratio of PICC in comparison to that of USA, Japan, and UK markets (non-life), 1980–95	240
12.3	Insurance penetration in China, 1987–95	241
13.1	Geographical distribution of China's outward direct investment, 1979–94 (%)	275
13.2	Geographical distribution of China's 'non-trade' outward direct investment, 1979–92 (%)	275
13.3	Geographical distribution of China's 'total' outward direct investment, 1979–92 (%)	276
13.4	Sectoral distribution of China's outward direct investment, 1980–94 (%)	277

Tables

1.1	China's external trade, 1980–96	9
1.2	Hong Kong's external trade, 1975–96 (HK$m)	13
1.3	Hong Kong re-exports by origin, 1975–95 (HK$m)	14
1.4	Re-exports of China origin by country of destination, 1975–95 (HK$m)	15
1.5	Re-exports through Hong Kong by destination, 1975–96 (HK$m)	16
1.6	Re-exports destined for China by country of origin, 1977–95 (HK$m)	17
1.7	Re-export trade through Hong Kong to/from China, 1978–95 (US$m)	19
1.8	Importance of outward processing trade for Hong Kong, 1989–95	20
1.9	Reported trade between the European Union and China, 1978–95 (US$m)	22
1.10	Adjusted EU trade surplus with China, 1978–95 (US$m)	23
1.11	Importance of Sino-EU trade to both partners, 1978–95	25
1.12	Foreign direct investment in China, 1979–95 (US$m)	27
1.13	Foreign direct investment in China, by country of investor, 1985–95	28
1.14	China's foreign trade, by type of foreign-investment enterprise, 1993–96 (US$m)	31
1.15	China's foreign trade involving foreign-investment enterprises, by customs regime, 1995–96 (US$m)	33
3.1	Benefits to China under the EU Generalised System of Preferences, 1981–95	66
3.2	EU anti-dumping investigations concerning imports from China, 1979–96	70
4.1	Statistical profile of the member countries of ASEAN, ECO, and SAARC, 1994	82
4.2	China's trade with the member countries of ASEAN, ECO, and SAARC, 1995	94
5.1	China's technology import contracts by mode, 1981–95	104

Tables ix

5.2	China's technology import contracts from five European nations, the United States and Japan, 1985–95 (US$m)	105
5.3	Average values of China's technology import contracts from five European nations, the United States and Japan, 1987–95	106
5.4	Technology import contracts and realised foreign direct investment in China, 1983–95 (US$m)	107
5.5	Alternative forms of foreign direct investment in China, 1989–95 (US$bn)	108
5.6	China's top joint ventures in 1994	110
6.1	China's trade (according to China's customs statistics) with selected partners, 1981–96 (as % of total China trade)	116
6.2	Importance of re-exports through Hong Kong for China's total trade, 1980–96	117
6.3	China's imports (adjusted for re-exports through Hong Kong) from selected trading partners, 1988 and 1994	119
6.4	China's exports (adjusted for re-exports through Hong Kong) to selected trading partners, 1988 and 1994	120
6.5	Technology composition of China's imports from selected trading partners, 1988 and 1994 (as % of total exports to China for each exporting country)	121
6.6	Technology composition of China's exports to selected trading partners, 1988 and 1994 (as % of total imports from China for each importing country)	123
6.7	Technology composition of re-exports to/from China through Hong Kong from/to selected trading partners, 1988 and 1994	124
6.8	Importance of re-exports relative to total exports to China for selected trading partners, 1988 and 1994 (as % of total exports of each type of commodity by the country concerned)	125
6.9	Importance of re-exports relative to total imports from China for selected trading partners, 1988 and 1994 (as % of total imports of each type of commodity by the country concerned)	126
8.1a	World exports of toys and indoor games (SITC 8942), 1970–93 (US$m)	151
8.1b	World exports of toys, sporting goods etc. (SITC 894, 1989–95 (US$m)	152
8.2	Numbers of establishments and persons employed in Hong Kong's toy industry, 1960–95	153
8.3	Hong Kong's domestic exports and re-exports of toys, 1982–96 (HK$m)	154
8.4	EU imports of toys from China, 1992–94 (million ecu)	
9.1	Structure of the Swiss watch industry (1970s)	172

9.2	Production levels and export prices for the watch industries in Switzerland, Hong Kong and Japan	178
9.3	Hong Kong's larger watch companies	183
10.1	Key European entrants in Chinese telecommunications equipment manufacturing and construction operations, and main foreign rivals	199
10.2	Key European entrants in Chinese telecommunications services, and main foreign rivals	202
11.1	Capital and assets requirements for the different types of foreign financial institutions in China	211
11.2	Scope of business for foreign-funded banks and foreign-funded finance companies in China	212
11.3	Growth of representative offices and management set-ups of foreign-funded financial institutions in China	213
11.4	Management set-ups of foreign-funded financial institutions in China	213
11.5	European banks with branches and representative offices in China	216
11.6	European banks with joint ventures in China	217
11.7	European banks with representative offices in China	218
11.8	Country risk rankings for selected countries	220
12.1	International entry modes in the insurance industry	230
12.2	Major companies in China's insurance market	242
12.3	Licensed foreign insurance companies in China	248
12.4	Strategies to obtain operating licences, analysed by nationality of the foreign insurer	251
12.5	Selection criteria for joint venture partner, analysed by nationality of the foreign insurer	254
12.6	Determinants of location choice, analysed by nationality of the foreign insurer	257
12.7	Favoured locations for representative offices, analysed by nationality of the foreign insurer	258
13.1	China's outward direct investment, 1985–95	273
13.2	Ratio of outward to inward investment for China, 1985–94 (outward investment as % of inward investment)	273
13.3	Outward investment by developing Asian countries in the European Union, 1980 and 1992	278
13.4	Inward investment flows and stocks from China to Europe, by country, 1984–93	279
13.5	Cumulative FDI in Central and Eastern European countries in which China is a principal investor (US$m)	279
13.6	Numbers of Chinese students studying overseas, 1976–94	280

13.7	Numbers of Chinese students studying in three Anglophone countries (USA, UK, Australia), 1988–94	280
A1	Calculation of EU exports to China, 1978–95 (US$m)	291
A2	Calculation of EU imports from China, 1978–95 (US$m)	292
A3	Adjusted bilateral trade balances for selected EU Member States with China, 1978–95, (US$m)	293
C1	Representative offices and branches of foreign insurance companies in China	296
C2	Representative offices and branches of foreign insurance brokers in China	301

Contributors

Jian Chen is a PhD student at King's College London, a research assistant at the London School of Economics, and a consultant in the MTM partnership whose business focuses on the Chinese economy. He holds an MBA from a leading university in China, and has been an Associate Professor at Henan University of Finance and Economics, China. He has also been a consultant to the Henan Provincial Government and other Chinese governmental organisations. He has published widely in China, and his current research interests focus on corporate governance, corporate finance, capital markets, and international trade.

Jeremy Clegg is Jean Monnet Senior Lecturer in European Integration and International Business Management at the Centre for International Business, University of Leeds (CIBUL). His publications are in the subject area of foreign direct investment (FDI) and the multinational enterprise, particularly in the context of the European Union. His current research focuses on the relationship between EU market integration and FDI by US, Japanese, and European multinational firms. His collaborative research embraces the internationalisation of services, and market entry modes of multinational banks in Central and eastern Europe. He is a co-editor of *Internationalisation Strategies* (Macmillan, 1997).

Howard Davies is a Professor in the Department of Business Studies at the Hong Kong Polytechnic University where, at various times, he has been Head of Business Studies, Dean of the Faculty of Business, and Associate Dean. He is an economist by training and his published work includes textbooks on Managerial Economics and an edited book on *China Business: Context and Issues* (Longman Asia, 1995), as well as journal papers and book chapters on technology development, technology transfer, industrial policy, and business education.

M. John Foster is Assistant Dean of the Faculty of Business at Kingston University. He has worked in both the commercial and academic sectors, since studying Mathematics at Warwick and Liverpool. In 1990–93 he was

Senior Lecturer in Business and Management at the City University of Hong Kong. His research interests lie on the cusp between corporate strategy and operations research. Current projects include work on corporate strategy in East and Southeast Asia, the evaluation of FDI projects, and planning effectiveness measures.

Peter Chi-Ming Fu graduated from the University of Western Ontario, Canada, and also holds an MBA from the University of Hong Kong and a Postgraduate Diploma in Education from the Chinese University of Hong Kong. He is currently Senior Lecturer in the Division of Commerce at the City University of Hong Kong, and has been the subject leader of the Economics and Banking team and programme leader of the Higher Diploma in Banking and Financial Services. Prior to joining the City University he had experience of foreign exchange dealing and training in commercial banking. His research area is multinational banking in China.

Syed Kamall is a Strategy Consultant in the London consultancy firm OMEGA Partners, and was formerly an Economic and Social Research Council (ESRC) Management Research Fellow in International Business at the Centre for International Business, University of Leeds (CIBUL). He is an expert on the telecommunications industry worldwide, and was the recipient (with Jeremy Clegg) of an award financed by the Carnegie Bosch Institute for Applied Studies in International Management for research on 'Foreign Direct Investment and Organizational Change in the Hungarian telecommunications Industry'. He is the author of *Spicer's European Union Policy Briefings: Telecommunications* (Cartermill, 1996).

Wai-Shau Mary Leung is a postgraduate research student at the Centre for International Business, University of Leeds (CIBUL). Her research focuses on the telecommunications industry in China. She is currently involved in a project entitled 'The Prospects for Liberalisation and Foreign Investment in the Telecommunications Services Market in China: A Comparative Study of the UK and Hong Kong Experience' jointly financed by the UK/Hong Kong Joint Research Scheme of the British Council and the Research Grants Council of Hong Kong. She is the co-author of several papers on foreign business activity in the Chinese telecommunications industry.

Jim Newton is Lecturer in International Business at the University of Hong Kong's School of Business. He holds a PhD from the London School of Economics and, prior to taking up an academic career, was employed in a number of managerial positions in various countries. His research interests focus on the interaction of firm strategies and state policies in internationally traded sectors of the World Economy. He has a particular interest in travel and tourism, and also in those sectors that are of interest to the Asian economies.

Notes on contributors

Richard Pomfret has been Professor of Economics at the University of Adelaide since 1992. From 1979 to 1991 he was at the Johns Hopkins School of Advanced International Studies, and taught in Baltimore, Washington, Bologna and Nanjing. In 1993 he spent a year with the United Nations Economic and Social Commission for Asia and the Pacific, and he has worked as a consultant for the UNDP, the World Bank, and other international agencies. He has written fourteen books, most recently *The Economics of Regional Trading Arrangements* (Clarendon Press, 1997), and numerous journal articles on international trade and economic development.

Gordon Robinson teaches at the University of Birmingham's Business School and Department of Politics, and is also a Visiting Lecturer at Cranfield University. His main interests are in the fields of International Business, European Business and Politics, and Europe–Asian Business Relations which he teaches on a wide range of postgraduate courses outside the UK. He also consults to UK business.

Jim Slater is Director of the Graduate Centre for Business Administration at the University of Birmingham and has, since 1985, been responsible for the development of the MBA programme. He has extensive research and management education links in Europe, South East Asia, Africa and Latin America. His consultancy experience includes a number of private and public institutions in various countries. His present research is focused on foreign direct investment, and he is the co-editor of *Business Relationships with East Asia: The European Experience* (Routledge, 1997).

Ian Stones is a Marketing Analyst for the Electrical and Electronics Division of LucasVarity, one of the world's largest automotive components companies. Previously, he was an Analyst in the Corporate Strategic Planning Department, where part of his role involved analysis of developing markets, including China, in support of the company's operating business. He met his co-author, Gordon Robinson, while studying for his MBA at Birmingham Business School.

Roger Strange is Senior Lecturer in Economics, and formerly Head of the Management Centre at King's College London. He was the co-organiser of the conference held at King's College London in April 1996, at which most of the chapters in this volume were presented as papers. He has also edited a book containing some of the other papers from the conference, entitled *Management in China: The Experience of Foreign Businesses* which was published by Frank Cass in 1997, and which also appeared as a Special Issue of the *Asia Pacific Business Review*. He is the co-editor of *Business Relationships with East Asia: The European Experience* (Routledge, 1997) and the author of *Japanese Manufacturing Investment in Europe: Its Impact* *on the UK Economy* (Routledge, 1993). His research interests focus on trade and foreign direct investment, in particular with regard to the Chinese and Japanese economies.

Lai-hing Tse is an Assistant Research Officer at Lingnan College, Hong Kong. She was educated at the University of Hong Kong from where she received her B.Soc.Sci and M.Phil degrees. Her research interests include enterprise reform in China and the global production process. At present she is working on several projects that focus on service industry developments in Hong Kong.

Limin Wang obtained her BSc in Management Science from Northern Jiaotong University, Beijing in 1984, and was awarded her PhD in Economics from Southampton University in 1994. She has worked as a Research Officer on the China programme at the Suntory-Toyota International Centre for Economics and Related Disciplines (STICERD) at the London School of Economics, analysing the economic reforms in China. Subsequently, she held a lecturing position in the Economics Department at the University of Kent at Canterbury, before taking up her present position at the Management Centre, King's College London.

Paul Whitla is Lecturer in Marketing and International Business at Lingnan College, Hong Kong. He received his MBA from Manchester Business School and is currently a PhD candidate at the Hong Kong Polytechnic University. His current research interests centre around the internationalisation and globalisation of service industries, and the development of organisational capabilities within Chinese firms.

Xiaohong Wu is a PhD candidate at the Management Centre, King's College London. Her current research interests relate to international trade and investment, focusing on the strategic issues concerning foreign insurance businesses in China. She is a regular contributor to *Reactions* (a leading London-based insurance/reinsurance magazine) on insurance/reinsurance matters in Greater China, and has also contributed to the magazine's monthly newsletter, *Insurance in China*.

Abbreviations

AFIA	American Foreign Insurance Association
AFTA	ASEAN Free Trade Area
AIA	American International Insurance
AIG	American International Group
ANOVA	analysis of variance
APEC	Asia Pacific Economic Cooperation
ASEAN	Association of Southeast Asian Nations
ASEM	Asia–Europe meeting
bn	billion (1000 million)
CAD/CAM	computer-aided design/computer-aided manufacture
CER	Closer Economic Relations between Australia and New Zealand
CFBs	Chinese family businesses
cif	cost including insurance and freight
CIS	Commonwealth of Independent States
DTCs	deposit-taking companies
EAEC	East Asian Economic Caucus
EAGA	East Asian Growth Area
EC	European Community
ECO	Economic Cooperation Organization
ecu	European currency unit
EC92	European Community 1992 – i.e. the Single European Market programme
EIU	Economist Intelligence Unit
ETDZ	Economic and Technological Development Zone
EU	European Union
EU(12)	The twelve Member States of the European Union before 1995
EU(15)	The fifteen Member States of the European Union after 1995
EUROSTAT	Statistical Office of the European Union
FDI	foreign direct investment
FEAC	foreign exchange adjustment (swap) centre

FHKWTI	Federation of Hong Kong Watch Trades and Industries
FIE	Foreign investment enterprise
FMA	Factory Mutual Association
FMSS	foreign market servicing strategy
fob	free on board
FTC	foreign trade corporation
GATS	General Agreement on Trade in Services
GATT	General Agreement on Tariffs and Trade
GCC	Gulf Cooperation Council
GMS	Greater Mekong Sub-region
GDP	gross domestic product
GNP	gross national product
HDTZ	High-Technology Development Zone
HK	Hong Kong
HKCSD	Hong Kong Census and Statistics Department
HKPC	Hong Kong Productivity Council
HKQAA	Hong Kong Quality Assurance Association
ICCT	Industrial and Commercial Consolidated Tax (China)
IMF	International Monetary Fund
IPE	international political economy
JETRO	Japan External Trade Organization
JV	joint venture
LCD	liquid crystal display
LED	light-emitting diode
LIMRA	Life Insurance Marketing and Research Association
LOMA	Life Office Management Association Inc.
m	million
MFA	Multi-Fibre Agreement
MFN	most favoured nation
MNE	multinational enterprise (cf. TNC)
MOFERT	Ministry of Foreign Economic Relations and Trade (China)
MOFTEC	Ministry of Foreign Trade and Economic Co-operation (China)
MPT	Ministry of Posts and Telecommunications (China)
NAFTA	North American Free Trade Agreement
nes	not elsewhere specified
NIEs	newly industrialising economies
NIMEXE	Nomenclature of Goods for the External Trade Statistics of the European Community
OBM	own brand manufacturing
ODI	outward direct investment
OECD	Organisation for Economic Cooperation and Development
OEM	original equipment manufacturing
OJEC	*Official Journal of the European Communities*
OP	outward processing

OTA	Office of Technology Assessment (United States)
PBOC	People's Bank of China
PCBC	People's Construction Bank of China
PICC	People's Insurance Company of China
PPP	purchasing power parity
PRC	People's Republic of China
PTA	preferential trading arrangement
PTBs	post and telecommunications bureaux
R&D	research and development
Rmb	Renminbi
ROC	Republic of China
SA	Société Anonyme
SAARC	South Asian Association for Regional Cooperation
SAFE	State Administration of Foreign Exchange (China)
SAFIC	State Administration for Industry and Commerce
SCMP	*South China Morning Post*
SEM	Single European Market
SEZ	Special Economic Zone
SITC	Standard International Trade Classification
SME	small and medium enterprises
SMH	Société Suisse de Microeléctronique et d'Horlogerie
SRZ	sub-regional economic zone
TME	Toy Manufacturers of Europe
TNC	transnational corporation (cf. MNE)
UBAH	Union des Branches Annexes d'Horlogerie
UK	United Kingdom
UNCTAD	United Nations Conference on Trade and Development
US	United States
VAT	value-added tax
VNPT	Vietnam Posts and Telecommunications
WFOE	wholly foreign-owned enterprise
WTO	World Trade Organization
WWII	World War II

INTRODUCTION

How important is China as an economic partner for Europe? How important is Europe as an economic partner for China? How is the bilateral relationship likely to evolve? These are the key issues addressed in this book. The aggregate data provided by Roger Strange in Chapter 1 have suggested that European firms have not as yet engaged with China to the same extent as their US and Japanese counterparts. But there are two important caveats to this simple conclusion. The first is that the situation varies significantly by industrial sector and, in some sectors (e.g. automobiles), European firms are already playing a major role. And the second is that Sino-European relations are developing fast, and each partner is becoming more important for the other.

The chapters in this book are divided into three sections. The five chapters in the first section examine the policy framework for trade and investment relations between China and Europe, and the environment within which the relationship needs to develop. In Chapter 2 John Foster details the emerging policy framework within China with regard to foreign trade and foreign direct investment. He notes that the 'open-door' might perhaps be better categorised currently as a 'door which is not closed' but that, notwithstanding the plethora of detailed policies and attendant regulations, the underlying reality is that everything is 'open to negotiation'. The bottom line for the Chinese authorities is that foreign trade is perceived as vital to the continued development of the Chinese economy, and that increased FDI is seen as vital to growth of foreign trade.

The European Union is China's main economic partner within Europe, and EU firms have provided the overwhelming majority of European investment in China. In Chapter 3 Roger Strange traces the evolution of EU trade policy towards China from the early 1970s, through the establishment of official diplomatic relations in 1975 and the conclusion of the 1978 Trade Agreement, to the complex situation that exists in the mid-1990s. In so doing, he draws attention to the fact that the European Union is increasingly taking a much tougher stance on imports from China notwithstanding official rhetoric to the contrary, and to the confusion as to whether China should be classified as a developing economy or as a state-trading economy.

In Chapter 4 Richard Pomfret considers the issue of regionalism in Asia, and the options which would be available to China should its application for WTO membership be frustrated. He examines the increased interest in formal regional integration in Asia in the early 1990s, stimulated both by the spectre of regionalism in Western Europe and North America, and by the dissolution of the Soviet Union and the Eastern bloc. In addition, he considers the emergence of sub-regional economic zones which cross national boundaries but do not involve entire national economies. China's growth and opening-up have provided several examples of these new forms of economic integration (e.g. the Pearl River Delta, the Tumen River Area Development Project, and the Greater Mekong Subregion), and they in turn have facilitated the expansion of China's foreign trade and the development of neighbouring regions.

'The essence of the Open Door is a quest for accelerated economic development through the adaptation and diffusion of foreign technology' (Ho and Huenemann 1984: vii). But there are many different ways in which foreign technology may be brought in. In Chapter 5 Paul Whitla and Howard Davies consider the various possible channels through which technology transfer may be effected (e.g. FDI, licensing, equipment supply contracts), and the appropriateness of each in the Chinese situation. They outline China's historical experience of technology transfer since the formation of the People's Republic, and highlight various distinctions between European technology transfers and those from other foreign countries. Their broad conclusion is that Europe appears to have been 'punching beyond its weight', and has made a more significant contribution to Chinese technology imports than their share of funds flows would suggest.

The vital role of Hong Kong in China's trade has been noted, as has the differing commodity composition of the re-export trade to and from China. There are also major differences in the commodity composition of China's direct exports and imports. And these differences vary according to the trade partner. In Chapter 6 Jian Chen, Roger Strange and Limin Wang use unpublished disaggregated data on the re-export trade to/from China through Hong Kong to examine the technology intensiveness of China's trade with the European Union, the United States and with Japan, in comparison to China's trade with its Southeast Asian neighbours. Furthermore, they contrast the commodity composition of China's direct trade with that of the re-export trade through Hong Kong, and draw conclusions about Hong Kong's likely future role as an entrepôt.

The second section includes six detailed studies of Chinese industries where trade and investment with/from Europe have already proved significant, or where European firms have the potential to play a significant role in the future. Three of these studies are of manufacturing sectors (automobiles, toys, watches); and three are of service industries (telecommunications, banking, insurance). The toy and watch industries have been mainstays of China's industrial activity for some time, but it is in the other three industries where the future provides immense possibilities for European trade and economic cooperation. Needless to say, however, such possibilities have also come to the attention of other foreign businessmen.

Gordon Robinson and Ian Stones in Chapter 7 trace the development of China's car industry and examine the role that EU car producers and EU components suppliers have come to play in the domestic automotive industry. European firms (in particular Volkswagen, Peugeot and Citroen) have been in the vanguard of foreign investment in the car sector, and there is also huge potential demand for trucks, buses, coaches, and components. Robinson and Stones suggest that European firms are better placed to take advantage of these opportunities in one of China's 'pillar' industries than many of their US and Japanese counterparts, because political relations with most European governments are rather less fraught than relations between China and both the United States and Japan. Furthermore, they emphasise that the Chinese market is vital to the European car producers, as they do not have a volume presence in either North America or Pacific Asia and are in danger of being globally marginalised. These wider strategic considerations provide an additional imperative to entry into the Chinese market.

More than half the world's toys are now made in China. Ten years ago, the dominant production site was Hong Kong, but this position has changed as production has steadily been relocated to China. HK firms continue to play a significant role in the industry, however, through their widespread ownership of factories in China, and through their distribution (as part of the re-export trade) of Chinese-made toys to world markets. The European Union is a major importer of Chinese-made toys, and it has been estimated that almost half the toys sold in Europe have been made in China. In 1994, the EU trade policy towards China was amended, and restrictions imposed upon Chinese-made toys in the form of sudden and punitive quota reductions. This produced an apparently perverse reaction from European manufacturers who simultaneously supported Chinese protests and brought court actions against the European Commission and the European Council. In Chapter 8 Jim Newton and Lai-hing Tse explain the rationale for these policy changes and the subsequent reaction by the European manufacturers by identifying the nature of the commodity chain that links the elements of the toy production process. In so doing, they outline the structure of the toy industry in China, and review the structures and processes by which toys are supplied to the European market.

The upsurge in the development of sub-national economic zones in Asia has already been catalogued in the chapter by Richard Pomfret. At the industry level, such zones involve production networks of small firms, and have been presented as a new form of industrial organisation which offers a viable alternative to the hierarchy of the vertically integrated corporation. At the same time, the literature on strategic management has become increasingly interested in the concept of 'capabilities', which are difficult to reproduce resources which allow firms (or nations) to secure profitable market positions in the face of competition. In Chapter 9 Howard Davies uses the example of the watch industry in Switzerland and Hong Kong to show that production networks in the same industry in different locations can display widely different capabilities. Those capabilities are long-lived, arising from the accumulated experience of the firms involved, and they allow the participating firms to compete successfully as long as there are significant market niches for which those capabilities are well suited. However, if market conditions or technologies change significantly, requiring the development of new capabilities, the supposedly flexible networks tend to fail and it is only the larger and vertically integrated hierarchical firms which have been able to achieve flexibility in this broader sense. In the Jura region of Switzerland, the production network has an established capability in precision and micro-mechanical engineering but this has proved less valuable in the volume segment of the watch industry. In Hong Kong (and the adjoining Special Economic Zone of Shenzhen), the production network also has a well-established capability, but in 'merchant-manufacturing', which allows it to coordinate order-taking with the acquisition and assembly of components. Here, in a mirror-image of its Swiss counterpart, the network has been unable to upgrade itself to address higher value-added segments. In both cases, only the larger and more vertically integrated firms have shown the ability to assemble new and different sets of capabilities. Davies' conclusion is that, both in Europe and Hong Kong/China, a discriminating mix of sub-systems containing elements of both networked production and vertically integrated hierarchies is required for a high-performance industrial system.

In Chapter 10 Jeremy Clegg, Syed Kamall and Wai-Shau Mary Leung review the current state of multinational entry strategy in the telecommunications service industry in China, and seek to relate this to developments in the economic and regulatory environment. The Chinese telecommunications industry has seen a considerable amount of liberalisation in respect of inward FDI in manufacturing equipment supply and construction, but as yet the telecommunications service industry is highly constrained in respect of foreign participation. In the equipment manufacturing sector, around 90 per cent of foreign participation is in the form of joint ventures with domestic firms, and foreign participation is governed by a clear legal framework. In services provision, however, there is virtually no formal regulation, and actual commercial developments have tended to outrun the law and regulations. For example, several foreign firms have set up offices in China to provide services to the two domestic telecommunications services companies, i.e. to provide services by an indirect route. In particular, it is feasible to enter the market indirectly by providing products such as network building and construction. After construction of the network, operation in principle passes to the Chinese corporation, but it is possible for the foreign firm to maintain an interest in the operation and provision of services even after the completion of construction.

As international trade and investment activities in China continue to grow and diversify, there will be an increased need for foreign banks, particularly those from developed countries, to facilitate such activities both by channelling funds and by providing potential customers with information about Chinese industry and the economy. The presence of foreign banks in China will also promote competition, and provide models to their Chinese counterparts and hence stimulate efficiency gains. The banking sector in China has undergone significant changes in recent years, as the functions of the People's Bank of China have been clarified, the commercialisation of the specialised banks has progressed, and as restrictions on the participation of foreign financial institutions have been relaxed. In Chapter 11 Peter Chi-ming Fu outlines the liberalisation process of the Chinese banking sector, assesses the possible market entry modes for foreign banks, and details the European involvement to date.

The development of an insurance industry in China is also crucial to the future development of the domestic economy, not only as a means of generating funds for investment but also as a requirement for the reform of the social security system.[1] For foreign insurers, the potential of the market is enormous but, by the mid-1990s, the process of opening-up to foreign participation has been slow and partial as the Chinese authorities fear an adverse impact on economic development if entry is not 'orderly'. Licences to operate through branches or joint ventures are coveted by the foreign insurers, but approval by the Chinese authorities is far from automatic and must be earned. In Chapter 12 Xiaohong Wu and Roger Strange outline the development of the Chinese insurance industry up to the mid-1990s, and report the results of a questionnaire survey regarding the strategies adopted by foreign insurers in pursuit of these licences, their criteria for the selection of Chinese partners in joint ventures, and their criteria for deciding where to locate within China. They find some interesting differences between the responses of European insurers, and their US and Japanese counterparts.

The third and final section considers the future prospects in the bilateral relationship between China and Europe, and contains two chapters by Jim Slater. The first details the development of China's outward investment, in terms of both financial and human capital. This is a phenomenon which has received little attention, particularly in comparison to the volumes which have been written on inward investment, yet Chinese firms are increasingly looking to invest overseas in support of their wider corporate objectives. Furthermore, the burgeoning numbers of Chinese students studying abroad may give rise to a reverse transfer of tacit technological expertise if or when they eventually decide to return to their homeland – a form of technology transfer which does not show up in any statistics. The second pulls together the evidence presented in this book on the European experience of trade and investment in China, and speculates about the future development of the bilateral relationship into the twenty-first century.

NOTE

1 And reform of the social security system is essential for the further reform of Chinese State-owned enterprises. See Hussain and Zhuang (1997).

REFERENCES

Ho, S. and Huenemann, R. (1984) *China's Open Door Policy: The Quest for Foreign Technology and Capital*, Vancouver: University of Columbia Press.

Hussain, A. and Zhuang, J. (1997) 'Chinese State Enterprises and their Reform', in R. Strange (ed.) *Management in China: The Experience of Foreign Businesses*, Ilford: Frank Cass, pp.20–37.

1 Trade and investment in China

Roger Strange

INTRODUCTION

The past decade has witnessed many momentous events and far-reaching developments in the world economy. There has been the successful, if belated, conclusion of the Uruguay Round of multilateral trade negotiations in December 1993. The Round – the eighth and final to be held under the aegis of the General Agreement on Tariffs and Trade (GATT) – involved many developing countries for the first time. It resulted in a wide range of agreements – including one on textiles and clothing to replace the Multi-Fibre Agreement (MFA) – which were to be implemented from 1 January 1995. It also established a permanent body, the World Trade Organization (WTO), to oversee world trade in the future. There has been a proliferation of regional trading agreements of varying degrees of scope and ambition,[1] not only in Europe but also in North America, Central America, South America, Australasia, and Asia. The disintegration of the former Soviet Union, the reunification of Germany in October 1989, and the fall of the communist regimes in Bulgaria, Czechoslovakia, Hungary, Poland, and Romania have redrawn the political and economic map in Eastern Europe. Asia has become the most dynamic economic region in the world, although debate still continues over the reasons for the 'East Asian Miracle' (World Bank 1993) and over the role of trade and inward investment.

Foreign direct investment (FDI) has emerged as a major form of economic linkage not only between developed economies, but also between the developed and the developing economies. This emergence may be attributed to five major stimuli (Strange 1997). First, there has been a phenomenal expansion of FDI from Japan – initially towards Asia, then towards North America, then towards Europe, and latterly again towards Asia (and particularly towards China) – reflecting the growing internationalisation of the Japanese economy. Second, there have been moves towards regional integration which have given rise not only to greater intra-bloc FDI but also to greater FDI from firms outside the emerging blocs seeking to gain insider status. Third, there has been widespread liberalisation, notably of service industries, in many countries. Fourth, there has been a sea-change in the attitude of many developing countries, notably in South America and East Asia, towards FDI and, in particular, towards FDI as a source of capital, technological know-how, and managerial skills. As technology has become more sophisticated and the importance of tacit knowledge has increased, so too has the popularity of FDI as a vehicle for technology transfer. And fifth, there have been substantial developments in information technology which have not only made existing markets more accessible, but have also enabled the creation of new products and services and the development of new markets.

As the foremost trading bloc and the largest trading entity in the world, the European Community (EC) had a considerable influence on the outcome of the Uruguay Round, has been a significant catalyst in the evolving pattern of regional trading agreements, and is a major source of exports and direct investment to, as well as a major market for imports and direct investment from, the rest of the world. Recent events have reinforced the status of the European Union (EU): the completion of the Single European Market (SEM) in January 1993; the accession of Spain and Portugal (in 1986), and of Austria, Finland and Sweden (in 1995); the entry into force of the Treaty on European Union on 1 November 1993;[2] and the conclusion of the Europe Agreements with Bulgaria, Hungary, Poland, Romania, and the Czech and Slovak Republics in 1992–93, to name but a few of the more important developments. Furthermore, the completion of the internal market has also heralded a more *communautaire* approach to the Community's relations with third countries.

But perhaps the most significant development of all has been the emergence of the People's Republic of China (PRC) as a significant economic and political power. Since the instigation of its wide-ranging programme of economic reforms in the late 1970s, including the measures adopted to promote foreign trade and investment commonly referred to as the 'open-door' policy, the economic performance of China has been startling. Economic growth has averaged about 10 per cent p.a., and GDP per capita has trebled. With a GDP of US$630bn in 1994, China was already the seventh largest economy in the world[3] and optimistic predictions suggest it might become the largest early in the twenty-first century. Foreign trade has increased dramatically not only in absolute terms, but also in proportion to GDP and to world exports (see Table 1.1). In 1980, China's exports accounted for 6.0 per cent of GDP and only 0.9 per cent (ranked 27th in the world) of world exports. By 1995, China was a much more open economy with exports accounting for almost one-quarter of GDP, and 3.0 per cent (ranked 11th in the world) of world exports. This impressive growth of China's foreign trade has been accompanied by major changes in the domestic economy and by substantial inflows of foreign investment, and has been marked by significant changes in the provenance of China's imports and the destination of her exports. However, as will be discussed below, much of this trade growth has been associated with the establish-

Table 1.1 China's external trade, 1980–96

Year	Exports				Imports	
	Value US$m (a)	Growth rate (%)	as % of GDP (b)	as % of world exports (c)	Value US$m (a)	Growth rate (%)
1980	18,119	—	6.0	0.9	20,017	—
1981	22,007	21.5	7.7	1.1	22,015	9.9
1982	22,321	1.4	8.0	1.2	19,285	−12.4
1983	22,226	−0.4	7.5	1.2	21,390	10.9
1984	26,139	17.6	8.3	1.4	27,410	28.1
1985	27,350	4.6	9.5	1.4	42,252	54.2
1986	30,942	13.1	11.2	1.5	42,904	1.5
1987	39,437	27.5	13.0	1.6	43,216	0.7
1988	47,516	20.5	12.6	1.7	55,275	27.9
1989	52,538	10.6	12.2	1.7	59,140	7.0
1990	62,091	18.2	16.6	1.8	53,345	−9.8
1991	71,910	15.7	18.6	2.0	63,791	19.6
1992	84,940	18.2	18.5	2.3	80,585	26.3
1993	91,744	8.0	16.7	2.5	103,959	28.9
1994	121,006	31.9	23.6	2.9	115,615	11.3
1995	148,780	22.9	21.2	3.0	132,084	14.2
1996	151,066	1.5	18.5	2.9	138,838	5.1

Sources:
(a) *China's Customs Statistics* (various issues)
(b) *Almanac of China's Foreign Economic Relations and Trade 1994/95*, p. 498
   Almanac of China's Foreign Economic Relations and Trade 1996/97, p. 998
   Almanac of China's Foreign Economic Relations and Trade 1997/98, p. 967
(c) *Almanac of China's Foreign Economic Relations and Trade 1996/97*, p. 528
   Almanac of China's Foreign Economic Relations and Trade 1997/98, pp. 1000–7

ment of processing and assembly facilities in the southern provinces of China, and the effects upon domestic growth and development may well be relatively minor.

The sheer size of the Chinese economy and its enormous potential as a market have attracted the attention of businessmen, politicians, academics, etc. from all over the world.[4] No discussion of trade with China, or of direct investment in China, would be complete without a proper appreciation of the role that Hong Kong (HK) has played in China's 'open-door' policy. Indeed, it is perhaps more realistic to refer to the roles that Hong Kong has played: as financier, trading partner, middleman, and facilitator.[5] The financier role refers to Hong Kong's function as a provider of direct investment and foreign loans, and as a centre for loan syndication. The trading partner role refers to Hong Kong's domestic exports to, and imports retained from China, both in commodities and in services. In addition to this direct trade, however, Hong Kong also plays a vital and increasingly important role as a middleman both in commodities and services trade.[6] In commodity trade, Hong Kong functions both as an important entrepôt for China's indirect trade with the rest of the world and as a vital centre for transhipments. Furthermore, HK firms perform a significant brokerage function in China's direct trade. And Sung (1991a: 26) notes that:

> The dominant role of Hong Kong in direct foreign investment also conceals a middleman function. The investments of Taiwan and South Korea in China are concealed through Hong Kong subsidiaries, and multinational companies also like to test the Chinese investment environment through their Hong Kong subsidiaries.

Finally, the facilitator role refers to Hong Kong's function as a contact point for China with the outside world (and vice versa), as a conduit for market information and technology transfer to China, and as a market and production training ground for Chinese businesses.

This introductory chapter starts with an assessment of the vital middleman role that Hong Kong has played in trade with China, with particular attention given to the outward processing (OP) activities of HK firms. Estimates are provided for the bilateral trade balance between China and the European Union (EU), taking into account entrepôt trade through Hong Kong. The chapter continues with an assessment of the development of FDI in China, and the contribution of European firms to the inflow of investment. The importance of foreign-investment enterprises (FIEs) for China's trade is highlighted. Finally, the history of China's application to join the GATT/WTO is outlined, and suggestions made as to the likely outcome of the negotiations on China's accession.

THE ROLE OF HONG KONG

Hong Kong has long been an important trading partner for China. Between 1931 and 1938, imports from China accounted for 37 per cent of Hong Kong's total imports, and the Chinese market accounted for 40 per cent of Hong Kong's total exports. Four-fifths of the imports, and nine-tenths of the exports represented entrepôt trade, and accounted for 25 per cent and 19 per cent of China's exports and imports, respectively.[7] After World War II, HK exports (domestic and re-export combined) grew dramatically from US$71m in 1948 to US$221m (38 per cent of total Chinese imports) in 1950, stimulated by the Korean War and the closure of major Chinese ports after the 1949 revolution. However, on 18 May 1951, the UN introduced an embargo on the export of strategic commodities to China following the PRC's entry into the Korean War, and this led to a sharp fall in HK exports to the mainland. Furthermore, the establishment of the People's Republic presaged a reorientation of China's trade towards the communist countries, and a reduction in the import of consumer goods. HK exports to China dwindled to insignificant levels through the 1950s, the 1960s and the 1970s. In response, Hong Kong developed its own manufacturing base so as to generate domestic exports with the result that, by 1978, domestic exports accounted for over three-quarters of total HK exports. Re-exports to/from China accounted for a mere 7 per cent of total HK exports.

In contrast, the situation regarding HK imports from China proved remarkably stable. Throughout the 30-year period from 1948 to 1978, China supplied about 20 per cent of Hong Kong's total imports, largely consisting of foodstuffs and other necessities. In 1978, it was estimated that two-thirds of Hong Kong's imports from China were retained for domestic consumption, and that this trade accounted for about 15 per cent of China's total exports. Thus was the nature of trade between Hong Kong and China before the introduction of China's 'open-door' policy in December 1978. Since then, the overall volume of trade in both directions has increased considerably, not only in absolute terms but also in relation to each partner's trade with the rest of the world. Furthermore, there have been marked changes in the nature of the trade.

The Hong Kong trade statistics have, since 1959, differentiated between those goods which are exported from the domestic HK economy and those goods which originate in another country, are imported into Hong Kong, and are then sold in a third country. These latter goods are referred to as re-exports,[8] but are still regarded as part of the trade of Hong Kong because they are cleared through customs and a HK buyer takes legal possession of them. The imported goods may then be processed by the HK buyer before the goods are subsequently re-exported. The extent of the processing must, however, be relatively minor as otherwise the item would be classified as being of HK origin, and this might lead to its inclusion in quotas (as in the case of textiles and clothing) or to the granting/withdrawal of generalised and other preferences. In contrast to re-export, transhipment means that the goods are consigned directly from the country of origin to the buyer in the country of destination, though they may be stored temporarily or even change mode of transportation in Hong Kong. Transhipped goods do not clear customs in Hong Kong, and are therefore not registered as part of the trade of Hong Kong.

The Hong Kong Census and Statistics Department (HKCSD) has, since 1989, carried out an annual survey of re-export trade with a view to establishing the re-export margin, i.e. the difference between the value of goods imported into Hong Kong, and their value when subsequently re-exported from Hong Kong. This margin includes any processing costs in Hong Kong and the traders' profits and, as a percentage of the gross value of the re-exported goods, the HKCSD (Census and Statistics Department, Hong Kong 1996) found:[9]

- that the margin on goods of China origin was generally much higher than that on goods originating in other countries. This, the HKCSD suggested, was due to the fact that a large proportion of Hong Kong's re-exports of China origin was related to outward processing activities in China (see below).
- that the margin on goods of China origin had increased from 11.5 per cent in 1989, to 26.1 per cent in 1993, before dropping back to 24.9 per cent in 1994.
- that, in contrast, the margin on goods originating in other countries had decreased from 10.3 per cent in 1989 to 5.7 per cent in 1994.
- that the margins varied widely among different types of goods, and that consumer goods had the highest margin while raw materials and semi-manufactures had the smallest margin.

The HK statistics on imports include not only goods for domestic consumption but also those goods which are destined for re-export. Unfortunately, the aggregate data are not sub-divided, because traders are not required (and often it would be impossible) to provide information on whether imported goods are for local consumption or for re-exportation. Nevertheless, the value of imports for re-export may be estimated by subtracting the re-export margin from the value of re-exports; the imports retained for domestic consumption may then be estimated by the difference between the value of total imports and the value of imports for re-export. Estimates[10] of retained imports, and of imports for re-export, are provided in Table 1.2 for the years 1975–96.

Two points stand out. The first is the dramatic increase in the scale of Hong Kong's re-export trade, particularly since the mid-1980s. The share provided by domestic exports fell from over three-quarters of total exports in 1978, to under one-fifth by 1995. The second is the less dramatic, but still ever-increasing, proportion of Hong Kong's imports that are destined for re-export. This proportion has risen from less than 20 per cent in 1978, to more than 60 per cent in the mid-1990s. In short, these observations underscore Hong Kong's increasing importance through the 1980s and early 1990s as an entrepôt.

A substantial proportion of the contemporary re-export trade through Hong Kong is linked to China, either as a source (see Table 1.3), or as a market. Since the mid-1960s, China has always been the single most important source of HK re-exports although it only supplied just over one-quarter of Hong Kong's re-exports in 1975. Since then, China has risen steadily in importance and, by the mid-1990s, it was the source of almost 60 per cent of the total. If re-exports destined for China are deducted from the total, goods of China origin have accounted for over 80 per cent of the re-export trade destined for third countries from 1992 onwards. Much of this trade is linked to outward processing arrangements commissioned in Guangdong Province by HK companies (see the next section).

Table 1.2 Hong Kong's external trade, 1975–96 (HK$m)

Year	Exports			Imports				
	Total	Re-export	% of total	Domestic	Total	For re-export	% of total	Retained
1975	29832	6973	23.4	22859	33472	6276	18.7	27196
1976	41557	8928	21.5	32629	43293	8035	18.6	35258
1977	44833	9829	21.9	35004	48701	8846	18.2	39855
1978	53908	13197	24.5	40711	63056	11877	18.8	51179
1979	75934	20022	26.4	55912	85837	18020	21.0	67817
1980	98242	30072	30.6	68171	111651	27065	24.2	84586
1981	122163	41739	34.2	80423	138375	37565	27.1	100810
1982	127385	44353	34.8	83032	142893	39918	27.9	102975
1983	160699	56294	35.0	104405	175442	50665	28.9	124777
1984	221441	83504	37.7	137936	223370	75154	33.6	148216
1985	235152	105270	44.8	129882	231420	94743	40.9	136677
1986	276530	122546	44.3	153983	275955	110291	40.0	165664
1987	378034	182780	48.4	195254	377948	164502	43.5	213446
1988	493069	275405	55.9	217664	498798	247865	49.7	250934
1989	570509	346405	60.7	224104	562781	308466	54.8	254315
1990	639874	413999	64.7	225875	642530	352552	54.9	289978
1991	765886	534841	69.8	231045	778982	449744	57.7	329238
1992	924953	690829	74.7	234123	955295	571668	59.8	383627
1993	1046250	823224	78.7	223027	1072597	672269	62.7	400328
1994	1170013	947921	81.0	222092	1250709	789090	63.1	461619
1995	1344127	1112470	82.8	231657	1491121	929568	62.3	561553
1996	1397917	1185758	84.8	212160	1535582	989767	64.5	545815

Sources: *Hong Kong Review of Overseas Trade* (1977–1990)
 Annual Review of Hong Kong External Trade (1991–1995)

Notes:
Imports for re-export are estimated by deducting the re-export margin from the value of re-exports.
Retained imports are estimated as follows: = total imports − imports for re-export.

Japan has traditionally been the second largest source of HK re-exports, and its share rose above 20 per cent over the period 1981–85. Both the European Community and the United States accounted for about 12 per cent of re-exports in 1978, but the subsequent rise of OP trade from China has led to an approximate halving of the respective shares of these three countries/areas. In absolute value terms, re-exports from these three sources have all grown substantially but have been overshadowed by the massive growth of re-exports originating in China. Only Taiwan, of the major source countries, has increased its percentage share of total re-exports: 90 per cent of the re-exports originating in Taiwan are destined for China.

A breakdown of the destinations of the re-exports of China origin (see Table 1.4) shows that Indonesia and Singapore were the main markets in the mid-1970s, together accounting for almost 30 per cent of the total. The European Community only received 7 per cent of the Chinese re-exported goods in 1978, and the United States and Japan each accounted for about 8 per cent in 1975. The general pattern was that re-exports from China were

Table 1.3 Hong Kong re-exports by origin, 1975–95 (HK$m)

Year	Total re-exports	Percentage share of re-exports originating in:					HK re-exports destined for countries other than China (b)	Re-exports from China as % of HK re-exports destined for third countries
		China	Japan	Taiwan	USA	EU (a)		
1975	6973	25.0	17.3	2.8	13.9	—	6836	25.5
1976	8928	26.9	13.7	2.9	13.9	—	8805	27.3
1977	9829	25.4	17.7	3.7	12.7	—	9654	25.8
1978	13197	27.7	17.0	3.0	12.1	11.9	12983	28.2
1979	20022	28.3	16.9	4.5	11.4	9.8	18707	30.3
1980	30072	27.9	19.6	7.1	10.5	7.4	25430	33.0
1981	41739	30.7	20.1	8.1	9.7	6.4	33695	37.2
1982	44353	33.1	20.5	5.6	11.1	6.9	36361	38.9
1983	56294	35.0	20.7	4.6	10.7	7.0	44111	42.4
1984	83504	33.7	22.4	6.1	10.2	6.3	55440	46.9
1985	105270	32.9	21.4	9.1	9.0	7.1	59247	53.3
1986	122546	42.1	15.2	7.1	8.5	6.7	81652	58.0
1987	182780	46.1	13.5	6.9	7.4	5.9	122610	63.7
1988	275664	47.7	13.7	7.7	6.9	5.6	180510	67.9
1989	346406	54.3	11.3	7.8	6.4	5.3	242913	72.5
1990	413999	58.1	10.2	7.3	5.9	5.1	303091	74.7
1991	534841	59.0	10.7	7.8	5.0	4.7	381523	78.4
1992	690829	58.4	12.3	7.9	4.6	4.8	478724	80.1
1993	823224	57.6	13.4	7.9	4.5	5.3	548663	82.4
1994	947921	57.6	12.9	7.6	4.6	5.2	625086	83.0
1995	1112470	57.2	11.7	7.5	5.0	5.1	728427	82.4

Sources: *Hong Kong Review of Overseas Trade* (1977–1990)
Annual Review of Hong Kong External Trade (1991–1995)
Notes:
(a) The data for the European Union (EU) relate to the twelve Member States prior to 1995.
(b) Excluding goods from China re-exported to China.

mainly destined for other economies within Pacific Asia (including Australia), and that the European Union and the United States were of minor importance. One year after the adoption of the open-door policy and the situation was quite different. The United States took over as the main destination in 1979 (although Japan enjoyed a brief surge of popularity in 1978), and the proportion of Chinese re-exports routed to the United States climbed quickly to about one-third by the mid-1980s: a level which has remained relatively steady ever since. Meanwhile, the importance of Indonesia, Singapore and Taiwan has declined drastically. Apart from a brief surge in the late 1970s, Japan's share has been relatively steady at about 6–9 per cent of the total. As regards the European countries, Germany, the United Kingdom, France and the Netherlands have all emerged as major consumers of re-exported goods from China, and the European Community/Union has accounted for over one-fifth of the total since 1990. Thus, the United States and the European Union are now the major destinations for re-exports of China origin, while the Pacific Asia countries are of much reduced importance. Much of the goods re-exported to the United States, Japan and the European Union are clothing and apparel, footwear, toys, and other miscellaneous manufactured goods.

China is also a major destination for re-exports through Hong Kong (see Table 1.5) and, furthermore, its relative importance has increased significantly over the past twenty years. During the late 1970s before the adoption of the open-door policy, the proportion of Hong Kong's re-export trade destined for China was minimal (approximately 2 per cent of re-exports originating in third countries). The open-door policy had an immediate impact, and China took over 20 per cent of the re-exports originating in third countries in 1980 and over 60 per cent in 1985. Although there was a subsequent dip in this upward trend, the figures for 1996 show China as a destination for over 80 per cent of Hong Kong's re-export trade originating in third countries. As with the re-export trade originating in China, these

Table 1.4 Re-exports of China origin by country of destination, 1975–95 (HK$m)

Year	Total re-exports of China origin	Percentage share of re-exports destined for:						
		USA	Japan	Taiwan	EU	China	Singapore	Indonesia
1975	1743	8.0	7.8	7.4	—	—	13.8	15.9
1976	2402	10.2	9.4	8.0	—	—	10.5	16.7
1977	2492	11.3	10.1	6.0	—	—	11.4	16.7
1978	3659	10.2	18.7	6.0	7.0	—	9.4	12.1
1979	5663	13.0	12.4	4.9	9.1	—	8.9	12.0
1980	8394	20.1	7.0	4.7	9.3	—	7.1	11.9
1981	12834	21.9	8.9	3.3	8.8	2.3	6.4	10.0
1982	14694	24.3	6.1	3.7	6.9	3.8	6.4	10.4
1983	19680	28.0	5.6	3.5	6.3	5.0	6.0	8.3
1984	28107	31.2	7.6	3.6	6.7	7.5	4.2	5.4
1985	34628	32.5	8.3	2.6	9.1	8.9	3.5	3.7
1986	51597	36.2	6.3	2.2	10.8	8.2	3.1	3.5
1987	84266	32.9	6.7	2.7	15.5	7.3	2.4	2.2
1988	131525	32.9	8.5	2.8	18.1	6.8	2.1	1.6
1989	188271	35.1	8.0	2.4	19.2	6.4	1.8	1.3
1990	240410	34.0	6.7	2.5	23.3	5.8	1.6	1.4
1991	315689	32.9	6.6	2.8	24.6	5.2	1.6	1.0
1992	403782	34.7	7.1	2.2	23.7	5.0	1.6	0.8
1993	474007	35.5	7.5	1.8	23.6	4.6	1.8	0.8
1994	545831	35.9	8.3	1.8	21.9	5.0	2.1	0.8
1995	636392	33.6	9.3	1.9	21.7	5.7	2.5	0.7

Sources: *Hong Kong Review of Overseas Trade* (1977–1990)
Annual Review of Hong Kong External Trade (1991–1995)

Note:
The data for the European Union (EU) relate to the twelve Member States prior to 1995.

Table 1.5 Re-exports through Hong Kong by destination, 1975–96 (HK$m)

Year	Total re-exports	Percentage share of re-exports destined for:					HK re-exports originating in countries other than China	Re-exports to China as % of HK re-exports originating in third countries
		China	Japan	Taiwan	USA	EU (a)		(b)
1975	6973	2.0	13.8	8.6	8.0	6.9	5230	2.6
1976	8928	1.4	16.8	9.1	9.6	6.9	6526	1.9
1977	9829	1.8	13.6	8.9	9.0	7.2	7337	2.4
1978	13197	1.6	17.3	9.3	9.3	6.6	9538	2.2
1979	20022	6.6	12.4	8.6	10.0	8.8	14359	9.2
1980	30072	15.4	7.3	7.4	10.3	8.5	21678	21.4
1981	41739	19.3	6.7	5.8	11.5	6.5	28905	26.8
1982	44353	18.0	5.8	6.0	12.7	5.6	29659	25.1
1983	56294	21.6	5.6	6.1	14.3	5.3	36614	30.6
1984	83504	33.6	5.5	5.8	14.5	4.5	55397	46.9
1985	105270	43.7	5.2	4.1	14.0	4.9	70642	60.8
1986	122546	33.4	5.4	4.8	18.2	7.3	70949	51.7
1987	182780	32.9	5.3	5.3	17.8	9.7	98514	54.8
1988	275405	34.5	6.3	5.1	18.0	10.7	143880	59.7
1989	346405	29.9	6.4	4.8	20.8	12.1	158134	57.8
1990	413999	26.8	5.9	5.1	21.2	15.2	173589	55.8
1991	534841	28.7	5.5	4.6	20.7	15.9	219152	62.5
1992	690829	30.7	5.4	3.8	21.5	15.0	287047	66.9
1993	823224	33.4	5.4	2.7	21.9	14.5	349217	72.4
1994	947921	34.1	5.8	2.4	22.2	13.5	402090	73.6
1995	1112470	34.5	6.3	2.5	20.8	13.4	476078	73.1
1996	1185758	35.2	6.8	2.2	20.4	13.4	502244	83.2

Sources: *Hong Kong Review of Overseas Trade* (1977–1990)
Annual Review of Hong Kong External Trade (1991–1996)

Notes:
(a) The data for the European Union (EU) relate to the twelve Member States prior to 1995.
(b) Excluding re-exports to China that originated in China.

developments are linked to the growth of outward processing arrangements in Guangdong Province. The rising shares of re-exports destined for the European Union and the United States reflect the increased importance of these two markets as destinations for goods of China origin.

The main sources for the re-exports to China have been Japan, Taiwan, the United States, the European Union and the Republic of Korea (see Table 1.6). Except for a few years in the early 1980s, Japan and Taiwan have together provided over 40 per cent of the re-exports destined for China. Sung (1991a: 141) notes that the Taiwanese share soared in 1980 when China abolished tariffs on Taiwanese products – on the grounds that Taiwan was a part of China although tariffs were still levied on goods from Hong Kong. The resultant surge of orders put a strain on production

Table 1.6 Re-exports destined for China by country of origin, 1977–95 (HK$m)

Year	Total re-exports destined for China	Percentage share of re-exports originating in:					
		Japan	Taiwan	USA	EU	China	Korea
1977	175	12.6	0.1	15.4	—	—	—
1978	214	18.7	0.1	15.0	8.9	—	—
1979	1315	27.6	8.1	10.0	10.0	—	2.2
1980	4642	19.5	26.0	7.3	4.5	—	4.8
1981	8044	18.3	27.1	7.0	5.7	3.6	10.1
1982	7992	20.7	15.8	12.9	6.5	6.9	4.2
1983	12183	27.8	10.1	12.1	7.9	8.1	2.7
1984	28064	33.8	11.9	10.4	7.3	7.5	4.5
1985	46023	31.6	16.7	9.7	8.7	6.7	6.0
1986	40894	21.8	15.5	10.8	8.6	10.3	5.3
1987	60170	21.5	15.9	10.3	7.7	10.3	7.0
1988	94895	24.4	18.4	10.1	8.0	9.4	10.1
1989	103492	22.7	21.8	9.9	8.0	11.7	7.5
1990	110908	22.4	23.1	9.3	7.8	12.7	6.8
1991	153318	23.5	23.7	8.7	8.2	10.7	7.0
1992	212105	26.2	23.1	8.6	8.5	9.5	6.8
1993	274561	28.4	21.5	9.0	10.4	8.0	6.1
1994	322835	28.1	20.6	8.9	10.2	8.4	6.7
1995	384043	24.2	20.1	10.0	9.8	9.4	7.2

Sources: *Hong Kong Review of Overseas Trade* (1977–1990)
Annual Review of Hong Kong External Trade (1991–1995)
Note: The data for the European Union (EU) relate to the twelve Member States prior to 1995.

capacity, and many defective and low quality products were exported to China to meet demand. Taiwanese exports thus fell in 1983, but increased again in 1985. Taiwan's liberalisation of trade with China in 1988 prompted another rise in the Taiwanese share (Imai 1990; Wakabayashi 1990). The United States has provided 10 per cent on average of total re-exports destined for China, the European Union about 8–10 per cent, the Republic of Korea around 6–7 per cent, and China itself about 10 per cent. A substantial proportion of the trade to/from China consists of textile yarn, fabrics and clothing accessories.

Three final points should be stressed. First, re-exports through Hong Kong amounted to HK$1,112,470m (US$143,804m) in 1995. Some 54 per cent of these re-exports originated in China and were destined for third countries; 31 per cent originated in third countries and were destined for China; and a further 3 per cent came from China and were then re-exported back again. Thus, over 88 per cent of the re-export trade through Hong Kong in 1995 was linked to China, either as a source or as a destination. The comparable figure in 1978 was 29 per cent.

Second, the European Union and the United States together account for a modest 20 per cent of the re-exports destined for China, whereas they are the recipients of 50–60 per cent of the re-exports of China origin. In contrast, Japan and Taiwan account for almost half the re-exports destined for China, but are the destinations for only 10 per cent of the total re-export trade of China origin. In value terms (see Table 1.7) both the European Union and the United States are far more important as destinations for HK re-exports originating in China than as sources for HK re-exports destined for China. Japan, Taiwan and, to a lesser extent, Korea are rather more important as sources of re-exports to China than as markets for re-exports of China origin. Clearly, HK firms fulfil a different function *vis-à-vis* Sino-EU and Sino-US trade than they do in trade with Japan and Taiwan.

Third, the commodity composition of the re-export trade destined for China is quite different from that originating in China and, moreover, it varies by country of origin (see Chapter 6 for analysis). The main re-exports from China to the European Union, the United States and Japan are apparel (SITC84) and miscellaneous manufactured articles (SITC89), while re-exports in the opposite direction consist largely of electrical machinery, office machinery and telecommunications equipment (SITC75, 76 and 77). In contrast, textile yarn and fabrics make up about one-third of the re-exports from Taiwan to China, and plastics and specialised machinery are also important (SITC65, 57, 58 and 72). Textile yarn and fabrics account for almost 40 per cent of Korean re-exports to China.

PROCESSING AND ASSEMBLY ARRANGEMENTS IN CHINA

The legal framework for processing and assembly arrangements in China was established in 1979. Thereafter the State has sought to promote such arrangements through the priority approval of foreign exchange for the necessary imports, the direct allocation of the imported materials and components to the relevant export-producing firms, and the guarantee of appropriate supplies of domestic raw materials for these firms (Lardy 1993: 42). In 1984, the State Council approved two new schemes to promote exports based on processing and assembly arrangements, namely, 'processing with supplied materials' and 'processing with imported materials'. Under the former scheme, a Chinese enterprise is entitled to import free of duty all raw materials, components, etc. provided by a foreign supplier as part of an export contract. The Chinese enterprise does not take ownership of the imported components, but is paid a per unit fee for the processing activity it undertakes. The foreign firm is responsible for the marketing of the finished goods. The value of the exported goods is equal to the sum of the imported components plus the processing fee. In contrast, under the latter scheme, the Chinese enterprise is responsible for the marketing of the final products but does not take ownership of the materials, etc. – the materials, etc. may, however, still be imported free of duty (Lardy 1994: 112–14).

The importance of these two schemes for China's trade is considerable. Data for 1996 show that 'processing with supplied materials' ventures accounted for over US$17bn of imports (13 per cent of total imports) and

Table 1.7 Re-export trade through Hong Kong to/from China, 1978–95 (US$m)

Year	European Union			United States			Japan			Taiwan		
	To China	From China	EU surplus	To China	From China	US surplus	To China	From China	Japan surplus	To China	From China	Taiwan suplus
1978	4	55	−51	7	80	−73	9	146	−137	0	47	−47
1979	26	103	−77	26	147	−121	73	141	−68	21	56	−34
1980	42	156	−114	68	340	−272	182	118	64	242	79	164
1981	81	202	−121	101	503	−401	263	203	60	390	76	314
1982	85	164	−79	170	589	−418	273	148	125	208	90	118
1983	132	172	−40	203	758	−555	466	153	313	169	96	73
1984	262	240	+21	375	1123	−748	1213	273	939	426	128	298
1985	511	405	+106	575	1445	−870	1867	370	1497	988	116	872
1986	452	711	−258	567	2392	−1825	1143	420	723	811	144	667
1987	591	1679	−1087	792	3558	−2766	1658	727	931	1227	289	938
1988	967	3050	−2082	1228	5540	−4311	2968	1440	1527	2240	478	1762
1989	1062	4623	−3561	1316	8461	−7144	3008	1923	1086	2897	587	2310
1990	1115	7196	−6080	1320	10482	−9162	3195	2057	1138	3283	766	2516
1991	1613	9995	−8383	1712	13377	−11666	4633	2678	1955	4685	1130	3554
1992	2337	12361	−10025	2349	18083	−15734	7178	3682	3496	6336	1127	5208
1993	3706	14438	−10731	3180	21759	−18579	10197	4611	5486	7648	1113	6535
1994	4251	15436	−11185	3709	25336	−21627	11723	5846	5877	8597	1304	7292
1995	4851	17828	−12977	4982	27604	−22622	12027	7642	4384	9965	1587	8377

Sources: See Appendix A
Note: The data for the European Union (EU) relate to the twelve Member States prior to 1995.

over US$24bn of exports (16 per cent of total exports), while 'processing with imported materials' ventures accounted for US$44bn of imports (32 per cent of total imports) and over US$60bn of exports (40 per cent of total exports).[11] Together, therefore, the two schemes account for about half of China's total trade.

Much of this processing activity/trade is associated with firms from Hong Kong[12] who have sub-contracted all or part of their manufacturing activities to business entities in China in order to take advantage of the lower production costs. About 94 per cent of the outward processing activities commissioned by Hong Kong companies in China[13] are located in Guangdong Province, with over 60 per cent located in Shenzhen and Dongguan.[14]

The development of these OP activities is reflected in the statistics on Hong Kong's exports to China (both domestic exports and re-exports), on the re-exports of China origin through Hong Kong, and on Hong Kong's imports from China. The following conclusions emerge from the data presented in Table 1.8:[15]

- OP trade accounts for about 70 per cent of Hong Kong's domestic exports to China, although this percentage has declined from almost 80 per cent in 1990. This decline reflects the fact that an increasing proportion of Hong Kong's exports are destined for the domestic Chinese market.
- OP trade accounts for about 40–50 per cent of re-exports through Hong Kong to China.
- OP trade accounts for a steadily increasing proportion of re-exports of China origin through Hong Kong (over 82 per cent in 1995).
- OP trade accounts for a steadily increasing proportion of Hong Kong's total imports from China (although the proportion fell from 76 per cent to 74 per cent in 1995). However, as the import figures include the (import) value of goods of China origin which are to be subsequently re-exported, this trend says little about the importance of OP trade for domestic consumption in Hong Kong. Indeed, the value of OP imports for domestic consumption in Hong Kong would appear to be small and declining.

Table 1.8 Importance of outward processing trade for Hong Kong, 1989–95

Category of HK trade	Outward Processing trade as a percentage of total HK trade						
	1989	1990	1991	1992	1993	1994	1995
Domestic exports to China	76.0	79.0	76.5	74.3	74.0	71.4	71.4
Re-exports to China	43.6	50.3	48.2	46.2	42.1	43.3	45.4
Re-exports of China origin (except to China)	n. a.	n. a.	74.1	78.3	80.8	82.0	82.2
Imports from China	58.1	61.8	67.6	72.1	73.8	75.9	74.4

Sources: Census and Statistics Department, Hong Kong (1995: F5)
    Hong Kong Monthly Digest of Statistics, March 1997: 41

The growth of re-exports from China thus appears to be closely related to OP activities, though a sizeable amount (>HK$100,000m) originates elsewhere. In contrast, the greater proportion (approximately 50–60 per cent) of re-exports destined for China is not earmarked for subsequent outward processing but consists of capital goods, such as road vehicles, industrial machinery and equipment, that are to be used domestically.

TRADE BETWEEN THE EUROPEAN UNION AND CHINA

A major difficulty in trying to assess the quantitative importance of EU–China trade has been the increasing value of entrepôt trade passing through Hong Kong, and the asymmetric nature of this trade. It is instructive to compare the statistics on bilateral trade published, on the one hand, by the General Administration of Customs of the People's Republic of China and, on the other hand, by the IMF (for the European Union) (see Table 1.9). Several points emerge from a scrutiny of the data:

- The Chinese Customs statistics consistently value China's imports from the European Union rather higher than the IMF reports EU exports to China. This is mainly[16] because the former series includes goods of EU origin re-exported to China through Hong Kong, whereas the latter series does not. The IMF statistics thus understate EU exports to China.
- The IMF statistics consistently[17] value EU imports from China *substantially* higher than the Chinese Customs report Chinese exports to the European Union, particularly since the mid-1980s. This too is mainly because the former series includes goods of Chinese origin re-exported to the European Union through Hong Kong, whereas the latter series does not.[18] The Chinese Customs statistics thus understate Chinese exports to the European Union.
- It is not valid to rely on the two sets of import statistics because these figures include value added as the goods pass through Hong Kong.
- The extent of the discrepancies in the corresponding series depend largely upon the value of goods re-exported, in both directions, through Hong Kong. As has been shown above, the scale of the re-export trade from China to the European Union (US$17,828m in 1995) is considerably greater than that of the re-export trade in the opposite direction (US$4,851m in 1995). Furthermore, the imbalance on EU–China re-export trade has grown substantially since the mid-1980s, related in large part to the growth of processing and assembly operations in Southern China.
- These statistical niceties give rise to a situation where both partners may claim to be simultaneously running a trade deficit with the other. Thus, according to the IMF data, the European Union has moved from a bilateral trade surplus in the early 1980s to a substantial bilateral trade

Table 1.9 Reported trade between the European Union and China, 1978–95 (US$m)

Year	EU exports to China (IMF)	China imports from the EU (PRC)	EU imports from China (IMF)	China exports to the EU (PRC)	EU trade surplus with China (IMF)	(PRC)
1978	1979	—	1289	—	+690	—
1979	3010	—	1984	—	+1026	—
1980	2478	—	2753	—	−275	—
1981	2217	2772	2583	2534	−366	+238
1982	2105	2222	2437	2198	−332	+24
1983	2574	3417	2485	2516	+89	+901
1984	2929	3527	2638	2354	+291	+1173
1985	5482	6108	2971	2254	+2511	+3854
1986	6403	7661	4105	3993	+2298	+3668
1987	6429	7267	5946	3888	+483	+3379
1988	6771	8148	7718	4722	−947	+3426
1989	6901	9128	9159	4854	−2258	+4274
1990	6701	8351	12312	5813	−5611	+2538
1991	6942	8402	16917	6739	−9975	+1663
1992	8651	9803	19454	7601	−10803	+2202
1993	13264	14410	21403	11694*	−8139	+2716*
1994	14645	16938	25051	14580*	−10406	+2358*
1995	16981	19070	32450	18350*	−15469	+720*

Sources: IMF, *Direction of Trade Statistics Yearbook*
General Administration of Customs of the People's Republic of China, *China's Customs Statistics*

Notes:
(a) Data are provided for the twelve countries of the European Union prior to the accession of Austria, Finland and Sweden in 1995. The data include the former German Democratic Republic from July 1990.
(b) Chinese trade data for 1980 and earlier years were collated on a different basis by the Ministry of Foreign Trade and Economic Cooperation, and are therefore not reported above – see Lardy (1992) for further details.
* There is a change in the collation of the Chinese export statistics from 1993 onwards – see text for details – so that data for 1993–95 are not strictly comparable with earlier years.

deficit with China since 1988. In contrast, the Chinese Customs data point to a considerable EU trade surplus throughout the period.

To assess the bilateral trade balance between the European Union and China, it is thus necessary to adjust the data presented in Table 1.9 to take account of this re-export trade. The appropriate calculations are shown in detail in Tables A1 and A2 in Appendix A, and are summarised in Table 1.10. The following comments may prove useful:

- Reported EU exports to China (as reported by the IMF) have been supplemented by the ex-EU value of goods re-exported to China through Hong Kong. This ex-EU value has been constructed by deducting, from the gross re-export value, the re-export margin earned by firms in Hong Kong.
- EU imports from China (as reported by the IMF) have been reduced by the value added by HK firms on re-exported goods of China origin.

- The result of these two adjustments has been to reduce the EU trade deficit (as reported by the IMF) with China.
- It is worth re-emphasising that these estimates are highly approximate, and rely crucially on the many simplifying assumptions made (i.e. that the re-export margin on goods of EU origin is the same as the average margin estimated by the HKCSD for all (except China) supplying countries; and that no adjustments are made for time lags in transportation or for the costs of freight and insurance).

Re-exports between the European Union and China were negligible in 1978 and, through 1984, accounted for less than 10 per cent of direct trade in both directions. In fact, trade between the two partners stagnated during this period despite the signing of the 1978 Trade Agreement and the extension of Community GSP benefits to China from 1980 onwards (see Chapter 3 for details of EU trade policy towards China). Demand for each other's exports was dampened by the recession in Western Europe and by the period of economic 'readjustment' in China. There was a sudden surge of direct EU exports in 1985 following the liberalisation of the Chinese foreign

Table 1.10 Adjusted EU trade surplus with China, 1978–95 (US$m)

Year	EU exports to China			EU imports from China			Adjusted EU trade surplus with China
	Direct	Re-exports through Hong Kong	Total	Direct	Re-exports through Hong Kong	Total	
1978	1979	4	1983	1234	49	1284	+699
1979	3010	24	3034	1881	93	1974	+1060
1980	2478	38	2516	2597	141	2737	−222
1981	2217	73	2290	2381	182	2563	−273
1982	2105	77	2182	2273	148	2421	−239
1983	2574	118	2693	2313	155	2468	+225
1984	2929	236	3165	2398	216	2614	+551
1985	5482	460	5942	2566	365	2930	+3012
1986	6403	407	6810	3394	640	4034	+2776
1987	6429	532	6961	4267	1511	5778	+1183
1988	6771	870	7641	4668	2745	7413	+228
1989	6901	952	7853	4536	4091	8627	−774
1990	6701	989	7690	5116	5944	11060	−3370
1991	6942	1463	8405	6922	7946	14868	−6463
1992	8651	2120	10771	7092	9531	16623	−5853
1993	13264	3417	16681	6965	10669	17635	−954
1994	14645	4009	18654	9615	11592	21207	−2554
1995	16981	4608	21589	14622	13371	27993	−6404

Sources: See Appendix A
Notes:
(a) The data for the European Union (EU) relate to the twelve Member States prior to 1995.
(b) The data on re-exports are net of the estimated value-added by Hong Kong firms.

trade system the previous year, but then only very slow growth up to the early 1990s. Direct EU exports then doubled between 1991 and 1994. Meanwhile, the value of EU goods re-exported through Hong Kong grew steadily from the mid-1980s onwards, and its relative importance also increased so that re-exports accounted for about one-quarter of total EU exports to China in 1995.

EU imports from China have, in contrast, developed in a quite different manner. Direct imports grew steadily from 1984 onwards, but have been overshadowed by the growth of re-exports through Hong Kong. Whereas re-exports accounted for about 8 per cent of total EU imports from China in 1984, this percentage rose to 50 per cent in 1989-90, and to over 60 per cent in 1993. Direct imports then doubled in value between 1993 and 1995, while re-exports grew by 'only' 30 per cent. This is a manifestation of a wider trend away from the re-export of Chinese goods towards simple transhipment through Hong Kong, and results from improvements in China's port facilities and its greater maturity in product processing and auxiliary services.[19] In the longer term, it seems likely that this trend will continue, and that Hong Kong's role as an entrepôt will diminish while its role as a control centre for trade financing and servicing will increase.

The net result is that bilateral trade through the open-door period may be divided into four distinct phases. The first (1980-84) was a period of slow growth in trade in both directions for the reasons cited above, and of rough balance. The second (1985-86) was a phase of strong growth in EU exports as the Chinese foreign trade regime was liberalised, and showed a healthy EU trade surplus on its bilateral trade. The third (1987-91) was a phase when the growth rate of EU imports from China substantially outpaced that of EU exports to China, with the result that the healthy EU trade surplus was converted into a substantial trade deficit from 1989 onwards. The fourth phase (1992-present) shows a strong EU export performance, but imports also growing quickly and the trade deficit (despite some respite in 1993-94) becoming larger. The asymmetric importance of re-export trade reflects the fact that HK firms play a major role in the sale of Chinese products, particularly toys, clothing, footwear, and watches (see Chapters 8 and 9 for case studies of the toy and watch industries respectively), but have a much more limited role in the sale of EU goods to China. A similar pattern is evident from the data on trade between China and the United States (Lardy 1994: 75).

It is also instructive to look at the bilateral trade balances for individual EU Member States with China (see Table A3 in Appendix A). The most striking feature is the complete turn-around in the Sino-German trade balance since the late 1980s: in the early to mid-1980s, Germany ran a substantial trade surplus with China, but the surplus has changed into a massive trade deficit in the 1990s. Other substantial deficits have also been shown through the 1990s by France, the Netherlands, Spain, and (particularly in 1995) the United Kingdom. But what is the significance of such deficits? It is impossible to answer these questions on the basis of the aggregate data, but it is likely that part of the explanation relates to the fact that German, etc. firms have been particularly active in importing Chinese goods for onward sale in the European Union, and thus the trade deficits with China may well be offset by surpluses generated elsewhere.

In conclusion, the existence of the substantial and increasing re-export trade through Hong Kong renders the data on trade between the European Union and China reported by both the IMF and the Chinese Customs Administration rather meaningless for any assessment of the bilateral position. The calculations above – notwithstanding the various simplifying assumptions that need to be made – enable a more realistic picture to be presented not only of the bilateral trade balance but also of the importance of Sino-EU trade to both partners (see Table 1.11).

Table 1.11 Importance of Sino-EU trade to both partners, 1978–95

Year	Importance of China trade for the European Union		Importance of EU trade for China	
	EU exports to China as % of total EU exports	EU imports from China as % of total EU imports	China exports to EU as % of total China exports	China imports from EU as % of total China imports
1978	0.9	0.5	—	—
1979	1.2	0.6	—	—
1980	0.8	0.7	—	—
1981	0.8	0.7	12.3	12.5
1982	0.8	0.7	10.5	11.5
1983	1.0	0.8	12.0	15.9
1984	1.1	0.8	9.8	12.8
1985	2.1	0.9	9.6	14.3
1986	2.1	1.2	15.0	17.8
1987	1.8	1.5	13.7	16.7
1988	1.8	1.6	15.7	14.6
1989	1.7	1.8	17.0	15.3
1990	1.4	1.9	18.9	15.4
1991	1.6	2.4	20.4	12.9
1992	1.9	2.6	20.2	11.9
1993	2.9	3.1	19.2	13.6
1994	2.9	3.3	17.5	14.4
1995	2.8	3.6	18.8	14.3

Sources: Appendix A for EU exports and imports
China's Customs Statistics for Chinese exports and imports
The Hong Kong Census and Statistics Department for data on re-exports through Hong Kong

Notes:
(a) EU exports to China and EU imports from China both include re-exports through Hong Kong (see Table 1.10).
(b) Total EU exports and total EU imports exclude intra-EU exports and imports.
(c) China exports to the EU and China imports from the EU both include re-exports through Hong Kong. (Chinese exports to the EU in 1993–95 are estimated by EU imports from China as given in Table 1.10, as the Chinese export data are not consistent with earlier years.)

Three points stand out from a scrutiny of the data. First, trade with the European Union has been much more important for China throughout the period 1981–95 than trade with China has been for the European Union. Second, the European Union has increased in importance as a market for Chinese goods, particularly since the mid-1980s. In contrast, the relative importance of the European Union as a supplier of imports to China has remained remarkably constant throughout the period. Third, the importance of China for both EU exports and imports has grown considerably, albeit from a low initial base, since the late 1980s. Indeed, on the basis of the adjusted data for 1995, China was the fourth largest supplier to the European Union (after the United States, Japan and Switzerland) and the fifth largest export market (after the United States, Switzerland, Japan, and Norway).

However, it is worth emphasising the limitations of bilateral trade data. As Lardy (1994: 79) has noted, 'bilateral trade data are of diminishing value when capital is highly mobile and where foreign-invested firms, processing and assembly operations, and other types of foreign participation are so important in generating exports'. This point is taken up in more detail in the next section. Much of the increase in China's exports has been due to the liberalisation of China's foreign investment regime, and a sizeable proportion of the profits from increased exports accrue to foreign firms. Sung (1991b: 15.8) has estimated that China earns only 20 cents for every dollar of goods exported under processing and assembly arrangements, yet the full dollar of exports shows up in the trade data.

Finally, and even more fundamentally, it is important to acknowledge that a bilateral trade deficit (surplus) is not necessarily bad (good). The EU trade deficit with China arises in large part because European consumers purchase huge quantities of Chinese clothes, toys, etc. that are being produced at low cost and which cannot be produced more cheaply elsewhere. The fact that Chinese consumers do not purchase a similar value of EU exports is only of consequence if, as the European Commission believes, China adopts 'structures and practices which are not compatible with free and fair trade rules'.[20] But what really matters is the EU global trade balance, and whether consumers somewhere buy enough EU exports to pay for the goods that EU consumers wish to import.

FOREIGN DIRECT INVESTMENT IN CHINA

The growth of FDI in China since the advent of the 'open-door' policy has been dramatic, particularly since the mid-1980s and even more explosively since the early 1990s (see Table 1.12). At the end of 1995, a total of 258,788 projects had been agreed with a cumulative investment value of almost US$400bn. The amount of FDI actually realised was US$133bn. Provisional figures put the amount of realised investment at US$177bn at the end of 1996.

Table 1.12 Foreign direct investment in China, 1979–95 (US$m)

Year	Contracted FDI		Realised FDI	
	Projects	Value	Average size	Value
1979–82	922	6,010	6.52	1,166
1983	470	1,732	3.69	636
1984	1,856	2,651	1.43	1,258
1985	3,073	5,931	1.93	1,658
1986	1,498	2,834	1.89	1,875
1987	2,233	3,709	1.66	2,314
1988	5,945	5,297	0.89	3,194
1989	5,779	5,600	0.97	3,393
1990	7,273	6,596	0.91	3,487
1991	12,978	11,977	0.92	4,366
1992	48,764	58,124	1.19	11,008
1993	83,437	111,436	1.34	27,515
1994	47,549	82,680	1.74	33,767
1995	37,011	91,282	2.47	37,521
Total	258,788	395,859	1.53	133,156

Source: Almanac of China's Foreign Economic Relations and Trade (various issues)
Notes:
(a) The figures include FDI in equity joint ventures, contractual joint ventures, wholly foreign-owned enterprises, and joint exploration. Excluded is 'other foreign investment': i.e. projects involving international leasing, compensation trade, and processing assembly.

Over 80 per cent of the projects have been contracted since 1992 – the year of Deng Xiaoping's tour of southern China – and over 96 per cent since 1988. The amount of new contracted investment appears to have peaked at US$111bn in 1993,[21] but the average value of the FDI in each project is on the increase. Furthermore, the amount of FDI actually realised continues to grow each year and, according to the provisional figures given above, amounted to US$44bn in 1996.

HK firms have been overwhelmingly the most active investors in China, accounting for 59 per cent of the total realised FDI over the period 1985–95 (see Table 1.13). It was noted above that Hong Kong developed its own manufacturing base in response to the effective closure of the Chinese market in the 1950s. This was heavily concentrated in six industrial sectors, namely, wearing apparel, textiles, paper products, plastic products, metal products and machinery, and electrical and electronic products. As Lee and Davies (1995: 25) note:

> in the 1960s and 1970s these industries competed in world markets largely on the basis of cost. Companies used mature or obsolete production technologies to combine relatively cheap inputs of land and well-disciplined labour in order to manufacture products designed by customers in overseas markets. However, by 1978, the combination of rising labour costs, the emergence of lower-cost locations and the threat of protection led to significant doubts about the continuing viability of that approach.

Table 1.13 Foreign direct investment in China by country of investor, 1985–95

Country	Realised FDI (1985–95)		Contracted FDI (1990–95)		
	Value (US$m)	As % of total	Number of projects	Value (US$m)	As % of total
Hong Kong	76,820	59.0	134,976	212,998	58.8
Taiwan	10,472	8.0	28,472	26,752	7.4
Macau	1,880	1.4	4,904	7,541	2.1
Singapore	3,909	3.0	5,456	16,653	4.6
Thailand	911	0.7	2,024	3,367	0.9
Chinese diaspora	94,263	72.5	175,832	269,310	74.4
United States	10,394	8.0	18,763	24,321	6.7
Japan	9,923	7.6	12,197	18,435	5.1
South Korea	1,069	0.8	2,147	3,097	0.8
United Kingdom	2,084	1.6	1,380	8,851	2.4
Germany	1,166	0.9	1,156	3,876	1.1
France	815	0.6	894	1,438	0.4
Italy	748	0.6	812	1,093	0.3
The Netherlands	401	0.3	366	1,199	0.3
Spain	279	0.2	266	168	—
Belgium/Luxembourg	166	0.1	221	327	0.1
Denmark	125	0.1	82	616	0.2
Ireland	3	—	16	59	—
Portugal	2	—	19	8	—
Greece	2	—	7	3	—
EU(12)	5,793	4.5	5,219	17,639	4.9
Austria	219	0.2	288	238	0.1
Sweden	140	0.1	228	242	0.1
Finland	112	0.1	45	59	—
EU(15)	6,264	4.8	5,780	18,178	5.0
Switzerland	235	0.2	212	717	0.2
World	130,096	100.0	237,012	362,093	100.0

Source: *Almanac of China's Foreign Economic Relations and Trade* (various issues)

Notes:
(a) The figures include FDI in equity joint ventures, contractual joint ventures, wholly foreign-owned enterprises, and joint exploration. Excluded is 'other foreign investment': i.e. projects involving international leasing, compensation trade, and processing assembly.
(b) FDI from Macau in 1985–87 is included in the Hong Kong total, and not in the Macau total.
(c) FDI from Taiwan and South Korea was not recorded before 1992, and the totals for these two countries thus refer to the period 1992–95.

The advent of the open-door policy in China provided many HK manufacturing firms with a timely means by which they could prolong their cost competitiveness by moving their production operations into southern China (particularly Guangdong Province) to take advantage of the lower labour and land costs available there. In the ensuing years, many HK firms established manufacturing facilities in China, though the extent of any significant technology transfer is questionable. Interestingly, this relocation of manufacturing activity has not led to the development of new and different manufacturing sectors in Hong Kong. The traditional industries have continued to dominate, but with greater emphasis on the higher value-added service activities within the territory. The contemporary manufacturing sector in Hong Kong thus employs fewer people than in the late 1970s, in smaller establishments, and at higher capital intensities.[22] A sophisticated division of labour has been effected within a sub-regional economic zone around the Pearl River Delta (see Chapter 4 for further discussion).

In comparison, the United States has provided 8.0 per cent, Japan 7.6 per cent, and the European Union only 4.5 per cent of the total realised FDI during 1985–95. The most active EU countries have been the United Kingdom, Germany, France and Italy. FDI from non-EU European countries has been minimal, with only Switzerland showing a significant interest. Taiwan has provided 8.0 per cent of the total, and this figure only includes investment over the period 1991–95 as earlier data on FDI from both Taiwan and South Korea were not recorded by the Chinese authorities (Wakabayashi 1990; Kohari 1992).

The data on contracted FDI over the period 1990–95 provide some guidance to future trends. HK firms continue to dominate with just under 60 per cent of the total value of contracted FDI. The shares provided by the United States (6.7 per cent) and Japan (5.1 per cent) are rather lower, while that of the EU(12) has risen to 4.9 per cent. This apparent increase in the relative importance of investment from the European Union is, however, entirely due to greater interest by UK and German investors, while most of the other European countries (particularly Spain) have not followed suit. The data also suggest that European investments are of rather larger scale (US$3.4m per project) than those undertaken by Hong Kong ($1.6m), Japanese ($1.5m), US ($1.3m), and Taiwanese ($0.9m) investors. Perhaps European FDI in China is a case of 'less but more' (see Chapter 5). Provisional data suggest that FDI from the European Union increased considerably in 1996 and that, by the end of the year, the amount of realised EU investment had risen to US$8.94bn – over 5 per cent of the total.[23]

Four final points should be borne in mind when interpreting these figures. First, Tracy (1995: 4) reports a marked tendency for overseas Chinese in Southeast Asia to route their investments in China through Hong Kong.

> in the case of the Taiwanese, government restrictions on direct investment in the mainland made it imperative until recently to use a third country, Hong Kong being the obvious choice. Even now that restrictions have been removed some Taiwanese prefer to continue to invest through that route in order to evade government scrutiny. In the case of the Chinese from other parts of South East Asia, the internationalisation of their operations over the last decade has led to the opening of branch offices in Hong Kong in many instances and even the establishment of second headquarters in the case of some of the more prominent regional

conglomerates from Singapore, Malaysia, Indonesia and Thailand. These branch offices and second headquarters serve several purposes. First, they allow these companies to more readily tap the Hong Kong market for funds. Secondly, they permit the spreading of risk for a group whose economic power is not matched by similar social or economic power in their home base. Thirdly, Hong Kong's position as the gateway to Southern China makes it the obvious base from which to launch their companies in China.

Thus Tracy concludes that the published figures overstate the numbers of projects and amounts of capital emanating from Hong Kong, while understating considerably those from Taiwan and the other countries of the 'Chinese diaspora' in Southeast Asia. In particular, he suggests that Taiwanese investment might be double the level reported.[24] Ash and Kueh (1993: 735) report a survey conducted by the Ministry of Economic Affairs in Taipei which cited a cumulative Taiwanese FDI stock in the People's Republic of US$750m as of April 1991. It is also likely, as Sung (1991a: 26–7) has noted, that many Japanese, US and European multinationals have used HK subsidiaries to test the investment climate in China. Unfortunately, no hard data are available on the scale of this phenomenon.

Second, there is evidence that the flow of investment into China has been inflated by the practice known as 'round-tripping'. This involves an outflow of capital from China (in many cases to HK affiliates of Chinese firms) and the subsequent 're-investment' of the 'foreign' capital in China. Thus Chinese investors circumvent the regulatory regime governing domestic investment and, moreover, benefit from the fiscal incentives offered to foreign investors. Recent policy reforms have, however, both reduced the incentives for round-tripping and improved the monitoring procedures (UNCTAD 1995: 59–69). In addition to round-tripping, the FDI figures may be subject to over-valuation in that about 70 per cent of the reported inward investment is 'in kind', i.e. in the form of equipment and technology. For the foreign investor, there is an incentive to overstate the cash valuations of these assets so as to maximise its equity stake and share of dividends in any joint venture, and to take advantage of lower taxes arising from the 'larger' capital expenditures. Again, however, recent policy reforms have acted to discourage over-valuation.[25]

Third, much of the early investment projects were in labour-intensive manufacturing ventures but, since 1992, the Chinese authorities have progressively opened up various service sectors of the economy to foreign investment (see Chapters 10, 11 and 12 for case studies of developments in the telecommunications, banking and insurance industries) while simultaneously strengthening the requirements to be met by potential investors (see Chapter 2 for further details). These changes generally favour investors in high-technology and capital-intensive industries, and should lead to larger-scale FDI projects which may well favour EU, US and Japanese investors. The moves have predictably had a mixed reception from foreign investors, with many complaints both about the slow pace of liberalisation and about the withdrawal of various preferential incentives. But it is China's prerogative to amend the FDI environment in its domestic economy as and when it sees fit, though it is constrained by its wish to meet the requirements for accession to the WTO, and it is for foreign companies (particularly those with technology and/or expertise which China requires) to leverage their proprietary assets to their own strategic advantage.

Fourth, the amounts of money invested in the Chinese economy by foreign firms are substantial, notwithstanding the fact that much FDI is 'in kind', yet they are still relatively insignificant (certainly in national terms) compared to domestic savings. It is not therefore through the provision of scarce capital that FIEs have had their most profound impact upon the Chinese economy, but rather through the introduction of more efficient management and production practices, the upgrading of technology and product ranges, and through their effects upon foreign trade (Hussain and Zhuang 1997: 24–5). FIEs accounted for over 40 per cent of China's exports in 1996, and over 54 per cent of her imports (see Table 1.14). Furthermore, these shares had increased substantially since 1992, when the corresponding figures were 20 per cent and 34 per cent. Given the praise which is lavished upon FIEs as the engine behind China's export growth and, more tangibly, the fiscal incentives with which FIEs have been provided, it is interesting to note that not only do FIEs account for a higher percentage of total imports than of total exports, but also that their imports have exceeded their exports

Table 1.14 China's foreign trade, by type of foreign-investment enterprise, 1993–96 (US$m)

	1992	1993	1994	1995	1996
EXPORTS					
Contractual joint ventures	—	3,878	5,355	6,791	7,949
Equity joint ventures	—	14,117	18,075	22,689	29,750
Wholly foreign-owned enterprises	—	7,242	11,283	17,396	23,807
Total FIE exports	17,356	25,237	34,713	46,876	61,506
Total China exports	84,940	91,744	121,006	148,780	151,066
FIE exports % China exports	20.4	27.5	28.7	31.5	40.7
IMPORTS					
Contractual joint ventures	—	7,037	9,200	9,010	9,290
Equity joint ventures	—	25,904	29,880	34,818	41,094
Wholly foreign-owned enterprises	—	8,891	13,853	19,114	25,219
Total FIE imports	26,371	41,833	52,934	62,943	75,603
Total China imports	80,585	103,959	115,615	132,084	138,838
FIE Imports % China imports	32.7	40.2	45.8	47.7	54.5

Source: *China's Customs Statistics* (various issues)

in aggregate value terms in each of the five years (1992–96) for which data are available. All types of FIEs seem to incur such trade deficits, though the wholly owned enterprises are least at fault.

This curious situation is largely explained by the fact that equipment, parts and other materials imported by FIEs as part of their initial investments show up in the data on imports (see Table 1.15). The sums involved are quite significant: FIE equipment/materials investment accounted for over 30 per cent of total FIE imports in 1995–96, and the FIEs would have shown a comfortable trade surplus if these amounts were excluded. Presumably these sums are also recorded in the statistics on realised FDI. If so, then a comparison of imports of FIE equipment/materials investment for 1995–96 (US$43.6bn) with realised FDI for 1995–96 (US$82bn) would suggest that the proportion of FDI 'in kind' certainly exceeds 50 per cent.[26]

The major contribution of FIEs to China's foreign trade comes from processing arrangements with imported materials: these account for about 80 per cent of FIE exports and about three-quarters of FIE imports (excluding FIE equipment/materials investment). Given Sung's estimate (cited above) that China earns a meagre 20 cents for each dollar of goods exported from processing and assembly ventures, the direct benefits[27] to China from the expansion of FIE trade seem rather uninspiring. It is also interesting to note that FIEs provide only a small proportion of 'ordinary' exports, and that the major share is provided by the much-maligned State-owned enterprises.

CHINA AND THE WORLD TRADE ORGANIZATION

China was one of the original twenty-two Contracting Parties of the General Agreement on Tariffs and Trade (GATT) in 1947 (Qin 1993: 79). Soon afterwards, however, the Government of the Republic of China (ROC) was deposed by the communists, and relocated to Taiwan where it continued to claim its status as the legitimate government of China. This claim was supported by a majority of nations both at the time and for a considerable time thereafter, notwithstanding the founding of the People's Republic of China on 1 October 1949. Thus, when the ROC Government notified the UN Secretary General on 6 March 1950 of China's withdrawal from GATT, its authority to do so went unchallenged.[28]

The PRC Government showed little interest in GATT during the subsequent three decades,[29] and the first official contact was not made until 1980. China obtained observer status in 1982. On 10 July 1986, the PRC Government formally requested resumption of China's contracting party status in GATT, and set out three basic principles for its entry, namely, that its application should be treated as a resumption rather than accession as a new member;[30] that it should join as a developing country; and that there

Table 1.15 China's foreign trade involving foreign-investment enterprises, by customs regime, 1995–96 (US$m)

	1995			1996		
	FIE trade	Total trade	FIE trade % total trade	FIE trade	Total trade	FIE trade % Total trade
EXPORTS						
Ordinary trade	4,355	71,366	6.1	7,523	62,839	12.0
Processing with supplied materials	2,870	20,660	13.9	4,487	24,240	18.5
Processing with imported materials	39,177	53,043	73.9	48,596	60,094	80.9
Warehousing trade	463	1,283	36.1	890	1,998	44.5
Other	11	2,418	—	10	1,895	—
Total exports	46,876	148,780	31.5	61,506	151,066	40.7
IMPORTS						
Ordinary trade	5,294	43,365	12.2	6,873	39,359	17.5
Processing with supplied materials	2,662	16,226	16.4	3,736	17,803	21.0
Processing with imported materials	34,409	42,143	81.6	37,757	44,472	84.9
FIE equipment/ materials investment	18,736	18,738	—	24,861	24,861	—
Warehousing trade	1,797	5,950	30.2	2,344	7,234	32.4
Other	45	5,656	—	33	5,109	—
Total imports	62,943	132,084	47.7	75,604	138,838	54.5

Source: *China's Customs Statistics*, nos 76 and 88 (December 1995 and December 1996)
Notes:
(a) 'Processing with supplied materials' refers to processing activities in which foreign suppliers provide raw materials, parts or components under a contractual arrangement for the subsequent re-exportation of the processed products. The imported inputs and the finished outputs remain the property of the foreign supplier.
(b) 'Processing with imported materials' refers to processing activities in which raw materials or components are imported for the manufacture of products for export.
(c) 'Warehousing trade' refers to goods imported into or exported from customs-bonded warehouses.
(d) 'FIE equipment/materials investment' refers to imports of equipment, parts or other materials by a foreign-invested enterprise as part of its total initial investment.
(e) 'Other' includes *inter alia* compensation trade, border trade, barter trade, equipment imported for processing and assembling, and outward processing. See the definitions in the Introduction to *China's Customs Statistics*.

should be no special discriminatory provisions attached to the protocol. In March 1987, a GATT Working Party on China's Status as a Contracting Party was established to examine the application. The Working Party met nineteen times during the period 1988–94,[31] yet despite attempts by China to force the issue (Harrold 1995: 143) following the conclusion of the Uruguay Round, agreement on the terms of resumption/accession was not reached. Thus China's hopes of becoming a founder member of the WTO were dashed.

China had placed great store in becoming a founder member of the WTO, not only for the trade benefits[32] it would bring but also because it craved the political recognition of its status as a major economic power (and because it was insistent that it be granted membership before Taiwan – see below).[33] In contrast, the three major trading powers with whom China was obliged to negotiate (the European Union, the United States and Japan) had all insisted that membership was a commercial contract to be effected on 'commercially viable terms' rather than an act of political recognition. Negotiators were unable to reconcile the different positions, though substantial progress was made on many key reforms: centralisation of foreign trade rules; lowering of customs duties; reductions in the numbers of import licences and quotas; elimination of the import regulatory tax; elimination of the dual exchange rate system;[34] reform of the taxation system; reform of State-owned enterprises (Commission of the European Communities 1995: 34).

The Chinese authorities reacted to this snub by announcing that China would no longer participate in bilateral talks, but it nevertheless took part in two rounds of meetings of the WTO China Working Party in March and July 1995.[35] The failure of these meetings to achieve a breakthrough finally extinguished China's hope that it might still, retroactively, be regarded as one of the founding members of the WTO, though it was granted observer status at all WTO meetings.

The extent of the gulf between China and the major trading powers was set out in stark terms in a secret 'road map' presented by the US Deputy Trade Representative, Charlene Barshefsky, in November 1995. According to this document, the main issues[36] requiring resolution before WTO accession by China were:

- Tariff reductions and market access. Average tariff rates were deemed to be too high by the major trading powers and, furthermore, China had expressed a reluctance to liberalise import restrictions and foreign investment regulations in the telecommunications and automobile industries (see Chapters 10 and 7, respectively). It is worth noting in this regard the offer made by China at the November 1995 APEC meeting in Osaka, to reduce tariffs on 4,000 items, eliminate import quotas and licences on 170 products, and reduce its overall level of protection by 30 per cent.[37]
- Developing country status. Developing countries in the GATT/WTO are subject to less exacting requirements regarding trade liberalisation than are developed members, and are permitted to retain discriminatory measures in favour of their domestic industries for longer transitional periods. China has long insisted (see above) that it should be admitted to the GATT/WTO as a developing country because of its low *per capita* income. The developed countries respond by pointing out the substantial share of world trade already enjoyed by China, and

its potential for disruption of world trade patterns on account of its huge size.
- Trading rights. Exports and imports in China are controlled through a system of trading rights under which approval is required from central authorities. Tariff concessions can thus in principle be negated through the withholding of import licences. In December 1995, China offered to phase out trading rights over a period of five years, but the United States still insisted on a shorter period.
- Industrial policy. China prohibits FDI in certain industries (see Chapter 2) and discriminates against foreign firms in the granting of trading rights. Furthermore, China's rules on minimum export requirements, local content requirements, and the transfer of patented technology in foreign-investment enterprises all contravene agreements reached under the Uruguay Round.
- Import quotas. Taking Poland's 1968 GATT accession as a precedent, the 'road map' envisaged China increasing its imports from WTO members by an agreed amount each year. China's response to what it perceives as an attempt to pry open its domestic market was that import quotas were inappropriate as it was in transition from a planned economy to a market economy.
- Safeguards. Whereas the three major trading powers have essentially been in agreement over the issues above, there are some differences of opinion over the use of safeguards against surges of imports. Under WTO rules, such safeguards are permitted in certain circumstances, but must be applied equally to imports from all countries. Both the European Union and the United States, however, want WTO members to be allowed to impose safeguard measures selectively against Chinese exports or against specific Chinese products. The EU position has appeared to harden on this issue as its bilateral trade deficit with China has increased through the 1990s. Japan does not regard safeguards as a major issue. For its part, China has pointed out that the use of selective safeguard measures is a violation of the MFN principle, but has not objected to the inclusion of a general safeguard clause.

In addition to the primarily economic issues above, there is also the sensitive political issue of Taiwan's application to join the WTO. Taiwan submitted an application in January 1990 to participate in GATT as 'The Customs Territory of Taiwan, Penghu, Kinmen and Matsu' or 'Chinese Taipei'. By all accounts, the negotiations[38] on the application have proceeded further and faster than those on China's application, aided by the fact that Chinese Taipei has indicated its willingness to join the WTO as a developed country. Indeed (at the time of writing), it is likely that the outstanding issues regarding the accession of Chinese Taipei will be resolved long before those regarding the accession of China. China does not object to the accession of Chinese Taipei, and has even expressed its willingness to sponsor Taiwan's membership once it has become a member. But China is adamant that Chinese Taipei will not accede to the WTO before China as it considers accession to amount to political recognition.

The reality of the situation in the mid-1990s is that not only the European Union, but also the majority of the other WTO members, will risk incurring the wrath of the People's Republic and jeopardising the difficult negotiations on PRC accession over the 'Taiwan issue'. The most likely outcome is the simultaneous accession of China and Chinese Taipei, as and when negotiations with China have been successfully concluded. Perhaps the question that is crucial to the successful conclusion of the negotiations on the Chinese application is whether reform of the Chinese economy is more or less likely if China is granted early membership. The current EU (and US) position appears to be that China's Protocol of Accession should contain substantial and verifiable commitments on trade liberalisation, etc. An alternative strategy would be to hasten China's WTO entry on the basis that reform and liberalisation would be both easier to accomplish and more likely to endure within a framework of WTO membership.

For its part, as the WTO Director-General Renato Ruggiero (1997: 5) notes:

> [an] outward-looking China cannot afford to stand on the sidelines while others write the rules of the game. A China with growing export interests cannot afford to be left without secure and expanding access to growing access to global markets – security which only the multilateral system provides. And perhaps most important, a China dependent upon technology and modernisation cannot afford to fall behind the fast-moving pace of globalization – particularly in sectors like information technologies, telecommunication, or financial services which will be the key building blocks of the new economy.

CONCLUDING REMARKS

On 1 July 1997, Hong Kong reverted to Chinese sovereignty after more than 150 years of British rule.[39] Under the Sino-British Joint Declaration of December 1984, the two governments agreed that Hong Kong would be ruled under the 'one country, two systems' principle, and that Hong Kong's economic and social systems would remain in place for fifty years after the handover. Hong Kong would become a Special Administrative Region of China, but it would continue to be autonomous in all areas except foreign affairs and defence: it would keep its own currency and exchange rate system, operate a separate customs area (keeping its status in the WTO) with an independent trade policy, and permit free movement of capital and foreign exchange.

In the absence of an unheralded shift in policy by the Chinese authorities, therefore, the economic effects of the transfer of government should be relatively small in the short term. There was significant economic integration between Hong Kong and the mainland for many years prior to 1997, and there appears to be no reason why this should change although, as noted above, it seems likely in the longer term that Hong Kong's role as an entrepôt will diminish while its role as a control centre for trade financing and servicing will increase. Even as Shanghai develops as a major financial centre (Liu and Strange 1997), Hong Kong should still retain its pre-eminent position for many years to come.

NOTES

1 See JETRO (1997: 16–21) for details.
2 The European Community was renamed the European Union when the Maastricht Treaty came into effect on November 1st 1993. In this chapter, the terms European Union and European Community are both used as appropriate, but all data relate to the twelve Member States prior to 1995 except where otherwise indicated.
3 *The World Bank Atlas 1996*, pp.18–19.
4 China's size also underscores its political, strategic and environmental importance, not just with regard to its neighbouring countries but to the whole world. Such issues are not addressed in this volume. See Commission of the European Communities (1995) for further details.
5 This summary is taken from Sung (1991a: 15–28).
6 Including financial services, business consultancy and tourism.
7 Sung (1991a: 21) citing Tom (1957).
8 The official definition of a re-export is 'a product which had previously been imported into Hong Kong and which is re-exported without having undergone in Hong Kong a manufacturing process which has changed permanently the shape, nature, form or utility of the product'. Sung (1991a: 15) suggests that the processing may include packaging, sorting, grading, bottling, drying, assembling, decorating, diluting, or even minor manufacturing (such as the pre-shrinking of grey cloth).
9 Other studies have come up with different estimates. A widely quoted survey undertaken in 1988 by the Hong Kong Development Council estimated that the gross re-export margin on goods originating in China was 16 per cent, and that on goods originating elsewhere was 14 per cent. See Sung (1991b: 15.6) and Lardy (1994: 77). Ash and Kueh (1993: 713) assume a re-export margin of 25 per cent on goods of China origin.
10 These estimates are constructed using the re-export margins calculated by the HKCSD for 1989–94:

	1989	1990	1991	1992	1993	1994
China origin	11.5	17.4	20.5	22.9	26.1	24.9
Other countries	10.3	11.3	9.3	9.3	7.8	5.7

A constant margin of 10 per cent has been used for the years before 1989 for all re-exports, whether from China or elsewhere. For 1995 and 1996, margins of 25 per cent and 5 per cent, respectively, are used for re-exports from China and from third countries. The following possible sources of error should be borne in mind when interpreting the estimates: (a) there is a time lag between the import of goods into Hong Kong and their subsequent re-export (and registration in the HK re-export statistics); (b) the estimates for the re-export margins for 1989–94 are based on a 'small' sample of traders, and it was not feasible to estimate margins for individual countries other than China (Census and Statistics Department, Hong Kong 1996: F5). There is no guarantee that the margins will be the same across all countries; (c) the margins for 1975–88 and for 1995–96 are extrapolations from the survey estimates – the earlier estimates in particular should be treated with extreme caution. Furthermore, the margins vary widely across different types of goods and thus, as the commodity composition of trade changes, so too will the aggregate re-export margin.

11 *China's Customs Statistics*, 88 (December 1996) p.13.
12 Sung (1991b: 15–18) suggests that HK firms account for roughly 60 per cent of the foreign investment in processing/assembly operations in China.
13 Some HK firms also undertake OP trade with Indonesia, Thailand, Singapore and Vietnam to diversify investments and spread business risks. The scale of this trade is, however, small as these countries lack the cultural and linguistic bonds that link Hong Kong with neighbouring Guangdong.
14 Census and Statistics Department, Hong Kong (1995: F15).
15 This data emerges from three quarterly surveys undertaken by the Hong Kong Census and Statistics Department, namely, the *Survey on Exports to China for Outward Processing*, as from the third quarter of 1988; the *Survey on Imports from China related to Outward Processing*, as from the first quarter of 1989; and the *Survey on Re-exports of China origin (except to China) involving Outward Processing in China*, as from the first quarter of 1991. See Census and Statistics Department, Hong Kong (1995) and the articles since 1991 in the *Annual Review of Hong Kong External Trade*.
16 The export and import series will also differ because of (a) time lags in transportation, and (b) the cost of insurance and freight, but these factors cannot explain the full amount the observed discrepancies.
17 Except in 1983, when the Chinese Customs Statistics valued EU imports (US$2516m) higher than do the IMF statistics (US$2485m).
18 The Chinese Customs authorities did adjust the method of statistics collation from 1993, so as to include re-exports from China through Hong Kong to the European Union (and to the United States) *where they were able to identify the final destination of the goods*. It appears, however, that the 1994 and 1995 export data do not include *all* goods re-exported through Hong Kong to the European Union. *Almanac of China's Foreign Economic Relations and Trade 1994/95*, p.475. See also the note above about time lags in transportation, and the costs of insurance and freight.
19 Economist Intelligence Unit, *Hong Kong and Macau: Country Profile 1995–96*, p.39.
20 Commission of the European Communities (1995: 35).
21 The slowdown in 1994 coincided with attempts by the Chinese authorities to calm an overheating domestic economy and to clamp down on real estate speculation.
22 'The "Chinese mainland factor" has also revitalized Hong Kong's manufacturing industry. Incomplete statistics show that 90 per cent of its electronics industry, 80 per cent of its garment industry and 70 per cent of its shoe and toy industries have shifted their production bases to China's interior areas' *China Daily* (23 June 1997) p.4.
23 At the end of 1996, China had approved a cumulative total of 7,318 EU projects involving US$27.3bn contracted capital *China Daily Business Weekly*, 22–28 June 1997, p.2.
24 On the basis of detailed analysis of enterprises in Shenzhen, Nanhai, and Panyu in Guangdong Province. See Tracy (1995: 5).

25 UNCTAD (1995: 59–69) notes that 'round-tripping gives rise to an inefficient use of resources by Chinese TNCs. It retards the commitment of domestically generated capital to productive uses, requires expenditures on the international networks through which round-tripping capital flows, and diverts the attention of Chinese managers away from "real" competitiveness enhancing initiatives.' Moreover, overvaluation 'lowers tax revenues for the Government as well as the share of revenues accruing to the local partners in joint ventures with TNCs'.
26 The announcement that tax relief for FIEs on imported capital equipment was to be withdrawn from April 1996 is likely to have brought forward certain imports for FIE equipment/materials investment in both 1995 and 1996.
27 Foreign trade, and international competition, may also bring indirect benefits, but these are notoriously difficult to quantify.
28 Except by Czechoslovakia. Qin (1993: 80).
29 Qin (1993: 80) reports that the PRC Government expressed its appreciation of the 1971 GATT decision to remove the observer status that the ROC Government had obtained in 1965, following the passing of UK General Assembly Resolution No. 2758 recognising the PRC Government as the sole legal representative of China to the United Nations, and expelling the representatives of Chiang Kai-Shek from all UN-related organisations.
30 Qin (1993: 77–8) notes that China and GATT both understood that the resumption would serve as a legal formality only, and that the ensuing negotiations were conducted in the typical manner of accession. Harrold (1995: 143) suggests that the issue of accession or resumption was still relevant to WTO entry, as all GATT members had automatically become WTO members.
31 See Lardy (1994: 141–3) for a chronology. The first meeting was in February 1988; the nineteenth in December 1994. The eighth meeting, originally scheduled for July 1989, was cancelled because of the Tiananman Square events, but eventually took place in December 1989.
32 See Harrold (1995: 143–4) for details of various empirical studies of the welfare gains arising from WTO membership.
33 Segal (1994: 326) suggests that 'Chinese membership in the General Agreement on Tariffs and Trade (GATT) is especially desired by Beijing because if membership requires the regions to provide more reporting of data, then the centre will gain power over otherwise freer enterprise in coastal regions. The same transparency that GATT requires of China as a whole will be required by Beijing of its provinces. Indeed, Beijing and international institutions often share common interests. The most egregious cases of Chinese enterprises receiving GATT-violating subsidies or flouting intellectual property rules are to be found at the provincial or township and village enterprise level. Beijing may want to abide by international agreements on these matters, but it simply does not control that part of the economy.'
34 Lardy (1994: 106) credits the European Union for pressurising China into hastening the convertibility of its currency.
35 Negotiations for WTO entry take part not only in the Working Party but also in bilateral discussions on tariff reductions and market access with individual WTO members. Failure to conclude the bilateral discussions to the satisfaction of the WTO members effectively prevents agreement on a Protocol of Accession.
36 There are other contentious issues, such as the application of the US Jackson-Vanik Amendment (Lardy 1994: 47, 136–7).
37 Strange (1996: 160) has suggested that China's dramatic package of Initial Actions at Osaka was a face-saving way of introducing measures required for its WTO entry without being seen to bow directly to international pressure.

38 GATT appointed a Working Party in September 1992 to review the application of Chinese Taipei. The first meeting was held in November 1992 (Lardy 1994: 142–3).
39 China lost control of Hong Kong Island under the Treaty of Nanking (29 August 1842) following the defeat of the Qing Dynasty in the Opium War, and later ceded the Kowloon Peninsula under the Treaty of Tianjin (24 October 1860). The New Territories, and the surrounding 235 islands, were leased to the United Kingdom for a period of 99 years in 1898 under the Convention Regarding an Extension of the Hong Kong Territory. See Ito (1997: 2).

REFERENCES

Ash, R. and Kueh, Y. (1993) 'Economic Integration within Greater China: Trade and Investment Flows between China, Hong Kong and Taiwan', *The China Quarterly*, 136, December: 711–45.

Census and Statistics Department, Hong Kong (1993) 'Review of Hong Kong's Re-Export Trade', *Hong Kong Monthly Digest of Statistics*, May: 117–28.

Census and Statistics Department, Hong Kong (1995) 'Trade Involving Outward Processing in China 1989–1994', *Hong Kong Monthly Digest of Statistics*, June: F1–F15.

Census and Statistics Department, Hong Kong (1996) 'Analysis of Hong Kong's Retained Imports, 1989–1994', *Hong Kong Monthly Digest of Statistics*, February: F2–F18.

Chan, R. (1994) 'Re-Emergence of Re-Export Trade between Hong Kong and China', *Asian Economies*, 23(3): 66–79.

Chen, E. and Wong, T. (1995) 'Economic Synergy: A Study of Two-way Foreign Direct Investment Flow between Hong Kong and China', in Nomura Research Institute and Institute of Southeast Asian Studies, *The New Wave of Foreign Direct Investment in Asia*, Singapore: Institute of Southeast Asian Studies, 243–77.

Commission of the European Communities (1995) *A Long Term Policy for China–Europe Relations*, COM(95)279 final, Luxembourg: Office for Official Publications of the European Communities.

Economist Intelligence Unit (1996) *Hong Kong and Macau: Country Profile 1995–96*, London: EIU.

General Administration of Customs of the People's Republic of China (1996) *China's Customs Statistics*, Beijing: General Administration of Customs of the People's Republic of China.

Harrold, P. (1995) 'China: Foreign Trade Reform: Now for the Hard Part', *Oxford Review of Economic Policy*, 11(4), Winter: 133–46.

Ho, S. and Huenemann, R. (1984) *China's Open Door Policy: The Quest for Foreign Technology and Capital*, Vancouver: University of Columbia Press.

Hussain, A. and Zhuang, J. (1997) 'Chinese State Enterprises and their Reform', in R. Strange (ed.) *Management in China: The Experience of Foreign Businesses*, Ilford: Frank Cass, pp.20–37.

Imai, S. (1990) 'New Developments in the Mainland's Relations with Taiwan', *JETRO China Newsletter*, 89, November–December: 2–9.

Ito, S. (1997) 'The Future of Hong Kong as Seen on the Eve of Handover: A Review of Political, Social and Economic Issues', *RIM: Pacific Business and Industries*, 2(36), June: 2–9.

Japan External Trade Organization (1997) *WTO and Regional Economic Unions: New Trade Environments Taking Shape*, Tokyo: JETRO.

Kohari, S. (1992) 'Chinese–South Korean Economic Relations: An Update', *JETRO China Newsletter*, 97 (March–April 1992): 13–18.

Lardy, N. (1992) 'Chinese Foreign Trade', *The China Quarterly*, 131, September: 691–720.

Lardy, N. (1993) *Foreign Trade and Economic Reform in China, 1978–1990*, Cambridge: Cambridge University Press.

Lardy, N. (1994) *China in the World Economy*, Washington, DC: Institute for International Economics.

Lee, J. and Davies, H. (1995) 'Transforming Hong Kong: From Manufacturing to Services', in H. Davies (ed.) *China Business: Context and Issues*, Hong Kong: Longman Asia, pp.22–36.

Leung, H., Thoburn, J.; Chau, E. and Tang, S. (1991) 'Contractual Relations, Foreign Direct Investment, and Technology Transfer: the Case of China', *Journal of International Development*, 3(3), June: 277–91.

Liu, Y-C. and Strange, R. (1997) 'An Empirical Ranking of International Financial Centers in the Asia-Pacific Region', *The International Executive*, 39(5): 651–74.

Ministry of Foreign Trade and Economic Cooperation, (various years) *Almanac of China's Foreign Economic Relations and Trade*, Beijing: China Economics Publishing House.

Qin, Ya. (1993) 'China and GATT: Accession instead of Resumption', *Journal of World Trade*, 27(2), April: 77–98.

Ruggiero, R. (1997) 'China and the World Trading System', *WTO Focus*, 19, May: 5–6.

Segal, G. (1994) 'Deconstructing Foreign Relations', in D. Goodman and G. Segal (eds) *China Deconstructs: Politics, Trade and Regionalism*, London: Routledge pp.322–55.

Strange, R. (1996) 'Asian Consensus or Pragmatic Realism: APEC at Osaka', *Asia Pacific Business Review*, 2(3), Spring: 152–62.

Strange, R. (1997) 'Trading Blocs, Trade Liberalisation and Foreign Direct Investment', in G. Chryssochoidis, C. Millar and J. Clegg (eds) *Internationalisation Strategies: Current Research*, London: Macmillan, pp.19–42.

Sung, Y-W. (1991a) *The China–Hong Kong Connection: The Key to China's Open Door Policy*, Cambridge: Cambridge University Press.

Sung, Y-W. (1991b) 'Foreign Trade and Investment', *China Review 1990*, Hong Kong: The Chinese University Press, 15.1–15.21.

Tang, K. (1995) 'The Chinese Economic Area: Hong Kong–China Trade and Investment Relations', in OECD, *Foreign Direct Investment: OECD Countries and Dynamic Economies of Asia and Latin America*, Paris: OECD, pp.41–51.

Tom, C. (1957) *Entrepot Trade and the Monetary Standards of Hong Kong, 1842–1942*, Chicago: University of Chicago Press.

Tracy, N. (1995) 'Transforming Southern China: the Role of the Chinese Diaspora in the Era of Reform', in H. Davies (ed.) *China Business: Context and Issues*, Hong Kong: Longman Asia, pp.1–21.

United Nations Conference on Trade and Development (1995) *World Investment Report 1995: Transnational Corporations and Competitiveness*, Geneva: United Nations.

Wakabayashi, M. (1990) 'Relations between Taiwan and China during the 1980s, viewed from the Taiwan Perspective', *JETRO China Newsletter*, 87, July–August: 6–16.

World Bank (1993) *The East Asian Miracle: Economic Growth and Public Policy*, New York: Oxford University Press.

World Bank (1994) *China: Foreign Trade Reform*, Washington, DC: the World Bank.

World Bank (1995) *The World Bank Atlas 1996*, Washington, DC: the World Bank.

Section I

The trade and investment environment

2 Foreign trade and investment
Policy reforms in China in the mid-1990s

M. John Foster

INTRODUCTION

The history of the 'open-door' policy in the People's Republic of China (PRC) is well documented, and the effects upon the flows of trade and foreign direct investment (FDI) have been striking. China has evolved from being a largely self-sufficient, inward-looking country, to being one of the foremost recipients of inward FDI and one of the major traders in the world in the mid-1990s (Harrold 1995: 133). The precise scale of the changes can be seen from the tables of trade and FDI data presented in Chapter 1. What is also very clear from those tables is just how important Hong Kong is as a conduit for China's trade.

The challenge for China through the remainder of the 1990s and into the twenty-first century is to build upon this impressive performance and to develop a 'market-oriented' system which is consistent with their long-term goals of independence, self-reliance and, some would argue, their ultimate goal of dominance in the global market-place. To this end, the Chinese authorities had embarked upon a series of ambitious reforms by the mid-1990s with regard not only to FDI policy and the foreign trade system, but also *inter alia* to the foreign exchange system and the taxation system. These reforms are outlined in this chapter, and consideration is given to their effects upon future flows of trade and direct investment. It is worth emphasising that these reforms are only part of a wider package of reform (see, for example, Chapter 11 for details of the reforms to the banking system) which touch upon almost all aspects of economic activity in China, and any comprehensive assessment of their impact should take these wider considerations into account.

REFORM OF THE FOREIGN TRADE SYSTEM

The traditional objective of foreign trade planning in China[1] was to establish which essential materials and commodities were in short supply domestically and thus needed to be imported, and then to arrange for suitable quantities of selected exports to be produced in order to generate the necessary foreign exchange to fund these imports. Thus the plan was geared towards satisfying import requirements. Furthermore, at the inception of the 'open-door' policy in 1978, foreign trade was monopolised by twelve national Foreign Trade Corporations (FTCs) and their branches. As Harrold (1995: 136) notes,

> All transactions with producers took place at domestic prices, on the basis of 'balancing' domestic supply and demand. The exchange rate was merely for accounting purposes, but was so overvalued that losses were around 2 per cent of GDP. Thus the FTCs operated an 'economic buffer' shielding the domestic economy from external influences.

The foreign trade system was considerably decentralised in 1984, when each province was allowed to create its own FTCs and the provincial branches of the national FTCs were permitted to operate as independent bodies. As a result, the number of FTCs rose to 1,200 in 1986, and to over 5,000 in 1988.[2] The foreign trade plan also became more export-driven. The objective of the planning exercise became one of keeping imports within the foreign exchange constraint implied by the export plan. This latter had two components: a command plan and a guidance plan.

> The command plan was mandatory, fixed in quantitative terms, applied to specific products, and was accompanied by an assured supply of necessary inputs to the producing enterprises. In contrast, the guidance plan contained value targets assigned to provincial authorities, which were accorded considerable flexibility in determining how to achieve them.
> (World Bank 1994: 24–5)

All export transactions had to be routed through FTCs and, at least in the case of the command plan (to which 60 per cent of exports were subject in 1986), were effected at fixed prices. There was thus only a weak indirect link between international prices and the prices received by exporters. The import plan had three components: a mandatory plan for key raw materials whose import was to be handled only by designated national and/or provincial FTCs; a system of foreign exchange allocation for investment projects; and an import licence system. All mandatory imports took place at fixed prices, but an agency system was instigated for non-mandatory imports under which importers were free to choose any FTC and would pay the import price plus the FTC's commission.

The FTCs were thus bound by their obligations under the mandatory export and import plans, but were also required to buy or sell selected goods and commodities at domestic prices which were higher or lower than the corresponding international prices. They thus ran up substantial financial losses, which needed to be covered by direct fiscal subsidies.

In 1988, a further round of reforms initiated a contract system between the Ministry of Foreign Economic Relations and Trade (MOFERT)[3] and the FTCs under which targets were given to each FTC for foreign exchange earnings, the amount of foreign exchange earnings to be remitted to the central government, and the amount of subsidy that the centre would provide to cover losses on export sales. One of the main rationales for the contract system was its attempted limitation of the export losses for which the central government was responsible, while the latter still maintained indirect control over the increasing amount of decentralised trade. The contract system was modified in 1991 and targets for the value of exports, foreign exchange earnings, and foreign exchange to be remitted to the central authorities were thereafter fixed on a 'bottom-up' basis by the enterprises and local authorities after negotiation with the centre. Furthermore, all specialised national FTCs and all provincial administrative units were made responsible for their domestic currency profits and losses on exports.

The import plan also was scaled down after 1988, though not to the same extent as the export plan, and the coverage of the trade plan fell (from 40 per cent in 1988) to under 20 per cent by 1992. A large proportion of non-mandatory plan imports were still, however, subject to administrative regulation through tight control of foreign exchange allocations.

The new Foreign Trade Law of the People's Republic of China, which was promulgated on 12 May 1994 and which came into effect on 1 July 1994, was a very significant piece of legislation as it ended mandatory planning for all foreign trade enterprises. The Law abolished foreign trade subsidies, and help for exporters has since been provided through internationally acceptable channels such as export refunds, risk funds, and the establishment of specialised financial institutions to promote foreign trade. Administrative restrictions on imports were also abolished, and replaced by internationally acceptable anti-dumping and anti-subsidy legislation. Notwithstanding the above, however, the Law did not preclude State management of exports and imports, only insisting that it should be transparent and WTO-consistent (China's application to rejoin GATT/WTO is discussed in Chapter 1), and actually laid down detailed rules for the importation and exportation of selected goods and technologies (see below). In addition, the Law set down major principles to be followed by those engaged in international service-related trade (i.e. trade in finance, transport, tourism, telecommunications, consulting services, and contracted-out projects).

The General Provision of the Law states that China will conduct trade under a 'unified' foreign trade system, i.e. irrespective of Special Economic Zones (SEZs), Economic and Technological Development Zones (ETDZs), open cities, etc. In a sense there is a contradiction or paradox here for, while it may be policy to operate a unified system, the tax incentives available in the SEZs and other zones may be seen as inimical to the notion of a unified policy. At the top level of this unified system is the Ministry of Foreign Trade and Economic Cooperation (MOFTEC) which has been charged by the State Council with the macro-regulation of foreign trade for the whole country and the construction of an appropriate legal system for foreign trade. MOFTEC has responsibility for formulating both a development strategy and policy for foreign trade, and for organising their supervision and enforcement. In addition, the Ministry is in charge of external negotiations and is empowered to sign treaties on behalf of the Chinese Government. Various Departments under the State Council may also be involved in managing activities relating to the import and export of goods and technology. For example, the State Planning Commission is in charge of the management of import quotas for general goods; the State Economic and Trade Commission is in charge of the export and import of machine-building and electronic products; and the State Science and Technology Commission, together with the Commission of Science, Technology and Industry for National Defence, oversee and monitor the import and export of high technology.[4]

At the provincial level, or in autonomous regions or centrally administered municipalities, the local Foreign Trade and Economic Commission (or Bureau) has responsibility for foreign trade, and its role is to implement measures consistent with the Foreign Trade Law and appropriate to the local situation under the guidance of the local government. Finally, there are the organisations, firms and/or individuals who produce the exports or purchase the imports. The Law abolished various foreign trade subsidies, and explicitly stipulated that managers should take responsibility for their own profits and losses. Each manager who is engaged in the import/export of goods and/or technology must be approved by the appropriate (State Council) Department; otherwise trade may be undertaken through authorised foreign trade managers. By the end of 1994, more than 7,000 Chinese enterprises had been approved to undertake foreign trade (either as principal or as agent), and over 200,000 foreign investment enterprises (FIEs) also had foreign trade rights. As about half of the FIEs were in operation, over 100,000 enterprises were thus permitted to engage directly in foreign trade. According to Madam Wu Yi, the Minister in charge of MOFTEC, the approval system for foreign trade rights was a transitional measure, which would be relaxed in stages and eventually replaced by a register system. No timescale was set for this development though the approval system had in practice been speeded up and simplified by the end of 1997.

Trade in a number of goods and technologies has been restricted by the Law, and may only be carried out under conditions stipulated therein. Thus eighteen machine-building and electronic products (including cars, motorcycles, video cassette recorders, computers, and air conditioners) are subject to import quotas.[5] Other goods, as specified in *The Catalogue of General Goods Subject to Import Quota Management*, may also be subject to quotas.[6] Currently, the list includes twenty-six commodities, including crude oil, timber, cotton, grain, and pesticides.

Export quotas are also set by MOFTEC for a variety of products, and are administered under one of three schemes: plan quota management, active quota management, or passive quota management. The main difference between plan quota management and active/passive quota management is the degree of involvement of the State. Some thirty-eight commodities (including rice, tea, crude oil, finished oil products, coal, and cotton) are subject to plan quota management, under which MOFTEC[7] sets national quotas for exports, and allocates local quotas to each region. The Economic and Trade Commission (or Bureau) within each region (such as the local Foreign Trade Corporation) then assigns the local quotas to individual businesses. A further fifty-four commodities are subject to active quota management.[8] These quotas are determined by MOFTEC according to the prevailing supply conditions in the domestic market and the needs of the international market, and are published in a catalogue which also details countries or regions to which each of the commodities may be exported. The local Economic and Trade Commission is charged with assigning and redistributing the local active quota. Some twenty-four commodities are currently subject to passive quota management. These commodities are divided into two categories: 'textiles' and 'non-textiles'. In both cases, MOFTEC announces the export quota for each region in accordance with *The Textile Export Quota Management Methods*, and these amounts are allocated by the local Economic and Trade Commissions. There are nineteen textile products (including cotton yarn, woollen yarn, knitting wool, and chemical fibres) covered by passive quotas, together with the quota amounts. These are stipulated in the various bilateral, textile-trade agreements between China and its partner countries (Chapter 3 discusses textile agreements between China and the EU).

In February 1994, MOFTEC introduced a new method for allocating export quotas, under which enterprises must tender for the quota rights.[9] The tenderer must be a foreign trade manager approved by MOFTEC. Productive enterprises and FIEs may only tender for quota rights for their own products. Import/export companies must first join the relevant Import/Export Chamber of Commerce for the product in question. Some thirteen types of commodity (including logs and ramie gauze) were included in the scheme from March 1994, and this figure was expanded to twenty-four commodities in 1995. The introduction of the tender scheme marks a move from a strictly administrative system of State management of export quotas towards a greater reliance on competitive market forces.

The allocation of a quota is the first, but not sufficient, step for an enterprise which wishes to import or export the commodities in question. The enterprise must also apply for a licence.[10] MOFTEC is in sole overall charge of the export goods licence system, while the import goods licence system is managed by MOFTEC together with the State Planning Commission and the State Commission for Economics and Trade. Responsibility for the examination, approval and verification of licences is delegated to the Quota Licence Affairs Bureau of MOFTEC and to local authorities in each region. Technology imports and exports are also subject to licence management by MOFTEC,[11] and its authorised departments. The State Planning Commission is in charge of the examination and approval of the introduction of technology; the State Science and Technology Commission is in charge of technical examination;[12] and MOFTEC is in charge of contract examination.

As we saw above, FIEs are becoming an increasingly important element, in terms of enterprise numbers, of the trading structure of the PRC. Many have a strong export focus and others have requirements for imported goods or technologies. Table 1.14 on p. 31 illustrates the precise scale of the role of FIEs in China's foreign trade, up to 41 per cent of exports and 55 per cent of imports by 1996. Data relating to the PRC's economic activities are notoriously unreliable, not least in this case because of a booming 'black' economy, but the figures quoted are significant by any standards.

An FIE will then necessarily have a keen interest in the evolution of trade regulations. Further, any 'overseas' company planning some sort of FDI in China will need to be fully aware of these facts, whether they seek to establish wholly foreign-owned enterprises (WFOEs) or to undertake joint ventures with Chinese firms.

REFORM OF THE FOREIGN EXCHANGE RATE SYSTEM

China had dual exchange rates, official and secondary, between 1981 and 1984.[13] The former was set under a system of managed floating, while the latter (also termed the internal settlement rate) was fixed at a lower rate, and was used for the settlement of payments between FTCs and their supplying enterprises. In January 1985, the official exchange rate was set equal to the secondary rate, and the latter was abolished.

In addition, China also operated a rigid system of exchange control under which domestic exporters had to surrender all their foreign exchange earnings to the Bank of China in exchange for domestic currency. Foreign exchange to finance imports was allocated to would-be importers by the State Planning Commission according to the annual import plan. In contrast, FIEs could retain 100 per cent of their foreign exchange earnings.

In late 1986, Foreign Exchange Adjustment (swap) Centres (FEACs) were established, and this led to the re-emergence of a dual exchange rate system. The official rate was used for foreign trade and other external transactions included in the annual foreign exchange plan, while the (lower) swap market rate was determined by supply and demand in the FEACs. Foreigners were required to use the official rate when valuing their inward investment, but were subject to the swap market rate when converting local currency to foreign currency for repatriation of profits.

Through the 1980s, local authorities and domestic enterprises, where authorised, were gradually permitted to retain ever-larger proportions[14] of their foreign exchange earnings. These retention quotas were transferable between enterprises and were initially transacted at the official exchange rate but, by 1988, all domestic enterprises and FIEs were permitted to trade retention quotas in the FEACs. In February 1991, the retention system was subject to several important modifications. A uniform retention rate was set for the whole country, although special rates were retained and adjusted upwards for favoured sectors – another example of the paradox of 'uniformity' mentioned earlier. Also, the central government reserved the right to purchase up to 30 per cent of the foreign exchange retained by local authorities and enterprises to meet its own requirements. In years when this option was fully exercised, exporters were left with no foreign exchange with which to buy non-plan imports.

On 1 January 1994, the dual exchange rate system was abolished and a managed floating of the Renminbi was introduced. The daily rate was set by the People's Bank of China (PBOC) on the basis of average prices at the major swap centres. Furthermore, the management of the system was reorganised so that the State Administration of Foreign Exchange (SAFE), the China Foreign Exchange Trade Network (located in Shanghai) and fourteen banks were thereafter permitted to conduct foreign exchange transactions. This has been viewed as a major step towards the establishment of a full national foreign exchange market where enterprises will be able to purchase foreign exchange directly from banks, and should lead to the eventual elimination of the swap markets. In the meantime, banks and FEACs operate parallel foreign exchange markets, and FIEs are permitted to use either. Since 1 July 1996, FIEs have been permitted to sell their RMB earnings to purchase hard currency at selected banks, and thus repatriate their profits, dividends and interest earnings. According to Prime and Park (1997: 8), China considers these changes as meeting the IMF requirement for current account convertibility.

Elsewhere, it was reported[15] that, from 1 December 1996, the RMB had become convertible 'under the current account'. This included trade, labour, tourism and short-term banking facilities, but direct investment, international loans and securities trading were still restricted. The indirect process for the remission of FIE RMB earnings is part of this set of restrictions which arguably make the RMB less than truly convertible.

A development which may be expected to facilitate foreign exchange dealing for foreign investors in China was the announcement in early 1997 by the PBOC that, subject to certain qualifying criteria, some foreign banks would be allowed to conduct business in Renminbi. Initially, this facility was limited to banks in the Pudong area of Greater Shanghai, but in June 1997, it was announced that this scheme would be extended to foreign-funded banks in Shenzhen.

REFORM OF THE FOREIGN DIRECT INVESTMENT REGIME

The 1990s have also witnessed significant changes in the PRC policy towards foreign direct investment. Previously, the Chinese Government had favoured a policy of regional preference for FDI, but the new emphasis envisaged FDI supporting a unified national industrial policy geared towards the promotion of selected sectors. This new industrial policy was outlined by the State Council in April 1994 and, as Chen (1997: 158) notes, the main points included:

- the further strengthening of agriculture as a foundation for the expansion of the rural economy;
- the construction of more basic industry, in order to ease the lack of basic industrial products and infrastructure;
- an acceleration in the development of the mechanical and electronic engineering industries, the petrochemical industry, the construction industry, and the automobile industry (see Chapter 7), in order to revitalise the national economy;
- adjustment of the structure of China's foreign economic relations in order to enhance China's competitiveness in world markets;
- faster development of new high-technology industries;
- continued development of the service sector;
- the development of an export-orientation in the coastal areas, building on existing strengths, by concentrating on industries able to make use of foreign capital and resources, and focus on high value-added products which can in turn earn foreign exchange.

The role of FDI within this new industrial policy was clarified by the *Provisional Guidelines on Foreign Investment Projects*, which took effect on 27 July 1995. In line with the domestic industrial objectives, priority was to be given to FDI projects in agriculture, infrastructure, communications, energy, transportation, basic raw materials, and high-technology industries. The *Guidelines* further stipulated that all FDI projects would be classified as either 'encouraged', 'restricted', 'prohibited', or 'permitted', according to the *Guiding Catalogue of Foreign Investment Projects*.[16] Those projects which were to be 'encouraged' would be allowed to sell up to 100 per cent of their output in the domestic market and/or would retain certain tax advantages, but would be required to:

- use new/advanced technology to upgrade product function, save energy and/or raw materials; or
- manufacture new equipment/materials for which there was excess demand; or
- use new technology/equipment which economised on natural and/or renewable resources, and/or prevented/controlled pollution; or
- make use of human/natural resources in the inland areas in the Central and North-West regions of China; or
- be export-oriented.

'Restricted' projects were those that used standard technologies, or where there was already excess domestic supply (Division A); and those under some degree of State Control (Division B). Most Division A projects concern investments by overseas Chinese from Hong Kong, Macau, and Taiwan, and require approval by provincial or higher-level planning authorities. Approval would only be granted if the project has a projected export/sales ratio of greater that 70 per cent, or if it permitted the development of resources in the favoured inland areas. The 'prohibited' list applies to projects which are deemed to be against the national interest, and include investments in various industries including postal and network telecommunications operations (see Chapter 10 for further discussion), although Cable and Wireless' new deal (in June 1997) may mark a softening of policy in this area.

'Permitted' projects were not explicitly defined in the *Guiding Catalogue*, but are those not classified as 'encouraged', 'restricted' or 'prohibited'. Restrictions on investment in various service industries were eased, notably in insurance (see Chapter 12), the retail trade, advertising, engineering and financial services (Prime and Park 1997: 7). Furthermore, as a further move towards decentralisation, the maximum size of project which may be approved by local authorities was raised from US$10m to US$30m by the State Council in September 1996.

Control over the process of approval of FDI contracts and the registration of foreign enterprises was also tightened when MOFTEC and the State Administration for Industry and Commerce (SAFIC) issued, in November 1995, the *Circular on Issues relating to Strengthening the Examination and Approval of Foreign-Funded Enterprises*.[17] Foreign investors have since been required to pay in their registered capital within a prescribed time limit, or else lose their business licence. The *Circular* also made allowance for penalties to be applied to phoney ventures set up to take advantage of favourable tax incentives.

Looking back to the data in Chapter 1, Table 1.12 on p. 27 shows the dramatic scale of FDI development since the beginning of China's economic reforms. Numbers of contracted new projects peaked at just over 83,000 in 1993. However, average value per project and aggregate realised value were higher in 1994 and 1995 than had been the case in 1993, although the scale of projects is still relatively modest in many cases – average contracted value per project was just US$2.47m in 1995.

Where much of the early impetus was in the southern coastal area and Shanghai, FDI projects are now pervasive in China. For example, as Pu and Foster (1996) report, the north-eastern province of Jilin could boast just one such project in 1984, but by 1994 this had risen to almost 3,000 projects with a paid in foreign capital of US$1,530m.

The complementary question to the last point is, whence does the foreign investment come? Again, the early pattern was that much of the investment came from Taiwan and Hong Kong and the pattern continues, as Table 1.13 on p. 28 shows very clearly. Table 1.13 shows almost 60 per cent of contracted FDI for the period 1990–95 coming from Hong Kong, 7.4 per cent from Taiwan (*more* than the 6.7 per cent from the United States!) and some 5 per cent from the European Union. The United Kingdom accounts for almost half of the EU figure. What these figures tend to suggest is that the overseas Chinese of Southeast Asia are unequivocal investors, while the Triad members are increasingly present but on a more limited scale.

Notwithstanding the developments detailed above, some commentators still consider that China does not have a policy of an 'open-door' so much as 'a door which is not closed'. Foreign investors are allowed in, but very much on China's terms, and they are subject to many regulations and have to overcome many difficulties (Chan 1991). This idea and the comparatively limited scale of Triad direct investment in China fit well with the wealth of anecdotal evidence that businesses in Europe and the United States feel obliged to 'be there' but also feel that they are going to have to play a long game if they are eventually to make big money from investing in China.

REFORM OF THE TAXATION SYSTEM

Towards the end of 1993, a series of new tax laws[18] were published with a view to introducing a new system of 'tax-sharing' between central and provincial governments (Chen 1997: 160). These reforms endeavoured to put foreign and domestic firms on an equal footing, while also increasing central government revenues. The outmoded industrial and commercial consolidated tax (ICCT) was replaced by a range of indirect taxes: a 17 per cent value-added tax (VAT), a 3–5 per cent business tax (on some service industries), and a 3–45 per cent Consumption Tax.[19] Tax revenues were to be divided between the central government and the provincial governments in such a way as to make the provincial governments bear the costs whenever they granted unauthorised tax concessions to foreign firms. For example, under the April 1991 Income Tax Law of the People's Republic of China for Enterprises with Foreign Investment and Foreign Enterprises, only 122 investment zones approved by the State Council were allowed to levy reduced income tax rates on foreign enterprises (see below). In practice, however, hundreds of other zones and non-zones did the same, at the expense of central government revenues. As from January 1994, however, the central government aimed to derive most of its income from the Consumption Tax and from its 80 per cent share of the VAT receipts, while the provincial governments collect the enterprise income taxes. If a provincial government outside an approved zone levies tax at a reduced rate, then it must now pay directly for its generosity.

The reforms cut the number of tax categories affecting FIEs and foreign employees to eleven, of which the most significant are enterprise income tax, local income surcharge, personal income tax, real estate tax, fees for land use, and tax on the licence plates of vehicles.

As regards enterprise income tax, the preferential policies granted to FIEs remained essentially unchanged under the new system. Thus, according to the 1991 Income Tax Law,[20] FIEs are subject to a 30 per cent tax rate on their profits together with a local income surcharge of 3 per cent, unless they meet one of the following criteria:

- the rate of tax will be 15 per cent if the FIE is located in one of the SEZs, or is a manufacturing concern in one of the ETDZs;
- the rate of tax will be 15 per cent if the FIE has been designated a high-technology enterprise, and is located in a High Technology Development Zone (HTDZ);
- the rate of tax will be 15 per cent if the FIE is engaged in energy, transportation, or other projects encouraged by the State and/or in large (i.e. foreign capital subscription over US$30m) infrastructure projects located in any part of the country;
- the rate of tax will be 24 per cent if the FIE is a manufacturing concern located in one of the coastal open economic zones, or in the old urban districts of cities where the SEZs and ETDZs are located;
- the rate of tax will be 10 per cent for FIEs which export at least 70 per cent of their total production value, once their period of tax reduction/exemption expires;
- the rate of tax will be zero for manufacturing FIEs in the first two years of profit-making, and will be reduced by half in the following three years, provided that they are scheduled to operate for more than ten years;
- the rate of tax will be reduced by 15–30 per cent for a further ten years for manufacturing FIEs which are engaged in agriculture, forestry or animal husbandry, or which are located in remote underdeveloped areas of China;
- the rate of tax will be 15 per cent for foreign capital banks or Sino-foreign joint venture banks located in one of the SEZs, or any other area approved by the State Council, and which have foreign capital in excess of US$10m and which are scheduled to operate for more than ten years. Furthermore, such banks will be exempt from tax in their first profit-making year, and their tax rate will be halved in the two succeeding years.
- the rate of tax will be zero for the five years after first making a profit for any FIE located either in Hainan Province or in the Pudong area of Shanghai engaged in infrastructure projects, and for any FIE, in operation for fifteen years or more, located anywhere engaged in harbour or wharf projects.

In addition, tax relief for FIEs is available when profits are reinvested and losses may be offset against future profits for up to five years. Post-tax profits of FIEs, commission fees, and other intermediary/consultancy income may be remitted freely abroad, and are exempt from withholding taxes.

As regards personal income tax, the rate applicable to wages and salaries has been reduced by 50 per cent for foreign employees, who also pay tax at a reduced rate of 10 per cent on their service remuneration, royalties, interest, dividends, rent from property, and other income. Income arising from scientific and technical inventions and from publications is tax-free.

Each local government body may (subject to the provisos noted above) grant FIEs reductions and exemptions from their local surcharges, fees for land use, real estate taxes, and taxes for vehicle licence plates. In practice, such favourable treatment is more likely to be accorded to FIEs producing goods for export or which bring in advanced technology, or which promote the development of infrastructure and basic industries, the technical improvement of existing enterprises, or which facilitate the growth of industries where there is already some local expertise.

CONCLUDING REMARKS

In this chapter, we have seen that foreign trade from and direct investment into China have continued to grow rapidly in the 1990s within a changing and developing policy framework. The changes in policy have been designed *inter alia* to make the PRC economy more export-oriented; to change FDI policy from a regional to a more sectoral orientation; and overall to make its activities consistent with WTO rules – thereby facilitating its application for membership of same. Reference has been made to a 'unified' industrial policy.

The notion of a unified policy for all of China, be it in respect of trade or FDI, does not sit altogether easily with the continued existence of preferential treatments available for various categories of enterprise in different areas of China (e.g. the continued tax breaks in SEZs and other types of development zone). There have been 'reports' that these sorts of preferential treatments may be phased out within the foreseeable future, but no concrete steps seem to have been taken yet by the central authorities. It is of course also axiomatic that, if the Beijing Government honours the Basic Law for Hong Kong, there will be a different set of policies operating in Hong Kong for the next fifty years.

The continuing, differential benefits may be unsurprising if, as one assumes, it continues to be policy to encourage foreign investors into China. There are a great number of foreign-invested projects already, and new ventures continue to be announced. At the same time anecdotal evidence suggests that, tax breaks and the like notwithstanding, many FIEs are finding it hard going to make any serious money from their ventures. This is as true of EU businesses as any others: it is not hard to find businessmen in Europe who talk of the necessity to 'take a long-term view of their Chinese projects'.

One of the important features of the evolving policy frameworks for the areas discussed here is their very existence. The fact that there are detailed policies and attendant regulations would seem to make it easier for foreigners to trade with or invest in the PRC. In a sense this is true, but the difficulty rests in the fact that often in China things are not what they seem to the untutored observer. According to Western precepts, the standard of draftsmanship in regulation is often relatively loose and there is the underlying reality that everything is 'open to negotiation' – for a vivid illustration of this point, involving a Chinese-owned overseas company, see Foster (1997). This explains in part why so many Western businesses find the going tough when they enter China.

Overall, the scale of many of the non-Chinese-owned foreign investments in China is relatively modest by world standards, and the rates of return achieved have been relatively modest. However, the continuing concern for many businessmen in Europe and elsewhere is whether they can afford not to 'be there' as the world's fastest growing economy forges ahead. The market may be a difficult one in which to trade in 1997, but will that still be true in 2007? Were it to be much easier then and one had ceded one's place at the economic table, frustration would be inevitable!

From the perspective of China's economic managers, trade is the engine of their desired, continuing growth and they have a self-interest in being accepted as trading within WTO guidelines, if they are to achieve the acceptance into the wider world economy which they seek. Continued FDI into China is likely to be a major support for and/or stimulus to enhanced trading operations for two reasons. First, FDI can bring technological benefits to the PRC economy more quickly than might be the case were they to be internally developed. Second, and perhaps more importantly, foreign investors bring with them both immediate foreign currency capital and improved access to capital markets. Finally, it may be the case that working with foreign companies will give China access to more efficient management and working practices, but the jury is still out on whether such foreign methods will be resisted as inimical to Chinese cultural mores.

NOTES

1 The early part of this section draws heavily on World Bank (1994: 24–8).
2 Some 1,400 FTCs were closed down in 1988–89.
3 Later to be renamed the Ministry for Foreign Trade and Economic Cooperation (MOFTEC).
4 For a more detailed description of these arrangements, see Pu and Foster (1996).
5 The quotas are set by the Import and Export Office of the Ministry of Machine-building and Electronics Industry, and are assigned to local regions after approval by the State Council. The local authorities in the regions are then responsible for the award of import quota certificates to successful applicants.
6 The *Catalogue* is produced by the State Planning Commission and MOFTEC, and the quotas are set by the State Planning Commission. These are then assigned by the State Planning Commission to the authorities in the local region, who then issue import quota certificates to the successful applicants.
7 The plans for eighteen of the thirty-eight commodities are handled jointly by MOFTEC and the State Planning Commission, and the quotas are managed by the State Planning Commission.
8 The *Detailed Rules and Regulations for Enforcing Export Commodity Active Quota Management* were promulgated by MOFTEC on 10 April 1993.

9 See *The Export Commodity Quota Inviting Tenders Method* promulgated by MOFTEC in February 1994. The Inviting Tenders Commission comprises MOFTEC and the relevant State Import/Export Chamber of Commerce.
10 The first administrative rules concerning licence management were set out in *Import Goods Licence System, Temporary Provision, PRC* which came into force on 10 January 1984.
11 See the *Detailed Performance Rules of Contract Management Regulation for the Introduction of Technology* promulgated by MOFTEC in 1988.
12 And of a list of technologies in which trade is limited and/or prohibited.
13 The early part of this section draws heavily on World Bank (1994: 24–34).
14 These proportions varied by province, by industrial sector, and according to whether or not earnings were above planned targets. The retained earnings would generally be split between the firms producing the exported good and the FTC handling the transaction.
15 *China–Britain Trade Review* (January 1997) p.3.
16 See Wu and Strange (1997: 204–6) for further details.
17 MOFTEC, *International Business*, issue 4 (April 1995) pp.63–4.
18 The *Detailed Implementing Rules for the Provisional Regulations of the People's Republic of China concerning Value Added Tax*; the *Detailed Implementing Rules for the Provisional Regulations of the People's Republic of China concerning Business Tax*; and the *Detailed Implementing Rules for the Provisional Regulations of the People's Republic of China concerning Consumption Tax* were all promulgated on 25 December 1993, and became effective on 1 January 1994.
19 Tax rates vary according to the category of the goods: for example, 3–8 per cent for small motor vehicles, and 30–40 per cent for tobacco products.
20 See also the October 1986 *Provisions of the State Council of the People's Republic of China for the Encouragement of Foreign Investment*.

REFERENCES

Chan, H. (1991) *China's Road to Free Enterprise*, Business and Management Working Paper 91-4, Hong Kong: City Polytechnic of Hong Kong.
Chen, C. (1997) 'The Recent Changes in PRC's Economic Development Strategy and their Impact on Foreign Direct Investment in China', in J. Slater and R. Strange (eds) *Business Relationships with East Asia: The European Experience*, London: Routledge, pp.151–70.
China Britain Trade Group (1997) *China–Britain Trade Review*, 387, January.
Foster, M.J. (1997) 'Straight Business Chinese Style', *Asian Case Research Journal*, 1 (1): 43–51.
Harrold, P. (1995) 'China: Foreign Trade Reform: Now for the Hard Part', *Oxford Review of Economic Policy*, 11, 4: 133–46.
Prime, P. and Park, J. (1997) 'China's Foreign Trade and Investment Strategies: Implications for the Business Environment', paper presented at the Conference on International Business in China, Beijing, 25–28 June 1997.
Pu, Z. and Foster, M.J. (1996) *How to do Business in China*, Business Paper 33, Kingston: Kingston Business School.
World Bank (1994) *China: Foreign Trade Reform*, Washington, DC, The World Bank.
Wu, X. and Strange, R. (1997) 'FDI Policy and Inward Direct Investment in China', in J. Slater and R. Strange (eds) *Business Relationships with East Asia: The European Experience*, London, Routledge, pp.199–217.

3 EU trade policy towards China

Roger Strange

INTRODUCTION

In July 1995, the European Commission (1995) published a document entitled *A Long-Term Policy for China–Europe Relations*. The document was part of a wider Asian strategy which emphasised the need for the European Union to take a more pro-active approach towards all countries in the region so as to protect its economic interests against competition from Japan, the United States, etc. As with all such documents, it contained a heady combination of lofty principles, flattering statistics, and ambitious objectives. Thus:

> the time has come to redefine the EU's relationship with China, in the spirit of the "new Asia strategy" endorsed by the Essen European Council. Europe must develop a long-term relationship with China that reflects China's worldwide, as well as regional, economic and political influence. Europe's relations with China are bound to be a cornerstone in Europe's external relations, both with Asia and globally. Europe needs an action-oriented, not a merely declaratory policy, to strengthen that relationship.
> (Commission of the European Communities 1995: 1)

The aim of this chapter is to examine the reality behind the upbeat rhetoric, and to clarify the current situation with regard to official EU trade policy towards China by tracing the evolution of that policy since the early 1970s. In so doing, attention is drawn *inter alia* to the fact that the European Union is increasingly taking a much tougher stance on imports from China notwithstanding the official rhetoric to the contrary, and to the confusion as to whether China should be classified as a developing economy or as a state-trading economy.

THE ESTABLISHMENT OF OFFICIAL RELATIONS

Trade between the European Community and China was limited up until the 1970s for a number of reasons. First, Mao Zedong's policy of self-sufficiency did not encourage trade with other countries, particularly countries outside the communist bloc. Second, China lacked the foreign exchange needed for foreign trade transactions. Third, China did not produce many exportable items which could be used to finance imports. China's interest in the Community was, however, kindled in the early 1970s as the Cultural Revolution began to falter, and as China started to view the Community as a cohesive economic and political unit. Not only could the Community supply China with necessary imports thus easing the latter's dependence on Japan and the United States as suppliers of resources, but it could also act as an 'intermediate zone' to prevent the domination of the world by the two superpowers.[1]

Various Chinese diplomatic initiatives towards the Community ensued. The most significant of these was the personal invitation extended in the autumn of 1973 to Christopher Soames, the Commission Vice President in charge of Foreign Affairs, to visit China. Kapur (1986: 29) suggests that

> the Chinese did not wish to give an official character to the invitation since the textile accord, concluded between the Community and the "Republic of Taiwan" on 1 October 1970 and valid for three years, had just expired, and Beijing was not at all sure what the Commission's future intentions were regarding its relations with Taiwan. The fear of creating a 'two Chinas' precedent was too great to permit a formal invitation being extended as long as EEC–Taiwan relations were not clear.

The Commission's response to the invitation was positive, and was favoured by its impending acquisition of a new mandate to negotiate commercial treaties with state-trading countries on behalf of all its Member States.[2] Kapur (1986: 31) notes that the Chinese signals 'could hardly be ignored as the establishment of relations with them could only contribute to the further enhancement of the Commission's role in the ongoing process of becoming an international participant'. Furthermore, general circumstances were favourable for increased contact between the Community and China. First and foremost, China was perceived – not only by assorted politicians and bureaucrats but also by Western businessmen – as a huge potential market. Second, the Sino-US relationship had thawed somewhat following the official visit of President Nixon to China in February 1972 (although formal diplomatic relations were not established until 1978). Japan, however, had formally resumed diplomatic relations with China in September 1972,[3] and there was European concern that US and Japanese firms might establish a dominant presence in the Chinese market unless prompt action was taken. Third, all the Member States of the Community (with the exception of Ireland) had already established diplomatic relations with China.

Notwithstanding the friendly Chinese overtures, it was the European Commission who took the first concrete steps. In November 1974, the Commission forwarded a memorandum to China, together with an outline draft of a possible trade agreement.[4] And the Commission accepted the invitation for Soames to visit China although it insisted that the visit be official. The Soames visit took place between 4 May and 11 May 1975, and marked the establishment of official relations between the European Community and China (Yue 1993: 4). One sensitive issue was the status of Taiwan. China refused to have official relations with any State or organisation which acknowledged Taiwan as an independent state, and wanted the Community to declare formally its support for the view that Taiwan was an integral part of the People's Republic. The Community was reluctant to do so, but a compromise was reached with Soames publicly stating that the Community had no official relations or agreements[5] with Taiwan (Kapur 1986: 37; Yue 1993: 6–7).

The Soames visit was a turning point in Sino-EC interaction, and formal talks soon opened (January 1976) on a trade agreement between the two parties. The subsequent negotiations were interrupted by Mao's death in September 1976 (and that of Zhou Enlai in January 1976) and the associated political turbulence in China, but thereafter proceeded fairly rapidly. On 3 April 1978, the two sides signed an agreement[6] on bilateral trade which entered into force on 1 June 1978.

THE 1978 TRADE AGREEMENT

The 1978 Trade Agreement was initially scheduled to last five years, but was renewed[7] at the instigation of the Community before being replaced by the 1985 Trade and Cooperation Agreement. The signing of the 1978 Agreement was hailed as a triumph for both parties. It was the first trading agreement to be concluded by the Community with a State-trading country while, for China, it formalised relations with an increasingly important trading partner and political power.

The Agreement contained various statements of good intentions, but was short on specific objectives. Thus Article 1 contained a commitment to promote and intensify trade; Article 2 bound both parties to giving the other Most Favoured Nation (MFN) treatment; Article 3 expressed a vague commitment to balanced trade; Article 4 promised favourable consideration by both parties for the other's exports; Article 5 included a safeguard clause under which the Commmunity could tighten quotas in the event of a sudden influx of Chinese imports, but only after friendly consultation with the Chinese authorities; Article 6 voiced an undertaking to promote economic and commercial visits; and Article 7 specified that trade should take place at market-related prices. The other Articles dealt with the institutional arrangements, such as (Article 9) the establishment of a Joint Committee to monitor the functioning of the Agreement. In practice, one of the main functions of the Committee was as a forum for the negotiation of liberalisation of quantitative restrictions imposed by the Community on Chinese imports.

The Agreement included a number of restrictive clauses regarding imports from China, reflecting European worries of a surge of low-cost Chinese imports on to the EC market. The MFN clause excluded China from the favourable treatment accorded by the Community to its neighbouring countries, and to associated customs unions and free trade areas. Thus China was placed in a disadvantageous position relative to many Mediterranean countries, the European Free Trade Area (EFTA) countries, and the African, Caribbean and Pacific (ACP) countries under the Lomé Convention (Yue 1993: 23). The safeguard clause, notwithstanding the requirement for friendly consultations, allowed the Community to unilaterally impose or tighten quotas. The price clause (Article 7) sought to address the problem of low-cost Chinese imports undercutting competing EC products. As Yue (1993: 38) has noted, the clause failed to acknowledge the principle of comparative advantage but rather provided a basis for allegations of dumping.

The trade balance clause was, however, included at the insistence of the Chinese. It is ironic, in the light of the escalating Chinese trade surpluses with the European Union through the late 1980s and 1990s, that China had favoured the adoption of an automatic mechanism for correcting any trade imbalance (Kapur 1986: 48), but that the EC negotiators insisted on the commitment for each party to attain a balance of trade by its own means.

The Trade Agreement was as much a political statement as an economic accord, and was the first step in cementing relations between two emerging forces in the world economy. China, in particular, emphasised this point repeatedly, stressing the fact that the European Community symbolised the emergence of the Western European countries outside the superpower framework. It provided a general framework for relations between the Community and China, but trade in both directions was circumscribed by more specific legislation. EC imports from China were subject to two separate pieces of legislation, depending upon whether imports of the products in question were subject to quantitative restrictions or had been liberalised.[8]

Rules specific to China were promulgated soon after the conclusion of the 1978 Agreement for products which were not subject to restriction. Regulation (EEC) No. 2532/78[9] entered into force on 3 November 1978 and replaced previous rules[10] applicable to all State-trading countries. It listed in an Annex those products originating in China which could be imported into the Community without quantitative restriction, but also provided for surveillance of import trends because of the special 'economic structure' of China and fears of a flood of low-cost Chinese goods on to the EC market. Furthermore, it empowered Member States to take protective action if they thought it necessary. The Regulation was subsequently replaced by Regulation (EEC) No. 1766/82[11] which established more precise criteria (Articles 6–9) for claims of injury and a Community procedure for investigating such claims, although Member States were still permitted to impose interim protective measures pending the results of any investigation. The list of liberalised products was extended in 1985 and in 1986.[12] Nevertheless, Yue (1993: 47–8) notes that the provisions of these Regulations were more restrictive than those in the analogous Regulations relating to imports from market economies,[13] and that both the Community and the Member States were granted much more freedom to impose protective measures than was envisaged under the 1978 Agreement.

As regards imports which were subject to quantitative restrictions, the Community had progressively standardised its arrangements regarding all State-trading countries since the early 1970s. Regulation (EEC) No. 3286/80[14] established import arrangements for products from the following twelve State-trading countries (Albania, Bulgaria, Hungary, Poland, Romania, Czechoslovakia, the German Democratic Republic, the People's Republic of China, North Korea, USSR, Vietnam, and Mongolia). In the case of China, it covered all products not listed in the Annex to Regulation (EEC) No. 2532/78 or covered by specific rules for textiles. The quotas were to be administered by the Member States, and were to be announced by 1 December each year for the following year. Regulation (EEC) No. 3286/80 was subsequently updated and replaced by Regulation (EEC) No. 3420/83.[15]

GENERALISED SYSTEM OF PREFERENCES

The Generalised System of Preferences (GSP) is designed to give developing countries more favourable access to the markets of the developed countries. It was conceived by UNCTAD in the 1960s, and was subsequently implemented by means of various national schemes. It offered developing countries an alternative to the GATT for obtaining tariff reductions, and was a useful instrument when the developed countries had relatively high levels of tariff protection. The Community scheme was introduced on 1 July 1971 and was initially adopted for a period of ten years (1971–80), then renewed in 1980 for a further ten years (1981–90). Concessions were granted on an annual basis within the 10-year periods of application.

Under the GSP scheme throughout this period, the Community unilaterally granted a series of generalised reductions in duty for imports originating in developing economies. The detailed arrangements varied according to whether the imports were industrial products, textiles, steel, or agricultural products. Importation of industrial products (and of steel products) was free of customs duty for amounts not exceeding certain quotas and ceilings;[16] additional imports were still permitted but at the full rate of duty. Importation of textile products was circumscribed by tariff quotas, and dependent upon potential beneficiary countries having concluded export-restraint agreements within the framework of the MFA or bilateral agreements of a non-preferential nature.[17] Importation of the (relatively small number of) agricultural products covered by the scheme was subject to reduced customs duties without any restrictions on quantity, though some products (e.g. unmanufactured tobacco, pineapples, coffee extracts) were subject to quantitative restrictions. A further preference, introduced for the first time in 1990,[18] involved reductions in levies for a number of products covered by the Common Agricultural Policy, within the limits of fixed quotas.

Imports from GSP beneficiaries could thus be roughly divided into three categories: products which entered the EC market duty-free because the MFN rate was zero; products which were specifically excluded from the GSP scheme (primarily agricultural products and certain sensitive industrial goods); and products which were covered by the GSP scheme. The benefits of the scheme accrued to the exporting countries in the form of duty not paid because of the preferential treatment.[19] GSP concessions were, as a rule, granted to all developing countries[20] but the concessions were rather less generous than those granted by the Lomé Convention and the Mediterranean Agreements (Commission of the European Communities 1990: 2.4). Thus, the only developing countries that made use of the GSP scheme through the 1970s and 1980s were those from the Middle East, Latin America and Asia.

At the first meeting of the Joint Committee established under the 1978 Trade Agreement, the Commission proposed that China should be included in its GSP scheme. China became a GSP beneficiary as from 1 January 1980, although its inclusion was conditional upon the conclusion of an agreement on trade in textiles.[21] Kapur (1986: 64) notes that several products (e.g. leather articles, basketware, wickerware, footwear, and furniture) that China had been successful at exporting to the Community were among the forty categories of manufactured goods excluded from the benefits of the GSP. The general list of products covered by the GSP concessions was progressively extended through the 1980s although China was often explicitly excluded, but preferential treatment was extended to China for several products where it had previously been denied.[22]

In 1985, concern about the distribution of the benefits from the GSP scheme led the Community to adopt a policy of greater differentiation between the exporting countries in its preferences.[23] Those countries which had attained a high level of competitiveness (Brazil, Hong Kong, Singapore, South Korea) suffered cuts in their quotas of sensitive industrial products from 1986 onwards.[24] The structure of the scheme for textiles covered by the MFA was drastically revised, and a policy of differentiation introduced for 1988, but these changes did not come into full operation until the following year. Although one of the major textile exporters to the Community, China was granted more flexible exclusion criteria because of its relatively low GNP.[25] Nevertheless, China did suffer a 50 per cent reduction in its preferential amounts for two MFA categories, and for some sensitive industrial goods in 1990.[26]

The GSP scheme was due for renewal for a new 10–year period in 1991, but was extended annually pending the conclusion of the Uruguay Round of GATT negotiations. In the meantime, various new beneficiary countries were announced: Hungary, Poland, Czechoslovakia, Bulgaria and Romania from 1991;[27] four Andean countries (Bolivia, Colombia, Ecuador and Peru) from 1991 as part of a plan to help combat drug abuse;[28] the three Baltic States (Estonia, Latvia, Lithuania) and Albania from 1992;[29] six Central American countries (Costa Rica, El Salvador, Guatemala, Honduras, Nicaragua, and Panama) from 1992;[30] Croatia, Slovenia, Bosnia-Herzegovina, and Macedonia from 1992;[31] and the other twelve independent States of the former Soviet Union from 1993–94.[32]

In December 1994, the European Union implemented a radical shake-up of its GSP scheme for industrial products and textiles.[33] The stated rationale was to make the scheme more development-oriented by focusing the benefits on the poorest countries, and a graduation scheme was to be set up to transfer preferential margins from the advanced to the less-developed beneficiary countries. The new 4–year GSP scheme took effect on 1 January 1995, and applied to products falling within Chapters 25 to 97 of the Common Customs Tariff. These products were classified as being either 'very sensitive', 'sensitive', 'semi-sensitive', or 'non-sensitive', and preferential rates of duty were allocated, thus replacing the previous mechanism of fixed duty-free amounts and ceilings. The preferential rates of duty varied from 85 per cent of the full rate for sensitive products, to 0 per cent for the least sensitive products. Thus the preferential margin for 'sensitive' products was thereafter only 15 per cent instead of 100 per cent as it had previously been.

Duties were suspended in their entirety on products from the least developed countries (e.g. Myanmar, Laos, Kampuchea) and from countries conducting campaigns to combat drugs. In contrast, the preferential margins for the most advanced countries (e.g. Hong Kong, Singapore, South Korea) were to be reduced by 50 per cent with effect from 1 April 1995 and abolished from 1 January 1996. The preferential margins for all other countries (including China) were to be reduced by 50 per cent from 1 January 1997 and abolished from 1 January 1998. Furthermore, the preferential margin was to be abolished:

- as from 1 January 1996 on products from countries whose GSP exports exceeded 25 per cent of the total GSP exports to the European Union in that particular sector. As regards China, the sectors affected were chemicals excluding fertilisers (Chapters 28–30, 32–38), clothing (61–63), and glass and ceramic products (68–70).
- as from 1 January 1995 for products where the phased implementation of the graduation mechanism would result in more favourable access to the EU market than under previous arrangements. As regards China, the sectors affected were leather articles and fur skins (42–43), footwear (64–67), base metals, non-ECSC, and miscellaneous items (94–96).

The scheme was scheduled to last for four years until the end of 1998, with special incentive arrangements concerning social and environmental measures coming into play from January 1998. A similar scheme for agricultural

Table 3.1 Benefits to China under the EU Generalised System of Preferences, 1981–95

Year	Value of imports from China enjoying EU GSP benefits (bn ecu)	As share of total EU GSP benefits (%)
1981	0.6	6.9
1982	0.6	5.9
1983	0.6	6.1
1984	0.7	5.8
1985	0.9	5.7
1986	1.0	8.5
1987	1.5	9.6
1988	2.1	13.2
1989	2.9	15.0
1990	3.8	17.2
1991	6.2	19.9
1992	6.6	21.9
1993	9.2	28.1
1994	11.6	28.6
1995	14.1	26.1

Source: EUROSTAT, *External Trade: System of Generalised Tariff Preferences (GSP). Imports* Volume 2 (various years)

products covering a 3–year period up to the end of June 1999 was adopted on 20 June 1996.[34]

China has for many years been by far the major beneficiary of the GSP scheme (see Table 3.1) notwithstanding substantial increases in the total value of imports from all countries eligible for GSP benefits (Commission of the European Communities 1994: 3). Furthermore, a wider range of industries have benefited in China than in most other countries. So although all but the least developed of the current beneficiary countries will find it harder to export to the European Union, it is China who stands to lose the most. It remains to be seen, however, whether the loss of the preferences will undermine China's competitiveness which has been manifest in its fast-growing exports to the European Community throughout the 1990s.

THE TEXTILE AGREEMENTS

Trade in textiles and clothing world-wide has for many years been regulated by bilateral agreements negotiated under the aegis of the Multi-Fibre Agreement (MFA).[35] The necessity of special arrangements for the sector arises because the manufacture of clothing, in particular, is very labour-intensive and thus is an ideal activity for many developing countries in the early stages of industrialisation. MFA1 was negotiated under the auspices of GATT and was introduced in 1974 with the objective (Article 1) of liberalising world trade in textile products in an equitable way while avoiding any disruptive effects. The MFA permitted importing countries to impose quantitative restrictions on imports of textiles (including man-made and synthetic fibres) and clothing if they were faced with disruption of their domestic markets, but required that these quotas be increased annually. MFA1 ran to the end of 1977, and has been replaced in turn by modified agreements as follows: MFA2 (1978–81); MFA3 (1982–86); MFA4 (1986–91). MFA4 extended the product coverage to include vegetable fibres (linen, jute, ramie) as well as silk and silk blends (National Consumer Council 1990: 2–4; Grimwade 1996: 171–4).

The European Community negotiated MFA agreements with twenty countries, thirteen of which were in Asia. These twenty countries, and those which had concluded similar agreements with the Community, were entitled to export fixed quantities of textiles and clothing to the EC market duty-free under the GSP scheme,[36] but these duty-free quantities were typically rather smaller than the quotas permitted under the bilateral agreements.

The MFA agreements expired at the end of 1994, and trade thereafter has been governed by the WTO Agreement on Textiles and Clothing. The WTO Agreement (Grimwade 1996: 181–4) provides for the textile and clothing sector to be gradually integrated into the GATT over a 10-year transitional period from January 1995. Quantitative import limits were to be eased steadily through this period according to pre-set formulae, though most of the liberalisation will take place in the later years. A transitional safeguard mechanism was also established under which importing countries could either negotiate export restraints or impose unilateral import restrictions should they be faced with serious disruption to their domestic industries. Furthermore, all countries were obliged to improve market access for textile and clothing products, avoid discrimination against imports, and ensure fair and equitable trading conditions. The WTO Agreement was hailed as a significant achievement for the developing countries although, as Grimwade (ibid.: 184) notes, the textile and clothing sectors in the developed countries will still be highly protected even after the phasing-out of the quotas because the Uruguay Round did little to reduce their high tariff rates.

The 1978 Sino-EC Trade Agreement did not refer explicitly to textiles, trade in which had been a major source of disagreement between the Community and China. Textiles were one of China's most important exports, and were a major source of foreign exchange earnings. China desperately needed to increase its textile exports[37] so as to fund its modernisation plan without a concomitant requirement for large debt or large inflows of foreign capital. The Community, on the other hand, was anxious to protect its own textile industries. Negotiations between the two sides proved very difficult. China wanted an increase in its exports from the then existing level of 20,000 tons per year, to 60,000 tons per year (Kapur 1986: 60). The Community was not prepared to accept such an increase, as the output of its own textile industries had been falling.

An Agreement on textile trade[38] was eventually finalised on 18 July 1979, and was fully implemented with effect from 1 January 1980. It limited China's exports to 40,000 tons per annum, but this still represented significantly increased access for Chinese textile products to the EC market. Redmond and Lan (1986: 142–3) note that it was more generous than the standard MFA-type agreement, and that it enabled China to double its exports during a period (1979–81) when most Third World textile producers experienced only a modest increase in their textile exports to the EC market.

But the Textile Agreement also included a number of concessions to EC wishes. There was a safeguard clause permitting the Community to restrict imports of Chinese textiles and clothing, even of products not subject to quota, should the need arise. There was a price clause that permitted the Community to suspend imports of a product should its price fall below a fixed level. This clause had two consequences (Yue 1993: 72). On the one hand, it meant that textile products from China could never be sold at the lowest possible price in the EC market no matter how competitive they might be. On the other hand, it rendered superfluous the application of EC anti-dumping legislation since any problems arising from low-priced imports of Chinese textiles could be eliminated through unilateral action. Finally, there were two clauses designed to benefit EC textile producers directly. The first (Article 11) was an undertaking by China to supply minimum guaranteed quantities of certain textile raw materials (such as pure silk, cashmere and angora) to the EC industry at the normal trade price. As Yue (1993: 73) notes:

> In order to have a strong position in the highly competitive international textile and clothing market, it was very important for the European manufacturers to have constant access to raw materials from China. The agreement provided that, before the end of each year, the Community might submit to the appropriate Chinese authorities a list of the interested producer/processing companies and, if appropriate, the quantities of raw materials required by them. The Chinese authorities, bearing in mind China's export capabilities, had to give favourable consideration to these orders in order to satisfy the Community textile industry's requirements.

The second (Article 12) was a commitment by China to encourage and facilitate the importation of EC textile products into its own market, even in preference to other countries.

The Textile Agreement was extended for a further five years in 1984[39] with some additional restrictions on imports of Chinese textiles, and some amendments to legal mechanisms – including the abolition of the price clause – to bring the Agreement into line with MFA3, which China had joined in January 1984.[40] A new 4-year Agreement[41] was negotiated in 1988 to take account of the provisions of MFA4, and this increased the quotas on certain Chinese textiles while introducing new restrictions on certain other textile products which had not previously been covered. An amended

Agreement[42] in the form of an exchange of letters was initialled on 8 December 1992, and ran – subject to modification to take account of the enlargement of the Union – to the end of 1995. New administrative arrangements were also introduced in 1993 (see below) as part of the more *communautaire* approach to external relations. The 1988 Agreement was renewed[43] for the period 1996–98, and included *inter alia* a series of undertakings by China concerning measures to combat fraud.[44] It also included an important addition to the text of Article 11 regarding the assured provision by China of certain textile raw materials (silk, cashmere, angora). Whereas previously China had simply guaranteed to export given minimum annual quantities to the Community but with no stipulation as to price, it was thereafter required to 'ensure that the supply to the Community industry of raw materials be made at conditions not less favourable than to domestic users'. Thus, price discrimination against EU purchasers was prohibited. The terms of renewal also specified that the quota restrictions would be phased out in the framework of the WTO Agreement on Textiles and Clothing should China become a WTO member before the end of 1988.

THE 1985 TRADE AND ECONOMIC COOPERATION AGREEMENT

The 1978 Trade Agreement dealt exclusively with trade matters, and it eventually became apparent that it provided an insufficient legal framework for coping with the ever-increasing economic interactions (e.g. EC financing of development projects in China) between the two parties. Thus, on 21 May 1985, a Trade and Economic Cooperation Agreement[45] was concluded to replace the 1988 Agreement. This came into effect on 1 October 1985 and was initially scheduled to last for five years, but has been subject to automatic annual renewal[46] and was still in place at the end of 1997.

The first part of the 1985 Agreement related to bilateral trade, and was virtually identical to its predecessor. But the new Agreement was much broader in scope, with the Community promising to cooperate (Article 10) with China to promote the growth and modernisation of the Chinese economy in areas such as industry and mining; agriculture; science and technology; energy; transport and communications, and environmental protection. In order to achieve these objectives, both parties agreed to promote (Article 11) joint production and joint ventures; common exploitation; the transfer of technology; cooperation between financial institutions; technical assistance (including the training of staff); and a continuous exchange of information relevant to commercial and economic cooperation. And Article 14 recognised the power of Member States to undertake their own bilateral economic activities with China, and that these powers should not be circumscibed by the Agreement. Redmond and Lan (1986: 152) have noted that the new provisions simply formalised what was already taking place and that – as with the 1978 Agreement – the 1985 Agreement was more symbolic and political, than economic and practical.

ANTI-DUMPING PROCEEDINGS

One increasingly contentious issue in Sino-EU relations[47] has been the incidence of Community anti-dumping proceedings against imports of Chinese products. During the 1990s (see Table 3.2) when the initiation of new proceedings[48] seems to be generally declining, the corresponding figures for China appear to be on the increase. Indeed, China has taken over from Japan in the 1990s as the most popular target on the basis of new proceedings and measures in force. However, a more realistic measure of the impact of anti-dumping measures would be the value of trade affected, and here Japan – by virtue of the fact that it has been found guilty of dumping various high-technology, high value-added products – has long occupied first place.[49] In contrast, the majority of the proceedings targeted on Chinese products have involved chemicals and metals.[50]

Table 3.2 EU anti-dumping investigations concerning imports from China, 1979–96

Year	Investigations initiated against imports from China			Total investigations initiated
	number	products	analogue economy	number
1979	2	saccharin and its salts	South Korea	
		mechanical alarm clocks	Mexico	
1980	1	furfural	South Korea	25
1981	2	oxalic acid	Spain	48
		paracetamol	India	
1982	4	canned pears	South Africa	58
		magnesite (caustic-burned)	Austria	
		magnesite (dead-burned)	—	
		barium chloride	United States	
1983	2	lithium hydroxide	United States	38
		artificial corundum	Yugoslavia	
1984	2	silicon carbide	Norway	49
		roller chains for cycles	Spain	
1985	1	hammers	—	36
1986	2	potassium permanganate	United States	24
		paint & similar brushes	Sri Lanka	
1987	0			39
1988	7	calcium metal	United States	40
		small-screen colour television receivers	Hong Kong	
		barium chloride	EC prices	
		ammonium paratungstate	South Korea	
		tungstic oxide and acid	South Korea	
		tungsten metal powder	—	
		tungsten carbide	South Korea	
1989	5	tungsten ores and concentrates	Australia	27
		silicon metal	EC prices	
		polyolefin woven bags	India	
		pure silk typewriter ribbon fabrics	EC prices	

Table 3.2 (cont.)

Year	Investigations initiated against imports from China			Total investigations initiated
	number	products	analogue economy	number
1990	4	espadrilles dihydrostrepto-mycin video tapes in cassettes artificial corundum polyester yarn (man-made staple fibre) gas-fuelled non-refillable pocket flint lighters	Uruguay Japan Hong Kong Yugoslavia Japan Thailand	43
1991	4	magnesium oxide deadburned (sintered) magnesia bicycles magnetic disks (3.5" microdisks)	Turkey Turkey Taiwan Taiwan	20
1992	8	unwrought manganese paint and similar brushes antimony trioxide fluorspar book-bound photo albums ferro-silicon gum rosin colour television receivers	— — United States South Africa South Korea Norway Brazil Thailand	39
1993	4	refractory chamottes furfuraldehyde furazolidone microwave ovens	United States Argentina India South Korea	21
1994	5	cotton fabric butt-welded tube or pipe fittings persulphates activated powdered carbons coumarin	India Thailand Japan United States United States	43
1995	5	footwear (textile uppers) footwear (leather or synthetic uppers) furfuryl alcohol glyphosphate ring binder mechanisms	* * Thailand * *	33
1996	4	unbleached cotton fabrics travel goods briefcases and school bags handbags	* * * *	

Sources: The fourteen Annual Reports from the European Commission on the Community's anti-dumping and anti-subsidy activities, viz: COM(83)519; COM(84)721; COM(86)308; COM(87)178; COM(88)92; COM(89)106; COM(90)229; SEC(91)92; SEC(91)974; SEC(92)716); COM(93)516; COM(95)16; COM(95)309; COM(96)146.
Vermulst and Graafsma (1992)
Notes:
1996 data relates to January–June only.
* awaiting publication of the outcome of the proceeding.

Notwithstanding the increasing numbers of proceedings, the really contentious issue concerns the methods used by the Community to establish dumping and to calculate the dumping margin. An anti-dumping proceeding usually starts with a complaint from the EU industry or a firm therein to the European Commission. The complaint must contain *prima facie* evidence of the existence of dumping and of resulting injury to the EU industry. The Commission will then either reject the complaint because it does not contain sufficient evidence, or will initiate a proceeding. This involves an investigation (using *inter alia* detailed questionnaires to various interested parties) at the end of which the proceeding may be terminated[51] in one of five ways, namely:

- no protective action on the basis of absence of injury;
- no protective action because dumping has not taken place;
- withdrawal of the complaint by the EU industry;
- imposition of provisional/definitive dumping duties which are sufficient to remove the injury but do not exceed the dumping margin;
- acceptance of undertakings from the exporter regarding export prices/ volumes to the extent that the Commission is satisfied that either the dumping margin or the injurious effects of the dumping have been eliminated.

The determination of dumping consists of a comparison between the export price of the product (i.e. the price paid by an independent EC importer) and its 'normal value'. In the case of countries (e.g. China) defined as being non-market economies, domestic costs and prices are deemed to be unreliable and the 'normal value' has to be constructed using data from an analogue market economy wherein a similar product has been manufactured under roughly comparable conditions. The dumping margin is then the difference between this normal value and the export value. As Vermulst and Graafsma (1992: 16–17) note, this 'presumption implies that a State-controlled economy can never have a comparative advantage that is larger than that of the analogue market economy used for the determination of normal value'.

The choice of analogue country is thus vital to the outcome of the proceeding, and it is often the case that there is no clear candidate as to what country is quite like China. Of the fifty proceedings[52] brought to a conclusion before the end of June 1996, the United States was used as the analogue country in eight; South Korea in seven; India and Thailand in four; Japan and the European Community in three; and Spain, South Africa, Yugoslavia, Norway, Hong Kong, Turkey and Taiwan in two. The use of developed countries in many of these proceedings is questionable in the extreme, as their high production costs (and prices) will give rise to a high 'normal value' – and thus to a large dumping margin. Hu and Watkins (1996: 11–12) cite the example of the investigation into the alleged dumping of Chinese video cassettes where the Commission first used EC firms to provide the analogue data. When a HK firm was later used (as proposed by

China) to provide the analogue data, the difference in the dumping margin was about 100 per cent. Such substantial, and essentially arbitrary, determinations do not promote good relations, whatever the validity of the dumping allegations.

TIANANMAN SQUARE

Economic relations between the Community and China developed apace through the late 1980s with, in particular, substantial increases in EC imports of Chinese goods and much greater interest by EC firms in direct investment in China. However, the events in Tiananmen Square on 4 June 1989 led to EC condemnation[53] and a dramatic change of attitude. The Community cancelled an arranged meeting with MOFERT officials, and later announced limited sanctions against China.[54] These sanctions included *inter alia*:

- the interruption of military cooperation and an embargo on trade in arms with China;
- the suspension of bilateral ministerial and high-level contacts;
- the postponement of new cooperation projects;
- limitations on cultural, scientific and technical cooperation;
- advocation of the postponement of the examination of new requests for credit insurance, and of new credits by the World Bank.

Yue (1993:10) suggests that the sanctions had a marked effect on bilateral economic relations. EC exports to China fell in 1990. FDI by EC firms slowed due to a combination of the difficult economic and political situation, and the suspension of export insurance by the Member States. Work on a number of existing projects was suspended due to Member States not extending any new soft loans to China. Relations began to improve towards the end of 1990 with the gradual lifting of the suspension of export credits and guarantees. Economic sanctions were gradually removed following a meeting of EC foreign ministers in October 1990, but it was not until April 1993 that top-level discussions resumed.[55]

EU TRADE POLICY IN THE MID-1990S

In July 1995, the European Commission (1995) published the document entitled *A Long Term Policy for China–Europe Relations*. The document called for early Chinese entry to the WTO while acknowledging that many issues still needed to be resolved before membership was possible. Additional expenditure was foreshadowed for promoting trade relations, scientific and cultural exchanges, and assistance with poverty alleviation and the environment. Closer cooperation was suggested to help China develop its legal and judicial system. The issue of human rights was sidestepped by calling for a separate political dialogue on the issue.

Despite the upbeat rhetoric of the document, the European Union had in practice began to adopt in the 1990s a much tougher stance on imports from China. This was evidenced *inter alia* by:

- the EU decision to withdraw GSP preferences from China, notwithstanding the concomitant withdrawal of preferences for many other countries;
- the increasing EU use of anti-dumping legislation against imports from China;
- the EU insistence on the inclusion in China's Protocol of Accession to the WTO of a clause permitting importing countries to introduce safeguard measures on a selective basis (see Chapter 1 for a discussion of China and the WTO);
- the liberalisation of EU trade with many Eastern European countries through the various Europe Agreements, with the consequent trade diversion effects this will have on EU trade with China.

As regards this last point, the Council in March 1994 promulgated Regulation (EC) No. 519/94[56] to replace both Regulation (EEC) No. 1766/82 and Regulation (EEC) No. 3420/83, as well as Regulation (EEC) No. 1765/82.[57] The new Regulation was introduced to ensure consistency of treatment across Member States following the completion of the internal market, and applied to all products (whether liberalised or not, but excluding textiles) imported from China and nineteen other countries.[58]

A comparison of these twenty countries with the twelve State-trading countries initially cited in Regulation (EEC) No. 3420/83 reveals that only five countries appear in both lists, namely: China, Albania, North Korea, Mongolia, and Vietnam. The three Baltic states (Estonia, Latvia, and Lithuania) had been added in December 1991 though they were not made subject to any quantitative restrictions,[59] and the other twelve Republics from the former Soviet Union[60] were included in April 1992. Meanwhile Bulgaria, Czechoslavakia, Hungary, Poland, Romania, and the German Democratic Republic had all been excluded: quantitative restrictions[61] on imports from the GDR had been suspended indefinitely with effect from 1 July 1990,[62] and restrictions had been lifted for Poland and Hungary with effect from 1 January 1990,[63] and for Bulgaria, Czechoslavakia and Romania with effect from 1 October 1990.[64] Estonia, Latvia and Lithuania were subsequently removed from the list of countries in April 1995.[65]

In contrast to the legislation it replaced, Regulation (EC) No. 519/94 did not refer explicitly to 'State-trading countries' and the term would be hard to justify for China in the mid-1990s, but the rules/procedures were still more stringent than those applied to other countries.[66] Furthermore, the only country for which import restrictions were specified was China: quotas were applied to imports of gloves, footwear, tableware and kitchenware, glassware, car radios and toys; surveillance was introduced on a number of mainly chemical products, but including sports shoes, bicycles and toys.[67] The dwindling list of countries to which these more stringent import rules apply, together with its application in practice only to products originating in China, suggests a certain discrimination against the People's Republic.

As regards the textile sector, the Community established common rules for administering all its bilateral agreements[68] to take account of the completion of the internal market. Regulation (EC) No. 958/93[69] set down quotas for the years 1993–95 for textile imports from twenty-two countries including China and the Eastern European countries. Many of the quotas on Chinese raw materials also stipulated minimum quantities reserved for European industry. It was later replaced by Regulation (EC) No. 3030/93[70] which set out more sophisticated arrangements for monitoring and administering the quotas. Furthermore, specific rules were established for outward processing traffic with additional quotas permitted for re-imports into the Community of selected textile products from China and fifteen other countries.[71]

The quotas for 1995 were subsequently amended[72] to take account of the enlargement of the European Union, and provision was also made for the inclusion of several products (in particular silk, linen and ramie products) that had previously not been covered. The inclusion of the silk, etc. products followed lengthy negotiations (Islam 1995). In 1994, the European Union had unilaterally set a quota of 17,000 tonnes for imports of such goods from China. EU importers and retailers complained that such a figure was too low and that firms would not be able to meet either their contractual obligations with their Chinese suppliers or market demand. The quota for 1995 was thus more than doubled to 38,000 tonnes, and the 1996 quota raised to over 39,000 tonnes. The growth rates allowed for the quotas of other textile products were, however, cut by about 2 per cent and additional sub-limits applied to certain categories. This contrasts with the rather more favourable treatment accorded to the textile quotas for other countries. And, as regards fraud in textile trade, the Commission deducted 9 million shirts and 200,000 pullovers from the 1994/5 quotas because it claimed that some consignments carrying African and Arab labels had originated in China.[73]

The tougher EU stance regarding imports from China may thus be explained by a number of factors of varying importance: a lingering reaction to the July 1989 events in Tiananman Square; an understandable desire to favour neighbouring countries in trade relations; recognition of the increased competitiveness of many Chinese industrial sectors; and alarm at the substantial EU trade deficit with China. In addition, it is important to note legitimate EU concerns regarding the fairness of the Chinese trading system, in particular regarding issues such as fraud, dumping, protection of intellectual property, and the openness of the Chinese market to EU exports. Maybe a tough EU stance on imports from China is the best way of extracting concessions from the Chinese authorities, particularly when combined with the 'carrot' of conditional support for WTO entry. But it is surely time to clarify the situation where China is classified as a developing country with regard to the GSP, as a non-market economy with regard to anti-dumping proceedings, and as a State-trading economy with regard to the imposition of quantitative import restrictions.

NOTES

1 Redmond and Lan (1986: 135) note that China had begun to view parts of the developed Western world (Western Europe, Japan, Canada, and one or two other countries) as potential diplomatic allies against superpower hegemony. These countries constituted the second 'intermediate zone'; the first was the Third World.
2 The existing bilateral trade agreements between China and the EC Member States were due to expire at the end of 1974, and the EC Council had decided that thereafter the Community would lead trade negotiations with State-trading countries (Yue 1993: 5).
3 While terminating diplomatic relations with Taiwan, and recognising the Government of the People's Republic as the sole legal government of China.
4 The Commission also sent similar memoranda to all other State-trading countries but, whereas these memoranda were sent through normal diplomatic channels, Soames handed the outline agreement to the Chinese Ambassador to Belgium in person. Kapur (1986: 34) suggests that the 'decision to disciminate in favour of the Chinese by using a more personal and more direct channel was clearly intended as a gesture to place China in a privileged position in relation to the other socialist countries'.
5 As noted above, the textile accord between the Community and Taiwan had expired on 1 October 1973.
6 'Trade Agreement between the European Economic Community and the People's Republic of China', *Official Journal of the European Communities (OJEC)* no. L123 (11 May 1978). The Agreement was adopted by Council Regulation (EEC) No. 946/78 of 2 May 1978.
7 *Bulletin of the European Communities* 11–1982 point 2.2.79.
8 Agricultural products were governed by rules set down under the Common Agricultural Policy.
9 Regulation (EEC) No. 2532/78 on common rules for imports from the People's Republic of China, *OJEC* no. L306 (31 October 1978).
10 Regulation (EEC) No. 109/70, *OJEC* no. L19 (26 January 1970).
11 Regulation (EEC) No. 1766/82, *OJEC* no. L195 (5 July 1982).
12 Regulations (EEC) No. 268/85, *OJEC* no. L28 (1 February 1985); and (EEC) No. 1409/86, *OJEC* no. L128 (14 May 1986). See also (84/C181/03) in *OJEC* no. C181 (9 July 1984) for the Annex to Regulation (EEC) No. 1766/82 updated to take account of amendments to NIMEXE and other changes.
13 Regulation (EEC) No. 288/82, *OJEC* no. L35 (9 February 1982).
14 Came into force on 1 January 1981, *OJEC* no. L353 (29 December 1980). Later amended by Decision 81/248/EEC, *OJEC* no. L115 (27 April 1981) and Regulation (EEC) No. 3424/82, *OJEC* no. L361 (22 December 1982).
15 Of 14 December 1983. *OJEC* no. L346 (8 December 1983). The Annexes were later updated to take account of amendments to NIMEXE and other changes, see (84/C181/04) *OJEC* no. C181 (9 July 1984); to replace NIMEXE codes with CN codes see Regulation (EEC) No. 3049/91, *OJEC* no. L292 (23 October 1991); and to take account of the MFA classification of textiles, see Regulation (EEC) No. 2273/87, *OJEC* no. 217 (6 August 1987). The Regulation was also amended

by Regulation (EEC) No. 3784/85 to take account of the accession of Spain and Portugal, *OJEC* no. L364 (31 December 1985).
16 Global quotas and ceilings were abolished as from the scheme for 1981, when the principle of differentiation was first introduced. Thereafter each beneficiary country was guaranteed a specific volume of preferential imports: those from highly competitive countries (for a specified product) were administered through quotas, those from the least-developed countries were administered through ceilings. Ceilings were more flexible than quotas in that duty was not automatically re-established when the ceiling was reached, but a Member State or the Commission might ask that this be done at any time thereafter. The result, however, was great uncertainty for suppliers and importers concerning the fate of their consignments, and often inequality of treatment between beneficiary countries. *Bulletin of the European Communities,* 12–1980, point 2.2.19 (Commission of the European Communities 1990: 7).
17 By 1990, the European Community had concluded such bilateral agreements not only with China (see below) but with several other Asian and Latin American countries, and with ASEAN, the Andean Group and the Central America Common Market (Commission of the European Communities 1990: 2.5).
18 *Bulletin of the European Communities,* 12–1989, point 2.2.61.
19 The benefits could be assessed in terms of that part of the total dutiable imports (from the eligible country) that could in principle benefit from preferential treatment (the coverage ratio), or in terms of that part of the total dutiable imports that actually benefited from preferential treatment (the benefit ratio). The latter was typically lower than the former because of the impact of quotas/ceilings and/or non-compliance with rules of origin requirements (Commission of the European Communities 1990: 3.12).
20 Two significant exceptions were the Republic of Korea and Taiwan. Korea is a beneficiary country, but it was excluded in 1988 for discrimination against the Community in the field of intellectual property rights. It was re-admitted in 1992, but then excluded once again in July 1994 in retaliation for raising customs duties on goods in which the European Union was a major exporter to the Korean market, Regulation (EC) No. 1291/94, *OJEC* no. L141 (4 June 1994). Taiwan has never been granted GSP treatment because it does not belong to UN organisations.
21 *Bulletin of the European Communities,* 7/8–1979, point 2.2.19.
22 *Bulletin of the European Communities*, 12–1980, point 2.2.19; 12–1981 point 2.2.21, 11–1982 point 2.2 24.
23 *Bulletin of the European Communities,* 5–1985, point 2.2.42; and 11–1985, point 2.3.26.
24 Regulation (EEC) No. 3599/85 of 17 December 1985, *OJEC* no. L352 (30 December 1985)
25 *Bulletin of the European Communities,* 11–1987, point 2.2.42.
26 *Bulletin of the European Communities*, 12–1989, point 2.2.61.
27 Regulations (EEC) No. 831/90, (EEC) No. 3832/90, and (EEC) No. 833/90, *OJEC* no. L370 (31 December 1990). Hungary, Poland and Czechoslavakia were withdrawn from the list of GSP beneficiaries as from 1 March 1992 following the entry into force of their Interim Agreements on trade and trade-related matters with the Community, Regulation (EEC) No. 1509/92, *OJEC* no. L159 (12 June 1992). Bulgaria and Romania were removed following the conclusion of their Agreements in 1993, COM(92)586.
28 Regulation (EEC) No. 3835/90, *OJEC* no. L370 (31 December 1990).
29 Regulation (EEC) No. 282/92, *OJEC* no. L31 (7 February 1992).
30 Regulation (EEC) No. 3900/91, OJEC no. L368 (31 December 1991).

31 Regulation (EEC) No. 548/92, *OJEC* no. L63 (7 March 1992). Yugoslavia had been withdrawn with effect from 15 November 1991. Montenegro was initially included among the list of beneficiary countries, but was later removed.
32 Regulation (EC) No. 3667/93, *OJEC* no. L338 (31 December 1993).
33 Regulation (EC) No. 3291/94, *OJEC* no. L348 (31 December 1994).
34 *Bulletin of the European Union*, 6–1996, point 1.4.37. The delay had been due to problems relating to the implementation of the results of the Uruguay Round for the products concerned.
35 The Arrangement regarding International Trade in Textiles, as the MFA is formally known, was preceded by the Short-Term Arrangement on Trade in Textiles (1961–62), and the Long-Term Arrangement regarding International Trade in Cotton Textiles (1962–73).
36 The ACP and Mediterranean countries were entitled to essentially unrestricted access to the EC market under the terms of their agreements.
37 Import quotas applicable to the Member States for imports of textiles from China had been previously laid down unilaterally under Council Decision (EEC) 74/652 of 2 December 1974, *OJEC* no. L358 (31 December 1974). This decision was superseded by Council Decision (EEC) 75/210 on unilateral import arrangements for various products (including textiles) from State-trading countries, *OJEC* no. L99 (21 April 1975) p.7.
38 Regulation (EEC) No. 3061/79, *OJEC* no. L345 (31 December 1979).
39 The Community negotiated a supplementary Protocol to the 1979 Agreement, to be fully implemented from 1 January 1984 to 31 December 1988. Regulation (EEC) No. 3061/79 was repealed and replaced by Council Regulation (EEC) No. 2072/84 on 'Common Rules for Imports of Certain Textile Products originating in the People's Republic of China', *OJEC* no. L198 (27 July 1984).
40 China had had observer status since July 1981 in the discussions on the renewal of the MFA.
41 The 'Agreement between the European Economic Community and the People's Republic of China on trade in textile products' was initialled in Brussels on 9 December 1988, and ran from 1 January 1989 to 31 December 1992, *OJEC* no. L380 (31 December 1978).
42 The 'Agreement in the form of an exchange of letters amending the Agreement between the European Economic Community and the People's Republic of China on trade in textile products' was initialled on 8 December 1992. It was applicable until 31 December 1994, but provision was made for it to be automatically extended until 31 December 1995 unless a GATT agreement entered into force at an earlier date, *OJEC* no. L410 (31 December 1992).
43 Decision 96/225/EC, *OJEC* no. L81 (30 March 1996). The Agreement with China was initialled on 13 December 1995. The measures to combat fraud were annexed in Appendix 7.
44 Three main sources of fraud had been identified: the circumvention of quantitative restrictions through fraudulent declarations concerning origin; the non-payment of customs duties through fraudulent recourse to the provisions of preferential agreements; and the counterfeiting of, in particular, fashion articles, *Bulletin of the European Union*, 6–1995, point 1.4.35.
45 'Agreement on Trade and Economic Cooperation between the European Economic Community and the People's Republic of China', *OJEC* no. L250 (19 September 1985) pp.2–7. See also *Bulletin of the European Communities*, 5–1985, points 1.5.1–1.5.4.
46 The Agreement is tacitly renewed from year to year provided that neither party notifies the other in writing of its denunciation of the Agreement.

47 See the *Almanac of China's Foreign Economic Relations and Trade*, 1994/95 edition p.484, and 1995/96 edition p.472.
48 And the numbers of anti-dumping measures in force: 158 (20 for China) at end 1992; 150 (23 for China) at end 1993; 151 (26 for China) at end 1994; 147 (30 for China) at end 1995.
49 Interestingly, although the value of Japanese trade affected has fallen dramatically from 70 per cent of the total at the end of 1992 to only 27 per cent at the end of 1995, COM(93)516, p.10 and COM(96)146, p.2.
50 No such clear pattern is evident in US anti-dumping proceedings concerning Chinese products, Vermulst and Graafsma (1992: 6).
51 The proceeding may also be terminated early for a number of reasons (e.g. the discontinuation of EC production as in the 1992 proceeding on *unwrought manganese*).
52 Review proceedings have also been initiated for saccharin (1983); oxalic acid and paracetamol (1987); roller chains for cycles, potassium permanganate, and paint and similar brushes (1988); typewriter ribbons, lighters and calcium metal (1992); potassium permanganate and lighters (1993); silicon metal, colour televisions, tungsten ores, tungsten carbide, tungstic oxide and acid, and polyolefin woven bags (1995).
53 *Bulletin of the European Communities*, 6–1989, point 2.3.2.
54 *Bulletin of the European Communities*, 6–1989, point 1.1.24.
55 Sanctions were only lifted gradually, and the ban on arms sales is still in place. Commission of the European Communities (1995: 5). See also Islam (1993).
56 Regulation (EC) No. 519/94, *OJEC* no. L67 (10 March 1994). ECSC products were subsequently included by Regulation (EC) No. 168/96, *OJEC* no. L25 (1 February 1996).
57 Regulation (EEC) No. 1765/82 laid down the rules for imports, not liberalised at Community level, from State-trading countries other than China, and was the counterpart of Regulation (EEC) No. 1766/82, *OJEC* no. L195 (5 July 1982).
58 Albania, Armenia, Azerbaijan, Belarus, Estonia, Georgia, Kazakhstan, North Korea, Kyrgyzstan, Latvia, Lithuania, Moldova, Mongolia, Russia, Tajikistan, Turkmenistan, Ukraine, Uzbekistan, and Vietnam.
59 Regulation (EEC) No. 3859/91, *OJEC* no. L362 (31 December 1991).
60 Regulation (EEC) No. 848/92, *OJEC* no. L89 (4 April 1992).
61 Except those imposed under Regulation (EEC) No. 288/82.
62 Regulation (EEC) No. 1794/90 and Decision 1796/90/ECSC, *OJEC* no. L166 (29 June 1990).
63 Regulation (EEC) No. 3691/89, *OJEC* no. L362 (12 December 1989).
64 Regulation (EEC) No. 2727/90, *OJEC* no. L262 (26 September 1990).
65 Regulation (EC) No. 839/95, *OJEC* no. L85 (19 April 1995).
66 Regulation (EC) No. 518/94 replaced Regulation (EEC) No. 288/82 and covered imports from all other countries; it was in turn replaced by Regulation (EC) No. 3285/94, *OJEC* no. L349 (31 December 1994).
67 The quotas for some gloves and car radios were later abolished and replaced by Community surveillance with effect from 1 January 1996; surveillance of several other products was discontinued. Regulation (EC) No. 752/96, *OJEC* no. L103 (26 April 1996).
68 Common rules for imports of textile products not covered by bilateral agreements were set out in Regulation (EC) No. 517/94, *OJEC* no. L67 (10 March 1994).
69 Regulation (EEC) No. 958/93, *OJEC* no. L103 (28 April 1993).
70 Regulation (EEC) No. 3030/93, *OJEC* no. L275 (8 November 1993). Ten additional countries, plus the Czech Republic and the Slovak Republic replacing

Czechoslavakia, were included making a total of thirty-three. Later amended by Regulation (EC) No. 3289/94, *OJEC* no. L349 (31 December 1994) to take account of the WTO Agreement on Textiles and Clothing.
71 Bulgaria, the Czech Republic, Hungary, Indonesia, Macao, Malaysia, Pakistan, Philippines, Poland, Romania, Singapore, the Slovak Republic, Sri Lanka, Thailand, and Vietnam.
72 Council Decision 95/131/EC of 20 February 1995, *OJEC* no. L94 (26 April 1995). The draft agreement had been initialled on 19 January, *Bulletin of the European Union*, 1/2–1995, point 1.4.60.
73 Regulation (EC) No. 560/95, *OJEC* no. L57 (15 March 1995). See also Islam (1995).

REFERENCES

Commission of the European Communities (1990) *Generalized System of Preferences: Guidelines for the 1990s*, COM(90)329 final, July, Luxembourg: Office for Official Publications of the European Communities.

Commission of the European Communities (1994) *Integration of Developing Countries in the International Trading System: Role of the GSP 1995–2004*, COM(94)212 final, June, Luxembourg: Office for Official Publications of the European Communities.

Commission of the European Communities (1995) *A Long-Term Policy for China–Europe Relations*, COM(95)279 final, July, Luxembourg: Office for Official Publications of the European Communities.

EUROSTAT (various years) *External Trade: System of Generalised Tariff Preferences, Imports*, vol. 2, Brussels: Statistical Office of the European Communities.

Grimwade, N. (1996) *International Trade Policy: A Contemporary Analysis*, London: Routledge.

Hu, X. and Watkins, D. (1996) 'The Evolution of Trade Relationships between China and the EU since the 1980s', paper presented at the Second Conference on East Asia–EU Business, King's College London, April 1996.

Kapur, H. (1986) *China and the European Economic Community: The New Connection*, Boston: Martinus Nijhoff.

Islam, S. (1993) 'EC, China Restore Ties', *Far Eastern Economic Review*, 13 May: 71.

Islam, S. (1995) 'A New Deal: European Union Increases Quotas for Asian Exporters', *Far Eastern Economic Review*, 158(5), 2 February: 52.

Ministry of Foreign Trade and Economic Cooperation (various years) *Almanac of China's Foreign Economic Relations and Trade*, Beijing: China Economics Publishing House.

National Consumer Council (1990) *International Trade and the Consumer: Working Paper 2: Textiles and Clothes*, London: National Consumer Council.

Redmond, J. and Lan, Z. (1986) 'The European Community and China: New Horizons', *Journal of Common Market Studies*, 25 (2), December: 133–55.

Vermulst, E. and Graafsma, F. (1992) 'A Decade of European Community Anti-Dumping Law and Practice Applicable to Imports from China', *Journal of World Trade*, 26(3), June: 5–60.

Yue, X. (1993) *Current EC Legal Developments: The EC and China*, London: Butterworths.

4 Regionalism in Asia and its impact on Sino-European trade[1]

Richard Pomfret

INTRODUCTION

China's future role in the world economy, and its approach to trade policy concern all of China's trading partners, including those in Europe. China had observer status during the Uruguay Round of multilateral trade negotiations, but its application for reaccession to GATT and to become an original member of the WTO failed (see Chapter 1). This failure has led some observers (e.g. Wall 1996) to raise the prospect that the stalled WTO negotiations might drive China to conclude bilateral arrangements with its neighbours, to the detriment of its trading relations with the rest of the world.

This chapter considers the issue of regionalism in Asia, and the prospects for China's trade relations with Europe in the context of China's developing relations with its immediate neighbours. Despite much talk, the Asian response to the spectre of world trade becoming increasingly centred on regional trading blocs in the 1990s has been rather muted, and the main concern of the market economies within the region has been the multilateral forum of GATT/WTO. Two broad Asian trade groupings – the Asia Pacific Economic Cooperation (APEC) forum and the East Asian Economic Caucus (EAEC) – have been formed, but their mandates are still rather vague. Furthermore, narrower regional initiatives have been taken by three organisations – the Association of South-East Asian Nations (ASEAN), the South Asian Association for Regional Cooperation (SAARC), and the Economic Cooperation Organization (ECO). Table 4.1 provides details of the current membership of the latter organisations, together with some economic and social data.

The first three sections of this chapter examine regional trade developments within Asia, emphasising the distinction between *regionalism* based on discriminatory trade policies, and the *regionalisation* of trade. The following two sections provide two alternative scenarios for the future Asian trading regime: one based on regionalism and the other on multilateralism. The penultimate section addresses the options which would be available to China should a frustrated application for WTO membership

Table 4.1 Statistical profile of the member countries of ASEAN, ECO, and SAARC, 1994

Country	Population (million)	GNP per capita (US$)	Real GNP per capita at PPP (US$)	Exports (fob) (US$)	Imports (cif) (US$)
Association of Southeast Asian Nations (ASEAN)					
Brunei	0.3	14,240	—	2,200*	1,700*
Indonesia	189.9	880	3,690	40,376	36,088
Malaysia	19.5	3,520	8,610	54,571	52,127
Philippines	66.2	960	2,800	11,375+	14,628+
Singapore	2.8	23,360	21,430	71,960+	80,020+
Thailand	58.7	2,210	6,870	44,419	52,059
Vietnam	72.5	190	—	3,600	4,804
The Economic Cooperation Organization (ECO)					
Afghanistan	18.9	(c)	—	243	737
Azerbaijan	7.5	500	1,720	687	885
Iran	65.8	(d)	4,650	16,700*	30,662*
Kazakhstan	17.0	1,110	2,830	3,070	3,662
Kyrgyzstan	4.7	610	1,710	325	379
Pakistan	126.3	440	2,210	6,795	9,333
Tajikistan	5.9	350	1,160	263+	374+
Turkey	60.8	2,450	4,610	17,954	23,044
Turkmenistan	4.0	(d)	—	2,425	1,636
Uzbekistan	22.3	950	2,390	3,235	3,203
The South Asian Association for Regional Cooperation (SAARC)					
Bangladesh	117.8	230	1,350	2,535	4,135
Bhutan	0.7	400	400	—	—
India	913.6	310	1,290	25,605	28,431
Maldives	0.2	900	—	—	—
Nepal	21.4	200	1,080	397	1,071
Pakistan	126.3	440	2,210	6,795	9,333
Sri Lanka	18.1	640	3,150	3,186	4,688
CHINA	1190.9	530	2,510	115,169	122,591

Sources: World Bank, *The World Bank Atlas 1996*, for the data on population, GNP per capita, and real GNP at purchasing power parity
World Bank, *Trends in Developing Economies 1995*, for the data on exports and imports

Notes:
(a) The real GNP figures at purchasing power parity (PPP) are for 1994, and are expressed in 'international dollars'.
(b) All data are for 1994 except where identified by a * (1992) or a + (1993).
(c) Estimated by the World Bank to be low-income (US$ 725 or less).
(d) Estimated by the World Bank to be lower-middle-income (US$ 726 to US$ 2,895).
(e) The export and import figures for Afghanistan, Brunei, and Tajikistan are not strictly comparable with the other data. The figures for Afghanistan are 1991 data from the United Nations, *International Trade Statistics Yearbook* 1993; the figures for Brunei are estimates provided by the Economist Intelligence Unit; the figures for Tajikistan are measured on a customs basis.

lead it to abandon multilateralism. The final section draws some conclusions, and offers guidance on the appropriate European response to the developments in Asia.

REGIONALISM IN ASIA BEFORE THE 1990S

Regional trading arrangements have not been a significant feature of the Asian economy. The formation of customs unions and free trade areas in Europe, Latin America and Africa during the 1960s had no counterpart in Asia. Although ASEAN made some attempts at creating preferential trading links in the late 1970s, these were unsuccessful. The rapid growth of the first generation newly industrialising economies (NIEs) was based on trade policies which did not discriminate among trading partners, and the same was true in practice for the second generation NIEs (i.e. Indonesia, Malaysia and Thailand).

ASEAN was formed in 1967 by Indonesia, Malaysia, the Philippines, Singapore and Thailand.[2] The primary motivation was geopolitical, bringing together non-Communist countries which felt threatnd by the expansion of Communism in Indochina. Even after the end of the Indochina War, ASEAN continued to be a vehicle for common political action (e.g. in opposing a Vietnamese military presence in Cambodia after 1978).

In 1977, ASEAN launched two schemes to promote economic integration: a preferential trading arrangement (PTA) and the ASEAN Industrial Projects (AIP) Program. Although each member nominated a large number of items to be covered by the PTA, the included items were so selected and circumscribed that they still covered no more than 5 per cent of intra-ASEAN trade by 1989. Under the AIP Program, each member was allocated an industrial project which would benefit from shared financing and preferred access to ASEAN markets but, again, the implementation was limited as only Indonesia and Malaysia completed their initial projects, and they faced unwanted competition from an independent Thai project. Although the ASEAN members spoke of economic integration, they were reluctant either to reduce trade barriers, even preferentially, on protected activities or to purchase items from an ASEAN partner which was not the least-cost supplier of that item.[3]

By the late 1980s preferential trading within ASEAN was of trivial importance, and empirical studies of the PTA found its impact to have been minimal (Imada 1993: 4-8). The rapid growth enjoyed by Indonesia, Malaysia and Thailand after the early 1980s was associated with unilateral trade liberalisation on a multilateral basis. Intra-ASEAN trade as a per centage of members' total trade was lower in 1989 than it had been in 1970 (Ariff and Tan 1992: 254).

Bangladesh, Bhutan, India, the Maldives, Nepal, Pakistan and Sri Lanka launched SAARC in 1985. As with ASEAN, the main motive was political to provide a forum for discussion among countries in a region which had experienced wars and continued to be characterised by mistrust. The actual economic content was nil and, indeed, some intra-SAARC trade was conducted under worse than MFN conditions.

Iran, Pakistan and Turkey had been members of a regional organisation during the 1970s, although this had little economic content apart from some channelling of Iranian financial assistance to Pakistan during the final years of the Shah's regime. The organisation lapsed after the Iranian Revolution, but was then revived in 1985 as the Economic Cooperation Organization (ECO). The three ECO members signed a Protocol on Preferential Tariffs in May 1991, by which they agreed to offer a 10 per cent preferential tariff reduction on selected commodities. The original lists of commodities were extremely limited and little progress had been made by the original implementation date of May 1993 (Pomfret 1997).

In sum, none of the regional trading arrangements of mainland south and east Asia had any significant economic impact before the 1990s. Other Asian arrangements – especially the 1983 Closer Economic Relations between Australia and New Zealand (CER), the South Pacific Forum (at least in areas such as the negotiation of trade and aid and fishing rights) and, to a lesser extent, the Gulf Cooperation Council (GCC) – have had greater economic impact, but they involve small total populations and are more remote from China.

THE REVIVAL OF REGIONALISM IN ASIA

ASEAN, ECO and SAARC all renewed their efforts towards regional integration in the early 1990s. The dual stimuli were, on the one hand, the spectre of regionalism in Western Europe (the EC92 programme) and in the Americas (NAFTA) and, on the other hand, the dissolution of the Soviet Union in December 1991.

The creation of the Single European Market (together with the pre-existing EU preferential trade relations with various African and Mediterranean Countries), and the negotiations to extend the Canada–US Free Trade Area to include Mexico (and thereafter perhaps form a western hemisphere free trade area), fed concerns about the disintegration of the world economy into large regional trade blocs. In Asia, worries about being harmed by regionalism elsewhere and by its systemic effects inspired extensive discussion in 1988–9. This led to the establishment of APEC and EAEC and, with a time lag, to new plans for regional integration in ASEAN, ECO and SAARC.

In January 1992 the ASEAN members signed accords in Singapore which aimed at gradually establishing an ASEAN free trade area (AFTA). AFTA involves the reduction of intra-ASEAN tariffs on manufactured goods to 0–5 per cent within the fifteen years starting from 1 January 1993. It was also proposed to include the elimination of non-tariff barriers to intra-ASEAN trade, although the mechanism for achieving this has not yet been specified.

AFTA was accorded greater credibility than the earlier PTA scheme, because it specified mechanisms for moving towards the preferential tariff which required the listing of exclusions, rather than detailed negotiation of what should be included.[4] Nevertheless, the original announcement had not been preceded by sufficient preparation at the national level and, during the ensuing twenty months, the national governments responded to the concerns of protected domestic producers by drawing up long exclusion lists. A relaunch in October 1993 redressed the situation somewhat by bringing reductions on high tariffs (i.e. those over 20 per cent) forward to January 1994. The deadline for bringing intra-ASEAN tariffs down to 0–5 per cent was moved from 2008 to 2003 and then, at the July 1995 ASEAN summit, the deadline was brought forward again to 2000. Nevertheless, uncertainty remains over the extent to which members will follow through with preferential tariff reductions as deadlines draw closer.

Studies of the impact of AFTA build on earlier work on the PTA. Imada (1993) finds that liberalising intra-ASEAN trade in manufactures will lead to greater specialisation according to comparative advantage, and increased intra-ASEAN trade due to both trade creation and trade diversion. The quantitative changes in trade flows are not large, and Imada does not estimate the welfare effects. Imada's estimates do, however, show significant trade balance effects, as the lower tariff countries (Singapore and Malaysia) will increase their intra-ASEAN exports by more than their imports, while Thailand will experience a large deterioration in its intra-ASEAN trade deficit. A key issue in practice will be how far intra-ASEAN trade really is freed but, even if AFTA goes much further than the PTA, the potential gains are not large, given the similarity of most of the members' economies.

ECO was revitalised by the dissolution of the Soviet Union. The six Islamic former Soviet Republics, plus Afghanistan, joined ECO in 1992, forming a bloc containing all of the non-Arab Asian Islamic nations west of India.[5] The new members were encouraged to participate in the preferential trading arrangements, although there was no practical response to this call. A more promising route to regional cooperation within ECO lies in the trade facilitation measures, called for in the February 1993 Quetta Plan of Action, and in the coordination of transport projects, envisioned in the October 1993 Almaty Outline Plan.

SAARC announced in 1995 a similar PTA programme to that of ECO (i.e. a 10 per cent reduction of tariffs on intra-SAARC trade in selected items), but that will be still more difficult to implement than the ECO programme given enduring distrust between some SAARC members. The end of the Cold War has been a stimulus for India and Pakistan to begin to repair their bilateral relations, but that process is still at an early stage. Indeed, pressure on Pakistan to apply MFN treatment to its trade with India is coming from the WTO rather than from the regional organisation.

SUB-REGIONAL ECONOMIC ZONES

A striking economic phenomenon in East Asia has been the recent emergence of sub-regional economic zones (SRZs), which cross national boundaries but need not involve entire national economies (Pomfret 1996c). The prime example is the Singapore–Johor–Riau (Sijori) zone, which appeared with little governmental direction in the late 1980s. The Pearl River Delta, or other configurations involving southern China, Macau and Hong Kong, is also sometimes viewed as a SRZ. The SRZ concept has been widened by some commentators, especially those associated with the Asian Development Bank (Thant *et al.* 1994; Tang 1995), to include growth triangles and other dynamic regions.

The economic basis for the Sijori SRZ is the difference in factor endowments in Singapore, and in Johor and Riau, combined with agglomeration effects which lead economic activities to concentrate geographically. Singapore and Indonesia signed bilateral agreements on investment protection and joint development of water resources in Riau in 1990 and 1991, but these were after the market-driven development was well under way. Formal agreements between Johor and Singapore played even less of a role, and joint infrastructure such as the causeway linking Johor to Singapore has been overstrained, with public policy following rather than leading demand. Liberalisation of trade and other policies in Malaysia and especially Indonesia facilitated the emergence of the SRZ, but these were non- discriminatory policy changes.[6]

Establishment of cross-border links within the Pearl River Delta has a similar history. Liberalisation of Chinese foreign investment and trade policies (see Chapter 2) was a prerequisite, and specific measures such as the creation of the Special Economic Zones in Shenzhen (adjacent to Hong Kong) and Zhuhai (adjacent to Macau) also contributed. These were, however, not bilateral measures, nor did they generally discriminate in favour of trade with Macau and Hong Kong. The boom in the Pearl River Delta took off in 1983-84, when wages and rents in Hong Kong made the export of labour-intensive manufactures produced in the colony less competitive. Hong Kong entrepreneurs moved their assembly operations into China, and by the end of the decade were employing more workers in Guangdong Province than in Hong Kong. The effects quickly spread beyond Shenzhen and Zhuhai as foreign entrepreneurs sought low-wage locations with minimal government interference.

Both the Sijori SRZ and the development of the Pearl River Delta illustrate the importance of the distinction between regionalism and regionalisation (Lorenz 1991). Neither involved regionalism, in the sense of policies aimed at promoting regional integration. Regionalisation – i.e. the development of closer regional economic ties – occurred as a result of market forces, with entrepreneurs seeking low-wage production locations close to the dynamic metropoles of Singapore and Hong Kong. Similar spread and agglomeration effects are visible around Bangkok and Shanghai in the 1990s; these 'zones' cross provincial, rather than national, borders and thus do not qualify as SRZs, although the economic origins and functions of the Greater Bangkok and the Lower Yangtze zones are the same as those of Sijori or the Pearl River Delta SRZ.

The concept of growth triangles captured the public imagination in Asia in 1992.[7] The triangle image is a misleading picture of the Singapore-centred SRZ where links between Johor and Riau are minimal, but it led to the identification of other potential growth triangles. The Malaysian Government, in particular, embraced the concept as a route to regional integration without having to change national trade policies. It has actively promoted the Northern Growth Triangle (covering northern Sumatra, and parts of north-western Malaysia and southern Thailand) and the East ASEAN Growth Area (incorporating Brunei and parts of Indonesia, Malaysia and the Philippines).[8] These government-sponsored SRZs have had limited success so far.

The UNDP-sponsored Tumen River Area Development Project in North-East Asia is also an example of trying to create an SRZ from above. This could eventually be part of a broader North-East Asia economic region involving Japan, Korea, Mongolia, North-east China and the Russian Far East, but so far there has been little progress even in the narrowly defined Tumen River area.[9] Although there are potential complementarities between the Tumen River countries, the exploitation of which has been limited by prohibitive trade barriers, the reduction of the non-tariff barriers will take time. The earliest positive effects of the Tumen River Project are likely to be extremely limited, but still mutually beneficial, trade-facilitating measures such as easing border formalities and completing a rail link between China and the East Sea (Sea of Japan).

Another area much broader in geographical scope than the original SRZ is the Greater Mekong Subregion (Tan *et al.* 1995). The Greater Mekong Sub-region (GMS) also has its origins in attempts by international organisations to facilitate trade between neighbours which have discouraged trade. The prospects for the GMS as a growth area are completely different from those of the Tumen River project, because it involves such dynamic economies as Thailand, Yunnan Province of China, and Vietnam, as well as Myanmar (Burma), Laos and Cambodia. As with the Tumen River project, however, this is not a regional trading arrangement, and the biggest contribution of the GMS format is likely to be to facilitate planning of regional transport projects (under the aegis of the Asian Development Bank) and of trade facilitation (under the aegis of the United Nations Economic and Social Commission for Asia and the Pacific).

The various configurations discussed in this section are sometimes lumped together with the regional trading arrangements described in the previous section to paint a picture of growing regionalism in Asia. Tang (1995: 198) also includes APEC and the EAEC for good measure. This is not comparing like with like. The Sijori and Pearl River SRZs are market-driven phenomena, which have not involved any discriminatory trade policies. The Tumen River and Mekong projects are about trade facilitation through the provision of hard and soft infrastructure, and make no mention of discriminatory trade policies. The other growth triangles appear to have similar intent, although none has yet had much impact. APEC and EAEC have so far been talking shops without practical impact, although the stated goal of APEC is free trade on a multilateral non-discriminatory basis. The regional trading arrangements, on the other hand, intend to implement discriminatory trade policies which give preferential treatment to intra-regional trade.

THE REGIONALISM SCENARIO

Nightmare

It is easy to draw a map of Asia early in the twenty-first century divided into trading blocs. This section will sketch such a scenario, and the next section will discuss its plausibility.

The most certain part of the regionalism of Asia is the extension of ASEAN. Laos, Cambodia and Myanmar have all signed the Treaty of Amity and Cooperation (the first two in 1992, Myanmar in 1995), which has become the recognised first step to membership since Vietnam joined ASEAN in July 1995. It is probable that ASEAN will expand to include ten members by the end of the century, which is also the current target date for establishing the ASEAN Free Trade Area (AFTA). Further west, SAARC and ECO both have plans to create preferential trading areas. Establishment of preferential tariffs would encourage intra-regional trade in both cases, which could have a large impact given the repressed levels of bilateral trade between India and its neighbours, and between the former Soviet republics and other ECO members.

China's reabsorption of Hong Kong in 1997 and Macau in 1999 has stimulated extensive discussion of the Greater China region, especially as economic links between China and Taiwan have expanded. The official Chinese position is 'one sovereign state – separate customs zones' but, at least for Hong Kong and Macau, it is probable that they will receive preferential access to the Chinese market and that there will be some reciprocity (e.g. in Chinese access to public procurement contracts).

Korean reunification is an uncertain prospect. In view of the lack of information available about economic conditions in North Korea, drastic changes in status cannot be ruled out.

If all of the forces of regionalism came to pass, then from the Bosporus to the Bering Sea would be seven large trading units: ECO, SAARC, ASEAN, Greater China, unified Korea, Japan and the Russian Federation – the only loose bricks being Mongolia, Georgia and Armenia. Such an outcome could have positive consequences if regional free trade arrangements provided an anchor for unilateral trade liberalisation in formerly closed economies and if the large trading units had outward-looking policies towards non-members. The fear, however, is that preferential trading arrangements would lead to trade diversion fostered by trade policies discriminating against non-members.

Likely outcome

In practice, the extreme regionalism scenario is an unlikely outcome. Despite the changing circumstances of the 1990s, many of the forces which worked against regionalism in Asia in the past still exist. On the political level, mutual distrust remains strong between the large countries of South Asia. Pressures for continuing separation in North Korea and in Taiwan may be at least as powerful as the forces for reunification. Within ECO, the three original members are competing for influence in Central Asia, and for the transport and pipeline links between Central Asia and the Indian Ocean or Mediterranean Sea, as much as they are cooperating in building a coherent region.

The regionalism scenario also contains some awkward overlaps. Pakistan is a member of both SAARC and of ECO. Turkey has signed an agreement to form a customs union with the European Union. Simultaneous membership in two regional trading arrangements poses problems and, if they both evolve into customs unions, the problems are insoluble short of amalgamating the two unions, because a country cannot operate two different common external trade policies.[10] For the Central Asian members of ECO, their trade remains heavily oriented towards the Commonwealth of Independent States (CIS), and the status of the former Soviet Republics' trade policies *vis-à-vis* other CIS members remains in flux.[11]

The economic forces which thwarted the attempts at regional integration in ASEAN in the late 1970s and early 1980s are also important. The ASEAN members agreed in principle to preferential trading arrangements and even to integrated industrial policies, but then resisted attempts to implement the regionalism measures. Protected domestic industries had the political influence to prevent any measures leading to trade creation, while governments and users of imported inputs resisted measures leading to trade diversion. This is not just an Asian phenomenon; similar recognition of the economic costs of regional trading arrangements led to their collapse or to being stillborn in Latin America and in Africa in the 1960s and 1970s (Pomfret 1988: 143–8).[12]

If extreme regionalism is unlikely, what are the prospects for alternative trade regimes in East Asia? The most likely outcome is multilateralism with trade conducted under the rules of the WTO. Such an outcome is consistent with the existence of regional organisations which address trade facilitation issues and so forth, as long as they do not implement preferential trade policies which conflict with GATT Article XXIV. It is also consistent with the existence of wider regional bodies such as APEC, which might act as fora for discussion of new trade-related issues and promote trade liberalisation on a non-discriminatory basis.[13]

Within the context of a non-discriminatory trade regime, many Asian countries might be expected to unilaterally liberalise their trade policies. Unilateral tariff elimination has a strong basis in economic theory, but the main impetus in practice is the demonstration effect of the association between openness and rapid economic development in the high-performing Asian economies. Across-the-board trade liberalisation is often easier to implement in practice than preferential tariff reductions such as those involved in the ASEAN, ECO and SAARC preferential trading schemes; the selectivity of the latter leads to negotiations being mired in bilateral bargaining where vested interests can manoeuvre to ensure exemption of their products.

Most of the larger Asian trading nations are already WTO members, and most of the non-members have applied for membership. Working parties to consider accession have been established for China (1987), Nepal (1989), Taiwan (1992), Russia (1993), Cambodia (1994), Vietnam (1995), Kyrgyzstan (1997), Kazakhstan (1997), and other Central Asian countries have applications pending. If all of these applications were successful, then the common acceptance of WTO rules would provide a mutually beneficial basis for intra-Asian trade.

The mutual benefits provide the biggest reason for hoping that WTO-based multilateralism will in fact be the outcome. The most difficult of the WTO negotiations surrounds China's application, which was lodged over a decade ago. The difficulties arise from the problem of reconciling trade rules appropriate to trade between market economies with the still large administered elements of the Chinese economy. In particular, possibilities for discretionary trade actions and considerable non-transparency challenge basic WTO principles. Similar complications surround many of the other accession negotiations between former centrally planned economies and the WTO. The Chinese case, however, is politicised by the concerns in North America and Western Europe about non-economic issues related to China, and by economic fears based on the sheer size of the Chinese economy.

This is not the place to speculate on the outcome of China's WTO negotiations. Both China and the rest of the world would benefit from Chinese acceptance of the rules, obligations and rights of WTO membership, and this should be encouraged rather than obstructed. Nevertheless, the possibility of an unsuccessful outcome raises the question of whether China will reject multilateralism if it fails to be accepted into the WTO.

THE OPTIONS FOR CHINA

China is not a potential member of any regional trading arrangement, apart from the loose APEC and EAEC. It is currently pursuing WTO membership, and multilateralism is clearly the strongest option on economic grounds. But does China have alternatives, and especially if the WTO negotiations are not satisfactorily concluded, can China take a bilateral route?

One problem with bilateralism is that, even if China wished to conclude bilateral agreements with her neighbours, there may not be a positive response. With China's largest local trading partners, Japan and Korea, there is a historical divide. ASEAN's geo-political glue has changed from concern about Vietnamese expansionism to concern over Chinese expansionism. The latter concern would have to be resolved before China–ASEAN bilateral trading relations could be warm. Territorial disputes over the Spratley Islands involve China, Indonesia, Malaysia, the Philippines, Taiwan and Vietnam, but the concern among the ASEAN countries is that China may resort to the use of force in pursuit of its claims. The Chinese occupation of Mischief Reef shortly before Vietnam's formal accession to ASEAN highlighted the threat. The recent extension of Chinese links with Myanmar (Burma) has not improved feelings within ASEAN, and ASEAN enlargement to include Myanmar is likely before 2000, with one purpose being to reorient Burmese trade towards the south and east, rather than to the north.

Chinese trade with the former Soviet Republics and with Mongolia increased rapidly in 1991–92. It had a firm basis in comparative advantage as China provided cheap but good consumer goods, of which Soviet consumers had been starved. In Kazakhstan, the largest of China's Central Asian neighbours, imports from China soared from less than 4 per cent of the 1990 total to over 40 per cent in 1992, when the trade turnover of US$433m with China was more than double that with any of Kazakhstan's other trading partners except Russia (Pomfret 1995: 191, 201–2). Continued rapid growth of Chinese trade with its Central Asian neighbours was, however, not maintained in 1993 and 1994, apparently because of concerns in Kazakstan and Kyrgyzstan, as well as in Mongolia, over growing Chinese economic influence. In 1994, China's trade with Kazakhstan had fallen to US$219 million, and Kazakhstan imports from China ranked behind imports from Russia, Germany, Ukraine, USA and Turkey, at about the same level as imports from Belarus and from South Korea.[14]

Similar concerns underlie Russian caution within the Tumen River negotiations. Russian negotiators have opposed plans for supranational administration of an economic zone involving Russian territory. Such sensitivity on matters of sovereignty reflects concerns over the large demographic imbalance between the two sides of the Russo-Chinese border in the Tumen area and over Chinese acceptance of the current international border.[15]

A more acceptable option for China's neighbours, who may feel threatened by China's sheer size and weight of numbers, is for geographically limited trade expansion, along the line of the SRZs. The expansion of border trade with Russia, Mongolia, Kyrgyzstan and Kazakhstan could be viewed in that light. The Greater Mekong Sub-region is an alternative model. Whether this option is acceptable to China is, however, less clear. Even in the Tumen River negotiations the central Chinese Government has been careful to retain control over developments, rather than allow too much decentralisation of powers to the Yanbian autonomous prefecture, which is home to most of China's Korean minority.[16] Similar concerns about border provinces with minority populations apply to relations between Inner Mongolia and Mongolia, and between Xinjiang and Kazakhstan. The centrifugal tendencies may be hardest to control in the case of Yunnan Province, since improved transport links and trade facilitation would greatly increase the attraction of trading with the dynamic ASEAN countries, and of using Bangkok rather than Chinese ports as Yunnan's seaport.

CONCLUDING REMARKS

What are the implications of these recent developments for future trade patterns in East Asia, and for future trade between China and the rest of the world? Will changes at the global level and within Asia lead to regionalism rather than multilateral trade policies? In particular, what will be the role of China? Will China be at the centre of an East Asian economic region, or will there be a decentralisation process as North-east China becomes part of a North-East Asia zone, while Yunnan Province focuses towards ASEAN, Xinjiang Province towards the ECO countries of Central Asia, and so forth?

Despite the announcement of preferential trading arrangements by ASEAN, ECO and SAARC in the first half of the 1990s, the prospects for regionalism in Asia are dim. In ECO and SAARC, significant political obstacles to close regional integration remain. In all three cases, economic forces are likely to undermine preferential trading initiatives. A more plausible scenario is for continued reliance on the GATT-based system which has served the high-performing Asian economies so well in recent decades. The stability of this system will be related to the performance of the WTO, but commitments to open regionalism at APEC summits could be seen as an Asian statement of intent to maintain multilateralism even if the WTO falters.

The high profile of APEC summits has induced an ironic role reversal for the European Union. After initiating the new regionalism of the 1980s and creating 'omission anxiety' in Asia, the European Union now exhibits growing concern about being left out (or being left in a basket with slow-growing economies of Africa and South Asia). The European Union has reacted by seeking collocutors in Asia, for example with ASEAN or within the Asia–Europe (ASEM) meeting initiated in March 1996.[17] The European Union has been unwilling to react imaginatively to the APEC proposal for eliminating tariffs by 2020, which was matched by a similar declaration at the Summit of the Americas. EU commitment to the same target would enhance the momentum towards global free trade, and hence remove the prospect of discriminatory tariffs in future.

China's role in the spread of open non-discriminatory trading regimes in Asia has been passive. The Chinese economy has become substantially more open since the 1970s, although its own trade policies remain far from GATT-consistent. China has benefited from the extension of MFN treatment to it by the major trading nations, but has so far enjoyed this major right of GATT/WTO membership without meeting the obligations. Any tendency towards increased regionalism in world trade could undermine these benefits, as China does not fit into any regional grouping other than the broad umbrellas of APEC or the EAEC. Moreover, China's major trading partners, except Japan, are outside Asia (see Table 4.2).

The best outcome for China and for the world would be for China's WTO application to be successful, and for China to meet the obligations and enjoy the rights of a WTO member. If the WTO negotiations are unsuccessful, however, will China turn to a strategy of bilateral relations with its neighbours? Such an outcome is improbable, not least because all of China's neighbours are suspicious of closer bilateral ties. The Chinese central government may also be reluctant to encourage border trade to flourish, since it could exacerbate centrifugal tendencies, especially in provinces with minority populations. In sum, China is neither threatened by a resurgent regionalism in Asia, nor likely to be an instigator of bilateral alternatives to the multilateral trading system.

Nevertheless, China may feel uncomfortable within the evolving system of international economic relations in Asia. The regional organisations (ASEAN, SAARC, ECO and the CIS) may not turn into regional trading arrangements, but they may still have an impact as fora for discussion and as vehicles for negotiation on matters of joint concern to their members. China does not have the prospect of being a member of any of these groups, apart from APEC, which may engender a sense of isolation, although that should be uncalled for given China's size; only the largest regional grouping (SAARC) has a similar population to China, although ASEAN's combined trade (and GNP at market prices) exceeds China's (see Table 4.1).

A second cause for Chinese concern arises from the distinctions made in this chapter between regionalism and regionalisation and between top-down and bottom-up approaches to regionalism. Yunnan Province, in particular, is likely to feel the economic pull of the rapidly growing economies to its south. Thailand was the fastest-growing economy in the world in the decade from the mid-1980s, and Thai economic influence is spreading rapidly in Laos and Yunnan. Whether the central government in Beijing likes it or not, it will be difficult in the semi-reformed Chinese economy to prevent local authorities and economic agents from developing closer links with ASEAN.

Table 4.2 China's trade with the member countries of ASEAN, ECO, and SAARC, 1995

Country	Imports from China (US$m)	Exports to China (US$m)
Association of Southeast Asian Nations (ASEAN)		
Brunei	34.5	—
Indonesia	1438.1	2052.0
Malaysia	1281.0	2065.1
Philippines	1030.1	275.8
Singapore	3500.6	3398.0
Thailand	1751.7	1610.8
Vietnam	720.1	332.1
ASEAN total	9756.1	9733.8
The Economic Cooperation Organization (ECO)		
Afghanistan	31.6	16.6
Azerbaijan	1.1	2.7
Iran	277.9	226.6
Kazakhstan	75.4	315.5
Kyrgyzstan	107.5	123.5
Pakistan	788.6	222.9
Tajikistan	14.6	9.2
Turkey	44.4	2.6
Turkmenistan	11.3	6.3
Uzbekistan	47.6	71.0
ECO total	1400.0	996.9
The South Asian Association for Regional Cooperation (SAARC)		
Bangladesh	633.0	45.1
Bhutan	—	—
India	765.3	397.5
Maldives	0.7	—
Nepal	53.4	—
Pakistan	788.6	222.9
Sri Lanka	239.2	2.0
SAARC total	2480.2	667.5
Japan	28462.7	29004.8
United States	24711.3	16118.2
European Union	18348.6	19069.8
WORLD	148769.7	132078.2

Source: Almanac of China's Foreign Economic Relations and Trade 1996/97
Notes:
(a) The European Union refers to the twelve Member States prior to 1995.
(b) The data are not corrected for re-exports through Hong Kong or any other entrepôt – see Chapter 6.

Regionalism in Asia is an unlikely prospect, but regionalisation of Asian trade will be enhanced by trade liberalisation and rapid growth centred on some growth poles. The rest of the world will benefit from both non-discriminatory trade liberalisation and rapid growth in East Asia, but two facilitating attitudes are desirable. First, China will be more encouraged to play a positive role in this process if the WTO accession negotiations can be brought to a successful conclusion. That requires adjustment on China's part in making its trade policies more WTO-compatible, but the European Union could play a constructive role in the process. Second, intercontinental trade will be less disrupted if liberalisation in Asia is matched by liberalisation elsewhere, and by acceptance of the need for (and desirability of) structural adjustment in China's trading partners.

NOTES

1 The author is grateful to Ki Fukasaku, David Turnham and David O'Connor for helpful comments on an early draft of the paper, to Margot Schuerman for assistance in obtaining Bhutan data, and to participants at the April 1996 Second East Asia-EU Business Conference for a stimulating discussion. This paper is part of a larger research project on regional trading arrangements in the Asia–Pacific region, undertaken with financial support from the Australian Research Council.
2 Brunei joined ASEAN in 1984 and Vietnam in 1995.
3 Pomfret (1996b) provides more detailed analysis of these episodes and of subsequent ASEAN schemes to promote regional cooperation in industrial development, which were largely stillborn.
4 East Asia Analytical Unit (1994) contains an accessible statement of the contents of AFTA and early progress in implementing AFTA, as well as the text of the agreements. Lee (1994) also analyses the AFTA implementation mechanisms. The 'padding' of exclusions was addressed by agreeing that inclusions would be defined at the 6-digit level, while exclusions would be defined at the more disaggregated 8-digit level (Tan 1995: chapter 8). A cumulative local content requirement of 40 per cent has been set, but the enforcement of rules of origin – a special problem for ASEAN given that two member states (Singapore and Brunei) operate close to free trade policies – does not appear to have been adequately addressed.
5 The Turkish Muslim Community of Cyprus is not a member, but its representative often attends ECO meetings. To the west, Bosnia is the only non-Arab state with an Islamic majority which is not an ECO member.
6 Creation of the Batam duty free zone in 1978 and the subsequent liberalisation of Indonesia's policies towards foreign investment were important in establishing conditions favourable to foreign investment in Riau, but they were not targeted at creating special links with Singapore.
7 The catalyst was a conference at the National University of Singapore in April 1992, which was widely reported in the press although the papers were only published in the following year (Toh and Low 1993).
8 Turner (1995) analyses the East Asean Growth Area (EAGA) from the perspective of the Philippines.
9 Pomfret (1996a: 130–42) analyses the evolution of the Tumen River project during the first half of the 1990s. In December 1995, the two Korean governments, China, Mongolia and Russia signed three parallel agreements establishing the first inter-governmental organisations for development of North-east Asia; the secretariat to support these agreements is located in Beijing.
10 Turkey has already signalled in ECO meetings over the Protocol on Preferential Tariffs that it cannot make any commitments which conflict with its EU obligations. However, there is a chance that, in reaction to EU coolness over Turkey's long-standing quest for EU membership, Turkey could renounce its customs union in favour of closer ties with its Islamic neighbours; this is the stated

preference of Necmettin Erbakan, leader of the Islamic Welfare Party, who became Turkey's Prime Minister in June 1996.
11 Trade across national borders in Central Asia, especially those within the former USSR, remains poorly monitored apart from bulk arrangements concerning key primary products such as cotton, natural gas, oil and minerals. In January 1994, Kazakhstan, Kyrgyzstan and Uzbekistan signed an agreement to create a common economic space, the content of which is unclear. The broader conflict surrounds Russia's desire to formalize intra-CIS trade in a customs union; Kazakhstan and Kyrgyzstan signed an economic integration agreement with Belarus and Russia in March 1996, but some Central Asian countries (e.g. Uzbekistan) disagree over Russia's proposed common external tariff while others (e.g. Turkmenistan) resist the supranationality associated with a customs union.
12 The apparent exception of Western Europe reflects two important differences: the European customs union was formed in the context of substantial external trade liberalisation, and political commitment to integration led governments to accept the trade diversion costs associated with some common policies (notably agriculture). Winters (1993) argues that, compared with a likely alternative scenario of non-discriminatory trade liberalisation, the economic effects of the EC/EU were small. In sum, if a country is embarked on reducing its tariffs to low levels then preferential treatment of trade with its neighbours will make little difference, whereas if it embarks on a seriously discriminatory policy of preferentially reducing high general tariffs, then the economic consequences will be larger and the reactions of affected producers will undermine the programme.
13 China used the 1995 APEC Summit in Osaka to announce a package of tariff cuts which went some way to removing obstacles to China's WTO accession; the occasion allowed China to display constructive participation in trade liberalisation in the Pacific region, without appearing to bow to foreign pressure over the WTO negotiations.
14 The 1992 and 1994 trade figures are from the Kazakhstan State Committee on Statistics. A large, but by its nature unknown, amount of border trade between China and Kazakhstan is unmonitored. Low reported exports by Kazakhstan to China is in part due to under-reporting of exports of alcoholic beverages and casino services.
15 China does not have any formal territorial claims in the Tumen area, but does exert a right of access to the sea along the Tumen River, which can only be done in small craft. The existence of Vladivostok (whose name means 'ruler of the east') is, however, viewed by some Chinese nationalists as a provocation by a European power which has no place in the Pacific. China's relations with Tajikistan, and to a lesser extent Kyrgyzstan, are affected by irredentism; both the government in Beijing and that in Taipei disavow as an 'unequal treaty' the 1881 Treaty of Saint Petersburg by which China surrendered its claim to the Ferghana Valley.
16 A major setback to Chinese–North Korean cooperation arose when the Yanbian Government agreed to provide financial support for North Korea's construction of the Haeryong–Chongjin road running from the Chinese border to the sea. The Chinese central government, however, failed to authorise the prefecture's expenditures and the North Koreans did not receive any money, which the Koreans viewed as an act of bad faith on China's part. Whether the action in Beijing was prudent fiscal management or had other motives, the Chinese central government was willing to assert its power of final say even at the cost of undermining North Korean participation in the Tumen River project.
17 The second ASEM meeting is scheduled to take place in London in April 1998.

REFERENCES

Ariff, M. and Tan, G. (1992) 'ASEAN-Pacific Trade Relations', *ASEAN Economic Bulletin* 8(4): 258–83.
East Asia Analytical Unit (1994) *ASEAN Free Trade Area: Trading Bloc or Building Block?*, Canberra: Australian Government Publishing Service.
Imada, P. (1993) 'Production and Trade Effects of the ASEAN Free Trade Area', *The Developing Economies*, 31(1), March: 3–23.
Lee, T.Y. (1994) 'The ASEAN Free Trade Area: The Search for a Common Prosperity', *Asian-Pacific Economic Literature*, 8(1), May: 1–7.
Lorenz, D. (1991) 'Regionalization versus Regionalism – Problems of Change in the World Economy', *Intereconomics*, 26(1), January: 3–10.
Ministry of Foreign Trade and Economic Cooperation (1996) *Almanac of China's Foreign Economic Relations and Trade 1996/97*, Beijing: China Economics Publishing House.
Pomfret, R. (1988) *Unequal Trade,* Oxford: Basil Blackwell.
Pomfret, R. (1995) *The Economies of Central Asia*, Princeton, NJ: Princeton University Press.
Pomfret, R. (1996a) *Asian Economies in Transition: Reforming Centrally Planned Economies*, London: Edward Elgar.
Pomfret, R. (1996b) 'ASEAN: Always at the Crossroads?', *Journal of the Asia Pacific Economy*, 1(3): 365–90.
Pomfret, R. (1996c) 'Sub-regional Economic Zones', in B. Bora and C. Findlay (eds) *Regional Integration and the Asia-Pacific*, Melbourne: Oxford University Press, pp.207–22.
Pomfret, R. (1997) 'The Economic Cooperation Organization: Current Status and Future Prospects', *Europe-Asia Studies* (formerly *Soviet Studies*), 49(4): 657–67.
Tan, G. (1995) *ASEAN: Economic Development and Cooperation,* Singapore: Times Academic Press.
Tan, R., Pante Jr, F., and Abonyi, G. (1995) 'Economic Cooperation in the Greater Mekong Subregion', in K. Fukasaku (ed.) *Regional Cooperation and Integration in Asia*, Paris: OECD, pp.223–48.
Tang, M. (1995) 'Asian Economic Cooperation: Opportunities and Challenges', in K. Fukasaku (ed.) *Regional Cooperation and Integration in Asia*, Paris: OECD, pp.195–221.
Thant, M., Tang, M. and Kakazu, H. (eds) (1994) *Growth Triangles in Asia*, Oxford: Oxford University Press, for the Asian Development Bank.
Toh, M.H. and Low, L. (1993) *Regional Cooperation and Growth Triangles in ASEAN*, Singapore: Times Academic Press.
Turner, M. (1995) 'Subregional Economic Zones, Politics and Development: The Philippine Involvement in the East ASEAN Growth Area (EAGA)', *The Pacific Review*, 8(4): 637–48.
Wall, D. (1996) 'China as a Trade Partner: Threat or Opportunity for the OECD?', *International Affairs*, 72(2): 329–44.
Winters, L.A. (1993) 'The European Community: A Case of Successful Integration?', in J. de Melo and A. Panagariya (eds) *New Dimensions in Regional Integration*, Cambridge: Cambridge University Press, pp.202–28.
World Bank (1995a) *The World Bank Atlas 1996*, Washington, DC: the World Bank.
World Bank (1995b) *Trends in Developing Economies*, Washington, DC: the World Bank.

5 Europe's role in the transfer of technology to China

Paul Whitla and Howard Davies[1]

INTRODUCTION

In 1979 an editorial in the *People's Daily* gave the first hint of a shift away from technological self-reliance in China, which had been the central feature of policy since the Sino-Soviet rift of 1960. That was followed by Deng Xiaoping's confirmation that 'the Chinese people should learn from the merits of science and technology which are developed by the people in different countries', and commitment to that change in direction was re-affirmed in 1981 when Zhao Ziyang's Report to the Fifth National Party Congress emphasised the end of China's technological isolation by noting that 'We must abandon once and for all the idea of self-sufficiency' (Zhao 1982).

From that point onwards, despite Zhao's fall from political power in 1989, the acquisition of technology from abroad has remained a 'fundamental tenet of China's current modernisation strategy' (Conroy 1992: 212). The purpose of this chapter is to explore the role of Europe as a source of technology for China, paying particular attention to the modes of transfer involved, their amounts, and the differences which exist between the pattern of technology transfer from Europe and that from elsewhere. Before turning to that analysis, however, it is useful to define and categorise 'technology' and 'technology transfer', and to set out the context in which transfers to China have taken place.

DEFINING 'TECHNOLOGY' AND 'TECHNOLOGY TRANSFER'

Al-Ali (1995) suggests that there is a distinct lack of consensus on the definition of both 'technology' and 'technology transfer'. While that may be true, there is nothing particularly problematical about the definition used by Robock (1980), who states that technology is 'a perishable resource comprising knowledge, skills and the means for using and controlling factors of production for the purpose of producing, delivering to users and maintaining goods and services for which there is an economic and/or social demand'. Having defined technology in this way, expressed more concisely as 'information and the capability to use it' (Davies and Whitla 1995), it is possible to identify various taxonomies which are commonly used to differentiate between significantly different types of this perishable resource.

Perhaps the most common distinction is that between 'advanced' or 'high' technology, on the one hand, and 'low', 'mature', 'standard', 'backward' or even 'obsolete' technology, on the other. 'High technology' is a much over-used expression but it usually refers to information which is the result of relatively recent research and development activity. As most research and development takes place in the high-wage countries of the 'triad' – Europe, Japan and the United States – advanced technology tends to be associated with relatively capital-intensive techniques, while 'low' technology is more labour-intensive. Under Chinese regulations, imported technology is supposed to be 'advanced' (Wolff 1989), although there is little evidence of such transfers and the same regulations also require imported technology to be 'appropriate'.

This distinction between 'appropriate' and 'inappropriate' technology may be interpreted in a number of ways. Most obviously, it can refer to the factor-intensity of the techniques used in production, so that capital-intensive techniques are inappropriate in a labour-rich, low-wage economy like China (Lall 1981). More generally, 'appropriate' technology may be construed as the use of techniques which are capable of producing the outputs required at the lowest opportunity cost to the economy, when all costs are taken into account, including the social costs arising from pollution, social dislocation and the use of non-renewable resources.

A third set of categories into which 'technology' may be divided concerns the form of its embodiment. In this case, distinctions may be drawn between the technology embodied in 'hardware' (i.e. plant and equipment), and that embodied in 'software' (including manuals, operating procedures and routines, and the memories of individuals, teams and organisations).

Fourth, there is the distinction, not well supported by the Chinese legal system, between 'proprietary' technology, which is privately owned by an organisation or individual, and 'non-proprietary' technology which is in the public domain.

Finally, there is the important difference (Teece 1978) between technology which is 'explicit' or 'codified' and can therefore be easily recognised by its owner and fully disclosed in writing or graphically, and that which is 'tacit'. The latter may not be well understood or recognised, even by its owner and it cannot be made accessible to others without extensive interaction among the personnel who currently have it, and those to whom it is to be communicated.

Having defined 'technology' and identified some of the important distinctions to be made among different types, it is possible to define 'technology transfer' to China in the terms used by the US Office of Technology Assessment (OTA 1987), which are that it is 'a process whereby a government, company or institution provides the information necessary for China to improve its capability to design or produce goods and services'. This process may involve various 'channels' for technology transfer, each corresponding to a different set of organisational arrangements, governance structures and 'information content' (Davies 1993). These are considered below, first by outlining the Chinese experience to date, and then by examining the evidence on the role of Europe in that process.

CHINA'S EXPERIENCE OF TECHNOLOGY TRANSFER

China's experience of technology transfer to date can be divided into three very distinct periods, each corresponding to different development strategies, different valuations of foreign technology, different sources of technological assistance and different types of recipient enterprise.

In the period extending from Liberation until 1960, China was heavily involved in the import of technology from the Soviet Union and its client states. Attention centred upon the establishment of an industrial base through 256 very large construction projects, valued at US$ 2.7billion (Ho and Huenemann 1984). These focused on metallurgy, machinery, trucks, coal, petroleum and electricity. In keeping with Stalinist notions of development strategy, emphasis was placed upon the import of complete sets of plant and equipment, supported by 'turnkey' arrangements and the secondment of large numbers of Russian personnel.

While the emphasis on technology embodied in heavy 'hardware' transferred into a relatively primitive industrial environment might have left the Chinese with plant and equipment they could not use, that appears not to have been the case. The combination of Russian experts in China, thousands of Chinese students learning in Russian universities, and a wholehearted effort to induce 'learning-by-doing' provided the necessary 'software' and produced what has been described as 'the most comprehensive technology transfer in modern industrial history' (Barnett 1981).

This successful initial experience was brought to an abrupt halt, first by the disastrous industrial policies of the Great Leap Forward in 1958–60 and then by the political rift of 1960 between China and the Soviet Union. When the Soviet experts left, in many cases taking vital blueprints and codified information with them, the Chinese found themselves unable to complete a large number of projects (Zadoria 1962).

The second phase of technology import extended from 1962 until 1978, including the chaotic period of 1967–76 when the xenophobic attitudes of the Cultural Revolution rendered suspect any commitment to learning from abroad and the slogan 'better Red than Expert' indicated the low regard in which technological competence was held. In the years before those attitudes became firmly entrenched, the Chinese Government signed eighty-four technology transfer contracts with Japanese and European firms, following the earlier pattern of heavy industrial development. However, the value of those contracts was only a small fraction of that for the Soviet programme and many of these projects were abandoned or delayed (Huang 1987).

As the Cultural Revolution passed, the previous pattern re-emerged. Out of 220 contracts valued at US$3.8 billion in 1972–78, more than US$3 billion was accounted for by twenty-six very large projects (Conroy 1992). However, the de-skilling effect of the previous decade had destroyed China's 'software' and rendered the country incapable of absorbing these projects effectively. They were approved without proper feasibility studies, inappropriately advanced technologies were selected, and unskilled workers were allocated to run them, with the predictable effect. Nevertheless, in one of those almost unbelievably irrational twists of Chinese official behaviour, a further US$3billion of contracts were approved in the last ten days of 1978.

At the close of the 1970s, the Cultural Revolution was finally laid to rest as the 'Gang of Four' were ousted. Attention shifted away from politics towards economic development and successive Five Year Plans placed increasing emphasis on the need to import 'advanced and appropriate' technologies and managerial skills from other countries. Within this new policy environment a number of different strands have emerged with respect to technology import. First, there has been some continuation of the earlier approach, with a series of large 'hardware' projects involving complex industrial installations and a group of State Council initiatives designed to produce 'key sets of equipment' which had hitherto been imported. Second, there has been a new emphasis on 'technological renovation', improving existing facilities instead of commissioning new sets of plant. Third, the general emphasis has shifted away from heavy industry in the north of the country, towards light industry in the south and the eastern seaboard. Finally, and most significant of all, the gradual development of a 'socialist market economy' has given more autonomy to Chinese enterprises and radically enhanced access to China for foreign companies. As part of that development, technology has become a proprietary commodity (in form if not in substance) and legislation for the protection of intellectual property has been put in place. Enterprises have become responsible for their own technology development and are free to seek assistance from abroad, so that the pattern of technology import is increasingly determined by the autonomous decisions of individual enterprises, with much less involvement from the planning authorities at the centre.

The pace of change continues to be very rapid and an overall evaluation of technology import to date is difficult. On the one hand, the very rapid growth of Chinese output, income and productivity which has taken place has been led by the foreign-invested sector. Areas such as Guangdong Province, which were traditionally agricultural areas with no industrial capability, have been transformed through the establishment of joint ventures with foreign enterprises (most notably from Hong Kong) into export-driven development zones with the ability to compete in the global market place (Kueh and Ash 1996). In that sense, the overall judgement on technology transfer from abroad must be a positive one. On the other hand, the tone of most evaluations of technology import is noticeably negative, as revealed in Conroy's study for the OECD in 1992.

A first concern is that the level of technology imported has been 'low tech' rather than 'advanced', consisting of relatively unsophisticated information embodied in simple general purpose equipment. The majority of foreign-invested enterprises, especially those Hong Kong companies working in the southern and coastal regions, are engaged in small-scale labour-intensive assembly operations for export. They compete internationally on the basis of cheap Chinese labour using limited amounts of expensive equipment. This may be economically and commercially rational for the foreign investors, but very little 'advanced' technology is transferred and it may be argued that, in common with other developing countries (OECD 1993), China receives relatively little technological up-grading through these operations. In the terms used by Dahlman and Westphal (1983), China has received the 'production capability' which is required to operate fairly simple technology, and it may have received some of the 'investment capability' needed to expand existing capacity and build new facilities. However, it has not received any significant 'innovation capability', which would allow the country's enterprises to develop new products and processes.

A second problem associated with this type of enterprise is that it imports most of its processed materials and manufactured components, and then exports the final product. As a result, there are few vertical linkages with other parts of the domestic economy. Local suppliers are not encouraged to develop, and the output of the foreign-invested firms does not form an upgraded input to user enterprises. Higher level functions like design and marketing expertise are usually kept in the Hong Kong head office, and local partners may even be actively dissuaded from trying to learn about foreign customers and markets (Leung *et al.* 1991).

Third, for most enterprises and projects, the emphasis is placed on the import of 'hardware' for production purposes, with relatively little attempt being made to learn further from the imported equipment. Many projects have therefore remained dependent upon foreign sources for inputs, and relatively little import-substitution through reverse-engineering has taken place.

Fourth, Chinese importers of technology have tended to believe that technology 'can somehow be delivered in a tidy package, complete and ready to use' (Hendryx 1986). As a result, there has often been a failure to appreciate that significant local capability may be needed in order to make effective use of technological information provided from abroad and many projects have failed to reach their planned levels of production.

Finally, some commentators have argued that, even where effective technology transfer takes place, if the channel used is foreign direct investment the transferred knowledge remains within the investing firm and is rarely made available even to the local partner, much less the wider local community (Lan 1996; Lan and Young 1996).

Against this background it is possible to explore the evidence on the use of alternative channels for the import of technology to China, the pattern of European involvement and the importance of that involvement in the light of the concerns which have been expressed.

TECHNOLOGY TRANSFER THROUGH CONTRACTS

At the time of the Industrial Revolution in Europe and America, it was possible for significant transfers of technological knowledge to take place through the migration of skilled individuals (Scoville 1951). However, the complexity of modern technology and the highly specialised role played by individuals in the process of production mean that most useful knowledge today is held corporately, rather than in the minds of individuals (Gabriel 1967). Some degree of technology transfer may be achieved by hiring skilled and knowledgeable individuals, and China was estimated to have 20,000 'foreign experts' at work in the country in 1988 (Stewart 1990: 347) and 107,000 postgraduate students abroad in 1993 (State Statistical Bureau 1994: 563). Such skilled people certainly need to be available if an enterprise or an economy is to have the 'absorptive capacity' needed to make effective use of corporate information (Cohen and Levinthal 1990). However, technology transfer is fundamentally a process which takes place between and through organisations rather than individuals.

There are two main channels through which technology may be transferred across national boundaries from one organisation to another. The first is through contracts between independent organisations and the second is through foreign direct investment. Various forms of technology transfer through contract may take place. The simplest involves 'equipment supply', where the supplier simply sells plant and equipment to the technology importer, usually accompanied by elements of training, service and maintenance. In some cases, it may also involve a 'turnkey' arrangement where the supplier commissions the equipment and does not hand it over to the purchaser until full operations have been established. In either case, the focus is on 'hardware' and the relationship between supplier and recipient is of relatively short duration.

Longer-term contractual relationships between technology suppliers and recipients frequently take the form of licensing agreements. The most limited form of licensing involves nothing more than a 'covenant not to sue' whereby the licensee is given the legal right to use technical information which it could acquire without assistance, but which is proprietary to its owner. However, in almost all cases (apart from copyright licensing) the licensor provides technical information and assistance, as well as the legal rights.

The acquisition of technology through contract has the advantage of leaving overall control of the enterprise in Chinese hands. It may also be a relatively efficient way of transferring technology which is perfectly embodied in equipment, or well defined and well codified and hence easily transferred through a licensing agreement. However, contracts between independent parties are not an efficient way in which to transfer 'tacit' information, which is uncodified, difficult to identify, and difficult to communicate (Davies 1977, 1993, 1995). Licensors will also tend to fear the 'leakage' of their information to third parties and therefore be unwilling to transfer their latest and most commercially valuable information.

Table 5.1 shows the overall pattern of contracts for the import of technology into the PRC from all countries for the period 1981–95. 'Complete plant' and 'key equipment' together accounted for more than 60 per cent of the total contract numbers, and more than 80 per cent of the total value. 'Technical licensing' agreements accounted for a further 30 per cent of the number, but just 10.5 per cent of the value. However, it needs to be remembered that payments for plant and equipment cannot be directly compared to payments for licensing as payments for 'technology', because the value of contracts for plant and equipment includes the cost of both the technology and the equipment, whereas licensing payments are essentially payments for the technology alone. Crude estimates of the value of output arising from technology import through 'complete equipment' and through 'licensing' suggest that they have been around the same order of magnitude, with the value of output arising from licensing being equal to about 60–90 per cent of the value arising from complete equipment (Davies and Whitla 1995).

The information available for European technology import to China is insufficiently detailed to provide a breakdown corresponding to the categories in Table 5.1. However, Table 5.2 shows the total values of technology import contracts for five European countries and for China's other major suppliers, the United States and Japan. The five European countries have

Table 5.1 China's technology import contracts, by mode, 1981–95

Mode	Numbers of contracts	% of total contracts	Value of contracts (US$bn)	% of total value	Average value per contract (US$m)
Complete plant	3160	34.2	38.647	72.3	12.230
Key equipment	2525	27.3	4.622	8.6	1.830
Technical licensing	2842	30.7	5.629	10.5	1.981
Adv consultancy	222	2.4	0.274	0.5	1.234
Technical service	293	3.2	1.186	2.2	4.048
Co-production	204	2.2	3.120	5.8	1.529
Others	6	—	0.005	—	0.833
TOTAL	9252	100.0	53.483	100.0	5.781

Source: *Almanac of China's Foreign Economic Relations and Trade* (various issues)
Note: Co-production refers to the joint development of offshore oil projects.

Table 5.2 China's technology import contracts from five European nations, the United States and Japan, 1985–95 (US$m)

Year	Total	Europe							Japan	US	Others
		Germany	France	UK	Italy	Spain	Eur(5)	Eur(5) as % of total			
1985	2960	793	325	80	124	n.r.	1322	44.6	550	692	396
1986	4460	230	1150	420	260	n.r.	2060	46.2	n.r.	n.r.	2400
1987	2980	290	300	120	210	n.r.	920	30.8	710	670	680
1988	3550	419	576	437	815	n.r.	2247	63.3	272	256	775
1989	2923	430	374	n.r.	687	n.r.	1491	51.0	203	144	1085
1990	1274	133	n.r.	43	61	n.r.	237	18.6	92	322	623
1991	3459	265	n.r.	344	553	246	1408	40.7	269	n.r.	1782
1992	6590	733	383	n.r.	1444	388	2948	44.7	1376	1432	834
1993	6110	748	175	116	922	442	2403	39.3	1746	507	1454
1994	4110	1232	195	75	311	95	1908	46.4	770	594	838
1995	13033	1892	1706	718	977	275	5568	42.7	2249	2272	2944
85–95	51449	7165	5184	2353	6364	1446	22512	43.8	8237	6889	13811

Source: *Almanac of China's Foreign Economic Relations and Trade* (various issues)
Notes:
n.r. = not reported
Eur(5) = total for the five European countries listed (i.e. Germany, France, UK, Italy, and Spain)

provided a remarkably large proportion of the total value of technology import contracts, accounting for 44 per cent of the total for 1985–95, compared with only 16 per cent for Japan and 13 per cent for the United States. Furthermore, that share has stayed remarkably stable over the 11-year period, with the exception of 1990 which was affected by the aftermath of the Tiananmen Square events.

The figures also show that in 1995, which is the last year for which data are available, there was a sudden dramatic increase in China's technology imports. Both the numbers of contracts and the total value of contracts rose substantially, by more than 700 per cent and 200 per cent, respectively, over the previous year. Wu Zhenquan of the Department of Science and Technology at MOFTEC suggests that there were three causes for this sudden jump (Wu 1996). First, there was a substantial increase in the amount of technology imported by State-owned enterprises and for certain key State projects that year. Second, a number of previously agreed major projects came on schedule in that year, including thermal and nuclear power plants and subway systems. Third, there were improvements in the administration procedures for the facilitation and measurement of technology imports. The size and suddenness of the 1995 rise in technology imports suggest that it might well arise from these changes in the measurement system, and it will be difficult to judge whether 1995 was something of an outlier until the data for subsequent years are released.

The limitations of the data make it difficult to comment authoritatively on the mix of activities which make up Europe's very significant contribution to technology transfer through contract. However, Table 5.3 provides

Table 5.3 Average values of China's technology import contracts from five European nations, the United States and Japan, 1987–95

Transferor	1987–1990			1991–95		
	Number of contracts	Total value of contracts (US$m)	Average value of contracts (US$m)	Number of contracts	Total value of contracts (US$m)	Average value of contracts (US$m)
Germany	261	1272	4.87	672	4870	7.25
United Kingdom	75	600	8.00	125	1253	10.02
France	77	1250	16.23	143	2459	17.20
Spain	n.r.	n.r.	—	52	1446	27.81
Italy	110	1773	16.10	309	4207	13.61
Japan	314	1277	4.06	927	6410	6.91
United States	313	1392	4.44	1062	4805	4.52

Source: Almanac of China's Foreign Economic Relations and Trade (various issues)
Notes: n.r. = not reported

some clues by showing the average value of European technology transfer contracts in comparison with those of Japan and the United States. The average value of European technology transfer contracts was significantly higher than that of contracts involving Japan and the United States. In the sub-period 1987–90, both France and Italy were involved in contracts having an average value in excess of US$16m, which was four times the US and Japanese figures, while British contracts averaged twice the latter's size. In the later period 1991–95, the British, French and Italian figures remained very high while the newly-reported figure for Spain stood at nearly US$30m, more than six times the American figure.

If the figures in Table 5.3 are compared with those in Table 5.2, it seems legitimate to surmise that European technology contracts with China have been relatively more focused on the transfer of large sets of equipment while Japanese and American contracts have either been concerned with smaller sets of equipment or with licensing agreements.

TECHNOLOGY TRANSFER THROUGH FOREIGN DIRECT INVESTMENT

Although contracts have clearly been a significant channel for technology import from Europe into China, they are not normally regarded as the most important means by which corporate knowledge is transferred from place to place. Greater significance is usually ascribed to the 'internalised' transfers within the multinational enterprise (MNE), which provide the rationale for the MNE's existence (Davies 1979). According to the 'eclectic' model of the MNE (Dunning 1980), the internalisation of technology transfer avoids the costs and risks associated with contracts by replacing them with direct control through the managerial hierarchy. From the technology transferor's point of view, this avoids the costs of finding a partner with whom to transact, the costs of negotiation and drafting, and the risks arising from opportunistic behaviour which can only be overcome through considerable spending on monitoring and enforcement. Given the greater security of internalised transfer, technology suppliers will be more willing to channel information down this route and the wholly foreign-owned enterprise (WFOE) is likely to be the most effective channel for transfer.

While this division between 'contractual' and 'internalised' technology transfers is a fundamental one, the most important channel for technology transfer to China is difficult to assign to either category. That is the equity joint venture, which is a 'hybrid' form of organisation having some characteristics of both types of governance. As equity joint ventures involve relationships between independent organisations, they have some features of a contract, including the risk of technology 'leakage' and opportunistic behaviour on the part of the partners. On the other hand, the behaviour of a joint venture is under the managerial authority of the partners and, if the technology supplier is able to exert control, the dangers of opportunism may be reduced.

Given the wide publicity which has been accorded to the enormous flows of foreign direct investment (FDI) into China, it is startling to realise that only six years ago it was possible for the major study on technology development in China to conclude that FDI had been relatively unimportant as a vehicle for technology flows (Conroy 1992). However, that judgement was based on a comparison of technology contract values and FDI for 1986, at which point FDI had remained at modest levels. Table 5.4 shows the comparison between the realised values of foreign direct investment and the values of technology import contracts for the period 1982-92.

Table 5.4 Technology import contracts and realised foreign direct investment in China, 1983–95 (US$m)

Year	Realised FDI	Technology import contracts
1983	636	563
1984	1,258	951
1985	1,658	2,960
1986	1,875	4,460
1987	2,314	2,980
1988	3,194	3,550
1989	3,393	2,923
1990	3,487	1,274
1991	4,366	3,459
1992	11,008	6,590
1993	27,515	6,110
1994	33,767	4,110
1995	37,521	13,033

Source: *Almanac of China's Foreign Economic Relations and Trade* (various issues)

As Table 5.4 clearly illustrates, the cumulative value of contracts exceeded the value of realised FDI until 1989, after which the relationship changed very dramatically. In 1994[2] the value of realised FDI inflows was eight times the value of technology import contracts. This shift in the importance of FDI relative to contracts has been accompanied by a changing balance within the alternative forms of FDI, as illustrated in Table 5.5.

As Table 5.5 indicates, FDI into China has been dominated by the equity joint venture which continues to account for more than 50 per cent of the total. However, as the PRC Government has become more willing to allow wholly foreign-owned enterprises, they have begun to account for larger proportions of the total, being responsible for approximately 25 per cent in the most recent years for which figures are available.

The importance of Europe in this overall flow of investment was indicated in Table 1.13 on p.28. As regards the present discussion, the most salient point is the very much smaller contribution made by European firms to the flows of investment, in comparison with technology contracts. While the five main European countries were responsible for 44 per cent of the value of technology contracts during the period 1985–95, all twelve EU Member States were responsible for only 4.5 per cent of the realised FDI over the same period. That figure compared with 59 per cent for Hong Kong, 8 per cent for the United States and 7.6 per cent for Japan.

It is almost certain that the European contribution is under-estimated in Table 1.13 because the 'Hong Kong' figure is likely to include some investments made by European countries through their branches and subsidiaries in Hong Kong (see the discussion in Chapter 1). However, there are no statistics on which to base such an estimate and in any event, the same point applies with at least as much force to Japanese and American companies (and even more emphatically to the Taiwanese). Even the most significant adjustment to the figures would be unlikely to change the general conclusion, which is that European firms have been a quantitatively less important source of FDI into China than their rivals in the United States, Japan and 'Greater China'.

Table 5.5 Alternative forms of foreign direct investment in China, 1989–95 (US$bn)

Form of investment	1989	1990	1991	1992	1993	1994	1995
Equity joint venture	2.04	1.89	2.30	6.12	15.35	17.93	19.08
Contractual joint venture	0.75	0.67	0.76	2.12	5.24	7.12	7.54
Wholly foreign-owned enterprise	0.37	0.68	1.14	2.52	6.51	8.04	10.32
Joint development	0.23	0.24	0.17	0.25	0.42	0.67	0.59
Total	3.39	3.49	4.37	11.01	27.52	33.77	37.52

Source: *Almanac of China's Foreign Economic Relations and Trade* (various issues)

QUALITATIVE CONSIDERATIONS: IS EUROPE PROVIDING LESS BUT MORE?

The conclusion to be drawn from the summary statistics above appears to be that Europe has been an important source of technology transfer through contract, but a much less significant contributor in respect of foreign investment, which is acknowledged to be the more significant channel for transfer. However, that quantitatively based judgement on Europe's role in respect of FDI needs to be set in the light of more qualitative considerations. A number of factors suggest that European technology transfers to China have been of a higher quality than most others, in a number of respects.

In the first place, it has been noted that European technology transfer contracts tend to be much larger than those involving other technology suppliers. Such large contracts involve significant and relatively long-term interaction between relatively large organisations on both sides of the transfer, with correspondingly more opportunities for learning to take place. Furthermore, control of the technology importing enterprise remains in Chinese hands, improving the opportunities for indigenous development.

Second, the industrial distribution of European investment is different, being concentrated in sectors which are much less labour-intensive than the average and which involve a significantly higher technological content. According to a recent United Nations report (UNCTAD 1996), European investment into China has been relatively narrowly focused on sectors like automobiles, pharmaceuticals and chemicals. These are industries in which the application of technology is important, economies of scale and scope are very significant, and competitiveness requires the development of complex and sophisticated managerial hierarchies (Chandler 1990). Such enterprises are very different from the archetypal foreign-invested enterprise in China, which is a small Hong Kong-based joint venture in a labour-intensive and export-oriented industry.

Third, European technology transfers tend to be in industries which are vertically more 'upstream', or which require the development of significant networks of local suppliers. In this case, the learning process extends beyond the enterprise involved in the immediate transfer. Suppliers learn how to upgrade their own products in order to meet the needs of the foreign-invested enterprise, and user industries face enhanced opportunities to 'learn-by-doing' with the superior inputs provided.

This difference in the quality of European foreign direct investment into China is well illustrated by the preponderance of European firms in the listing of China's 'top ten joint ventures', published annually by the *China Daily* and the *Economic Daily*. Two European ventures, Shanghai Volkswagen and China Schindler have appeared on the list for eight consecutive years, thereby earning a special award, and were removed from the list for 1994 in order to make room for others. The only other company to achieve that status was Shanghai-EK Chor, a Thai joint venture. Table 5.6 sets out

Table 5.6 China's top joint ventures in 1994

Joint venture	Nationality	Industry	Rank	Employees 1992	Sales 1992 RMB bn	Gross profits 1992 RMB bn
Shanghai Volkswagen	German	Automobile	Special	5812	710.8	103.4
Shanghai EK-Chor	Thai	Motorcycle	Special	3182	85.4	15.0
China Schindler	Swiss	Elevators	Special	1460	22.1	3.5
Shanghai Bell	Belgian	Telecoms	1	1305	131.8	40.9
Xi'an Janssen	Belgian	Pharmaceut	2	583	55.2	23.8
Shenzhen Konka	Hong Kong	Electronics	3	2424	121.3	12.0
Shanghai Yaohua Pilkington	British	Building materials	4	903	34.0	10.0
Beijing Matsushita	Japanese	Electronics	5	2166	114.2	32.0
Shanghai Belling	Belgian	Electronics	8	363	10.2	2.2
Xinjiang Tianshan	Hong Kong	Textiles	9	2838	30.5	2.7

Source: SinoMarket Data 1996
Note: Data for Chun Lan (Hong Kong JV, ranked 6); Shanghai Dajiang (Thai JV, ranked 7); and China Bicycle (HK/US JV, ranked 10) are not provided.

some basic data for ten of the thirteen award-winning joint ventures (the 'top ten' plus the three special award-winners).

As Table 5.6 illustrates, six of the largest and most successful joint ventures originate in Europe, a proportion which is very significantly greater than the 3.5 per cent contribution made to the total value of FDI. Given their position in 'upstream' industries, these enterprises are helping to develop networks of buyers and suppliers, thereby helping to upgrade China's industrial infrastructure in a way which is much less evident among foreign-invested enterprises in general. In the case of Shanghai Volkswagen, for instance, 1994–96 has seen a flood of new investments into joint ventures designed to provide components, ranging from seats and paint to batteries, lights, and braking systems (Davies 1996). It has been estimated that at least fifty such ventures are in place, approximately 40 per cent of them involving German companies who are close to Volkswagen in Germany and other parts of the world. While Volkswagen's Shanghai plant at Anting is producing a very old model (the Santana), the company's Chinese engineers have successfully introduced an upgraded version, the Santana 2000, in collaboration with Volkswagen engineers in Brazil. It may not constitute a full 'innovation capability', but in the motor industry the development of such a capability requires an extended effort over many decades. To have developed a facility capable of producing 200,000 vehicles per year, supported by an extensive network of suppliers, represents a major achievement, not yet replicated by any major non-European investors.

CONCLUDING REMARKS

This chapter has examined the place of Europe in the transfer of technology to China, setting the inquiry in the context of China's experience to date.

The analysis suggests that European firms have been foremost in the transfer of technology to China through contract, being involved in projects and contracts which are distinctly larger than the average, representing Europe's industrial strength in complex, capital-intensive and relatively 'high-tech' sectors. In terms of their contribution to the volume of foreign direct investment, European firms have been much less significant, although that may be over-stated by the extent to which they have channelled investments through Hong Kong. In qualitative terms, however, European firms have made a contribution to Chinese technology imports which is more significant than their share of the funds flows would suggest. They provide a majority of China's largest and most successful joint ventures; they are in sectors which require the transfer of considerable technological capability if they are to be successful; their upstream position leads them to produce new opportunities for downstream industries; and their requirement for development in the supply chain has been instrumental in drawing further investment, particularly in the automobile sector and in chemicals. In this respect Europe appears to have been 'punching beyond its weight' in respect of technology transfer to China.

NOTES

1 The authors acknowledge financial support provided by the Research Grants Council of Hong Kong under grant No. HKP4/95H and by the Hong Kong Polytechnic University.
2 As noted above, the value of technology import contracts increased dramatically between 1994 and 1995, but the reasons are unclear and may be largely due to changes in the measurement system.

REFERENCES

Al-Ali, S. (1995) 'Developing Countries and Technology Transfer', *International Journal of Technology Management*, 10(7/8): 704–13.
Barnett, A.D. (1981) *China's Economy in Global Perspective*, Washington, DC: Brookings Institution.
Chandler, A.D. (1990) *Scale and Scope: The Dynamics of Industrial Capitalism*, Cambridge, MA: Harvard University Press.
Cohen, W.M. and Levinthal, D.A. (1990) 'Absorptive Capacity: A New Perspective on Learning and Innovation', *Administrative Science Quarterly*, 35(1): 128–52.
Conroy, R. (1992) *Technological Change in China*, Paris: OECD.
Dahlman, C. and Westphal, L. (1983) 'The Transfer of Technology: Issues in the Acquisition of Technological Capability by Developing Countries', *Finance and Development*, 20(4): 6–9.
Davies, H. (1977) 'Technology Transfer through Commercial Transactions', *Journal of Industrial Economics*, 26(2): 161– 175.
Davies, H. (1979) 'Transfers of Technology and the Multinational Enterprise, *Multinational Bibliographies and Reviews*, 5(3): 203–18.
Davies, H. (1993) 'The Information Content of Technology Transfers: a Transactions Cost Analysis of the Machine Tool Industry', *Technovation*, 13(2): 99–107.

Davies, H. (1995) 'Intra-firm versus Licensed Transfers of Machine Tool Technology', *International Journal of Technology Management*, 10(7/8): 941–54.

Davies, H. (1996) *Shanghai Volkswagen: A Major Joint Venture in the Motor Industry*, mimeo, Hong Kong: Hong Kong Polytechnic University.

Davies, H. and Whitla, P. (1995) 'Technology Transfers to China: The Experience to Date', in H. Davies (ed.) *China Business: Context and Issues*, Hong Kong: Longman, pp.190–214.

Dunning, J. (1980) 'Toward an Eclectic Theory of International Production', *Journal of International Business Studies*, 11(1), Spring–Summer: 9–31.

Gabriel, P. (1967) *The International Transfer of Corporate Skills*, Boston: Harvard University Press.

Hendryx, S. (1986) 'Implementation of a Technology Transfer Joint Venture in the People's Republic of China: A Management Perspective', *Columbia Journal of World Business*, 21(1), Spring: 57–66.

Ho, S. and Huenemann, R. (1984) *China's Open Door Policy: The Quest for Foreign Capital and Technology*, Vancouver: University of British Columbia Press.

Huang, F. (1987) 'China's Introduction of Foreign Technology and External Trade', *Asian Survey*, 27(5): 577–94.

Kueh, Y. and Ash, R. (1996) 'The Fifth Dragon: Economic Development', in B. Hook (ed.) *Guangdong: China's Promised Land*, Hong Kong: Oxford University Press, pp.149–92.

Lall, S. (1981) *Developing Countries in the International Economy*, London: Macmillan.

Lan, P. (1996) 'Role of IJVs in Transferring Technology to China', *Journal of Euromarketing*, 4(3/4): 129–53.

Lan, P. and Young, S. (1996) 'International Technology Transfer Examined at Technology Component Level: A Case Study in China', *Technovation* 16(6): 277–86.

Leung, H., Thorburn, J., Chau, E. and Tang, S. (1991) 'Contractual Relations, Foreign Direct Investment and Technology Transfer: The Case of China', *Journal of International Development*, 3(3), June: 277–91.

Ministry of Foreign Trade and Economic Co-operation (MOFTEC), *Almanac of China's Foreign Economic Relations and Trade*, Beijing, MOFTEC, various issues.

Office of Technology Assessment (OTA), United States (1987) *Technology Transfer to China*, Washington, DC: OTA.

Organisation for Economic Co-operation and Development (OECD) (1993) *Foreign Direct Investment Relations Between the OECD and the Dynamic Asian Economies*, Paris: OECD.

Pan, Y. (1994) 'Features of European Equity Joint Ventures in China: A Longitudinal Study', *Journal of Euromarketing*, 4(1): 5–21.

Robock, S. (1980) *The International Technology Transfer Process*, Washington, DC: National Academy of Sciences.

Scoville, W. (1951) 'Minority Migrations and the Diffusion of Technology', *Journal of Economic History*, 15–38.

State Statistical Bureau of the People's Republic of China (1994) *China Statistical Yearbook 1994*, Beijing: China Statistical Publishing House.

Stewart, S. (1990) 'Technology Transfer and the People's Republic of China', in M. Chatterji (ed.) *Technology Transfer in Developing Countries*, London: Macmillan, pp.345–52.

Teece, D. (1978) *The Multinational Corporation and the Resource Cost of International Technology Transfer*, Cambridge, MA: Ballinger.

UNCTAD, Division on Transnational Corporations and Investment (1996) *Investing in Asia's Dynamism: European Union Direct Investment in Asia*, interim version, March.

Wolff, A. (1989) 'Technology Transfer to the People's Republic of China', *International Journal of Technology Management*, 4, May: 449–76.
Wu, Z. (1996) 'China's Technology Transfer Grows Obviously in 1995', *Almanac of China's Foreign Economic Relations and Trade 1996/97*, Beijing: Ministry of Foreign Trade and Economic Cooperation, pp.60–5.
Zadoria, D. (1962) *The Sino-Soviet Conflict, 1956–61*, Princeton, NJ: Princeton University Press.
Zhao Ziyang, (1982) 'Persist in an Open-Door Policy', *Report to the 5th National Party Congress, 1981*, Beijing: Foreign Languages Press.

6 The technology intensiveness of China's trade with the European Union

Jian Chen, Roger Strange and Limin Wang

INTRODUCTION

The role of Hong Kong (HK) in China's trade with the rest of the world was outlined in Chapter 1 where it was established *inter alia* that:

- some countries/areas (e.g. the European Union and the United States) were much more important as markets for goods of China origin re-exported through Hong Kong, than they were as sources of re-exported goods destined for China, and that the reverse was true for many other countries (e.g. Japan, Korea, Taiwan);
- that the re-export margin on goods of China origin was markedly higher than the margin on goods originating in other countries, and that the difference was increasing over time;
- that published data involving bilateral trade with China are often misleading given that goods re-exported through Hong Kong (whether from China or elsewhere) are recorded by the country of consignment as exports to Hong Kong, rather than as exports to the country where they are eventually consumed;
- that the re-export trade is very significant in relation both to Chinese exports to the European Union, and to Chinese imports from the European Union, and – although no detail was provided – it is likely that the same will be true for other trading partners;
- that the commodity composition of the re-export trade destined for China is quite different from the commodity composition of the re-export trade originating in China and that, moreover, the composition varies by country of origin.

In this chapter we build upon this analysis in two ways. First, whereas the emphasis in Chapter 1 was primarily upon Hong Kong's role in the re-export trade, here the focus is upon China's trade with its major trading partners but taking the re-export trade explicitly into account. Second, the commodity composition of China's trade with its major partners is investigated more systematically.

The first part of the chapter is devoted to the identification of the major trading partners of China and to highlighting the countries which are, on the one hand, the principal sources of imports to the Chinese market and, on the other, the main destinations for Chinese exports. In particular, the importance of the European Union relative to Japan and the United States will be stressed, and the contrast between China's trade with these three 'developed' areas relative to her trade with the so-called Asian newly industrialising economies (NIEs) will be addressed. Trade between China and her major trading partners is then disaggregated into trade in high-technology, medium-technology, and low-technology goods, so as to provide an analysis of the technology composition of China's exports and imports. As might be expected given her factor endowments, China's exports to the world consist primarily of low-technology goods while her imports contain rather more medium- and high-technology goods. But this situation is changing and, in particular, China's exports are increasingly in higher-technology goods. Finally, the importance of the re-export trade through Hong Kong is assessed relative to China's total exports and imports from its major trading partners. Interestingly, this shows that the re-export trade through Hong Kong is rising in proportion to total trade with China for many countries – this suggests that Hong Kong's role as an entrepôt is perhaps assured, at least for the time being.

WHO ARE CHINA'S MAIN TRADING PARTNERS?

An analysis of China's Customs Statistics (see Table 6.1) suggests that Japan was China's principal trading partner in 1981,[1] accounting for over one-quarter of China's total trade (exports plus imports). In second place came Hong Kong (15 per cent), followed by the United States (14 per cent) and the European Union[2] (12 per cent). No direct trade was reported with either Taiwan or South Korea (Imai 1990; Wakabayashi 1990; Kohari 1992; Ferdinand 1996). At this time, the amount of re-export trade through Hong Kong originating in China was small (10.4 per cent in 1981) relative to China's total exports, as was the amount of re-export trade destined for China as a proportion of China's total imports (6.5 per cent in 1981) (see Table 6.2). The unadjusted data from Table 6.1 thus provide a reasonable picture of the geographical dispersion of China's foreign trade at the start of the 'open-door' period.

Thereafter, however, the situation changed dramatically and, throughout the 1980s, re-exports through Hong Kong accounted for ever-increasing proportions of both China's exports and imports. This trend continues throughout the early 1990s for China's imports, although it appears that re-exports may have peaked as a proportion of China's exports in 1993. As a consequence, China's statistics on her foreign trade have become less and less meaningful with regard to the destination of her exports and the provenance of her imports. In particular, the growth of the re-export trade through Hong Kong has been mirrored by the statistical finding that Hong Kong has become an ever more important trading partner for

China – accounting for about 30 per cent of China's total trade in 1988 and over 35 per cent in the early 1990s. Yet this re-export trade, by definition, consists of goods that neither originate in Hong Kong nor are destined for the HK market. The statistical picture painted by Table 6.1 therefore overstates the importance of Hong Kong as a trading partner, and increasingly so over the years as the importance of the re-export trade has increased, while simultaneously understating the relative importance of those countries from which the re-exported goods have been either originally consigned or ultimately destined.

Table 6.1 China's trade (according to China's customs statistics) with selected partners, 1981–96 (as % of total China trade)

Country	1981	1988	1990	1992	1994	1996
European Union (a)	12.05	12.52	12.27	10.51	13.32	12.66
Belgium/Luxembourg	0.59	0.61	0.58	0.61	0.80	0.73
France	1.58	1.46	2.00	1.37	1.42	1.43
Germany	5.04	4.78	4.29	3.90	5.03	4.54
Italy	1.40	2.23	1.65	1.72	1.97	1.75
Netherlands	1.33	1.09	1.13	1.03	1.26	1.54
United Kingdom	1.50	1.51	1.76	1.17	1.77	1.75
Other Europe (b)						
Austria	0.17	0.26	0.29	0.24	0.23	0.16
Finland	0.24	0.21	0.20	0.21	0.26	0.26
Sweden	0.42	0.41	0.35	0.42	0.56	0.61
Switzerland	0.69	0.67	0.49	0.41	0.57	0.48
USSR	0.64	3.12	3.79	—	—	—
Former USSR	—	—	—	4.02	2.78	4.32
North America						
Canada	3.14	2.19	1.65	1.56	1.37	1.44
United States	14.31	9.78	10.19	10.57	14.97	14.78
Japan	25.35	18.43	14.37	15.33	20.24	20.72
Asian NIEs						
Hong Kong	15.11	29.42	35.44	35.07	17.67	14.05
Korea (c)	—	—	1.68	3.06	4.95	6.90
Singapore	1.80	2.43	2.45	1.97	2.13	2.54
Taiwan (c)	—	—	2.23	3.97	6.90	6.55
WORLD	100.0	100.0	100.0	100.0	100.0	100.0

Source: *China's Customs Statistics* (various issues)
Notes:
(a) The data for the European Union (EU) relate to the twelve Member States prior to the accession of Austria, Finland and Sweden in 1995.
(b) 'Other Europe' excludes EU(12) in all years, but includes the Soviet Union (1981, 1988, 1990) and the countries of the former Soviet Union (1992, 1994, 1996).
(c) China did not report any statistics on direct trade with either South Korea or Taiwan before 1990. There was, of course, substantial indirect trade between China and South Korea, and between China and Taiwan, through Hong Kong and other third countries (e.g. Japan, Singapore, Guam).

Table 6.2 Importance of re-exports through Hong Kong for China's total trade, 1980–96

Year	Re-exports of China origin through Hong Kong as % of total China exports	Re-exports destined for China through Hong Kong as % of total China imports
1980	9.3	4.7
1981	10.4	6.5
1982	10.8	6.8
1983	12.2	7.8
1984	13.8	13.1
1985	16.3	14.0
1986	21.4	12.2
1987	27.4	17.9
1988	35.5	22.0
1989	45.9	22.4
1990	49.7	26.7
1991	56.5	30.9
1992	61.4	34.0
1993	66.8	34.1
1994	58.4	36.1
1995	55.3	37.6
1996	58.5	38.9

Sources: As Tables 1.1, 1.4, and 1.6

A further statistical complication is that the General Administration of Customs of the People's Republic of China have, since 1993, adjusted their methods of collation of trade statistics so as to classify goods re-exported through Hong Kong to the European Union (and the United States) as exports to the European Union and the United States, rather than as exports to Hong Kong.[3] As a result, the reported importance of Hong Kong as a trading partner for China fell dramatically between 1992 and 1994 (see Table 6.1), while the importance of the European Union and the United States increased. These changes are, however, statistical artefacts and should be discounted. Furthermore, the classification only applied to those re-exported goods whose final destination could be identified, and thus presumably some Chinese goods ultimately destined for the EU and US markets are still registered as exports to Hong Kong.

China's customs statistics do not therefore provide for the identification of her major trading partners. Rather, it is preferable to start from the records of those partners. Aggregate data on the trade of all countries with China are collated by the IMF in its *Direction of Trade Statistics Yearbook*, and data disaggregated by SITC heading are published by the United Nations in the various volumes of *Commodity Trade Statistics*. There are slight differences in the coverage of these two compendia, but these are relatively insignificant. The partner countries report their exports to China fob (i.e. before the inclusion of freight and insurance costs) and their imports cif (i.e. inclusive of freight and insurance), and this is one reason why these data differ from those in *China's Customs Statistics*. However, as the purpose of the analysis in this chapter is to examine the relative shares of each country in China's exports/imports, then the fob/cif distinction is not too important. By ignoring the distinction, we are implicitly assuming that freight and insurance costs are similar for China's trade with all her partners.[4]

The major correction that is required, however, is to incorporate estimates of the value of the re-export trade through Hong Kong, following the method outlined in Chapter 1.[5] Thus direct exports from the European Union, for example, to China need to be supplemented by the ex-EU value of goods that leave the European Union destined for Hong Kong, but which are subsequently re-exported to China. This ex-EU value is constructed by deducting, from the gross value of re-exported EU goods destined for China, an estimate of the value added as the goods pass through Hong Kong. This value added in Hong Kong certainly enhances the import bill for China, but it does not accrue to the EU exporters. An analysis of China's imports from selected trading partners, based on figures constructed in this way, is shown for 1988 and 1994[6] in Table 6.3. The figures show clearly that Japan was the principal supplier of goods to China in 1994, accounting for just over one-quarter of total imports. The European Union was the second largest supplier, and its share of the total had increased from 14.9 per cent in 1988 to 16.4 per cent in 1994.[7] Germany is the major exporter to China among the EU Member States, followed by Italy, France and the United Kingdom. In contrast to the European Union which has witnessed a small increase in its share of China's imports, the United States has shown a small fall from 12.7 per cent in 1988 to 10.7 per cent in 1994. Even though the European Union is a bigger entity than the United States (in terms of population, GDP, etc.), the figures still suggest that the European Union is out-performing the United States with regard to penetration of the Chinese market, though clearly it lags some way behind Japan.

The relative importance of Hong Kong is much diminished by the reallocation of re-exported goods to the country of original consignment. In 1988, HK domestic exports accounted for 9.6 per cent of China's total imports, but this proportion had fallen to only 6.7 per cent in 1994. Indeed, both Taiwan and South Korea now appear to be more important exporters to the Chinese market than Hong Kong.

Turning now to China's exports (see Table 6.4), the picture is rather different. In constructing this table, the data on imports reported by each partner country are reduced by the estimated amount of value added to goods passing through Hong Kong. This value added enhances the import bill for the importing country, but does not accrue to Chinese exporters. In 1988, Japan (21.6 per cent) was the pre-eminent overseas market for Chinese goods, followed closely by the United States (19.4 per cent) with the European Union some way behind in third place (16.1 per cent). By 1994,

Table 6.3 China's imports (adjusted for re-exports through Hong Kong) from selected trading partners, 1988 and 1994

Exporting country (a)	As % of total China imports	
	1988	1994
European Union (b)	14.9	16.4
Belgium/Luxembourg	0.8	0.9
France	2.0	2.3
Germany	6.0	6.5
Italy	2.8	2.6
Netherlands	0.5	0.7
United Kingdom	1.8	1.7
North America		
Canada	4.3	1.6
United States	12.0	10.7
Japan	23.8	25.1
Asian NIEs		
Hong Kong (c)	9.6	6.7
Korea (d)	2.2	7.5
Singapore	2.7	3.0
Taiwan (d)	4.0	7.0
WORLD (e)	100.0	100.0

Sources: United Nations, *Commodity Trade Statistics*
IMF, *Direction of Trade Statistics Yearbook*
Census and Statistics Department, Hong Kong

Notes:
(a) All data are as reported by the exporting country and recorded in the UN *Commodity Trade Statistics*, and adjusted to take account of re-exports through Hong Kong.
(b) The data for the European Union (EU) relate to the twelve Member States prior to the accession of Austria, Finland and Sweden in 1995.
(c) The figures for Hong Kong are for domestic exports only.
(d) Direct imports to China from both Taiwan and South Korea were assumed to be zero in 1988.
(e) The totals for world exports to China are taken from the IMF *Direction of Trade Statistics Yearbook*, and adjusted for re-exports through Hong Kong.

however, the United States had increased dramatically in importance as a market, and accounted for over one-quarter of total Chinese exports. The Japanese market had declined in importance, while the proportion of Chinese exports destined for the EU market had risen by a small amount. As with EU exports to China, Germany leads the way among the Member States with regard to EU imports from China. In Asia, the importance of the HK domestic market has also declined, while that of South Korea has increased in the wake of improved diplomatic relations. But the Taiwanese market does not appear to have developed as a major destination for Chinese exports.

The overall picture which emerges from the data in Tables 6.3 and 6.4 is that Japan is China's main trading partner, as befits its geographical

Table 6.4 China's exports (adjusted for re-exports through Hong Kong) to selected trading partners, 1988 and 1994

Importing country (a)	As % of total China exports	
	1988	1994
European Union (b)	16.1	16.7
Belgium/Luxembourg	0.5	0.7
France	3.1	2.7
Germany	5.3	5.9
Italy	3.1	2.0
Netherlands	0.9	1.0
United Kingdom	1.6	1.2
North America		
Canada	1.6	1.7
United States	19.4	25.4
Japan	21.6	18.8
Asian NIEs		
Hong Kong (c)	10.6	5.7
Korea (d)	1.7	3.8
Singapore	3.7	1.8
Taiwan (d)	1.0	1.1
WORLD (e)	100.0	100.0

Sources: United Nations, *Commodity Trade Statistics*
IMF, *Direction of Trade Statistics Yearbook*
Census and Statistics Department, Hong Kong

Notes:
(a) All data are as reported by the importing country and recorded in the UN *Commodity Trade Statistics*, and adjusted to take account of re-exports through Hong Kong.
(b) The data for the European Union (EU) relate to the twelve Member States prior to the accession of Austria, Finland and Sweden in 1995.
(c) The figures for Hong Kong are estimated using data on imports and re-exports provided by the HKCSD, and assuming re-export margins of 10 (1988) and 24.9 (1994) – see Chapter 1 for further details.
(d) Direct exports from China to both Taiwan and South Korea were assumed to be zero in 1988.
(e) The totals for world imports from China are taken from the IMF *Direction of Trade Statistics Yearbook*, and adjusted for re-exports through Hong Kong.

proximity (Krugman 1995) and the complementarity of the two economies. But the United States has gained in importance as an export market between 1988 and 1994, while simultaneously losing ground as a supplier to the Chinese market, with inevitable consequences for the Sino-US trade balance (Lardy 1994). Meanwhile, the European Union has consolidated its position as China's third most important trading partner while, in contrast to both Japan and the United States, retaining roughly equal shares of both China's exports and imports. In contrast, the importance of Hong Kong has declined dramatically, once the re-export trade has been reallocated to its 'rightful' owners, and South Korea may well now be China's fourth largest trading partner.

THE TECHNOLOGY COMPOSITION OF CHINA'S TRADE

We now turn to an analysis of the commodity composition of China's trade with her major trading partners. The categorisation of commodities according to whether they embody high, medium, or low technology is that used by the OECD (1986),[8] and is set out in Appendix B. Table 6.5 breaks down China's total imports, including re-exports through Hong Kong, from each country according to these categories.

All three 'developed' partners (i.e. the European Union,[9] Japan, and the United States) show similar trends:

- the largest share (38-50 per cent) of total exports is provided by medium-technology goods, but such goods have decreased slightly in importance between 1988 and 1994;
- a relatively high (20-30 per cent) share of high-technology exports in 1988, increasing by about 10 percentage points by 1994 (30–40 per cent);

Table 6.5 Technology composition of China's imports from selected trading partners, 1988 and 1994 (as % of total exports to China for each exporting country)

Exporting country (a)	1988			1994		
	High	Medium	Low	High	Medium	Low
European Union (b)	19.4	50.9	29.8	29.2	46.3	24.5
Belgium/Luxembourg	10.1	46.6	43.3	45.1	19.4	35.5
France	34.7	37.5	27.8	50.7	27.3	21.9
Germany	16.7	52.5	30.8	28.6	51.6	19.8
Italy	11.6	65.7	22.7	11.4	64.4	24.2
Netherlands	11.7	60.1	28.1	16.0	44.2	39.8
United Kingdom	32.5	42.4	25.1	20.7	43.9	35.4
North America						
Canada	2.1	18.8	79.1	30.9	21.6	47.5
United States	21.2	41.8	37.0	38.1	34.1	27.8
Japan	27.8	37.8	34.4	38.2	35.6	26.2
Asian NIEs						
Hong Kong	28.2	28.3	43.5	27.5	29.3	43.1
Korea	15.6	39.9	44.5	8.1	34.9	57.0
Singapore	15.9	29.7	54.4	18.4	23.8	57.7
Taiwan	11.5	37.2	51.3	—	—	—

Sources: United Nations, *Commodity Trade Statistics*
Census and Statistics Department, Hong Kong

Notes:
(a) All data are as reported by the exporting country and recorded in the UN *Commodity Trade Statistics*, and adjusted to take account of re-exports through Hong Kong.
(b) The data for the European Union (EU) relate to the twelve Member States prior to the accession of Austria, Finland and Sweden in 1995.
(c) The data for Hong Kong relate to domestic exports only.
(d) Direct exports from South Korea to China were assumed to be zero in 1988.
(e) Direct exports from Taiwan to China were assumed to be zero in 1988. Taiwan does not publish its trade data according to the SITC, so no figures are available for 1994.

- a rather higher initial share (30–40 per cent) of low-technology exports, reducing to about 25 per cent in 1994.

Exports from Hong Kong had a similar composition (high-technology = 28 per cent; low-technology = 44 per cent) in 1988, but these relative proportions had not changed much by 1994. In contrast, Korea, Singapore and Taiwan all exported much smaller shares (11–16 per cent) of high-technology goods and much larger shares (44–54 per cent) of low-technology goods in 1988, and there is some evidence of *increased* concentration on low-technology exports in 1994. Although comparable export data for Taiwan were not available for 1994, it was possible to form an idea of the technology composition of Taiwanese exports by looking at *China's Customs Statistics*. These showed that 58 per cent of China's imports from Taiwan in 1994 were low-technology goods; 26 per cent were medium-technology goods; and only 16 per cent high-technology goods. Overall, therefore, there appears to be some upgrading of the technological composition of China's imports from her three major suppliers who together account for about one-half of her total imports, while imports from the major Asian suppliers seem to be becoming more low-technology.

Japan, the United States and the European Union together were the destination for over 60 per cent of China's exports in 1994. Table 6.6 presents a similar analysis of the commodity composition of China's exports. High-technology goods featured much less in Chinese exports to these countries than they had in imports but, interestingly, the share of high-technology goods in China's total exports increased markedly between 1988 (1–10 per cent) and 1994 (7–18 per cent). Also, whereas low-technology goods still accounted for the largest part of Chinese exports to these developed markets, the proportions dropped quite markedly for both Japan and the United States between 1988 and 1994.[10]

Similar patterns emerge, i.e. larger shares of high-technology goods, and smaller shares of low-technology goods, from a scrutiny of the data on Chinese exports to Korea and, even more dramatically, to Singapore. Taiwan does not provide comparable data on imports from China but, as direct imports are insignificant relative to the re-export trade, it is reasonable to look at the technology composition of the latter. This shows very little change between 1988 and 1994. Overall, therefore, there appears to be an upgrading of the technological composition of China's exports to most destinations but, most importantly, to the three large developed markets. As Harrold (1995: 135–6) notes, 'this rapid evolution towards more sophisticated products is reminiscent of the path taken before by Japan and Korea, and currently being taken by Malaysia and Indonesia, indicating the likely evolution of China's future exports'. The analysis in this section thus appears to confirm that China is increasingly sourcing low-technology inputs from its Asian neighbours, and increasingly producing high-technology exports predominantly for the US, Japanese and EU markets, while

Table 6.6 Technology composition of China's exports to selected trading partners, 1988 and 1994 (as % of total imports from China for each importing country)

Importing country (a)	1988			1994		
	High	Medium	Low	High	Medium	Low
European Union (b)	10.1	29.2	60.6	17.3	16.3	66.4
Belgium/Luxembourg	10.6	16.8	72.6	3.3	18.2	78.5
France	15.3	13.8	70.9	19.8	14.7	65.6
Germany	9.7	63.7	26.7	18.3	16.9	64.8
Italy	6.1	6.4	87.5	16.2	13.0	70.9
Netherlands	10.0	18.1	71.9	9.8	18.5	71.7
United Kingdom	5.4	17.2	77.4	10.6	21.3	68.1
North America						
Canada	6.9	9.7	83.4	14.3	18.0	67.7
United States	8.2	12.4	79.4	18.0	14.0	68.0
Japan	1.3	6.3	92.4	7.6	6.8	85.6
Asian NIEs (c)						
Korea (d)	2.0	7.5	90.5	6.3	11.3	82.4
Singapore	3.4	10.3	86.4	21.0	23.2	55.9
Taiwan (e)	11.6	37.2	51.3	14.4	35.1	50.5

Sources: United Nations, *Commodity Trade Statistics*
Census and Statistics Department, Hong Kong

Notes:
(a) All data are as reported by the importing country and recorded in the UN *Commodity Trade Statistics*, and adjusted to take account of re-exports through Hong Kong.
(b) The data for the European Union (EU) relate to the twelve Member States prior to the accession of Austria, Finland and Sweden in 1995.
(c) No data are available on imports from China retained for domestic consumption in Hong Kong.
(d) Direct exports from China to South Korea were assumed to be zero in 1988.
(e) Direct exports from China to Taiwan were assumed to be zero in 1988. Taiwan does not publish its trade data according to the SITC, but direct imports from China so the figures for 1994 refer to re-export trade only.

importing more high-technology goods from these areas. It should be stressed, however, that China's exports are still largely of low-technology goods. Furthermore, it is not clear from the analysis whether the high-technology imports from Japan, the United States and the European Union consist of consumer goods for domestic consumption, or of capital goods for upgrading domestic industry.

THE IMPORTANCE OF THE RE-EXPORT TRADE THROUGH HONG KONG

We now turn our attention to the technical composition of the re-export trade through Hong Kong (see Table 6.7). As regards the re-exports destined for China, a small increase in the proportion of high-technology goods is evident between 1988 and 1994, offset by a reduction in the share

Table 6.7 Technology composition of re-exports to/from China through Hong Kong from/to selected trading partners, 1988 and 1994

	1988			1994		
	High	Medium	Low	High	Medium	Low
Re-exports destined for China from:						
European Union (a)	18.2	40.5	41.3	23.9	35.3	40.8
United States	23.9	41.6	34.5	33.6	30.1	36.3
Japan	47.2	34.5	18.3	53.5	28.5	18.0
Korea	15.6	39.9	44.5	7.6	29.0	63.4
Singapore	13.4	19.5	67.1	19.8	14.7	65.5
Taiwan	11.5	37.2	51.3	14.4	35.1	50.5
TOTAL	22.7	34.9	42.4	28.0	29.3	42.7
Re-exports originating in China to:						
European Union (a)	20.4	9.3	70.2	28.6	14.5	56.9
United States	13.1	12.4	74.5	21.6	12.1	66.3
Japan	7.4	3.4	89.1	21.2	6.1	72.7
Korea	2.0	7.5	90.5	20.9	10.1	69.0
Singapore	15.5	8.8	75.6	45.5	15.3	39.2
Taiwan	6.1	12.3	81.6	22.1	21.8	56.1

Source: Census and Statistics Department, Hong Kong
Notes:
(a) The data for the European Union (EU) relate to the twelve Member States prior to the accession of Austria, Finland and Sweden in 1995.

of medium-technology goods. Such changes are moreover exhibited by all the countries for which data have been tabulated (except for Korea where there has been a marked increase in low-technology goods). Re-exports from the European Union and the United States tend to involve fewer low-technology goods than re-exports from Korea, Singapore and Taiwan, but the composition of re-exports from Japan is markedly skewed towards high-technology goods. As regards re-exports originating in China, there have been major increases in the proportions of high-technology goods, and major reductions in the proportions of low-technology goods, exported to all the countries (particularly Singapore). Taken together, these figures suggest that the re-export trade through Hong Kong in general is moving away from a concentration on low-technology goods.

Finally, we look at how the importance of re-export trade through Hong Kong has changed relative to total trade between 1988 and 1994. The data clearly show (see Table 6.8) that Hong Kong's role in exports from the European Union (including all six Member States for which data have been tabulated), the United States and Japan was very much enhanced between 1988 and 1994, and that this conclusion holds true for high-technology, medium-technology, and low-technology goods alike. The only exceptions to this general conclusion were Korea and (probably) Taiwan, but these countries are exceptional in that direct trade was not permitted in 1988.

Table 6.8 Importance of re-exports relative to total exports to China for selected trading partners, 1988 and 1994 (as % of total exports of each type of commodity by the country concerned)

Exporting country (a)	Total trade		High-tech		Medium-tech		Low-tech	
	1988	1994	1988	1994	1988	1994	1988	1994
European Union (b)	11.6	20.7	10.9	17.0	9.2	15.8	16.1	34.3
Belgium/Luxembourg	9.4	12.6	16.1	4.3	6.9	22.6	10.5	17.6
France	10.8	19.3	4.1	5.7	8.5	13.8	22.3	57.8
Germany	8.6	17.3	10.8	21.9	7.1	15.6	9.9	15.4
Italy	9.7	25.2	10.7	28.7	7.8	13.9	14.6	53.8
Netherlands	21.7	35.4	50.8	26.8	16.7	34.9	20.5	39.4
United Kingdom	20.7	34.4	9.4	44.5	19.7	21.9	37.1	43.9
North America								
Canada	2.2	8.9	18.9	8.0	5.1	10.6	1.1	8.6
United States	18.1	27.6	20.4	24.4	18.0	24.3	16.9	36.0
Japan	22.0	37.2	37.4	52.1	20.0	29.8	11.7	25.5
Asian NIEs								
Korea (c)	100.0	29.8	100.0	27.7	100.0	24.7	100.0	33.2
Singapore	14.5	40.2	12.3	43.3	9.5	24.8	17.9	45.6
Taiwan (d)	100.0	98.4	100.0	—	100.0	—	100.0	—

Sources: United Nations, *Commodity Trade Statistics*
Census and Statistics Department, Hong Kong

Notes:
(a) All data are as reported by the exporting country and recorded in the UN *Commodity Trade Statistics*, and adjusted to take account of re-exports through Hong Kong.
(b) The data for the European Union (EU) relate to the twelve Member States prior to the accession of Austria, Finland and Sweden in 1995.
(c) Direct exports from South Korea to China were assumed to be zero in 1988.
(d) Direct exports from Taiwan to China were assumed to be zero in 1988. Taiwan does not publish its trade data according to the SITC, so no disaggregated figures are available for 1994.

Moreover, Hong Kong appears to play a significantly greater role in Japan's exports to China than in either EU or US exports, except with regard to low-technology exports.

A rather more confusing picture emerges from the data on re-exports originating in China (see Table 6.9). Generally, re-exports increased in importance between 1988 and 1994, but this finding was not universal over all countries or over all types of goods. As regards the European Union, for instance, re-exports accounted for over 50 per cent of total exports from China in 1994, up 12 percentage points on 1988 and despite a small fall in the proportion of low-technology goods that were re-exported. In contrast, re-exports play a much smaller role in China's exports to Japan, and there has been a marked fall in the proportion of high-technology exports being routed through Hong Kong. Exports to the United States too were less dependent upon Hong Kong in 1994 than in 1988, and especially so for high-technology goods.

Table 6.9 Importance of re-exports relative to total imports from China for selected trading partners, 1988 and 1994 (as % of total imports of each type of commodity by the country concerned)

Importing country (a)	Total trade		High-tech		Medium-tech		Low-tech	
	1988	1994	1988	1994	1988	1994	1988	1994
European Union (b)	38.0	50.3	76.6	83.1	12.1	44.8	44.0	43.1
Belgium/Luxembourg	—	59.1	—	—	26.6	55.2	47.0	42.8
France	21.2	33.9	31.6	45.7	18.7	32.6	19.5	30.7
Germany	36.3	46.6	83.7	75.3	4.5	40.6	95.1	40.0
Italy	25.8	36.5	92.4	55.9	34.2	35.4	20.5	32.3
Netherlands	67.2	—	4.6	—	44.8	71.6	81.5	68.3
United Kingdom	—	—	—	—	45.9	—	73.8	—
North America								
Canada	51.0	53.2	84.2	71.6	66.1	42.8	46.5	52.1
United States	57.3	54.3	91.9	65.1	57.1	46.9	53.8	53.0
Japan	13.4	16.9	76.4	47.4	7.2	15.1	12.9	14.3
Asian NIEs								
Korea (c)	100.0	11.8	100.0	39.0	100.0	10.6	100.0	9.9
Singapore	19.5	45.0	90.3	97.6	16.9	29.7	17.1	31.6
Taiwan (d)	100.0	63.8	100.0	—	100.0	—	100.0	—

Sources: United Nations, *Commodity Trade Statistics*
Census and Statistics Department, Hong Kong

Notes:
(a) All data are as reported by the importing country and recorded in the UN *Commodity Trade Statistics*, and adjusted to take account of re-exports through Hong Kong.
(b) The data for the European Union (EU) relate to the twelve Member States prior to the accession of Austria, Finland and Sweden in 1995.
(c) Direct exports from China to South Korea were assumed to be zero in 1988.
(d) Direct exports from China to Taiwan were assumed to be zero in 1988. Taiwan does not publish its trade data according to the SITC, so no disaggregated figures are available for 1994.

CONCLUDING REMARKS

The main aims of this chapter were to extend the analysis of Chapter 1, to present a clearer picture of China's trade with its major trading partners, and to identify how this trade had evolved over a 6-year (1988–94) period during which time both exports and imports had doubled in absolute terms. In considering the results of this analysis, three qualifications should be borne in mind. First, a number of assumptions had to be made regarding re-export margins, time lags in transportation, etc. in order to arrive at the estimates for bilateral trade. Those estimates are only as good as the assumptions were realistic. Second, the analysis concentrated on two years (1988 and 1994) which may well have been atypical. A more complete analysis would provide data for the intervening years, and ideally for the earlier years of the 'open-door' period. Third, the analysis has been purely statistical, and is subject to the vagaries of the classification of trade data.

Moreover, no attempt has been made to explain the observed changes in the trade patterns and the extent to which they are related, for example, to changes in factor endowments or the inflow of foreign direct investment. Such analysis awaits further research.

These qualifications notwithstanding, the analysis has certainly provided more insight into the development of China's trade than is apparent from the published statistics. As regards China's trade with the European Union, the following conclusions have been reached.

- The European Union is the second most important (after Japan) supplier of goods to the Chinese market, and its market share increased between 1988 and 1994.
- The European Union is the third most important (after Japan and the United States) market for Chinese exports, and its importance in this respect also increased between 1988 and 1994.
- EU exports to China primarily, and increasingly, consist of high-technology and medium-technology goods.
- EU imports from China primarily consist of low-technology goods, but the proportion of high-technology goods rose between 1988 and 1994.
- Hong Kong is playing an increasingly important role in EU exports to China in high-technology goods, medium-technology goods, and low-technology goods.
- Hong Kong plays an even more important role in Chinese exports to the European Union, and this role too became increasingly important between 1988 and 1994, particularly for high-technology and medium-technology goods.

In short, and notwithstanding the development of China's trade with her other partners, the Sino-EU trade relationship seems destined to increase in importance for both partners.

NOTES

1 Trade data for the years before 1980 were published by the Ministry for Foreign Economic Relations and Trade (MOFERT), but were collated on a different basis and are not comparable with the data in Table 6.1. See Lardy (1992: 693-5) for details and discussion.
2 The European Community was renamed the European Union when the Maastricht Treaty came into effect on 1 November 1993. In this chapter, the term European Union is used throughout even when referring to time before the Maastricht Treaty, and all data relate to the twelve Member States prior to the accession of Austria, Finland and Sweden in 1995.
3 See the *Almanac of China's Foreign Economic Relations and Trade 1994/95*, p.475. Apparently, this change in collation was not applied to trade with Japan, Korea, Taiwan, and most other countries.
4 This assumption is likely to be unrealistic given the different commodity compositions of China's trade with its various partners, but no reliable data are available with which to formulate alternative assumptions.

5 The reader is advised to take note of the various assumptions that had to be made in calculating the adjusted figures. These are explained in detail in Chapter 1 and are not repeated here.
6 1994 was the latest year for which the necessary data had been published, at the time of writing, in the *Commodity Trade Statistics*.
7 These percentages differ from those given in Table 1.11 because different figures for total imports have been used: the totals used here exclude any value added on re-exports through Hong Kong.
8 See also Hughes (1992) for a critical discussion of the link between technological specialisation and trade performance. She concludes that a shift into high technology is neither necessary nor sufficient for improved performance.
9 There are variations between the export composition of the individual EU Member States, but these are not explored here in any detail.
10 The share of low-technology goods in Chinese exports to the European Union increased between 1988 (60.6 per cent) and 1994 (66.4 per cent): this was largely due to a very low level of German imports of low-technology goods in 1988.

REFERENCES

Ferdinand, P. (1996) 'The Taiwanese Economy', in P. Ferdinand (ed.) *Take-off for Taiwan?*, London: Royal Institute of International Affairs, pp.37–65.
Harrold, P. (1995) 'China: Foreign Trade Reform: Now For the Hard Part', *Oxford Review of Economic Policy*, 11(4): 133–46.
Hughes, K. (1992) 'Technology and International Competitiveness', *International Review of Applied Economics*, 6(2): 166–83.
Imai, S. (1990) 'New Developments in the Mainland's Relations with Taiwan', *JETRO China Newsletter*, 89, November–December: 2–9.
International Monetary Fund (various years) *Directory of Trade Statistics Yearbook*, Washington, DC: IMF.
Kohari, S. (1992) 'Chinese–South Korean Economic Relations: An Update', *JETRO China Newsletter*, 97, March–April: 13–18.
Krugman, P. (1995) 'Growing World Trade: Causes and Consequences', *Brookings Papers on Economic Activity*, 1: 326–76.
Lardy, N. (1992) 'Chinese Foreign Trade', *The China Quarterly*, 131, September: 691–720.
Lardy, N. (1994) *China in the World Economy*, Washington, DC: Institute for International Economics.
Ministry of Foreign Trade and Economic Cooperation (1994) *Almanac of China's Foreign Economic Relations and Trade 1994/95*, Beijing: China Economics Publishing House.
OECD (1986) *Science and Technology Indicators 2: R&D, Invention and Competitiveness*, Paris: OECD.
Statistical Division of the United Nations (1988) *Commodity Trade Statistics According to the Standard International Trade Classification*, Statistical Papers Series D, New York: United Nations.
Statistical Division of the United Nations (1994) *Commodity Trade Statistics According to the Standard International Trade Classification*, Statistical Papers Series D, New York: United Nations.
Wakabayashi, M. (1990) 'Relations between Taiwan and China during the 1980s, Viewed from the Taiwan Perspective', *JETRO China Newsletter*, 87, July–August: 6–16.

Section II
Industry studies

7 European involvement in the automotive industry in China

Gordon Robinson and Ian Stones

INTRODUCTION

Perhaps one of the most symbolic consequences of China's 'open-door' policy has been the decision to develop a 'high quality, high technology, and mass production' car and motor vehicle industry (Takayama 1991). Still in its infancy and struggling to escape from antiquated production structures, low levels of technology and productivity, and a vestigial transport infrastructure, a volume car industry with a 1995 output of some 300,000 cars has nevertheless been created.[1] This fledgling industry is part of a wider and much longer-established automotive industry, which traditionally has concentrated on the production of trucks, heavy vehicles and buses. Pioneered originally with Soviet aid and later assisted by US, Japanese, and now a significant level of EU support, this industry currently produces some 1.5m units *per annum*, and it is hoped that this figure will rise to 6m by the year 2010. Excluding Japan, China produces or assembles one-fifth of all new cars in the Asia–Pacific, and it anticipates that this proportion will be increased to one-quarter by the year 2000 (EIU 1994). China intends to invest US$12bn in the sector during the period 1996–2000, three times the amount spent in the previous forty years. It is determined to make its mark in this industry, and to build upon its position as the third most important producer of motor vehicles in Asia–Pacific, after Japan and South Korea.

Given the saturated nature of most car markets around the world it is not surprising that China, with its rapid economic growth and vast unsatisfied consumer demand, should be targeted by the world's major car producers. Seen as one of the last frontiers for automakers, its potential as a car market has been described as 'breathtaking'.[2] China's suburban population is now around 300m people, which is similar in size to continental Europe and larger than the United States, and car ownership is still very low. There are only 2 cars per 1000 people (in comparison to the European Union where the figure is about 400) and 94 per cent of these are company-owned or State-owned. Furthermore, living standards in some parts of the country are beginning to reach the point where an increasing number of ordinary citizens can now realistically aspire to car ownership. If China were to consume cars at the rate of the average European country, it would

> suck in the entire present world production – and then some – a fully developed market in China would require 48m cars a year – 135 % of the present annual world production. At its present rate of growth China will become one of the most sought after and lucrative markets of all time.[3]

Nearly all of the major car manufacturers, along with the international investment community in general, have beaten a path to China's door. Driven by a 'China fever', they are aware not only of the great potential of this market, but the effect which success or failure in it could have on their global ranking and position. The car manufacturers are shoving each other aside in the effort to establish themselves. Indeed, it has been argued (Yukawa 1995) that they are 'almost forced to make products (in China) to remain competitive and (to) ensure their future survival'.

For EU car producers, in particular, China is a major challenge. Even though the Western European car market is still the largest in the world with approximately 12–13m cars sold annually, it is the market in which recent growth has been the most sluggish. Moreover, European car makers face rising costs and stiff international competition. The US vehicle manufacturers, Ford and General Motors, are organised on a more pan-European basis than nearly all of their competitors, while the Japanese companies are only held back from expanding their market share (which is already nearly half in some EU markets) by voluntary export restraint agreements which are due to expire by the end of 1999 (Strange 1993: 184).

Companies like Volkswagen, Fiat, and Peugeot-Citroen do not have the same global reach as their major competitors, who typically have a volume presence in all or most of the triad markets. Not only do Japanese companies virtually monopolise some Asian markets (90 per cent of Southeast Asian markets are held by Japanese car producers), they also have a strong presence in both Europe and North America. For instance, Honda generated 34 per cent of its consolidated sales in 1996 in North America,[4] and is now America's largest exporter of cars. Toyota aims to assemble in North America over 90 per cent of the cars it sells there. As regards the US companies, General Motors has a turnover three to four times that of Volkswagen, Europe's largest car producer. And Ford's turnover in 1991 was greater than the GDP of Norway, Portugal, and Greece (Rugman and Hodgetts 1995). There is a danger that European car producers, without either volume sales or a major presence in either North America (Volkswagen has only a 1 per cent share of the US market) or Asia–Pacific (except China), might find it increasingly difficult to break out from their intra-European orientation. Struggling, and perhaps failing, to achieve a global market presence (Peugeot only had 13 per cent of its sales outside the European Union in 1994), there is a danger that they will become increasingly subject to the competitive pressures of those that have. It is in this wider and more strategic sense that China is important to European car makers. If they wish to avoid being globally marginalised, they simply cannot afford to miss the opportunity which China and, by extension, the Asian market holds out to them.

This chapter traces the development of China's car industry and looks at the entry of EU car producers (particularly Volkswagen) and the role that they, and EU components suppliers, have come to play in the domestic automotive industry. It concludes with a brief discussion of the opportunities which China represents not just to European automotive manufacturers, but to EU industry and commerce in general which hitherto has been noticeable by its absence from the country and also from the Asia–Pacific, the most dynamic 'growth pole' of the world economy (Robinson 1997).

THE DEVELOPMENT OF CHINA'S AUTOMOTIVE INDUSTRY

It should come as little surprise that China, in pursuit of its economic modernisation, should want to emulate the success of its regional neighbours Japan and South Korea, and develop a capacity both to mass produce and to export cars. One of the most archetypal expressions of economic, social and cultural modernity, the motor vehicle is quite rightly regarded as 'the industry of industries' (Drucker 1946). Its significance, as Dicken (1992) points out, 'lies not only in its sheer scale but also in [the] immense spin-off effects [which it generates] through its linkages with other industries'. It is, to borrow a phrase used by Lord Rootes to describe the British motor vehicle industry, an integral prop of the nation's economy.

While steel mills and dams were the prestige projects of the 'heroic' phase of China's development, the modern car plant may be considered one of the symbols of its contemporary phase, summing up not only its industrial achievements and aspirations but also, perhaps, its desire to integrate itself ever more closely into a global society characterised by the possession and use of the motor car.

Until very recently, China was one of the last parts of the world untouched by the effects of the car. Indeed, the absence of the industry was both a token of China's isolation from the West, and a measure of its determination to develop its industries through its own endeavours. The decision to keep 'foreign forces' out of China was not only a clear statement of its intention to maintain its sovereignty, but also a recognition of the danger of the wider destabilising effects which might be unleashed by an industry which, perhaps more than any other, symbolises the possessive individualism and materialism of the West. This anxiety about the potentially subversive social and political effects of mass car ownership was well summed up by a Chinese official who, when asked in the 1970s why there were not any mopeds in China unlike the rest of Asia, replied: 'If some people have mopeds, everyone will want mopeds. Then they will want cars and, before we know where we are, we will have a capitalist system' (Bloomfield 1978).

Ever since 1949, China has realised that a domestic capacity to manufacture motor vehicles is of major economic and strategic importance. In the first half of the 1950s, during the period of the Sino-Soviet Pact, there was heavy reliance on the 'Socialist Camp' for capital equipment and technical assistance. The First Automotive Works (FAW) at Changchun, completed in 1956, was constructed with Soviet aid. China's minuscule demand for cars at this time was met from Polish and other East European imports. With the Twentieth Congress of the Soviet Communist Party in 1956 and the ensuing deterioration of Sino-Soviet relations, the Soviet technicians who had helped China to develop its automotive industry left the country. China's response to the withdrawal of Soviet assistance was to revert to strict self-reliance (The Great Leap Forward) although it should be noted that, even at this stage, the Chinese Government tried to arrange a deal with Berliet of France to manufacture trucks, although it came to nothing.

At this stage, the automotive industry was concentrated exclusively on the production of trucks with FAW at Changchun, and other facilities at Nanjing and Shanghai, producing the four-ton 'Jiefang' truck based upon a Soviet design and comprising 81 per cent Soviet parts (Harwit 1994). Car production capacity at this time was very limited and even basic materials, such as batteries and sandpaper for polishing cars, had to be imported (de Bruijn and Jia 1993). Nevertheless, assisted by a rudimentary support industry (steel production, metal forging, heat treatment, mould and die making, etc.), the automotive plants began to turn out their first cars and, in 1958, FAW produced the 'Red Flag' luxury limousine modelled on the Daimler-Benz 220 sedan. At the same time, the Shanghai Automotive Assembly Plant began producing the 'Phoenix' passenger car. Production numbers, however, were extremely small and intended for official use only, private use of cars being effectively illegal. As a result only ninety-eight cars were produced in the whole of China in 1960 (Harwit 1994).

With the worsening of China's relations with the Soviet Union, and increasing fears of a pre-emptive attack on its key industrial centres including its automotive facilities, China began building a Second Automotive Works in 1965. Located in Hubei province, and coming on stream ten years later, it embodied the lessons learned from the over-dependence on foreign partners and was based on the ideals of self-reliance, China's own experience, and the domestic provision of technology. Through a process called 'collecting the jewels', technicians and scientists were brought together from all over China to the remote city of Shiyan to design and build the plant. Its successful construction marked an important stage in China's manufacturing development, and contrasted sharply with the technological dependency of the earlier period when the Changchun plant had been built. As a result, its 'technology, production process, equipment, and development research

[were] the best [China's] automobile industry had to offer at that time' (Hishida 1987), something of which China was understandably proud.

It was not long, however, before the automotive industry, like the rest of China, was caught up in the turmoil of the Cultural Revolution. This gave rise not only to an emphasis on 'walking on two legs' (self-reliance), but also led to the dispersion of the automotive industry throughout the country to render it less exposed to attack. So, whereas in 1964 there were 417 plants producing automotive vehicles of all kinds, the number of factories had grown to 1,950 by 1976. Indeed, by the mid-1970s, there was barely a province which did not have an automotive plant of some description. While this might have made good strategic sense, it was hardly calculated to promote efficiencies of scale, and only about one-tenth of all major truck factories could produce more than 10,000 units a year (Harwit 1994).

THE AUTOMOTIVE INDUSTRY IN THE POST-MAO PERIOD

Even before the death of Mao-Tse Tung, a new course was being explored for China's automotive industry. At the top of the governmental, bureaucratic and technical structures, officials purged in the radical phase of the Cultural Revolution returned to positions of importance. Deng Xiaoping, a man convinced of the need both for reform and for a more constructive attitude towards the outside world, was joined by others of similar persuasion, including automotive experts like Chen Zutao who returned from rural exile to take over the running of the car plants.

The easing of tension with the Western world, which had been achieved towards the twilight of the Maoist period (the Sino-US *rapprochement*, better relations with some of America's more faithful European partners, the opening of EC–China diplomatic links in 1975,[5] etc.), also saw an improvement in contacts with foreign, initially Japanese, motor vehicle producers.

Helped by the restoration of Sino-Japanese diplomatic relations in 1972, Toyota was one of the first Japanese companies to benefit. Embarking on a path of global expansion and having chosen to modify its links with South Korea and Taiwan in order to accommodate China's diplomatic concerns, Toyota had, through a combination of trade and technical links, managed to carve out a 30 per cent share of China's truck imports by the mid-1970s. European producers, eager to take advantage of the warming of political relations, were not entirely absent either and France, the most active European partner, provided 17 per cent of China's truck imports at this stage. The Italians had also put down a marker with Agnelli's visit to Beijing in 1974 to discuss technical co-operation.

The real starting pistol for the motor industry, as for so many other Chinese industries, was only really sounded with the adoption of the 'open-door' policy in 1978. The abandonment of the previously rigid exclusion of foreign direct investment meant that the way was now open for collaboration with foreign partners as a means of radically developing China's automotive capacity, which was still only a few thousand passenger cars a year. There was also a recognition of the need to rationalise the myriad of small producers which had grown up in the period of self-reliance. China's desire to develop its automotive industry was reflected in the much higher priority given to it in the Sixth Five-Year Plan (1981–86) while, in the Seventh Five-Year Plan (1986–90), it was designated as one of the key props of the economy (Takayama 1991). Modernisation of the car industry would help meet the now rapidly growing domestic demand for cars, which was expected to rise to 160,000 by 1990, and to 400,000 five years later. Boosting domestic production would also assist in choking-off the extremely sharp rise in imports, which had grown from a mere 52 cars in 1977 to 19,570 cars in 1980 (Harwit 1994). This increase in imports was beginning to place a serious strain on the country's balance of payments. But to cut imports meant, above all, building an industry where the standards of quality, efficiency and competitiveness were at least within striking distance of the international car producers. If China was to achieve this, Western production technology as well as management expertise had to be brought in. It was therefore, at this stage, that China turned to the Western producers for help.

Discussions now began with foreign partners about possible joint ventures. One such venture was with the American Motor Corporation (later taken over by Chrysler) and which eventually became the Beijing Jeep Corporation. Another was with Volkswagen which, unlike its more parochial European rivals, was striving to develop a more extensive and systematic international strategy. As will be seen below, tortuous discussions between the Chinese Government and Volkswagen led eventually to the setting up of production facilities in Shanghai which would eventually allow the German car maker to emerge as China's largest producer with some 60 per cent of the market. Collaboration was also sought with Peugeot who, in 1985, entered into a joint venture with the Chinese Government which, when completed, represented the largest single investment by France in the country. By the middle of the 1990s, therefore, a number of key joint ventures had been formed. These were with the following partners: Volkswagen at Changchun (Audi 100/Jetta) and Shanghai (Santana); Peugeot at Guangzhou (Peugeot 504); Citroen at Wuhan (Citroen ZX); Mercedes on Hainan Island (minivans and multi-purpose vehicles); and Chrysler (Beijing Jeep). A fuller list would figure Toyota and Daihatsu producing minibuses at Tianjin and Shenyang, and Panda Motors' operations at Huizhou.

CHINA'S AUTOMOTIVE INDUSTRY POLICY IN THE 1990S

By the middle of the 1990s, many of the most formidable difficulties that had stood in the way of the creation of a viable car industry (political, technical, administrative, economic and even diplomatic) were well on the way to being overcome. Encouraged by the speed with which the industry had developed, and aware of the need to deal with problems which were still holding it back, the Chinese Government issued a new policy for the industry in 1994. This 'Policy for China's Automotive Industry Enterprises' aimed to put a freeze on all new joint ventures until 1997, in order to:

- allow existing operations a breathing space in which to achieve sufficient levels of both scale and technology;
- establish no more than 3-4 major centres of car production; and
- rationalise the tiers of suppliers in order to gain economies of scale.

From 1996, any new vehicle production ventures have had to commence with over 40 per cent local content, a policy innovation which led to prospective vehicle producers investing in component manufacturing operations as a means of gaining major contracts. It has also been government policy not to allow foreign companies to own more than 50 per cent of a joint venture, and to limit them to a fixed life span (25 years for Volkswagen). Also, no vehicle manufacturer will be permitted to have more than two joint ventures producing the same model.

Preferential treatment will also be given to suppliers holding over 25 per cent of the market for any particular component, and to any supplier that is able to fill any of the identified technology gaps. The government intends to ensure that investment in the components industry matches that for vehicles. The objectives of current policy are not only to make China self-sufficient, but also to enable it to export 10 per cent of its production (some 400,000 cars) by the year 2010.[6]

It was not long, however, before the targets built into this strategy began to look decidedly over-optimistic. Hit by difficult economic conditions, a credit squeeze, stagnation in output, a significant fall in exports (a drop of over 4 per cent in the first eight months of 1996), high rates of tax on cars (in some parts of China as high as 75 per cent of the purchase price), infrastructural constraints and, very significantly, continuing high levels of smuggled imports, car producers were barely selling half of their capacity. In the first part of 1996, one-third of the previous year's production remained unsold.[7] Matters were not helped by the much slower than predicted growth in the Asia–Pacific region: car sales slowed very significantly and predictions for future growth have had to be seriously pared back.[8] Not only has this downturn deflated the industry, it has also posed a serious dilemma for producers like Volkswagen for whom it could hardly have come at a more unfortunate time: 1996 production at Changchun had to be cut back by at least half, and at a time when Volkswagen was banking on buoyant sales to help it meet large-scale loan repayments which were due to commence in 1997.

Despite this, both the Chinese Government and its foreign partners remain optimistic about the future. Panglossian or not, they dismiss these difficulties as perfectly manageable. China, according to Mercedes is 'the most important industrial base in Asia'[9] – a market of long-term growth in which it would be a serious mistake to be underweight.

THE OPERATIONAL AND INVESTMENT ENVIRONMENT

The process of creating joint ventures in the automotive industry has been described by Yukawa (1995). It begins when the appropriate governmental agencies agree on a project and recommend it to the State Planning Committee, which may then accept it as a capital construction project. As of 1996, for any project to be approved, the provincial, municipal or central government organisation in charge has had to have filed an application directly with the Departments of Machine-Building, Electronics, Light Industry, or Textiles under the State Planning Commission. This is then passed to the Motor Vehicle Department of the Ministry of Machine-Building Industry where it is evaluated and returned to the State Planning Commission. If the proposed project is expensive, it has to be accepted by the State Council: whereas if the costs are less, it only needs the approval of the State Planning Commission. This means effectively that most decisions are made by the State Planning Commission in the light of the views of the Ministry of Machine-Building Industry and those of the relevant province or city.

Once the joint venture is agreed, the foreign partner will provide investment in one or a combination of the following forms: machinery and equipment, technological know-how, or currency: the sum of foreign capital must generally not be less than 25 per cent of the registered capital. The local firm will typically offer industrial property and the right to use the work site. The main objectives for the Chinese when entering such ventures are to gain foreign capital, access to export markets, and advanced technology and managerial expertise (Child 1994). The main pay-off for a foreign company entering the Chinese market in this way is that it allows them to cut through red tape and circumvent political and bureaucratic obstructions (something from which Volkswagen and Peugeot have clearly benefited). It might also allow the foreign company access to restricted industries or projects which might otherwise not be available. In addition, it provides a high level of political and legal security.

Enticed by this environment, new ventures in the Chinese automotive industry are being announced almost on a weekly basis, indeed, one of the problems of analysing the Chinese automotive industry is that of keeping abreast of its very rapid development. The enthusiasm of companies from the developed world to establish themselves has not gone unnoticed by the Chinese. Equity stakes held by foreign companies are becoming progressively smaller. Early entrants were able to negotiate stakes of over 60 per cent in their joint ventures. More recently, foreign investors have been lucky if they achieve over 50 per cent although, even with minority shareholdings, it is possible to have managerial control. Management control is considered to be of great significance since the quality of the workforce, production systems, goods and management is often very poor. Through more effective management, some foreign partners have raised efficiency very dramatically. Dana, for example, is reported to have raised productivity at its filter plant by over 600 per cent in only a few years (EIU 1996).

As from April 1996, tax relief has been removed from the import of capital equipment for foreign invested enterprises. This is expected to slow the pace of new investment and to ensure that only those truly committed to China will proceed. However, the general levels of import tariffs have been lowered as part of China's effort to join the World Trade Organization (WTO).[10] This is likely to further reduce the number of new joint ventures, while those that do go ahead will be larger thus increasing the average size of foreign investments (a trend which is already emerging).

Even although more joint ventures are planned, the Chinese automotive industry is becoming increasingly competitive, and foreign partners will have to choose their collaborators carefully. Many of the better Chinese companies are already committed to joint ventures and, as the threat of closure looms for many State-Owned Enterprises, they are moving into other activities in order to survive. Some of the country's aerospace companies, for example, are shifting into auto components as their traditional markets dry up. Despite the fact that these companies have little or no expertise in the industry they can, nevertheless, offer both facilities and relevant skills. They are also more likely to grant management control and larger equity stakes to their foreign partners. These type of ventures probably offer some of the best opportunities for future investment.

As competition increases and productivity rises, the quality of goods should improve. This will help boost the export drive which the Chinese Government is desperately keen to promote. The requirement placed on many ventures to expedite foreign exchange equality will also mean that many countries, including the European Union, will have to accept a growing quantity of reverse imports. This is especially likely to be the case with Germany and France, where the 'hollowing out' process is leading to the export of automotive jobs as strenuous efforts are made to cut costs and maintain international competitiveness. As global capacity of both vehicles and components increases, severe cost pressures may force the further downsizing of the automotive industry in the traditional centres of production. This drive for efficiency, pursued in the context of extremely demanding international competitive conditions, also means that vehicle manufacturers are no longer reluctant to break their ties with traditional partners in order to establish a sounder international position. This is the case with both German and particularly Japanese vehicle manufacturers as they pursue, or are driven towards, their strategies of delocalisation.

THE COMPONENTS SUPPLY INDUSTRY

Given that a modern car has something like 10,000 components which represent about three-quarters of its value, it is clear that the ambitious plans which China has for meeting 90 per cent of the demand for cars from domestic production by the year 2000 presupposes a vastly enhanced domestic capacity to manufacture components. The Chinese Government has identified a series of components technologies which it believes to be of strategic importance if this sector of the industry is to be competitive. The suppliers of these technologies are to be known as 'Dragon Heads', and one of the main reasons for holding up future vehicle ventures is to allow these to become established. Action in this sector will have to be very decisive and will have to be oriented towards radical technological upgrading and rationalisation. In 1994, it was reported that there were some 1,900 parts suppliers in China, and that their average productivity levels were less than half that of the engine makers and that their general performance was also very weak (Ishiro 1994).

Investment in the component sector is being encouraged by the vehicle manufacturers active in China, since each of their operations must be supported by a comprehensive network of components suppliers. Furthermore, they have an additional incentive either to encourage their suppliers to establish local operations or to produce components locally themselves, as higher local content means that the vehicle manufacturers are subject to lower customs duties. For example, moving from 40 per cent to 80 per cent local content gives rise to a reduction in duties from 37.5 per cent to just 20 per cent. This is of particular interest to Japanese and German companies which typically have extremely strong links with their long-term suppliers.

Due to the local strength of the EU vehicle manufacturers, many of the European components suppliers have established operations in China. A number of German components producers have established operations in and around Changchun and Shanghai in order to support the Volkswagen plants, while some PSA suppliers have set up operations near their plants in Guangzhou and Wuhan. This has resulted in these cities being touted as Chinese 'Detroits'. As new vehicle operations come onstream, these plants will be in an ideal position to exploit opportunities. The possibility of supplying a new customer in China may also result in potential business with vehicle manufacturers in other markets where access has been difficult due to close ties with traditional suppliers.

Bosch, the largest European components producer, has several joint ventures manufacturing a range of products, including diesel pumps and nozzles, engine management systems, petrol injection and electrical systems. Siemens, the longest-established European company in China with links going back to the 1870s, has over twenty-five joint ventures, though only a few are for automotive components (small motors and auto electronics). Other major German parts producers present in China include ZF (gearboxes and steering), Hella (2 lighting joint ventures), Temic (electronics), Ebersächer (exhausts), Bayer, Kögel, Brose, Illbruck and Plettac. Other major European auto parts producers are also present. Valeo of France has five joint ventures, and hopes soon to have one for each of its eight core businesses. Lucas and GKN each have two joint ventures (Lucas also has an aerospace joint venture), and Labinal, Connecteurs Cinch, Sogefi, Saiag, T&N, and Pilkington are also present.

The vehicle manufacturers each have their own substantial parts operations. ECIA, the PSA components arm, has several operations as does Volkswagen/Audi. The most significant component ventures, however, are those of General Motors and Ford who have established many operations in their battle to secure major vehicle production opportunities. A subsidiary of GM Delphi parts, which itself is the world's largest components producer, is reported to have over thirty ventures, and Ford has announced over a dozen. Other large US components firms are improving their already strong position. Tenneco, owner of Monroe shock absorbers, and Walker exhausts have several joint ventures, as do ITT, TRW, Varity and WABCO.

The Japanese are also improving their position after a slow and uncertain start. Because of the Chinese Government's insistence that increased local content is a condition for further joint ventures, the Japanese vehicle makers have recently been pressing affiliated parts makers to increase their presence in China. Even although there are problems for Japanese parts suppliers, firms like Koito Manufacturing are tripling their production in Shanghai, while Nippondenso, Nisseibo, NKO and Tokico are also increasing their investment (Ishiro 1994).

EU MOTOR VEHICLE OPERATIONS IN CHINA

Whether it is cars or their components, China clearly represents a great prize and in recent years it has witnessed the most dramatic levels of automotive investment of any country in the world. But China has been choosy about whom she wants to assist the development of her car industry, and relations with foreign manufacturers have been driven as much by China's diplomatic concerns as by economic and industrial interests. Both in the car, and latterly the aerospace industry, the European Union has benefited from China's desire to keep Japan at arm's length, and to punish the United States for its stubbornness over Taiwan and its use of the human rights issue as a lever over China's entry into the WTO. Suspicious of Japan, and convinced that the United States is deliberately obstructing China's rise to great power status (Yahuda 1996), China's aim has been to keep Europe as a balancing factor in Asia. This interest has been eagerly reciprocated by the European Union which has, at long last, produced a comprehensive policy towards Asia (Commission of the European Communities 1994) and has also entirely revamped its China strategy (Commission of the European Communities 1995). Even although China's first attempt at collaborating with foreign motor vehicle manufacturers was with Chrysler in the Beijing Jeep operation, it has been the EU's shoulder which China has largely chosen to lean on in this industry.

Within the European Union, the country which has been most active in its pursuit of the China market has been Germany. There are strong, high-level diplomatic links and relationships in the motor vehicle industry which go back to the late 1970s. The overtures, for what was later to become China's most successful joint venture in the motor vehicle industry, were first made by the First Machine-Building Vice-Minister on a visit to West Germany in 1978. Whilst also exploring the possibility of collaboration with Ford, General Motors and some other European partners, the Chinese Government hoped that collaboration with Volkswagen, Europe's largest car manufacturer, would help it promote the broad development of the industry as laid down in the Five-Year Plans. It was envisaged that Western production technology and management expertise would help China build an industry where the standards of quality, efficiency and competitiveness were at least within striking distance of those set by the international car manufacturers.

This was Volkswagen's window of opportunity. For Volkswagen, entry into China offered 'first mover' opportunities in what was clearly going to be a vast and rapidly growing market. It also represented a vital stage in the development of its global strategy, which needed to encompass not only China but the near-Pacific region as well. It was also a way of taking on the Japanese manufacturers in their own backyard. Finding an agreement between Volkswagen, the Chinese Government, the Bank of China, and the Chinese partner (Shanghai Tractor Factory) was not easy. Indeed, the whole process took six years, and thirty-six rounds of negotiations before its conclusion in 1984. The original visit of the Chinese Vice-Minister had seen Volkswagen moot the possibility of creating a plant in China capable of producing up to 200,000 vehicles. Volkswagen's preference was to produce the 'Santana' in kit-form, rather than its 'Golf' or 'Jetta' models, even though the 'Santana' had not been a success in Europe. Volkswagen hoped to recoup some of its huge development costs and saw the 'Santana' as an effective competitor to the models of Toyota and Nissan. Volkswagen calculated that the Santana would be competitive, as long as the Chinese Government protected the domestic market (de Bruijn and Jia 1993).

Preceded by the production of a small number of 'Santanas' at Anting, 30 miles from Shanghai, 'full-scale' production began at the Shanghai plant in 1985 with an output in its first year of 3,356 cars. By 1988, this figure had grown to over 10,000, while engine production had risen to over 13,000 in the same period (Harwit 1994: 99). It was not all plain sailing, however. Chinese workers constructing the facility seemed less than totally committed, the local banks were not particularly efficient, municipal planners were slow in raising funds for the project, and there were even reports of local officials selling cars as they came off the production line and pocketing the proceeds (ibid.). There were also differences of opinion about the amounts of locally produced parts to be incorporated, and about the speed with which China could effectively develop a reasonably high standard components industry. Unlike Chrysler, in its unhappy Beijing Jeep Project, Volkswagen's approach was to be patient and realistic, and this paid off with its Chinese partners. By 1993, the local content in the 'Santana' had reached 80 per cent, a scale and speed of localisation on a par with car production in other parts of the world. However, whether the quality would have met the standards of international markets is another matter. A decade after production began at Shanghai, Volkswagen had modernised 'Car Plant II' at Anting, the additional plant allowing it to raise annual production to 250,000 units and also to introduce the Santana 2000. A further increase in capacity to 300,000 units is planned for 1998, as is an output of 180,000 engines.[11]

The evidence would seem to indicate, therefore, that EU companies are in a relatively strong position. Volkswagen is the market leader, and PSA is also well established with its separate Peugeot and Citroen joint ventures. Recently Mercedes was awarded a major contract for a joint venture to produce multi-purpose vehicles and engines in Southern China, and this has further underlined the excellent prospects which European, and particularly German companies, have in the region. Other European vehicle manufacturers are also aiming to establish a foothold in China. Fiat has been in discussions with several potential Chinese partners and government officials to establish production of its 178 world car. BMW/Rover is considering local assembly, possibly of Range Rovers.

In addition, there are many EU enterprises involved in the production of commercial vehicles and engines. These include Iveco, Renault, Volvo, Perkins (classified here as an EU company despite the recent US involvement in its activities) and Mercedes Benz. Steyr, Renault and Iveco are all relatively strong in the light-van market with local production or licences. As the tourist industry develops, the need for luxury coaches is also likely to increase and, in line with that, Volvo is hoping to secure two further bus ventures in addition to its existing operation. Other coach and bus manufacturers are expected to follow suit. It should, however, be noted that competition from the Japanese and South Korean producers will be notably stronger than in the trucks sector.

THE FUTURE FOR EU MOTOR VEHICLE MANUFACTURERS IN CHINA

According to the European Commission, the rise of China is 'unmatched amongst national experiences since the Second World War' (Commission of the European Communities 1995). As a strategic actor, China is of increasing relevance to both Asia and the world at large, and it is clear that, increasingly, the central issues of global economic and political management cannot be satisfactorily addressed without reference to it. China is now playing a central role in the adjustment which the European Union is making in its relations with Asia. According to Sir Leon Brittan, China represents a major part in the *démarche* which the European Union is making towards the region (Commission of the European Communities 1994) and is destined to become one of the cornerstones of the European Union's relations, not just with Asia, but with the world as a whole. Particular attention has been paid by the European Commission to the part that China might play in the reversal of the EU's perceived loss of global competitiveness since there is a 'clear perception, both within the Chinese, European and foreign business communities, that EU companies are...less dynamic than their competitors' (Commission of the European Communities 1995).

If there is a silver lining to this cloud, it is in the automotive industry where the prospects for EU motor vehicle manufacturers in China are very encouraging. China is the only country in Asia where European vehicle manufacturers not only have a foothold but are dominant, and it is important that Volkswagen, as a standard-bearer, maintains its good reputation, raises its local content to 100 per cent, and stays out in front. The recently announced Mercedes venture will provide a Multi-Purpose Vehicle (MPV), which is a new product for the market and should do well. In addition, Fiat may be allowed to introduce its ambitious world car, a vehicle which is specifically designed for the needs of developing countries: robust, affordable but also having new technology and modern styling.

Further areas of opportunity for EU companies are represented by the potential demand for trucks, buses and coaches, components, and the aftersales service. The first offers huge potential. There is likely to be a tremendous increase in demand for light vans and pickups as market liberalisation leads to the creation of thousands of small companies. Many EU van producers are already present and have very competitive products. Renault and Iveco, in particular, are well placed and could build on their position to establish a stronger foothold in the region as a whole. Volvo, Scania, Mercedes Benz, Steyr, MAN and other large truck producers, as well as specialist vehicle builders, have excellent potential. It is in this market that EU producers are particularly strong on a global basis. As the Chinese economy develops further, and as new industries demand more goods, then new, bigger and more reliable trucks will be required. Older Chinese trucks will need to be replaced, while new emission standards, if introduced, could also create a demand for EU technology.

It is the components sector which, perhaps, offers the greatest possibilities for EU companies. As vehicle production grows, there will be a significant demand for components and new capacity will have to be created. As has already been suggested, most of the world's largest components producers are already present but some technologies, such as automatic braking systems (ABS), have yet to become established in China.

Components for trucks, buses and coaches will be required in large numbers, especially for those parts or systems which have not been needed before, such as large alternators, air conditioners, and certain types of interior fittings. Since the Chinese are not keen to see the development of monopolies, there may still be a gap in the market for those companies whose major competitors are already established.

There is little doubt, however, that much of China's potential will be lost if EU producers do not develop sales, distribution, and service networks. This is a major issue for EU producers since the development of after-sales and service channels is one of the most effective ways of cornering markets (something which has been done very effectively by the Japanese in the European Union, the United States, and in Asia–Pacific markets like Thailand). As the number of vehicles increases and the components which they use become more advanced, there will be a need for massive service networks. For this, and for distribution, the realisation of the possibilities will require partnerships between companies which are more used to being competitors. EU companies may not be as strong as some of their US competitors in this field but, even so, there is enormous potential for those with the scale and the commitment to succeed. The cooperative nature of many EU companies may turn out to be an important advantage over the competition, particularly from the United States. The creation of sales, distribution and service networks may be the toughest nut to crack, but it may ultimately offer the greatest rewards.

Overall, EU automotive companies are probably better placed than many of their US or Japanese counterparts, and difficult political relations between China and both the United States and Japan may increase their competitive leverage. Of late, there have been several high level visits by Chinese and EU leaders to each other's countries (the Germans have been particularly active) and these can only strengthen ties and improve relations. On China's part, there is a wish to see their partners commit themselves to long-term relationships and not just to pursue short-term gains. In China, it is an honour to be considered 'an old friend': as far as commerce is concerned, China must be reassured that it has many such 'old friends' in Europe.

NOTES

1 See the *Financial Times*, 29 October 1996.
2 *Business Week*, 30 January 1995.
3 *Lucas Automotive Market Information*, 29 August 1995.
4 *Financial Times*, 11 February 1997.
5 See Chapter 3 for further details.
6 See the *Financial Times*, 29 October 1996 and 5 March 1996.
7 *Financial Times*, 29 October 1996.
8 *Financial Times*, 28 November 1996.
9 *Financial Times*, 13 July 1995.

10 See Chapter 1 for further details.
11 *Business Week*, 30 January 1995.

REFERENCES

Bloomfield, G. (1978) *The World Automotive Industry*, London: David Charles.
Business Week, various issues as shown.
Child, J. (1994) *Management in China during the Age of Reform*, Cambridge: Cambridge University Press.
Commission of the European Communities (1994) *Towards a New Asia Strategy*, COM(94)314 final, Luxembourg: Office for Official Publications of the European Communities.
Commission of the European Communities (1995) *A Long-Term Policy for China–Europe Relations*, COM(95)279 final, Luxembourg: Office for Official Publications of the European Communities.
de Bruijn, E. and Jia, X. (1993) 'Managing Sino-Western Joint Ventures: Product Selection Strategy', *Management International Review*, 33: 335–60.
Deloitte Touche Tohmatsu (1995) *People's Republic of China: International Tax and Business Guide*, New York: Deloitte Touche Tohmatsu.
Dicken, P. (1992) *Global Shift: The Internationalisation of Economic Activity*, (2nd edition), London: Paul Chapman Publishing.
Drucker, P. (1946) *The Concept of the Corporation*, New York: John Day.
Economist Intelligence Unit (1994) *The Automotive Sector of the Pacific Rim and China*, London: EIU.
Economist Intelligence Unit (1996) *The Automotive Sector of the Pacific Rim and China*, London: EIU.
Financial Times, various issues as shown.
Harwit, E. (1994) *China's Automobile Industry: Policies, Problems, and Prospects*, New York: M.E. Sharpe.
Hishida, M. (1987) 'A Visit to China's "Second" Automobile Factory', *JETRO China Newsletter*, 71, (November–December): 2–8.
Ishiro, K. (1994) 'China's New Auto Industrial Policy', *JETRO China Newsletter*, 113, (November–December): 2–6.
Robinson, G. (1997) 'Is Europe Missing the Asia Boat?', in J. Slater and R. Strange (eds) *Business Relationships with East Asia: the European Experience*, London: Routledge, pp.73–84.
Rugman, A. and Hodgetts, R. (1995) *International Business: A Strategic Management Approach*, New York: McGraw-Hill.
Strange, R. (1993) *Japanese Manufacturing Investment in Europe: Its Impact on the UK Economy*, London: Routledge.
Takayama, Y. (1991) 'The Chinese Automobile Industry', *JETRO China Newsletter*, 94, (September–October): 16–21.
Yahuda, M. (1996) *The International Politics of the Asia–Pacific, 1945–1995*, London: Routledge.
Yukawa, T. (1995) 'Japanese Auto Parts in China', *JETRO China Newsletter*, 119 (November–December): 2–6.

8 Kids' stuff
The organisation and politics of the China–EU trade in toys

Jim Newton and Lai-hing Tse

INTRODUCTION

In March 1994, the European Union (EU) imposed Union-wide quotas on the import of Chinese-made toys. This decision was not unanimous, being opposed in the Council of Ministers by the UK Government, who then attempted to remove the quotas through the European Court of Justice. In September 1996, the Court ruled against the UK action, rejecting UK claims that the regime was protectionist. Involved in the debate was the toy industry's trade association, the Toy Manufacturers of Europe (TME), which represents 80 per cent of the manufacturers and distributors operating in Europe.[1] The TME had opposed the imposition of quotas, even before the UK Government had demanded their removal.

These observations raise two issues. The first concerns the apparently paradoxical behaviour of the European manufacturers in opposing measures which, at first sight, appear designed to protect European industry. The second, related, issue concerns EU trade policy, and the design and intent of policy especially towards China. The case is examined, first with an analysis of the structure and organisation of the industry, paying particular attention to the links between European firms and China-based production systems. Patterns of ownership and management are described and interpreted using the approach offered by 'global commodity chain' analysis. This approach reveals the fragmented nature of much of the production activity, not only spatially and functionally, but also in terms of the ownership of firms within the commodity, or production, chain. The analysis considers the specific reasons for this set of arrangements, and examines the choice of China as the production base. Trade relations between the EU and China are then considered (see also Chapter 3) with specific reference to the dispute over the toy quotas. To do this, a suitable approach is required that can capture the political and economic factors involved in the formulation of trade policy. This is done through the use of an 'international political economy' (IPE) framework, which adopts a bargaining approach to analyse outcomes in the global system. The 'global commodity chain' and IPE approaches are both necessary if the complexities of global production systems and the formulation of regional trade policies are to be interpreted successfully. The chapter concludes with a discussion of the implications for both trade theory and policy which emerge from the analysis of the China–EU trade in toys.

COMMODITY CHAINS IN THE INTERNATIONAL ORGANISATION OF PRODUCTION

In order to understand the nature of production in the toy industry, and the impact upon the European manufacturers' strategy and EU trade policy, there is a need for a framework that recognises organisational change and fragmentation. Not only technical, spatial and functional fragmentation, but also the fragmentation of ownership that leads to systems of production organised through networks of independent firms.

The concept of 'global commodity chains' advanced by Gereffi (1992) and Gereffi and Korzeniewicz (1994) offers insights into this form of organisation. Akin to New International Division of Labour approaches, the basis of 'global commodity chain' analysis is the presumption that nations specialise in different stages of production within a specific industry. This international division of labour is then integrated by core corporations who may not necessarily own the means of production. This is particularly so when physical production takes place in the specialising nations of the global periphery. The chains, with the corporations of the core economies as the key nodes, link the various activities of the participating firms. These may be further linked to technological, organisational and institutional networks, which together are used to develop, manufacture and market specific commodities or products. Gereffi (1992) highlights three main features. The first is the value-added chain of products, services and resources which are linked together across a range of relevant industries forming an input–output structure. Second, there exists a geographical separation of production and marketing networks into a distinct territorial structure. Finally, and most importantly, is the existence of a governance structure of authority and power relationships between participating firms. It is this governance structure that determines the allocation of financial, material and human resources within the chain.

Two types of governance structure have been identified. The first is a producer-driven structure which is found in capital and technology-intensive industries such as automobile and aircraft manufacturing. Here, control is exercised by the headquarters of large, transnational manufacturers over networks of component producers who supply the multinational enterprises (MNEs) through sub-contracting arrangements. The second form is a buyer-driven structure. Here large retailers, branded marketers and trading companies play a pivotal role in setting up decentralised production networks. Frequently the producers are located in developing countries where they concentrate on the production of labour-intensive consumer goods such as garments, footwear, consumer electronics and toys. Production takes place within locally owned factories which make finished goods to buyers' specifications. Thus, the buyers, while exercising ultimate control, do not normally own any production facilities. Instead, their crucial role is in the management of the dispersed production and trade networks. Such buyers are design and marketing-intensive firms who derive their power over the actual producers from their control over market access through, for example, high expenditures on advertising to establish brand identities.

Within the lower levels of the commodity chains, the producers may play different roles that form a spectrum of increasing technical competence. Such roles begin with simple assembly processes that are based on inputs of foreign components. The second level is that of component-supply subcontracting. This technologically more advanced production system yields components from the lower-level firms for final assembly in the core. The third stage is original equipment manufacturing (OEM), where contract manufacturers produce finished goods, generally in locally owned factories, for retailing or branding by the buyers. The highest stage is own brand manufacturing (OBM), where the local firm establishes its own brands, and thus begins to move out of the category of lower-level producer and approaches the status of a buyer–governor in its own right.

PRODUCTION AND TRADE IN TOY MANUFACTURING

Currently more than half the world's toys are made in China. This is a relatively recent phenomenon which followed the development of toy manufacturing in Hong Kong after World War II (WWII). In the 1940s, production began in Hong Kong using the territory primarily as an export platform, before being relocated to China in the 1980s. From insignificant origins, Hong Kong had become the world's leading exporter of toys by the 1970s, a position which has been lost to China in the 1990s. This section examines these developments in both production and trade through the perspectives offered by 'global commodity chain' analysis.

Before analysing the spatial disaggregation of production, however, the origins of the industry should be considered. Hong Kong's toy industry, and hence later China's toy industry, has its roots in the development of plastics manufacturing. The first plastics factory was established in Hong Kong in 1947, and the industry soon diversified into plastic flowers, toys, household decorations and utensils. Toys and flowers formed the bulk of the output. Both were manufactured predominantly for export, with over 90 per cent sold overseas, primarily in the United States (Riedel 1974). By 1960, Hong Kong had become the world's major producer of plastic flowers (Federation of Hong Kong Industries 1962) and, by 1964, had overtaken West Germany to become the second largest exporter of toys (Hong Kong Trade Development Council 1973).

Growth in both product lines can be accounted for in similar ways. Commodity chains were established early in the development of these industries, as a result of both domestic and international factors. Domestically, the plastics industry presented low barriers to entry. The industry required mainly low-cost labour which was readily available in the late 1940s and the early 1950s. The end of WWII in 1945 saw the first population increase from China, and the major influx that resulted from the Chinese Civil War of 1948–49 swelled the ranks of the unemployed (Federation of Hong Kong Industries 1962). Second, capital costs were low. Both flowers and toys require simple injection moulding machines for production, and these were available both locally and at low cost. Riedel (1974: 30) reports that the 'plastics industry is unique amongst other manufacturing industries in Hong Kong in that it employs locally produced machinery'. Virtually all the simple hand-operated moulding machines were made in Hong Kong and, by 1968, it was estimated that half the total domestic production of machinery was for the plastics industry. Riedel also considers that a major contributor to the price-competitiveness of the industry was the low price of the chief component of the machine, the mould.

Internationally, foreign sources provided the raw materials, none of which were available locally, and foreign buyers provided the impetus and access to overseas markets. The Federation of Hong Kong Industries (1962: 45) states that the production of plastic flowers 'began effectively in 1957 with the visit to Hong Kong of American businessmen who divined the advantage of using the colony's unique labour supply to produce flowers on a large scale'. Two years later, 70 per cent of Hong Kong's exports of plastic flowers were imported into the United States. The toy industry was established prior to this, largely through the link with British trading companies and the preferential tariff treatment offered through the Commonwealth Preference System (Tsui 1988). The trading companies' initial interest stemmed from their role as importers of raw materials for the plastics industry generally, and this connection later expanded into exports of finished toys.[2] By 1957, Hong Kong products accounted for 50 per cent of British imports of toys of all kinds (Federation of Hong Kong Industries 1962). Direct American involvement in the toy industry began in this period, utilising limited direct investment together with extensive subcontracting.[3] In 1957, in contrast to the British position, only 6 per cent of American toy imports were made in Hong Kong (ibid.). However, in 1968, just over ten years later, this share had risen to 26 per cent and, by 1972, Hong Kong accounted for 35 per cent of total American toy imports (Hong Kong Trade Development Council 1973).

This period represented a major growth phase of the industry in both output and share of world exports. The number of factories rose from 285 in 1962 to 1,395 in 1973, making the toy industry the third largest industry in Hong Kong after textiles (together with clothing) and electronics. Export values rose from HK$165m in 1962 to HK$1,389m ten years later, at which time Hong Kong replaced Japan as the world's leading exporter of toys. America was the major importer, taking 59.2 per cent of Hong Kong's total exports. The European Community (by then comprising nine Member States, including the United Kingdom) was the second largest recipient, taking 22.7 per cent of Hong Kong's exports (HK$315m) in 1972 (Hong Kong Trade Development Council 1973).

By 1980, as Table 8.1 shows, the value of Hong Kong's toy exports had quadrupled to HK$5,529m, and the number of establishments had almost doubled to 2,218. This growth, especially in the previous ten years, was partly due to the continued development of production chains. Manufacturers in developed countries, especially America, began to source from subcontractors or licensees in Asia to cut costs. This was especially marked in the toy industry, given the price sensitivity of the product. The pattern was thus established whereby Hong Kong firms became OEM manufacturers for overseas importers, many of whom established buying offices in Hong Kong (Tsui 1988).

Table 8.1a World exports of toys and indoor games, etc. (SITC 8942), 1970–93 (US$m)

Year	World	Hong Kong	China*	USA	Japan	Germany	Italy	UK
1970	655	183	—	70	213	80	73	99
1971	957	211	—	93	209	92	79	110
1972	1108	251	—	117	217	106	99	108
1973	1437	323	—	158	224	149	124	114
1974	1630	356	—	197	208	165	143	161
1975	1605	322	—	202	173	166	147	171
1976	2032	491	—	230	258	238	174	183
1977	2591	658	—	277	337	296	209	217
1978	3044	720	—	390	335	344	250	267
1979	3902	1037	—	538	361	399	329	338
1980	4685	1209	—	596	675	417	350	346
1981	4804	1331	—	636	700	384	314	277
1982	4864	1550	—	499	731	362	297	236
1983	4594	1270	—	509	593	333	253	228
1984	5123	1674	—	328	606	315	243	212
1985	5029	1629	—	271	688	355	259	227
1986	6344	2086	—	295	674	522	340	311
1987	8239	2765	886	403	688	614	392	442
1988	8894	3326	1183	535	718	639	467	470
1989	13585	3975	1524	849	746	681	446	519
1990	15793	4722	1831	1155	1151	902	587	590
1991	17118	5657	2241	1364	1567	942	595	602
1992	21035	7596	3132	1752	1695	1008	647	645
1993	22705	8122	3591	1888	1500	982	661	603

Source: International Trade Statistics Yearbook (various issues)
Note:
* data not available for 1970–86

Table 8.1b World exports of toys, sporting goods, etc. (SITC 894), 1989–95 (US$m)

Year	World	Hong Kong	China	USA	Japan	Germany	Italy	UK
1989	17272	4073	1638	1804	1096	1045	826	750
1990	22051	4871	1971	2208	1517	2666	1070	873
1991	23499	5906	2454	2558	1958	1413	1113	869
1992	28131	8007	3487	2984	2118	1484	1207	917
1993	30289	8648	4050	3292	1917	1385	1276	832
1994	32992	9702	5093	3690	1584	1512	1454	1109
1995	38737	11055	5862	4230	2097	1704	1806	1345

Source: *International Trade Statistics Yearbook* (various issues)

By 1987, between 75 and 80 per cent of industry sales were derived from contract manufacturing, either under licence or sub-contracting agreements. Overseas buyers provided the product specifications, undertaking product design, market research and marketing activities. Local manufacturers were thus able to avoid associated development and marketing expenses and risks. This did not apply to all Hong Kong firms, however. A relatively small number of companies have undertaken design and marketing, either producing under their own brand name or manufacturing open, or non-branded, items. In addition, Hong Kong trading firms developed an intermediate role between overseas buyers and local manufacturers, sourcing from a large number of local producers (Hong Kong Trade Development Council 1987).

This pattern of buyer-driven production chains has continued into the 1990s, with the major difference being the relocation of production to China. From its beginnings in the early 1980s, this relocation has led to a marked contraction of the industry in Hong Kong (see Table 8.2). After peaking in 1984, when 2,365 establishments were registered (Tsui 1988) and over 55,000 people were employed in Hong Kong in the manufacture of toys (Standard Chartered Bank 1988), the number of establishments fell to 554 in 1995 and employment dropped to 4,695.[4] In 1984, re-exports of China-made toys accounted for about 10 per cent of Hong Kong's total exports (including domestic exports and re-exports) (ibid.). In 1988, for the first time, re-exports of toys exceeded domestic exports. Of a total export figure of HK$26bn, HK$16bn were re-exports: toys worth HK$9bn were imported by the United States and HK$4bn by the European Community (Hong Kong Trade Development Council 1990).

By the early 1990s, of all Hong Kong's industries, the toy sector was the second most active investor in China's Pearl River Delta, next only to electronics. The labour-intensive nature of much of the production process meant that firms could clearly take advantage of the cheap labour supply in China. The shift of production was also prompted by rising wages, labour shortages, and rising land and rental costs in Hong Kong. The labour shortages, which arose in Hong Kong in the late 1980s, put additional

Table 8.2 Numbers of establishments and persons employed in Hong Kong's toy industry, 1960–95

Year	Number of establishments	Number of persons employed
1960	204	7430
1965	491	20227
1970	1137	39473
1975	1389	37333
1980	2128	55644
1985	2245	51078
1986	2264	56164
1987	2151	49034
1988	2003	39684
1990	1735	24734
1991	1431	18715
1993	1138	12246
1994	821	7884
1995	680	5689

Source: Hong Kong Government Industry Department, *Hong Kong's Manufacturing Industries 1996*

pressure on manufacturers already suffering from increasing wage costs. Toy manufacturing requires a large number of manual workers for the assembly processes, and the scarcity of labour therefore adversely affected the competitiveness of Hong Kong manufacturing compared to other Asian production locations (Federation of Hong Kong Industries 1992).

Thus, Hong Kong manufacturers began to establish a commodity chain, by extending production across the border, but leaving control largely in Hong Kong. Whilst such labour-intensive processes were relocated, other essential elements of the production chain remained in Hong Kong. Those elements of the manufacturing process requiring higher levels of technology or more refined skills have tended to be carried out in Hong Kong (ibid.), with shipments of components forming a significant part of Hong Kong's domestic exports to China.[5] The intangible elements of the production chain, i.e. the administration, design and marketing functions, also remain in Hong Kong, but the bulk of production is done over the border. The proximity of the Pearl River Delta also permitted the minimisation of transportation costs for both goods and technical/managerial staff, thus allowing easier management control. A desire for management control was also instrumental in the choice of wholly owned subsidiaries for the majority of ventures in China. Flexibility is important in the toy industry, which relies upon innovation and a rapid response to market trends for survival, and this could be compromised if joint venture partners were involved.

The result of this extension of the production chain into China has been the replacement of toys originating in Hong Kong by toys originating in

China. Estimates suggest that the majority of Hong Kong's toy factories have been relocated over the border and that, by 1995, there were around 3,000 factories in China, employing over 1.3 million people.[6] Management control remains very largely in Hong Kong hands, as too does the control over distribution: the majority of exports from China are routed through Hong Kong as re-exports. As Table 8.3 shows, Hong Kong's domestic exports of toys have plummeted since 1987 while total exports, including re-exports, have risen dramatically.

In 1994, Hong Kong's total toy exports had risen to HK$69bn, of which HK$65bn were re-exports of China origin. The proportion of toys produced under licensing or contract manufacturing arrangements with overseas firms declined somewhat from the 1980s, but still remained a high 70 per cent. The major overseas manufacturers were mostly American. The main firms acting as principals were Fisher-Price, Hasbro, Tyco and Ertl from the USA, followed by Bandai and Tomy from Japan.[7]

Other features of the production chain have, however, remained broadly unchanged, arguably since the inception of the toy industry in Hong Kong in the early 1950s. The governance structure of the toy industry fits well with Gereffi's concept of a buyer-driven chain. In this case, foreign buyers provide the access to markets along with designs and, in some cases, proprietary brands. The dominant buyers are, and have been from the early days of the industry, US firms. Their access to the large integrated US market ensures large shipments, and hence economies of scale. In addition, US firms also possess greater bargaining power than is found among buyers from either Japan or Europe.

Table 8.3 Hong Kong's domestic exports and re-exports of toys, 1982–96 (HK$m)

Year	Domestic exports	Re-exports		Total exports
		Total	Of which China origin	
1982	9191	389	187	9580
1983	8917	514	326	9431
1984	11621	1693	1421	13314
1985	9877	2838	2497	12715
1986	11753	4767	4478	16520
1987	11924	8571	8200	20495
1988	10000	15900	—	25900
1989	6975	24030	23468	31005
1990	5306	31468	30762	36774
1991	4641	39312	38279	43953
1992	3882	54638	53410	58520
1993	3118	59450	58040	62568
1994	2573	66631	65260	69204
1995	2509	75207	73306	77716
1996	1686	79536	77333	81222

Source: Hong Kong Trade Development Council, *Industry and Product Profile* (various issues)

Figure 8.1 shows the linkages in the global production chain. Thus the dominant roles are played by US manufacturers as the major governors of the chain, providing designs, brands and marketing. A closely similar role is played by the big retailers, of which Toys R Us is the dominant specialist firm globally, and which include the discount chains of K-Mart and Wal-mart and the main department stores, such as Sears and JC Penney. The second level of the chain is occupied by Hong Kong firms who provide services to both overseas buyers and to the producers in China. These may be trading firms who have little or no involvement in manufacturing, or may be the operators of manufacturing plant. The third level is the factory. Generally, as we have seen, factories are located in China, but with a high proportion of Hong Kong ownership and management. European toy manufacturers play a much less prominent role in the production chain. Due partly to the smaller size of the market and its fragmentation through language when compared to the USA, the Europeans source largely through importers who act as wholesalers to the trade. Thus, with the sole exception of the Danish company Lego, no large manufacturer exists that is comparable to Hasbro or Mattel of the United States, nor has any specialist retailer emerged to compete in any way with Toys R Us.

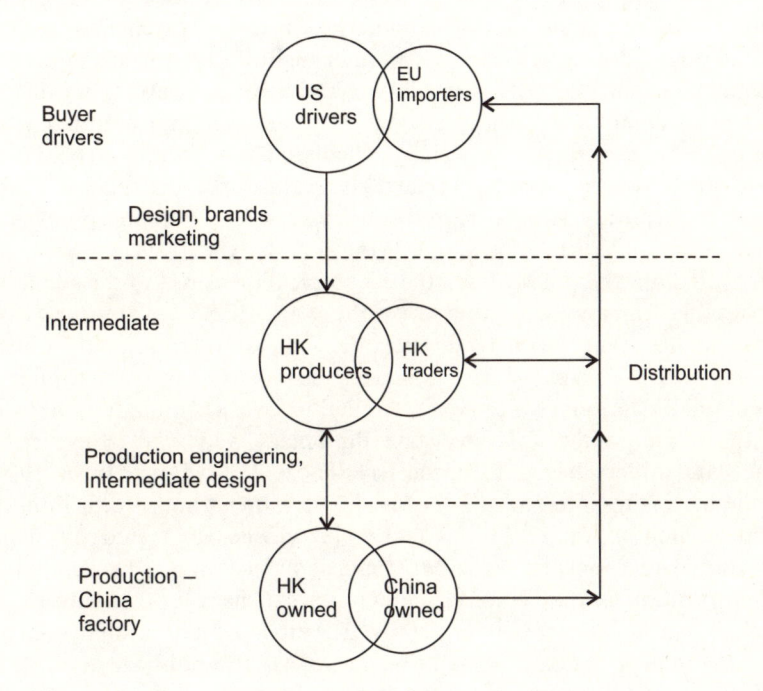

Figure 8.1 Levels of hierarchy in the commodity chain of the toy trade between the European Union and China

However, the US firms are multinational with a significant market presence and with regional headquarters in Europe. These firms, together with Lego and Bandai, dominate the TME, which was formed in the early 1990s as a political lobbying group serving the interests of the toy multinationals.[8]

From the preceding analysis, it is clear that these interests are being damaged by the EU quotas on Chinese-made toys. The China input is one element of a global commodity chain that starts and ends with the toy MNEs as buyer–governors. As these firms do not manufacture in Europe, their interest lies in maintaining open markets for countries that are the source of their production. As China is the dominant source of production, therefore, the imposition of quotas on Chinese toys was opposed by the TME.

TRADE RELATIONS: BEYOND COMMODITY CHAIN ANALYSIS

This, however, raises the question of why the quotas should have been imposed in the first place. If, as the TME contended, few if any European jobs were at stake and the limited manufacturing capability in Europe was not significant, what were the quotas designed to protect? One of the key issues facing the toy MNCs was the EU-wide nature of these barriers. Thus countries that had been quota-free under the prior arrangements, such as the United Kingdom and Germany, were brought into the protectionist net by the new system. 'Global commodity chain' analysis is no longer of help when approaching such issues and, hence, other tools are required when trade policy is considered, especially when policy is formulated in a regional, rather than a national, context. Given also the interplay of firms, and hence corporate strategies, and government policy in the practice of international trade, there is a need for an analytical system that can incorporate both the political and the economic dimensions of the situation.

A suitable framework is offered by the work of Susan Strange (1988, 1991) who has done much to develop the field of International Political Economy (IPE). This particular framework has its roots in the discipline of international relations which was, originally, overwhelmingly concerned with the 'high politics' of inter-state diplomacy and war. However, as Strange and others began to argue (see Tooze 1984; Barry-Jones 1983), with the increasing internalisation of trade, investment and production, the concept of international relations had to be widened to include all major international relationships, whether political or economic. The underpinning proposition is that empirical outcomes can have both political and economic causes, and this is especially true in the international domain. Hence theoretical perspectives that isolate either the political or the economic arenas are in danger of overlooking major causal factors. As early as 1970, Strange was first arguing this point, suggesting that the international political system itself was undergoing changes caused by shifts in the international economic system.

This view sparked a criticism of conventional paradigms that attempted to explain international political and economic behaviour. Both traditional international relations and neo-classical economics were attacked for limiting their analysis, the former to politics, the latter to the market with its concurrent dismissal of political action as an 'externality'. The attack was not confined to liberalism alone, however, but was also levelled at mercantilist and radical perspectives. The former was based upon assumptions of political hegemony over economic behaviour, and the latter for offering explanations based on a belief that the political agenda is dominated by the economic upper class. Both were criticised for their assumptions of a fixed hierarchy of political and economic forces and factors.

The major difference between IPE and the three foregoing perspectives (i.e. liberalism, mercantilism, and radical perspectives) lies in the assumption of a shifting balance of power between politics and economics, rather than there being either a separation of the two or, alternatively, a fixed hierarchy. Thus, the relationship between political and economic actors is central to IPE analysis. These actors are conceptualised as authorities, on the one hand, of which the organisations of the state are predominant and, on the other hand, as markets with producers playing the major role. Strange proposes a bargaining model. Fundamental to this is the role of power, with the relationship between markets and authorities conceptualised as negotiations, characterised by varying degrees of bargaining power. A further feature is a taxonomy of the global political and economic system. This classifies the system into four major elements: production, security, finance and knowledge. These are regarded as structures within the system, suggesting that there is therefore a degree of permanence attached to each. However, the relationship of actors within each structure is seen to vary, as does the influence of the structures on one another. Each is seen to have a possible influence on the others but in unspecified and varying ways. Indeed, this framework stresses change and inconsistency, directing our attention to variations in relationships and influences, both across the four structures and within each, as the bargaining relationships between authorities and markets shift with the situation. The following section examines the changes in EU trade policy towards China using the IPE framework as a means of analysis.

EU POLICY ON IMPORTS OF TOYS FROM CHINA

The imposition of EU-wide quotas on certain Chinese products in 1994, see Chapter 3, was in part a response to EU concerns over its growing trade imbalance with China. Prior to the introduction of the Single European Market (SEM), imports of more than thirty non-textile products from China were governed by national quotas in certain EU Member States. Such an import regime could not function within a single market, either conceptually or practically, as the absence of internal frontier controls would render separate national quotas impossible to enforce. A proposal for Union-wide quotas on nine product groups was drawn up in late 1992, but it was not until February 1994 that agreement was reached by the Member States.[9]

This final outcome was a compromise between two opposing views held by different Member States. Those proposing liberalisation included the United Kingdom, Germany, the Netherlands and Denmark.[10] In favour of a restricted trade regime were principally the southern EU States of Spain, Italy, and Greece, with support from France.[11] The resulting compromise reduced the number of quota categories to seven (gloves, footwear, tableware and kitchenware, glassware, car radios, and toys) from the nine originally proposed (bicycles and chloramphenicol were excluded). At the same time, a further twenty-seven products that had been under quota in certain Member States, became quota-free on a Union-wide basis.

Implementation of the proposal led to an extension of the quota system to previously quota-free countries. Denmark, Greece, France, Italy, Portugal and the United Kingdom – all of which had been quota-free – thus introduced quotas on toys of China origin. The final proposal imposed quotas on three types of toys: stuffed toys, including teddy bears (product type 9503 41); non-human toys, such as dinosaurs and Ninja Turtles (product type 9503 49); and other toys, including die-cast miniatures (product type 9503 90). Each category was allocated a separate quota, which together totalled 793m ecu.[12] By comparison (see Table 8.4), imports of these categories totalled 992m ecu in 1992 and 1,153m ecu in 1993. Not all toy products were included in the quota system. The proposal left untouched such categories as dolls and train sets which represented, in total, imports valued at 988m ecu in 1992 and 1,044m ecu in 1993 (Commission of the European Communities 1995).

The reaction from producers in China was predictably critical, with accusations of protectionism reported in the local press,[13] despite the selective nature of the toy quotas. A further major criticism concerned the speed with which the proposal had been implemented and the uncertainty over the mechanics of implementation.[14] The effective implementation date was 15

Table 8.4 EU imports of toys from China, 1992–94 (million ecu)

Product type	1992	1993	1994
9503 41	260	303	248
9503 49	111	171	89
9503 90	621	679	478
Total quota items	992	1153	815
Non-quota items	988	1044	1255
TOTAL TOY IMPORTS	1980	2197	2070

Source: Commission of the European Communities (1995)

March 1994; the regulations, however, were only published on 10 March 1994. The result was that goods consigned after 15 March would immediately be subject to the new quotas, although goods in transit would not be affected.[15] Adding emphasis to the industry criticisms, was the incomplete manner in which the regulations were imposed. As Hong Kong's Trade Development Council reported, the 'EU has yet to decide the methods of allocating quotas. Probably, quotas will be allocated on the basis of historical import performance, although an element of "first come, first served" will apply'.[16] The result of this delay was that goods awaiting consignment could not be imported into Europe until such allocations were made, and such allocations would not be made until Brussels had decided on the rules of allocation. Consequently, shipments were in danger of being delayed and of incurring storage charges while remaining in Hong Kong.[17]

At this stage in the dispute, the industry in China and Hong Kong was alone in challenging the European Union. If we now adopt the state/market balance central to Strange's IPE framework, we see a distinct imbalance in which the market was left in a very weak bargaining position. The fragmented nature of the organisation of production into many small firms, linked only through buyer-driven production chains, left producers without the power to launch a strong negotiation. The majority affected by the new quotas comprised Hong Kong firms operating in China. A critical feature of this form of production was that these firms were not able to seek the assistance of the Hong Kong Government. Hong Kong was unable to take up the case on behalf of manufacturing operations in China, irrespective of the location of ownership. At the same time, the Chinese authorities were more concerned about maintaining EU support for China's GATT membership application and were thus reluctant to lobby on behalf of the toy producers.[18]

This position changed, however, with the entry of the UK Government into the dispute. In May 1994, the British began to lobby on behalf of the toy producers. In June, this effort became more serious as the Department of Trade and Industry launched legal action against the European Union in the European Court of Justice. The UK Government accused the European Union of failing to give correct and/or adequate reasons for the imposition of quotas, of failing to carry out any appreciation of the facts, of imposing an arbitrary quota on the contested toys, and of breaching the principles of proportionality and equal treatment.[19]

The UK action proposed the annulment of the regulations imposing the quotas on Chinese toy imports. The British (state) action was a direct result of pressure from the industry body, the TME. As a result of this pressure from the state, the European Commission agreed to a retrospective increase in the quotas in August across all three categories, although the Council subsequently approved an uplift (of some 29 per cent) only for the category of stuffed toys.[20] This clearly illustrates the state/market bargaining processes that form a central element of the IPE framework. The bargaining chain at this stage was composed of European toy importers, whose major source of products lay in China. They were able to exert pressure on the UK Government to negotiate with the Commission. Without such bargaining pressure stemming from the buyers in the governance chain, it is unlikely that any revision of quotas would have been made. In contrast, the original quotas were left unchanged for other categories of Chinese products which faced similar unilateral quotas. This was so for ceramics and glassware, where no special representations were made by importers, and the original quotas set by the Commission were implemented in their original form.[21]

Following this move, the TME began lobbying in China. In August, their representatives met China's Minister of Foreign Trade, Madame Wu Yi, in Beijing to seek support for further anti-quota lobbying in the European Union. The focus of the argument was the lack of justification for the quotas.[22] In all the foregoing, the Commission put forward neither an economic justification for the quotas, nor any rationale for the levels of the quotas. When the toy quotas were first proposed, the level would have been such as to restrict imports in 1994 to 79 per cent of the value of imports in 1992.[23]

TRADE POLICY AND BARGAINING MODELS

It is therefore necessary to consider possible explanations for this apparently arbitrary decision. Again the state/market bargaining concept is useful in that it directs our attention to the political economy of the situation, rather than to a consideration only of the politics of the European Union, or alternatively just the economic position of traders and manufacturers. Two possible explanations exist, one at a Union-wide level and the second, related, explanation at the national level.

The broad aim of the Union-wide quotas was to prevent back-door entry for Chinese goods. When quotas were applied nationally, it was possible to gain access to such restricted national markets by first importing goods into Member States where there were no quotas for those goods.[24] As the Single Market reduced even further the border controls between Member States, quota controls at the national level could thus be readily eroded. The main thrust for the imposition of quotas on toys was orchestrated by the Spanish Government.[25] Europe's remaining toy manufacturing base lies in Spain and, to a lesser degree, in Germany. Initial support for the quotas was lent by Germany, but this was withdrawn later in the year, leaving Spain as the main protagonist.[26] Spain had emerged from a protectionist background and, together with the other 'southern' states of the European Union, was concerned about too much market liberalisation. The final outcome was the result of intra-EU bargaining carried out at the level of each Member State's Trade Minister, and was thus not necessarily technically rational. This would help explain why the initial quotas were set so low relative to the import values recorded two years earlier. It would also explain why a further paradox was created. One of the main categories of toys to be excluded from the quotas was dolls. Yet much of Spain's manufacturing capability lies in the production of these toys and, prior to the March quotas, Spain had stringent national quotas on dolls.[27] A bargaining process, which leads to losses traded for gains would offer an explanation for this paradox.

Opposing the Spanish position were the industry lobby groups led by the TME. Having achieved greater levels of state support in Britain, in China, and latterly in Germany, the industry then began to take a direct confrontational approach with the European Commission. The earlier analysis based on 'global commodity chains' may now be related to this state/market bargaining perspective to highlight the principal actors. The dominant buyers in the production chain were US brand holders, such as Hasbro and Mattel, and also similar Japanese companies such as Bandai. All are members of the TME.[28] Hence it would appear that the major thrust of the anti-quota movement was orchestrated by US and Japanese multinationals, whose principal production sites are located in China. This conclusion is reinforced by a separate court action brought against the Commission and the Council in December 1994 by the European subsidiaries of the American company, Tyco Toys Inc.[29] Again the pressure brought by the market, even prior to the action being heard in court, had an effect on the authorities. In March 1995, the EU Foreign Ministers agreed to raise the quotas for the year beginning January 1996. Quotas on stuffed toys would be increased by 36.8 per cent, on animals by 58.3 per cent, and the quota on other toys, such as die-cast models, would be increased by 27.8 per cent.[30]

No further liberalisation measures have followed this action, and the European Court of Justice, in 1996, rejected the UK Government's attempt to have the quotas removed. The question arises whether, after two and a half years, the bargain with Spain should not be breaking down even further in the face of continued opposition. Again, reference to the bargaining model may offer an explanation. The bargain in this case is no longer an intra-EU matter, but rather one between the European Union and China. Intentionally or not, the European Union has created a bargaining position that may be used in future trade negotiations with China. Thus toy quotas may in future, perhaps, be traded for Chinese concessions that permit greater market access for EU products and firms. The existence of toy quotas may follow from this position with respect to China as well as a result of Spain's continuing insistence on maintaining quotas.

CONCLUDING REMARKS

This chapter began with the observation of the apparently paradoxical behaviour being exhibited by the Toy Manufacturers of Europe in opposing EU quotas on China-made toys. Analysis of the international organisation of toy manufacturing has shown, however, that such behaviour is to be expected, given the extensive use made by these manufacturers of production sites in China. The complexity of international production was highlighted through the use of 'global commodity chain' analysis, which revealed the fragmented nature of the ownership of production. Thus, the European manufacturers are largely composed of US and Japanese toy multinationals, who source product from China using sub-contracting and licensing arrangements, before selling in Europe under their own brands. The complexity is increased by the way in which toy production is organised regionally. The analysis showed that by far the largest part of EU imports of toys was produced by HK-owned firms who have relocated their factories to China.

This suggests that trade policy, and the organisational structure of international production in such industries as toys, no longer map onto one another. Whilst this has been evident for some time in the extension of production within integrated multinational corporations, there have been relatively clear organisational boundaries even though these overlap two or more national boundaries. With the further extension of production in commodity chains in which there are multiple organisational boundaries, then the difficulty of formulating trade policy becomes more acute.

What is required therefore, for both analysts and policy-makers, is a conceptual framework that can accommodate these complexities at both the macro level of policy formulation and the micro level of the organisation of production. The framework offered by 'global commodity chain' analysis helps unravel the micro complexities, but is of little help in analysing the wider political and economic issues at the policy level. International Political Economy offered a means of examining the broader issues, especially through its emphasis on bargaining. This brought out the relative positions of the main actors in the situation in respect to their power to influence policy. To recap, the main actors were the European Union, the governments of Britain, Germany and Spain, the TME, the Hong Kong manufacturers with factories in China, and the Chinese Government.

The relative bargaining positions in this dispute were defined partly by the rules of the European Union, partly by conventions in international trade negotiations, and partly by the way in which production is organised. Thus, the Government of Hong Kong was unable to negotiate on behalf of its producers, because those producers no longer located production in Hong Kong. It follows that the Government of China was the only party able to influence the European Union formally on behalf of Asian producers. China's bargaining position in this specific area was, however, influenced by its on-going application to join the WTO, and the concomitant need to engender support from, among others, the European Union. The producers themselves, therefore, were left in a weak bargaining position. This was also true for the toy multinationals who were not formally party to the negotiations under the EU rules. The only recourse for the TME was to lobby, and to obtain the cooperation of individual governments. Only these bodies were able to take part formally in the negotiations. Hence the bargaining model helps in the analysis of the macro level issues inherent in this case. Unfortunately it is problematic to obtain hard data on bargaining positions taken by the main actors, namely, the Trade Ministers of the EU Member States and the Trade Ministry of China. Such negotiations are conducted in private, and hence a degree of speculation is required in interpreting observed empirical outcomes.

There are implications for theory and policy that emerge from this case and its analysis. In the first instance, it is clear that analysis of trade issues requires a theoretical framework that can operate at both the macro level of international politics and economics, and at the level of the global production process. The preceding analysis has adopted two distinct conceptual approaches in order to achieve this. What is needed is an approach that can blend the two. To some extent these two can be linked. The IPE taxonomy includes the production structure as one of the four constituents of the political economy, within which power is taken as a dominant variable. Whilst this power construct translates into a model of bargaining positions between states and firms, it is also within the purview of the model to consider power positions within production processes such as those outlined in this case. Thus the link with the 'global commodity chain' approach is established by first locating commodity chains within the production structure of the IPE framework. Second, the notion of the governance structure within the commodity chain is consistent with the emphasis on power in the IPE. The governors have power over the lower levels of production in the chain, and hence the same bargaining model can be applied at this level with conceptual consistency.

When considering policy implications, the prime issue in this particular case is, what constitutes a Chinese toy? Given the parties to the production bargain revealed by the 'global commodity chain' analysis, which national party should be considered the dominant actor? Toys are designed in one state, carry a brand name from another state, are made in factories in yet another, yet those factories are owned by actors from none of these states but from yet another. They are then sold in another state by a firm that has its ultimate locus of control in the state in which the design and branding functions take place. At the general level, the problem is that trade policy is nationally bounded, focusing on countries as the origin of products, rather than on organisations. As organisations have become more loosely coordinated, and as the linkages that bind the fragmented parts of the production process have become more diverse, it has become increasingly difficult for trade policy to capture this global diversity. As production processes continue to become more complex, more fragmented not only in terms of location but also in terms of the ownership and control of different functional elements of the process, it may no longer be possible for trade policy to be formulated on the basis of national models of organisation.

NOTES

1 *South China Morning Post*, 8 June 1994.
2 Industry sources.
3 Tsui (1988) notes that Louis Marx, known as the 'King of Toys', owned the then largest toy firm in the United States and was the first American to set up a factory in Hong Kong, against the mainstream tide of opinion.
4 Hong Kong Trade Development Council (1995) *Industry and Produce Profile*, no. 19.
5 Census and Statistics Department, *Hong Kong Trade Statistics: Domestic Exports and Re-exports: Annual Supplement 1994*.
6 BBC Monitoring Service: Asia Pacific, 14 June 1995.
7 Hong Kong Trade Development Council (1995) *Industry and Produce Profile*, no. 19.
8 Industry sources.
9 *Trade Watch*, March 1994.
10 *Trade Watch*, March 1994.
11 German industry sources.
12 *Trade Watch*, March 1994.
13 *China Daily*, 17 March 1994.
14 Industry sources.
15 *Trade Watch*, 18 March 1994.
16 *Trade Watch*, 18 March 1994: 1.
17 *South China Morning Post*, 19 April 1994.
18 *South China Morning Post*, 20 March 1994.
19 *Official Journal of the European Communities* no. L 25 November 1994.
20 *EU Monitor*, September 1994.
21 *EU Monitor*, March 1994.
22 *Agence Europe*, 27 August 1994.
23 *EU Monitor*, March 1994.
24 *EU Monitor*, March 1993.
25 Industry sources.
26 *South China Morning Post*, 13 December 1994.
27 *South China Morning Post*, 8 June 1994.
28 Industry sources and *South China Morning Post*, 13 December 1994.
29 *Official Journal of the European Communities*, no. L 23 December 1994.
30 *Reuters News Service*, 6 March 1995.

REFERENCES

Barry-Jones, R. (ed.) (1983) *Perspectives on Political Economy*, London: Frances Pinter.
Census and Statistics Department, *Hong Kong Trade Statistics: Domestic Export and Re-export*, Hong Kong: Census and Statistics Department, various issues.
Census and Statistics Department, *Hong Kong Trade Statistics: Domestic Export and Re-export: Annual Supplement*, Hong Kong: Census and Statistics Department, various issues.
Census and Statistics Department, *Quarterly Report*, Hong Kong: Census and Statistics Department, various issues.
Commission of the European Communities (1995) COM(95)614, Report from the Commission to the Council on the Surveillance Measures and Quantitative Quotas Applicable to Certain Non-Textile Products Originating in the People's

Republic of China, Luxembourg: Office for Official Publications of the European Communities.
Dicken, P. (1992) *Global Shift*, London: Paul Chapman Publishing.
EU Monitor, various issues as shown.
Federation of Hong Kong Industries (1962) *Industry in Hong Kong*, Hong Kong: The South China Morning Post Ltd.
Federation of Hong Kong Industries (1992) *Hong Kong's Industrial Investment in the Pearl River Delta: 1991 Survey Among Members of the Federation of Hong Kong Industries*, Hong Kong: Federation of Hong Kong Industries.
General Administration of Customs of the People's Republic of China (ed.) *China Customs Statistics Yearbook*, Hong Kong: Economic Information & Agency, (various issues).
Gereffi, G. (1992) 'New Realities of Industrial Development in East Asia and Latin America', in R.P. Appelbaum and J. Henderson (eds) *States and Development in the Asian Pacific Rim*, New Bury Park, CA: Sage Publications, pp.85–112.
Gereffi, G. and Korzeniewicz, M. (eds) (1994) *Commodity Chains and Global Capitalism*, Westport, CONN: Greenwood Press.
Government Industry Department, *Hong Kong's Manufacturing Industries*, Hong Kong: Hong Kong Government Industry Department, (various years).
Hong Kong Trade Development Council (1973) *Statistical Brief on Hong Kong's Toys Exports and Major Import Markets for Toys*, Hong Kong: Hong Kong Trade Development Council.
Hong Kong Trade Development Council (1987) *Brief on Hong Kong's Toy Industry*, Hong Kong: Hong Kong Trade Development Council.
Hong Kong Trade Development Council (1990) *Hong Kong's Major Exports: Statistical Yearbook Volume 2: 1990*, Hong Kong: Hong Kong Trade Development Council.
Hong Kong Trade Development Council *Industry and Produce Profile*, Hong Kong: Trade Development Council, various issues.
Murphy, C. and Tooze, R. (eds) (1991) *The New International Political Economy*, Boulder, CO: Lynne Reiner.
Official Journal of the European Communities, no. C202, 25 November 1994.
Official Journal of the European Communities, no. C254, 23 December 1994.
Riedel, J. (1974) *The Industrialization of Hong Kong*, Tübingen: J.C.B. Mohr (Paul Siebeck).
South China Morning Post, various issues as shown.
Standard Chartered Bank (1988) *The Toy Industry in Hong Kong*, Hong Kong: Marketing Research and Information Section, Corporate Banking Division.
Strange S. (1970) 'International Economic Relations: A Case of Mutual Neglect', *International Affairs*, 46(2): 304–15.
Strange, S. (ed.) (1984) *Paths to International Political Economy*, London: Allen & Unwin.
Strange, S. (1988) *States and Markets*, London: Pinter Publishers.
Strange, S. (1991) 'An Eclectic Approach', in C.N. Murphy and R. Tooze (eds) *The New International Political Economy*, Boulder, CO: Lynne Reiner, pp.33–49.
Tooze, R. (1984) 'Perspectives and Theory: A Consumer's Guide' in S. Strange (ed.) *Paths to International Political Economy*, London: Allen & Unwin, pp.1–22.
Trade Watch, various issues as shown.
Tsui, E. (1988) 'Marketing Strategies of the Toy Industry in Hong Kong', unpublished MBA dissertation, Hong Kong: University of Hong Kong.
United Nations. *International Trade Statistics Yearbook*, New York: United Nations Statistics Office, (various issues).

9 The persistence of key capabilities in flexible production networks
The watch industry in Switzerland and Hong Kong/China

Howard Davies[1]

INTRODUCTION

Recent years have seen a growing interest among economic geographers in the development of sub-national regional economies which achieve significant shares of the global market for some ranges of product through 'flexible specialisation' in production networks of small firms. Such networks have been presented as a new form of industrial organisation which offers a viable alternative to the hierarchy of the vertically-integrated corporation. At the same time, a different stream of literature, that on strategic management, has become increasingly interested in the concept of 'capabilities', which are 'difficult-to-reproduce' resources which allow firms to secure profitable market positions in the face of competition.

This chapter uses the example of the watch industry in Switzerland and Hong Kong to link these concepts by exploring the idea that localised production networks in different places may display widely different capabilities, even in the same industry. Those capabilities appear to be persistent, arising from the accumulated experience of the firms involved, and they allow the participating firms to compete successfully for as long as there are significant market niches for which those capabilities are well suited. However, if market conditions or technologies change to the extent where they require the development of new capabilities, the supposedly flexible networks tend to fail. Only the larger and more vertically integrated firms, working through hierarchies, have been able to achieve flexibility in this broader sense.

In the Jura Arc region of Switzerland, the production network has an established capability in precision and micro-mechanical engineering, which was traditionally a source of strength, allowing it to dominate the watch industry. However, when that capability was rendered less valuable in the volume segment of the watch industry, the production network of small firms was unable to respond effectively. The firms who survived within the old paradigm were those who focused on the high-price segment of the market in which the old capabilities remained valuable. The low-price segment of the market was abandoned until a large and vertically integrated firm was able to assemble a new and different set of capabilities. The economy of the Swiss Jura Arc became more diversified around the micro-technological capability which had previously been the foundation of the watch industry.

In Hong Kong (and its hinterland in mainland China) the production network in the watch industry has a very different but equally persistent capability. In this case, it lies in 'merchant-manufacturing', which allows it to coordinate efficient order-taking with the rapid acquisition and assembly of components. That gives it the ability to compete very effectively on price, product variety, and speed of delivery in the low-to-middle price segments of the market. However, faced with tightening margins and the need to address higher price segments, the vertically disintegrated production network has to date been unable effectively to 'upgrade' its technology and the quality of its products. Only a small number of much larger and more integrated firms have shown signs of such 'upgrading', although even they appear to remain constrained within the trading and merchant-manufacturing tradition.

FLEXIBLE PRODUCTION NETWORKS AS A MODEL FOR ECONOMIC DEVELOPMENT

The observation that networks of relatively small local firms have proved capable of taking and maintaining significant shares of the global market has prompted the view that such networks represent a new form of industrial organisation. The example of success stories from Italy like the network of firms coordinated by Benetton (Belussi 1992), the 'industrial districts' of Emilia Romagna (Beccatini 1990), and the ceramic tile industry around Sassuolo (Porter 1990), combined with American parallels in Silicon Valley (Saxenian 1990), Massachusetts (Castells and Hall 1994) and Hollywood (Powell 1990; Storper and Christopherson 1987) has led to the view that networks of small vertically disaggregated firms working in close proximity to each other represent a model for economic development which is superior to one based on large vertically integrated firms coordinated by their managerial hierarchies (Best 1990; Amin and Robbins 1990). Given its relationship to Porter's popular concept of the internationally competitive 'cluster' of industries (Porter 1990), and the extent to which it echoes Marshall's concept of the 'industrial district' where the 'secrets of industry are in the air' (Foray 1991), the idea of the localised production network of small firms as an efficient and effective form of organisation has received significant support, even as far afield as China, where some observers have suggested that it presents a more appropriate model for the development of Guangdong Province than that which is currently in place (Lau 1996).

This view has not gone unchallenged, particularly with respect to the adaptive and innovative abilities of a system composed entirely of small firms. Florida and Kenney (1990) aver that the success of small firms in Silicon Valley has been highly dependent upon their being sponsored by the large user firms which exist in the same area while Saxenian (1994) concludes that the Valley may lack the regulatory institutions needed for longevity. Ferguson (1990) suggests that innovative small firms frequently lose market share to technologically inferior units of large corporations, due to the latter's access to key marketing assets. Harrison (1994) points to the emergence of large, 'peak' organisations in proximity to production networks, which may be a response to their adaptive inadequacies. Others have gone further, suggesting that the much-vaunted flexibly specialised production networks may be little more than a modern form of 'outworking', securing market share on the basis of sweatshop conditions imposed on a fragmented workforce (Lazerson 1989; Shutt and Whittington 1987).

In this chapter, the key questions with respect to production networks made up of small firms concern the extent to which they are efficient substitutes for large corporations as mechanisms for adaptation and innovation, the nature of the capabilities they possess, and the extent to which their ability to change and develop is circumscribed by those capabilities.

THE ADAPTIVE EFFICACY OF PRODUCTION NETWORKS

Various conceptual frameworks are available for the analysis of production networks as a mode of organisation, and for the development of comparisons between them and other modes. Piore and Sabel (1984) use the distinction between 'flexible' production and 'mass' production, associating the former with product specialisation and variety, inter-firm networks and external economies of scale, and the latter with product standardisation, vertical integration and internal economies of scale. Salais and Storper (1992) develop a typology depicting 'four worlds of production', differentiated by markets, technologies and products having different characteristics. Commodity chain analysis (Hopkins and Wallerstein 1986; Gereffi and Korzeniewicz 1994) enables a focus on the organisation of production, the geographical location of each stage of the process, flows between those stages, and the distribution of surplus among the participants in the core and periphery of the world economy.

While these frameworks are useful for the purposes for which they were designed, none of them explicitly addresses the question of 'how effectively is adaptation achieved and what are its limits?' Williamson's development of transactions cost analysis as a means of analysing different types of adaptability mechanism (Williamson 1991), in combination with Chandler's analysis of scale and scope (Chandler 1990), provides such an opportunity and is therefore used here.

The starting point for the analysis lies in Williamson's distinction between two different types of adaptation. The first is 'autonomous adaptation'. This is the kind of adaptation which can be effectively carried out in a decentralised way by independent firms linked only by the market nexus. It will be effective when price signals contain all the information which is required for firms to make the necessary adjustments. The identity of individual buyers and sellers is immaterial, they have no dependency relations to each other, being able to deal with others at negligible extra cost, and transactions are self-liquidating – 'sharp in by clear agreement; sharp out by clear performance' (Macneil 1978: 738). This kind of adaptation is supported by classical contract law and represents the 'marvel of the market' as described by Hayek (1945). If demand for an existing commodity increases, to take the simplest example, prices will rise and independent firms will choose to increase output. Demand for inputs will rise and they will also be produced in greater quantity by the supplying sector. The intensity of incentives is strong as each party to the transaction directly appropriates the resulting net receipts, and administrative controls are not required.

If all disturbances could be effectively adapted through autonomous adaptation, the market alone would suffice to provide a high performance system. However, it will only be effective when there are no dependency relations among the different actors, when economies of scale or scope are insignificant, and when there are no important externalities. If dependency relations do exist, there is a need to coordinate investments because independent actions could be at cross-purposes with each other. Similarly, if there are economies of scope or scale, autonomous adaptation will fail because coordination between separable activities is required (in the case of scope economies), or it would be inefficient for more than a few investments to be made (in the case of scale economies). If externalities exist in the form of benefits (from R&D or labour force training, for instance), there will be under-provision of key assets, essentially because prices do not signal their full value.

In each of these cases, a different type of adaptation is necessary, described by Williamson as 'coordinated adaptation'. This is necessary whenever price signals alone are not sufficient to induce the requisite changes, as when scope, scale or externalities matter, the identity of the transactors is important, when they are not free to deal with others at low cost, and where the transaction is closer to a medium- or long-term relationship than a spot transaction. 'Coordinated adaptation' may be achieved within the managerial hierarchy, and it is that type of adaptation which Barnard (1938) and Chandler (1990) identify as the great strength of the corporation. Within the hierarchy incentives are weak, which encourages cooperation between employees and managers, and administrative controls are the major instrument through which desired ends are met.

The key factors which determine the relative efficacy of market and hierarchy, therefore, are the degree of asset-specificity, the extent of economies of scale or scope and the presence of externalities. In its simplest form this analysis takes no explicit account of production networks, focusing on markets and hierarchies, which are the polar cases. However, production networks may be characterised as 'hybrid' forms of governance occupying a space between the polar cases and sharing the characteristics of both (Williamson 1991: 281). Hybrids are 'semi-strong' with respect to both incentives and administrative controls. They are inferior to the market but superior to the hierarchy in respect of 'autonomous adaptation', but superior to the market and inferior to the hierarchy in respect of 'coordinated adaptation'. This intermediate status makes it possible for networks to be more effective than either the market or the hierarchy in an intermediate range of situations.

The extent of that range depends upon the threat of opportunistic behaviour within the network or, conversely, the degree of trust which members of the network are able to place in each other. If trust is well established, and supported by mechanisms for its continuous renewal, the dangers arising from opportunistic behaviour will be reduced. Such 'trust-enhanced networks' (Carney 1996) will be more effective mechanisms for 'coordinated adaptation'. They will be superior to the hierarchy up to a higher level of asset-specificities and in the face of more extensive externalities, and they may even be able to coordinate where there are economies of scale and scope. On the other hand, if trust is not well developed, the network is thereby 'unenhanced' and approximates more closely to a market system. As such, it will only be able to function effectively in situations where 'autonomous adaptation' will suffice and 'coordinated adaptation' is not required.

CAPABILITIES AND ADAPTATION MECHANISMS

Adaptation is required when disturbances take place, and disturbances vary in their significance. Small-scale disturbances may be thought of as those which may be successfully adapted to with existing sets of capital equipment, knowledge and skills. Medium-scale disturbances require investment in new capital equipment within the industry's existing knowledge base. Large-scale disturbances require the renewal of the industry's knowledge base and the development of new capabilities. The central question being considered here concerns the relative efficacy of hierarchies and production networks in adapting to large-scale disturbances. This may be addressed by considering the nature of capability and the analysis of production networks' adaptive efficacy set out above.

The capability of an industry and the firms within it may be seen as a set of knowledge, values and systems which is the outcome of a sequence of investments made in facilities and in learning (Leonard-Barton 1992; Prahalad and Hamel 1990). The development of a new capability requires new investments and if they involve asset-specificity, externalities, and economies of scale or scope, then it requires 'coordinated adaptation'. That coordination might be achieved in principle by a production network, especially one which is 'trust-enhanced'. However, the limits within which that is possible are not determined with any precision. It is clear that in the presence of very high levels of asset-specificity, externalities, and scale/scope economies, the hierarchy will prove superior. However, the extent to which the development of a new capability involves these conditions is unclear, and whether or not a production network can effectively change its own capabilities remains an empirical matter.

The remainder of this chapter therefore examines two production networks in the same industry, both of which have faced a need to change their key capability.

THE SWISS WATCH INDUSTRY: COMMITMENT TO PRECISION AND ITS LIMITS

In the first two decades of the twentieth century the Swiss dominated the world watch industry, having effectively adapted to meet competition from the United States in the previous twenty-five years (Dosi 1984; Landes 1979). The Swiss system, which was so effective, was made up of a discriminating mix of different types of organisation. Vertically integrated manufacturers of standard parts used versatile machines tended by skilled labour to achieve economies of scale at that level of the commodity chain. They combined with small, vertically disintegrated firms in design, case manufacture and assembly to give 'cost competitiveness, superior manufacturing competency, high levels of precision, and extraordinary attention to detail and style (Glasmeier 1991: 471). Firms made investments at an intermediate level of asset-specificity, purchasing assets which could be described as 'industry-specific', having no value if they had to be redeployed outside the industry, but retaining value if they had to be re-deployed from one firm to another within the sector.

This system was challenged by protectionism and the disruptions arising from the First World War, which led to drastic reductions in demand and a scramble among firms to reduce their inventory by price-cutting, and selling parts and movements abroad. Faced by a major threat to the value of their industry-specific investments, the larger firms sought to inject order into the industry through a process of regulation and cartelisation. The Swiss Watch Federation was established in order to govern both assemblers and component producers. The makers of movements were organised into a trust (EBAUCHE S.A) and other component makers into the Union des Branches Annexes de l'Horlogerie (UBAH). These industry-level organisations fixed output levels and prices, and attempted to restrict the transfer of watch technology abroad by limiting the export of parts. When this level of concerted action proved insufficient, the federal government worked with the leading firms and the banks to set up a holding company (ASUAG) bringing together all seventeen manufacturers of movements and most of the other component producers into a monopoly supplier.

This consolidation exercise was formalised in the Statut de l'Horlogerie which governed the sector from the 1930s until the 1960s (Jaquet and Chapuis 1970). Under that regime, Swiss watchmakers could only purchase from Swiss component suppliers, who were themselves only allowed to sell to Swiss customers. Permits were required for the construction or expansion of production facilities and machinery sales were controlled. The supply of watches was held down, ensuring high prices and wide margins for the Swiss industry. Those profits were re-invested in the development of process technology, and the Swiss industry became a byword for efficiency in the application of precision micro-mechanical capability.

As might have been anticipated, this system of cartelisation and control contained the seeds of its own demise in that the restriction of supply and consequent high prices attracted increasing competition, especially from America and Japan. The Swiss Government responded by gradually eliminating the restrictions on watch manufacturing, and the industry saw a series of mergers in the early 1970s.

The Swiss watch production system which emerged from the collapse of the cartel arrangements corresponded to a production system defined by Storper and Harrison (1991) as 'agglomerated network production with some large units'. There were a number of vertically integrated producers including the relatively large Rolex and the other high-end manufacturers like Patek Philippe, Piaget, Vacheron Constantin, Audemars Piguet, Ebel and Blancpain. There were also a number of movement producers employing around 200 workers each. However, the remainder of the industry's employment, and almost all of the activity in the low- and medium-price segments, was to be found in a vertically and horizontally disintegrated network made up of several hundred very small assemblers, parts and component suppliers. Table 9.1 shows the size distribution of firms, measured by the numbers of workers employed, as estimated for the 1970s (Glasmeier 1991: 474).

Table 9.1 Structure of the Swiss watch industry (1970s)

Size by employment	Percentage of establishments	Percentage of employment
1–9	35.1	4.6
10–19	22.8	6.2
20–49	17.5	12.4
50–99	12.3	15.4
100–199	6.0	15.4
200–499	5.6	30.1
500+	0.7	15.4
Total	100.0	100.0

Source: Adapted from Glasmeier (1991)

This activity was spatially concentrated in the Jura Arc region where physical proximity and constant personal interaction allowed the development of trust. The problems of scale economies and externalities in training were overcome through specialisation in the local education system, where the region's five technical colleges provided a supply of workers trained in the industry-specific precision metal-machining skills required. The industry-specific precision tools required were supplied by local manufacturers who were themselves pre-eminent in their field. The level of trust was sufficient for firms to fund collective research and development institutions and they also collectively financed training centres in major markets abroad (including Hong Kong) in order to support the servicing of their watches.

In the early 1970s, this production system provided a good example of a globally competitive production network made up of a 'cluster' of related and supporting industries (Porter 1990). In 1970, the industry employed almost 90,000 workers (Maillat *et al.* 1995: 254) and, in 1974, Swiss watches accounted for 40 per cent of world exports by volume. Swiss producers had significant market shares in both low and high-end parts of the market, the former held by the disintegrated production networks, and the latter by the more vertically-integrated firms.

By 1984, this apparently unassailable position had been lost. Employment fell by more than 60 per cent to a little over 32,000, and the 40 per cent share of world exports by volume had fallen to 10 per cent. The loss of employment, output and export share was almost wholly concentrated in the low to medium-price segments of the industry, where the production system took the form of a 'trust-enhanced network' of small firms.

The system had been thrown into disarray by what Tushman and Anderson (1986) would describe as a 'competence-destroying' technological change. The invention of the electronic watch, first in the 'tuning-fork' configuration at the beginning of the 1960s, and then in the form of the quartz movement in the 1970s offered the possibility of accuracy beyond that of the best mechanical movements, at very low cost, through the automated production of movements with very significant economies of scale. However, despite the fact that the 'tuning-fork' movement was invented by a Swiss, and that the Swiss also produced the first quartz watch movement, their production system was unable to take the innovation and put it to commercial use.

Examination of this failure clearly illustrates the rigidities associated with the key capability of the disintegrated Swiss production network. The first of these rigidities was cognitive and associated with both the industry's values and its organisational systems (Leonard-Barton 1992). Industry members were unable to perceive that the quartz movement differed from the many other 'innovations', most of them chimerical, which had been offered to them over the years. The years of regulation, during which movement producers were only allowed to sell inside Switzerland, had left them with poorly developed systems for gathering market intelligence abroad. Their 'fixation with precision' (Glasmeier 1991) and their confidence in their key capability made it impossible for many of them to imagine a wholly new way of keeping time. As Brusco (1990) notes of the Italian industrial district: 'the district [production network] is characterised by a strong, heavy inertia. It goes on learning the technology in a deep, personal and creative way, but it is very difficult to move this huge mass of people.'

Even if the cognitive weakness had been overcome, the structure of the production network made it extremely difficult to respond appropriately. Indeed, a few of the smaller firms were more open-minded in respect of the new technologies, launching electronic complements to their mechanical products (Gabus 1983). However, such a fragmented response could not suffice. In terms of the conceptual framework set out above, the requirement was for 'coordinated adaptation'. The extent of scale economies in the production of quartz movements is such that only a very small number of firms are required in that stage of production. There are also economies of scope to be had in the form of vertical integration. Furthermore, the key capability and accumulated investment in precision micro-mechanical engineering skills lost its ability to generate value for customers. In principle, as a 'hybrid' form of governance capable of operating over a range of circumstances, a trust-enhanced network might have been able to achieve a 'coordinated adaptation' to the new situation. In the event, it proved inadequate to the task. To be successful the system needed to commit to a single quartz movement design, or at most a few. However, in the face of competing designs in the early stages the Swiss movement suppliers had no means of knowing which could be sold to the hundreds of mechanical watch assemblers, and the assemblers provided no common signal. Prices failed to signal the most appropriate technological choice to make '*ex ante*' (Dosi 1982), so that the network could not adjust through autonomous adaptation and 'coordinated adaptation' was not achieved. The new technology required learning how to assemble watches cheaply in order to take maximal advantage of the new movements. However, that required a very different approach to production, involving high levels of automation and economies of scale, supported by significant levels of research and development expenditure, if it were to be successful in a high-wage environment. Despite a degree of information-sharing between watch designers, movement makers, and assemblers, the network failed to provide the design solution to low-cost quartz watch production and could not organise the concentration of low-cost production into a smaller number of larger units. The industry did have its collective R&D facilities, which were merged into the Swiss Electronics and Microtechnological Centre in 1984, but they were too distant from large-scale production to achieve the learning which was needed. As Crevoisier (1993) notes, the requirements of sports timing meant that Swiss researchers had considerable knowledge of quartz technology in that context, but it was regarded as a 'showcase' entirely separate from mainstream production.

The production network in the Swiss watch industry was unable to adjust to a situation where a change in its key capabilities was required. Those key capabilities were in precision micro-engineering, and they have exhibited very substantial persistence over time. While the Jura Arc region may no longer be described as an 'industrial district' based on the watch industry, it has become a 'technology district' based on technologies which are very similar to those previously employed in the watch industry. While Maillat *et al.* (1995) characterise that shift as a major one, and use it as an example of the region's strengths in respect of adaptability, the most salient feature of the change is the way in which the existing key capability has been retained and re-deployed in a production system which retains many features of the watch industry's organisational character. Certainly, the key capability has been changing, with elements of electronics and optics being fused with the traditional precision skills to produce a 'combinatory' capability. However, that new affiliation 'manifests itself mainly by the use of traditional know-how which has been renewed from contact with new know-how' (ibid., p. 254). The manufacture of products having similar features to watches, particularly in respect of the premium placed on precision, like heart pacemakers, measuring equipment and testing instruments exhibit very significant continuities. At the same time, the 'milieu' of the area is little different. As in the watch industry, a large proportion of firms are very small. The users of micro-technologies are highly concentrated in the Jura Arc, where their proximity enhances trust and they cooperate on joint projects. The technical colleges have amended their curriculum, moving from diploma courses in watchmaking engineering, to qualifications in micro-technologies. All in all, they remain within the same 'technological trajectory' which led from the cuckoo clock and the musical box in a production system which embodies the same capabilities. As Leonard-Barton (1992) notes, core capabilities bring with them core rigidities.

The failure of the production network within the Swiss watch industry is not, however, the whole story. There have been two very different but successful responses from elsewhere in the sector. The first of these is in the high-end part of the industry, where vertically-integrated manufacturers producing at relatively low volume on a craft basis have successfully retained almost total control of the most expensive market segment. That segment accounts for only 1 per cent of the watch market by volume. However, the difference in price between a low-end watch and a luxury watch is so great that dominance of that sector means that Switzerland continues to be the world's largest exporter by value. In this sector, mechanical watches (which are significantly less accurate than even the cheapest quartz models) are promoted and sold as expensive items of handcrafted jewellery (largely for men). By maintaining their commitment to mechanical precision, supported by heavy advertising spending, firms like Rolex, Patek

Philippe, IWC and Audemars Piguet have been able to hold their position. The development of brand-name capital, which embodies a high degree of asset-specificity (Williamson 1991), protected by in-house vertically-integrated movement production and assembly has enabled them to survive the paradigm shift brought about by the quartz revolution.

The other successful response came from the largest firm in the industry, providing a clear example of the ways in which the managerial hierarchy can provide 'coordinated adaptation'. The Société Suisse de Microélectronique et d'Horlogerie (SMH) was originally formed in the early 1980s by merging ASUAG with a number of other larger producers. Having noted that labour costs account for less than 10 per cent of the cost of production for a quartz watch, the Principal of SMH, Nicholas Hayek, oversaw the design of a watch with a standard movement, a standard case and fifty parts instead of more than one hundred, an example of 'coordinated adaptation' which would have been impossible among the non-integrated firms of the network. That allowed the SWATCH to be produced in high volume, with high product variety, at low cost, in highly automated Swiss facilities. By abandoning the craft tradition and precision engineering capability in favour of economies of scale through volume production in a single facility and aggressive marketing, SMH was able to sell the SWATCH at US$35 as a heavily branded fashion item, successfully giving the Swiss industry re-entry to the low-price segment. New collections of watches are launched twice per year, in 'limited editions' under the overall brand name. Total production is in the region of 30 million units per year, and the watches are marketed as youthful, stylish, provocative, and potential collectors' items. The latter strategy has proved so successful that SMH has been able to hold lotteries in which the winners are allowed to buy models produced in batches as large as 49,990 watches, and still be able to report that winners were able to re-sell their purchases at very significant mark-ups (Made in Italy Online 1996).

What is noticeable about both of these successful responses is that they required the development of new key capabilities. In the case of the high-end producers, they were able to retain their traditional approach to manufacturing, but success required a significant development of their marketing skills in order to direct heavy advertising spending and carefully targeted promotion of key sporting events. In the case of SWATCH, a new approach to marketing was also required, supported by an even more dramatic shift in the nature of production. In both cases, these major adaptations were achieved by managerial hierarchies and not by the production networks.

THE HONG KONG/CHINA WATCH INDUSTRY: 'MERCHANT-MANUFACTURING' AND ITS LIMITS

The watch industry in Hong Kong has a much shorter history than its Swiss competitor, demonstrating the development and use of a completely different key capability. Nevertheless, the watch production network in Hong Kong appears to share its Swiss counterpart's inability to adjust effectively when the existing key capability becomes a less useful source of competitive strength. In that sense, the industry's production networks display an important regularity across the two locations.

The watch industry in Hong Kong, together with its extension into the Chinese mainland, demonstrates in microcosm the history of the territory's manufacturing sector (Carney and Davies 1996). In the early 1950s, when Switzerland had a centuries-old tradition of watchmaking, Hong Kong had very little manufacturing activity and no domestic watch manufacturing capacity at all. Only the watch band sector was at all well established. As the region's premier entrepot, Hong Kong acted as the Swiss watchmakers' regional distributor, importing a recorded 2.07 million Swiss watches (worth HK$78.3m) in 1953 and re-exporting most of them to China, Malaysia and Indonesia. In keeping with the colony's freewheeling and somewhat piratical traditions, there were vast differences between the official figure for imports and those for exports (registered at HK$32.5m in 1953) which could not possibly be attributed to local sales, suggesting that 'sailors, tourists and smugglers became necessary agents of the booming trade' (FHKWTI 1993: 10).

As the 1950s progressed, Hong Kong's entrepot activities were curtailed by the US/UN embargo on trade with China. The territory's economic rationale was removed almost at a stroke, leaving an impoverished population of 2.4 million largely uneducated refugees, with few natural resources, no prospect of increased agricultural activity and a limited domestic market for manufactures. The only opportunity for the territory's erstwhile merchants lay in the development of export-oriented manufacturing in industries having low entry barriers where overseas sales could be made on the basis of cost-leadership (Carney and Davies 1996). In the watch industry, this development began with parts and components for mechanical watches, beginning with the wrist-band sector. By 1968, a watch band with the wonderfully redolent name of 'Kevin' was the first to be displayed at the prestigious international Basel Fair. In the 1970s, the industry began to produce and export low-price mechanical watches. However, these were rapidly replaced by electronic models and it was only when the shift to quartz movements became almost complete in the low price segment that the Hong Kong industry came into its own.

By 1978 or 1979, the Hong Kong watch manufacturing industry had developed to the point where it had the world's largest share of watch exports by volume, a position which it has retained ever since. In 1980, world production of complete watches was estimated at 342m, of which 119m (35 per cent) were produced in Hong Kong, and 88m (26 per cent) in Japan (FHKWTI 1993: 12). By 1994, world output had risen to more than 1 billion watches, with Hong Kong's share of production at 34 per cent, slightly behind Japan at 39 per cent. Table 9.2 illustrates the salient features of the industry in its three major centres. As Table 9.2 illustrates, the Hong Kong industry remains firmly entrenched in the low-price segment of the market.

Like its Swiss counterpart, the watch industry which achieved this dominant position for Hong Kong conforms to the Storper and Harrison (1991) definition of 'agglomerated network production with some large units'. In 1993, there were 1,477 establishments engaged in watch and clock manufacturing in Hong Kong. They employed 17,119 workers in total, giving an average of only 11.5 workers per establishment within the territory. However, most of them also have production facilities in China, with an average employment estimated by industry sources to be about 150 workers.

Most of these firms are Chinese family businesses (CFBs), which display a very particular set of characteristics (Redding 1990; Whitley 1992), arising partly from the historical and cultural circumstances of their development (Carney and Davies 1996). CFBs have very low levels of capitalisation, often raising their initial funding from informal family sources. As they are a long distance, both geographically and culturally, from their final product markets they cannot easily predict changes in those markets. They therefore avoid investing in highly specific assets, restricting their spending to very general purpose facilities and equipment which can be shifted to other uses if market demand should shift unexpectedly. Their activities are focused on vertically very shallow and highly disintegrated 'single-phase' functions, like assembly, case-making or band-making. They avoid the necessity, cost and transaction-specificity of investment or learning in product design and marketing by producing designs provided by customers and by imitating others. In terms of 'value-chain' analysis (Porter 1985), they focus on 'logistics', managing the procurement of inputs at low cost, limited transformation of those inputs and order-taking. A typical assembler will produce as many as 1,000 models of watch, differentiated by colour and style or by a host of ingenious but relatively trivial features. New designs come from customers or by 'shuffling the pack' of possible characteristics, and orders will be accepted for batches as small as 100 units. Delivery times are extremely short and the emphasis is upon 'quick money'.

Table 9.2 Production levels and export prices for the watch industries in Switzerland, Hong Kong and Japan

Country	Production by volume (millions)	Production by value (US$bn)	Average unit price of exports (US$)
Japan	392	2.7	30
Hong Kong	345	1.8	9
Switzerland	135	4.7	160
Global total	1070	n.a	n.a

Source: Citizen Watch Company, *Annual Review of the Watch Industry 1995*

Since the economy of the Chinese mainland began to open up in the early 1980s, this network of small firms has extended its activities from Hong Kong itself into China, with an estimated 85 per cent of the territory's watch firms shifting at least part of their production northwards. That shift has most often been explained in terms of helping firms to maintain their cost-competitiveness through access to cheap Chinese labour. However, it should also be noted that labour costs make up only 8 per cent of Hong Kong watch firms' overall costs, 86 per cent being accounted for by the cost of materials and components. Saving on labour achieves the reduction of a few percentage points on cost, as do savings on the cost of space. However, for many firms the most important advantage of the move to China lies in the increased flexibility provided by a migrant labour force which can be instructed to work in the evenings and at weekends, if the production schedule demands it.

In terms of the conceptual framework set out above, this network of small firms is extremely effective in terms of autonomous adaptation, described by Sit and Wong (1989) as 'mechanical market-response'. Indeed, the Hong Kong watch network is close to the 'market' form of transactional governance. Hierarchies are so shallow as to be almost non-existent, in a close approximation to the perfect market economy where all transactions are coordinated by price signals. Incentive-intensity is very high and firms are highly responsive to small changes in costs, prices and the pattern of demand. Family ownership and the ease of monitoring single-phase operations give tight control over direct costs so that such firms are models of parsimony. When prices signal the decline of profit opportunities in one area, the network responds very rapidly, shifting resources into other uses. As a result, the succession of changes from mechanical to light-emitting diode (LED) watches in the early 1970s, on to liquid crystal display (LCD) watches in the late1970s, and quartz analogue watches from the 1980s onwards was achieved with great speed and very little disruption. The key capability of the network may be described as 'merchant-manufacturing' or 'exchange, logistics and transactions management'. Provided that the adaptation to a new time-keeping or display technology could be achieved by using that established capability to identify sources of supply for new types of component, assembling those new components, and arranging for onward delivery, the Hong Kong production network could respond very effectively. In comparison with the Swiss production network of the 1970s, the Hong Kong network had no commitment to any particular technology, or to the industry as a whole (Glasmeier 1994). It existed in order to do business, not to make watches, and was therefore able to switch from one new product type to another, while leaving the technology development itself in the hands of the movement producers located in Japan. Whenever a new type of watch movement came into being, the Hong Kong firms would simply switch into purchasing those movements, having sunk only minimal investment into their predecessors.

While this production network has been extremely efficient in respect of autonomous adaptation, where independent responses to market signals are sufficient, it has come under increasing pressure as intense competition between the hundreds of firms has reduced margins, and as both producers in other low-cost locations and the Japanese have begun to seek market share in the low-end segment (Moore 1995). Industry leaders have identified the need to change, and have repeatedly called for a shift into higher-price market segments, supported by improvements in product and process technology and the development of significant brand-name capital. These calls have been amplified by reports to the Hong Kong Government, drawing attention to the undeveloped condition of the industry's manufacturing skills, and the Government has invested considerable effort and resources in seeking to help those firms who wish to follow the upgrading route. However, despite these pressures, the production network has shown a marked inability to develop and use new marketing and technological capabilities, preferring instead to risk staying within its merchant-manufacturing tradition. Two specific difficulties help to illustrate the general point.

First, the Hong Kong network of small firms has failed to develop the brand-name recognition which would allow it to secure higher prices for its products. Indeed, as production has shifted from Hong Kong itself into China, the price per unit of the watches exported has dropped even further and the industry's Federation has complained that 'what was lost from Hong Kong were high-end export markets (*sic*) and skilled jobs; what was gained through China were a low-end re-export share and service employment' (FHKWTI 1993: 16).

Industry sources report that some firms have begun to secure significant shares and buyer loyalty in peripheral markets like Iceland, but the fact that such a minor development is reported as significant simply emphasises the general weakness of the industry in this respect. When it is recognised that the development of significant brand-name capital involves economies of scale (too many brands necessarily dilute each other, concentration on a single brand for a wide range of watches was one of the keys to the SWATCH success) and requires investment in highly specific assets (Williamson 1991) which cannot be transferred to other uses without loss of value, it becomes clear that such a development cannot come easily for firms in a production network like that of Hong Kong.

If the Hong Kong network were significantly 'trust-enhanced', it might be possible for firms to cooperate on the introduction of a small but well-supported set of brand names. They could make more specific investments, secure in the knowledge that the enduring vertical relationships between firms which allow the production of specific product qualities signalled in a brand name are safe from opportunistic behaviour on the part of participants. However, lack of trust in non-family members is a hallmark of Chinese culture (Bond and Hwang 1986), and without a high level of trust such investments become impossible. In the Hong Kong case, the network part of the industry is so far away from developing its own brand identity that the most important signifier of quality on Hong Kong/China-made watches are the words 'Swiss Made' or 'Japan' which are applied to watches containing Swiss or Japanese movements. That practice runs counter to the traditional interpretation of international trade law whereby the stated name of origin is restricted to the country of assembly: it arose from unilateral action on the part of the Hong Kong Government in 1991 (Glasmeier 1994) and it may be vulnerable in the near future to a counter-ruling by the World Trade Organization.

An associated difficulty which has bedevilled the Hong Kong/China industry's development lies in the failure to cooperate effectively over the development of collective technological research and development facilities. In Switzerland, as described above, firms in the network part of the industry were sufficiently trusting of each other to establish, fund and operate such R&D facilities. That was insufficient to protect them from a radical change in the technological trajectory, but it did provide development within the confines of their original precision-focused capability. In Hong Kong, the Government has been aware of local industry's hesitance in respect of technological development, at least since 1967 and more particularly since a series of investigations and consultancy reports drew attention to the continuing weakness. It therefore assumes some of the responsibility for the provision of 'real services' to industry through the Hong Kong Productivity Council (HKPC). The HKPC's mandate is to assist Hong Kong manufacturing firms to improve their productivity, and it has had a number of watch-industry specific projects including the development of design and software skills, the introduction of CAD/CAM, metal-injection moulding, the replacement of nickel in electro-plating, and the promotion of ISO9000. Despite the provision of these subsidised facilities, progress has been very limited. By 1995, only one watch firm (Renley) had been certified to ISO9001 by the Hong Kong Quality Assurance Agency (HKQAA 1995), the replacement of nickel had made little progress because of the cost of its substitutes, and a proposal to establish a Watch and Clock Technology Centre foundered on companies' inability to agree on their share of the funding (Carney 1996).

Just as the production network in the Swiss watch industry was unable to adapt away from its key capability in precision mechanical engineering, thus has the Hong Kong network been unable to adapt away from its 'merchant-manufacturing' tradition. In both cases, the key capability of the production network has exhibited persistence or rigidity which has made it difficult for the networks to adapt to large-scale disturbance.

In the Swiss case, vertically integrated firms co-existed alongside the production network and these proved more capable of adaptation. Those in the luxury segment did not move away from their commitment to mechanical precision, but they were able to develop the marketing capability which allowed them to continue selling on the basis of that precision.

Only the largest vertically-integrated firm proved capable of the 'coordinated adaptation' which was needed to develop a wholly new key capability, based on a mutually reinforcing combination of marketing skill and automated manufacturing. It is useful then to consider whether the same pattern can be observed in Hong Kong, with larger firms proving better able to develop brand-name capital and upgraded products than the network, thereby moving beyond the traditional 'merchant-manufacturing' capability.

Hong Kong does have a small number of larger watch companies, including three which are very significantly larger than the others – Asia Commercial, Egana and Stelux. Table 9.3 sets out the salient features of these three companies in respect of their size, scope and their development of brand-name capital and new technology.

As Table 9.3 shows, these firms have all made significant moves in the direction of becoming more vertically-integrated, and acquiring brand-name capital or developing new technology. Asia Commercial continues to act as an OEM supplier for Citizen Watch of Japan, but it has also purchased the high-price segment Swiss brands, Juvenia and Leonard, while producing Montana, Perry Ellis and Carven under licence. It distributes the premium brands of Cartier, Breguet and TAG Heuer, while promoting TIMECITY as a retail brand through a chain of shops in China. Egana distributes twenty-two brand names in the medium-price range, and has product development bases in six countries, including Switzerland, Germany and Japan. Egana recently purchased Speidel of Germany in order to access its technology in jewellery production, and formed a joint venture with Junghans of Germany in order to source components for Junghans in Asia while giving Egana access to Junghans technology for radio-controlled watches (which are accurate to one second in one million years through updating by radio signal from a caesium atomic clock). Stelux owns the medium-range Swiss brand names, Solvil and Titus, Feuille d'Or, Universal Geneve and Cyma, while licensing the Adidas and Ellesse marks. Stelux has also integrated forwards into retailing through City Chain stores in six Asian countries, backwards into components where it supplies band and bracelet parts to some of the most expensive Swiss producers, and diversified into optical shops under the Optical 88 brand and children's wear retailing as HIP-fant.

It is clear that these companies are significantly different from the denizens of the production network, being prepared to become more vertically-integrated and to make the more asset-specific investments which are needed in order to develop new technology and acquire brand names. To that extent they illustrate the ability of the hierarchy to secure the coordinated type of adaptation which has evaded the network. At the same time, it is noticeable that their approach continues to bear some of the hallmarks of the 'merchant-manufacturer' and the Chinese family business. Brand-name capital and technology have been purchased, rather than being built

Table 9.3 Hong Kong's larger watch companies

	Size and markets	Scope of activities	Branding and technology development
Asia Commercial	HK$2bn turnover (93/4) 78% of sales in Asia, 96% from sales of watches and components	Manufacture of watches and watch parts in China and Switzerland. Watch trading. Distribution of high end jewellery. 30 principal subsidiaries. Diversified into property	Owns Swiss brands; Juvenia, Leonard. Joint venture with Citizen to produce watches in China. Produce Montana, Carven and Perry Ellis under licence. Distributes Cartier, Breguet and TAG Heuer. TIMECITY as retail brand in China
Egana	HK$1.3bn turnover (95/6)	Manufacture of watches and jewellery.	Distributes 22 brand names, including Bulova, Esprit, Stefanel, Nicole Miller, Haribo, Dugena. Successfully sued Benetton for compensation over ending the contract for 'Benetton by Bulova'. Product development bases in Switzerland, Germany, Japan, Hong Kong, India and the PRC. Purchased Speidel of Germany for access to advanced technology in jewellery. Formed joint venture with Junghans of Germany for sourcing of components and access to radio-controlled watch technology.
Stelux	HK$1.7bn turnover (93/4) 4,200 employees in 11 countries. 2,300 employed indirectly in 3 factories in Guangdong	Watch assembly, vertically integrated forward into retailing in Hong Kong and backward into components. 50 subsidiaries. Diversified into optical shops, children's wear and property.	Owns Swiss brand names (Solvil and Titus, Feuille d'Or, Universal Geneve and Cyma), licensing agreements with Adidas and Ellesse. City Chain as retail watch brand in Hong Kong, Taiwan, Singapore, Thailand, Malaysia, China. Optical 88 as retail brand in the region, HIPO-fant in children's wear in Hong Kong. Produces parts of bands and bracelets for top Swiss producers.

through internal development on the SWATCH model. Both Asia Commercial and Stelux have followed the traditional practice of the Chinese business and invested their profits in property, with disastrous results for Asia Commercial which recently took a multi-million dollar loss as a result of its property investments in China. In the mid-1990s, it still remains unclear whether the largest watch firms will lead the industry into the new millennium or become lost in the process.

There are other Hong Kong watch firms, apart from the three largest, who display some evidence of upgrading or successful branding. Renley, led by the Young Industrialist of the Year for 1994, is unusual, having ISO9001 certification, 100 workers in Hong Kong who regularly train with the firm's fifty workers in Switzerland, and three Swiss brands – Jean d'Eve, Sultana and Buler. Europe Supplies spent eight years pioneering the radio-controlled clock, securing significantly higher margins than those available for its 'novelty fruit clocks'. Crystal has secured recognition in Asia for its Bossini brand. Dailywin (listed in London) has secured a long-term relationship with Timex, involving investment by the American firm in the Hong Kong firm's Chinese manufacturing facilities, including high-precision digital lathing equipment. Dailywin has also increased its margins by developing its direct sales to Gap, Gap Kids, Banana Republic, Ann Klein and The Museum of Modern Art (Kohli 1996). However, when set against the behaviour of the many hundreds of firms in the industry, it is clear that these companies represent the exception, rather than the rule. Hong Kong's watch industry continues to be dominated by the 'merchant-manufacturing' approach.

CONCLUDING REMARKS

This chapter set out first to explore the idea that localised production networks in different places may display very different capabilities, but that they have in common an inability to adapt to disturbances which require the development of a new capability. Second, it set out to explore the idea that larger firms, working through hierarchies, are more successful in respect of this kind of adaptation.

With respect to the first issue, it seems clear from the analysis of the Swiss and Hong Kong watch industries that the production networks in these two locations have exhibited very different capabilities. Furthermore, both have faced the need to change and both have failed. With respect to the second issue, it is clear in the Swiss case that vertically-integrated firms were able to respond more effectively and they have secured sustainable positions for themselves. In the Hong Kong case, it is less clear whether the larger firms will be able to build on their initial investments in technology and brand names to secure such positions. As they have only recently begun to develop in that direction it may be some years before the outcome will be known.

The implications of this analysis for our evaluation of the role of production networks in economic development are negative. Such networks appear to be of limited value in the face of major disturbances, being unable to secure the 'coordinated adaptation' which is required. To hold them up as a superior form of industrial organisation, to be endorsed and supported by policy, would seem to be inappropriate, in either Europe or China.

NOTE

1 The author acknowledges financial support provided by the Research Grants Council of Hong Kong under grant No. HKP4/95H and by the Hong Kong Polytechnic University.

REFERENCES

Amin, A. and Robbins, K. (1990) 'Industrial Districts and Regional Development: Limits and Possibilities', in F. Pyke, G. Beccatini and W. Sengenberger (eds) *Industrial Districts and Inter-firm Cooperation in Italy*, Geneva: International Institute for Labour Studies, pp.185–219.

Barnard, C. (1938) *The Functions of the Executive*, Cambridge, MA: Harvard University Press.

Beccatini, G. (1990) 'The Marshallian Industrial District as as a Socio-economic Idea', in F. Pyke, G. Beccatini and W. Sengenberger (eds) *Industrial Districts and Inter-firm Cooperation in Italy*, Geneva: International Institute for Labour Studies, pp.37–51.

Belussi, F. (1992) 'Benetton Italy: Beyond Fordism and Flexible Specialisation. The Evolution of the Network Firm Model', in S. Mitter (ed.) *Computer-aided Manufacturing and Women's Employment: The Clothing Industry in Four EC Countries*, Berlin: Springer-Verlag, pp.73–91.

Best, M. (1990) *The New Industrial Competition: Institutions of Industrial Restructuring*, Cambridge, MA: Harvard University Press.

Bond, M. and Hwang, K. (1986) 'The Social Psychology of the Chinese People', in M. Bond (ed.) *The Psychology of the Chinese People*, Hong Kong: Oxford University Press, pp.213–66.

Brusco, S. (1990) 'The Idea of the Industrial District: Its Genesis', in F. Pyke, G. Becattini and W. Sengenberger (eds) *Industrial Districts and Inter-firm Cooperation in Italy*, Geneva: International Institute for Labour Studies, pp.10–19.

Carney, M. (1996) *The Competitiveness of Networked Production: The Role of Trust and Asset Specificity*, mimeo, Concordia University, Montreal.

Carney, M. and Davies, H. (1996) *From Entrepot to Entrepot via Merchant Manufacturing: Adaptive Mechanisms, Organisational Capabilities and the Structure of the Hong Kong Economy*, mimeo, Concordia University and Hong Kong Polytechnic University.

Castells, M. and Hall, P. (1994) *Technopoles of the World: The Making of 21st Century Industrial Complexes*, London: Routledge.

Chandler, A.D. (1990) *Scale and Scope: The Dynamics of Industrial Capitalism*, Cambridge, MA: Harvard University Press.

Citizen Watch Company (1995) *Annual Review of the Watch Industry*.

Crevoisier, O. (1993) *Région et Recomposition des Activités Industrielle: L'Emergence de Nouveaux Métiers dans l'Arc Jurassien*, Neuchâtel: EDES.

Dosi, G. (1982) 'Technological Paradigms and Technological Trajectories,' *Research Policy*, 11(3): 147–62.

Dosi, G. (1984) 'Technological Paradigms and Technological Trajectories', in C. Freeman (ed.) *Long Waves and the World Economy*, London: Butterworth, pp.78–101.

Federation of Hong Kong Watch Trades and Industries (1993) *The State of the Watch and Clock Industry in Hong Kong, 1993–94*, Hong Kong: FHKWTI.

Ferguson, C. (1990) 'Computers and the Coming of the US "Keiretsu"', *Harvard Business Review*, 68(4), July–August: 55–70.

Florida, R. and Kenney, M. (1990) 'Silicon Valley and Route 128 Won't Save Us', *California Management Review*, 33: 68–88.

Foray, D. (1991) 'The Secrets of Industry Are in the Air: Industrial Cooperation and the Organisational Dynamics of the Innovative Firm', *Research Policy*, 20(5): 393–405.

Gabus, A. (1983) 'Introduction de l'Electronique dans la Montre', in O. Hieronym and A. Gabus (eds) *La Diffusion des Nouvelles Technologies en Suisse*, St. Saphorin: Georgi, pp.35–114.

Gereffi, G. and Korzeniewicz, M. (1994) *Commodity Chains and Global Capitalism*, London: Greenwood Press.

Glasmeier, A. (1991) 'Technological Discontinuities and Flexible Production Networks: the Case of Switzerland and the World Watch Industry.' *Research Policy*, 20(5): 469–85.

Glasmeier, A. (1994) 'Flexibility and Adjustment: The Hong Kong Watch Industry and Global Change', *Growth and Change*, 25, Spring: 223–46.

Harrison, B. (1994) 'Concentrated Economic Power and Silicon Valley', *Environment and Planning A*, 26: 307–28.

Hayek, F. (1945) 'The Use of Knowledge in Society', *American Economic Review*, 35: 519–30.

Hong Kong Quality Assurance Association (1995) *ISO9000 Certification: Buyers' Guide*, Issue No. 43, 5 October 1995.

Hopkins, T. and Wallerstein, I. (1986) 'Commodity Chains in the World Economy Prior to 1800', *Review*, 10(1): 157–70.

Jaquet, E. and Chapuis, A. (1970) *Technique and History of the Swiss Watch Industry*, London: Spring Books.

Kohli, S. (1996) 'Dailywin Switches Tack to Lift Sales', *South China Morning Post*, 28 June, 2.

Landes, D.S. (1979) 'Watchmaking: A Case Study of Enterprise and Change', *Business History Review*, 53(1): 1–38.

Lau, C.K. (1996) 'Boom or Bust in the Delta Growth Zone', *South China Morning Post*, 18 February, 9.

Lazerson, M. (1989) 'A New Phoenix: The Return of the Putting-Out Mode of Production', *ILO Workshop on Industrial Districts*, Florence, April.

Leonard-Barton, D. (1992) 'Core Capabilities and Core Rigidities: A Paradox in Managing New Product Development', *Strategic Management Journal*, 13: 111–25.

Macneil, I. (1978) 'Contracts: Adjustments of Long-term Economic Relations under Classical, Neo-classical and Relational Contract Law, *Northwestern University Law Review*, 72: 854–906.

Made in Italy Online (http://www.made-in-italy.com/swatch/history.htm), *Watch my Swatch: How the Italians Turned a Plastic Watch into a Status Symbol*.

Maillat, D., Lecoq, B., Nemeti, F. and Pfister, M. (1995) 'Technology District and Innovation: The Case of the Swiss Jura Arc', *Regional Studies*, 29(3): 251–63.

Moore, W. (1995) 'Industry Review and Forecast: The Year in Review', *Watch Review*, 6: 12.

Piore, M. and Sabel, C. (1984) *The Second Industrial Divide*, New York: Basic Books.
Porter, M. (1985) *Competitive Advantage: Creating and Sustaining Superior Performance*, New York: Free Press.
Porter, M. (1990) *The Competitive Advantage of Nations*, New York: Free Press.
Powell, W. (1990) 'Neither Market nor Hierarchy: Network Forms of Organisation', *Research in Organisational Behaviour*, 12: 295–336.
Prahalad, C. and Hamel, G. (1990) 'The Core Competence of the Corporation', *Harvard Business Review*, 68(3): 79–91.
Redding, S.G. (1990) *The Spirit of Chinese Capitalism*, Berlin: de Gruyter.
Salais, R. and Storper, M. (1992) 'The Four "Worlds" of Contemporary Industry', *Cambridge Journal of Economics*, 16: 169–93.
Saxenian, A. (1990) 'Regional Networks and the Resurgence of Silicon Valley', *California Management Review*, 33: 89–112.
Saxenian, A. (1994) *Regional Advantage*, Boston: Harvard University Press.
Shutt, J. and Whittington, R. (1987) 'Fragmentation Strategies and the Rise of Small Units', *Regional Studies*, 21(1): 13–23.
Sit, V. and Wong, S-L. (1989) *Small and Medium Industries in an Export-Oriented Economy: The Case of Hong Kong*, Hong Kong: University of Hong Kong, Centre of Asian Studies.
Storper, M. and Christopherson, S. (1987) 'Flexible Specialisation and Regional Agglomeration: The Case of the US Motion Picture Association', *Annals of the Association of American Geographers*, March: 104–17.
Storper, M. and Harrison, B. (1991) 'Flexibility, Hierarchy and Regional Development. The Changing Structure of Industrial Production Systems and their Form of Governance in the 1990s', *Research Policy*, 20(5): 407–22.
Tushman, M. and Anderson, P. (1986) 'Technological Discontinuities and Organisational Environments,' *Administrative Science Quarterly*, 31(3): 439–65.
Whitley, R. (1992) *Business Systems in East Asia*, London: Sage.
Williamson, O. (1991) 'Comparative Economic Organisation: The Analysis of Discrete Structural Alternatives', *Administrative Science Quarterly*, 36(2): 269–96.

10 European multinational strategy in telecommunications services in China

Jeremy Clegg, Syed Kamall and Wai-Shau Mary Leung

INTRODUCTION

This chapter contains a study of the emerging forms of market entry strategy used by European and other foreign firms in the telecommunications sector in the People's Republic of China. It highlights the adoption of novel relationship-building approaches to accessing the Chinese market, and the evolution of coalitions between foreign and indigenous interest groups, with a view to promoting economic liberalisation.

In the early 1990s, the telecommunications industry in China was accorded priority status for development, but the environment in which foreign firms have to conduct strategic decisions is one dominated by powerful Chinese interest groups. The official position is that the telecommunications services market remains open to no-one bar the two domestic operators. No other firms can operate a public network. In this crucial respect the experience of the telecommunications industry contrasts markedly with those of other industries now able to receive inward FDI. This notwithstanding, the overarching consideration for foreign firms is that the Chinese market cannot be ignored, on account of its size and potential for growth.

Foreign multinational firms in China's telecommunications industry must contend with some formidable obstacles in formulating their market entry and investment strategies. They face a legal and regulatory vacuum filled by internal directives which make it is acutely difficult for firms to make long-term foreign direct investment plans. One commentator (Carver 1996: 11) has characterised the situation as one of 'legal and practical dysfunctionalism' between the business strategies of foreign firms and the interests of the Chinese Government. It is neither regulation nor law that forbids the foreign operation of public networks: rather, foreign operations are prohibited by an internal directive from the State Council in 1993 and by the *Provisional Guidelines on Foreign Investment Projects* which became effective in July 1995.[1] While these internal instructions do not have the status of law or regulations, the power of directives in China is nevertheless considerable.[2]

The phenomenal growth rate of the Chinese economy since 1979 has been noted in Chapter 1. However, a major problem facing China is that its communications networks are inadequate and simply out of date. There is a real danger that future growth in the twenty-first century may be hindered by the lack of adequate infrastructure. Without a modern and extensive telecommunications system, economic growth and modernisation will become increasingly difficult to achieve. From the point of view of global economic development, China's obsolete telecommunications system may act as a deterrent to inward investment and economic co-operation with other nations.

THE HISTORY OF TELECOMMUNICATIONS PROVISION IN CHINA

It can be argued that the historical neglect of telecommunications has been due to two main reasons. First, according to the central planners, telecommunications did not represent a force for production in the way that manufacturing industries did. Central planners decided on the 'essentials' to produce to meet the needs of the workers. However, the decision as to what constituted an 'essential' was a subjective one made by party apparatchiks. Telecommunications as a service did not appeal to the planners as much as heavy industry. A second reason was that the idea of hyperactive telephone networks with universal access did not appear attractive to China's leaders, who saw the free flow of information as a threat. In their view, the restriction of information to party members and state bodies was a way of maintaining control. For these reasons, all aspects of telecommunications were controlled by the Ministry of Post and Telecommunications (MPT). The Ministry combined three functions under its supervision: policy and regulation, service provision, and equipment manufacturing. The MPT monopoly power will not be eased substantially in the foreseeable future.

As a result of economic liberalisation and the opening of the economy to the outside world, China's leaders came to realise that the telecommunications infrastructure would have to be dramatically improved for the benefit of other sectors of the economy. Manufacturing, banking, tourism, and communications-intensive activities in general clearly required better communications services in order to achieve their full potential growth rates. In short, a modern telecommunications system was essential to sustain the level of economic growth that would allow China to realise itself as the economic giant that it yearned to become.

To this end, the MPT pursued the introduction of national digital telecommunications and data communications networks. Local post and telecommunications bureaux (PTBs) were granted increased financial autonomy and were allowed to retain part of their revenue for reinvestment. The MPT also encouraged the PTBs to seek investment from local governments and other local interests. As a result, the percentages of total telecommunications investment raised by PTBs and local government increased rapidly. This trend has become even stronger in recent years as many provincial PTBs have invested huge sums in the modernisation of their switching and transmission facilities (Tan 1994: 178).

In the short term, the MPT and PTBs have looked to cellular telephone technology to meet the demands of the business community. In comparison with fixed lines, it is possible for cellular telephone networks to be installed relatively quickly. Many businesses have been willing to pay the higher cellular prices where they require a telephone at almost any cost, i.e. their demand for telephony services has been highly price inelastic.

MODERNISATION, THE EMERGING LIBERALISED ENVIRONMENT AND FOREIGN PARTICIPATION

The State Council, China's parliament, in 1985 approved the Seventh Five-Year Plan, which stated that telecommunications had become a national priority (Zita 1987, cited in Ure 1994: 182). As a result, the number of telephone lines grew at an annual average rate of 17 per cent between 1986 and 1990. In 1993, nearly 11 million office exchange lines were installed, and almost 6 million new telephone subscribers were added (Zhu 1994: 19). By the end of 1993, the number of main lines totalled 17.33 million. However, this figure was equivalent to a line density of only 1.46 per cent. By contrast, the figure for the European Community was over forty lines per 100 population. China's leaders realise that there is still a long way to go. Official estimates claim that there will be 96 million telephone lines by the year 2000.[3] This is equivalent to installing a national network the size of that owned by BT in the United Kingdom, every three years.

There has been an increase in the quality, as well as the quantity, of the telecommunications system. There are now only a handful of manual local exchanges remaining. The construction of a digital trunk transmission network relying mainly on optical cable and linking large and medium-sized cities across the country was scheduled for completion by 1995 (Zhu 1994: 19). Modernisation of the telecommunications system has enabled subscribers to be offered a number of services that many Western customers take for granted: data communications, fax, radio paging, mobile phones as well as some value-added services such as videophone, videotex and electronic mail that are not subject to any restriction on foreign provision.

The tremendous growth in Chinese telecommunications has opened up a huge market to foreign manufacturers of telecommunications equipment. According to William Warwick, Chairman and Chief Executive of AT&T China: 'China will, in 1994 or 1995, be the largest single market in the world for telecommunications infrastructure equipment...It's going to be the largest market for the next 30 years at least – maybe 40' (Clifford 1994: 48).

China decided on a programme of importing foreign technology for several reasons. First, China's indigenous industry would be unable to meet the demand for equipment on its own. The second reason was one of speed. By importing technology 'off the shelf', coupled with the transfer of skills through training, Chinese industry might begin production and export much more quickly (Warwick 1994: 266). An additional consideration was that overseas investors would bring an influx of much-needed foreign capital.

Almost all the major international equipment suppliers (Alcatel, AT&T, Northern Telecom, Motorola, etc.) have representative offices in Beijing. They are involved in every aspect of telecommunication systems, from switching systems, transmission equipment and terminals, to components and materials. Some of these firms directly sell their products and transfer technology and know-how. Others set up joint ventures or wholly owned manufacturing ventures, or indeed both (Ure 1994: 180).

The rapid expansion in the domestic production of telecommunications equipment will save China foreign exchange, as currently most equipment has to be imported. China has vigorously pursued a policy of insisting that foreign equipment vendors also undertake local manufacturing of key components, on a joint venture basis. However, recently wholly owned subsidiaries have also been encouraged (ibid.: 186–7). The major equipment manufacturers are more than willing to transfer technology and skills to China in exchange for business. The foreign investors offer everything from network planning and training to after-sales support and financing (Clifford 1994: 48). Many of these firms have world-wide portfolios of business areas that encompass telecommunications operation. These multinationals would naturally be the first to be interested in providing this service in China.

Certain problems remain for foreign investors and equipment vendors looking to profit from China's plans to develop its infrastructure rapidly. Among these are bureaucratic turf wars, industrial protectionism, funding constraints, and political uncertainty. What is more, much of the current infrastructure boom still goes on in a legal and regulatory vacuum. Contrary to industry expectation, for instance, the Government has lately let it be known that the long-awaited Telecommunications Law will not after all be published in the foreseeable future.[4]

While the situation in the telecommunications equipment market is complicated, the telecommunications services environment exceeds even this. In terms of market dominance, the MPT still operates as a monopoly in the provision of services. However, a coalition of interests has developed to challenge the current monopoly, by pushing for a more competitive environment in telecommunications. This coalition includes:

- other State bodies who wish to share in the lucrative telecommunications and information technology markets currently monopolised by MPT. These include Ministries with private networks, State organisations at the central and provincial levels, and the interests of enterprising managers lower down the ladder.

- large customers such as State-owned enterprises and private commercial organisations who believe that more choice will lead to better services.
- foreign companies looking for investment opportunities.

In 1993, the Government finally gave in to political pressure and granted permission for a second national telecommunications network operated by Lian Tong (or Unicom), a joint venture between the Ministry of Power, the Ministry of Railways and the Ministry of Electronics Industry.[5] Lian Tong announced that it would offer voice and fax services along the private networks of its joint venture Ministries. In addition, by interconnecting to the local networks of PTBs, Lian Tong's second network will offer additional capacity at that level as well (Economist Intelligence Unit 1993: 1–2).

The increased power of the local PTBs and the distance, both physical and financial, between the MPT in Beijing and the provincial PTBs we making it difficult for the MPT to maintain its hold on the sector (ibid.: 1–2). The growing financial autonomy of the PTBs since the late 1980s has led to closer cooperation with provincial governments and provincial-level interest groups, at the expense of their relationship with the MPT. This growing gap has led the PTBs to make their own arrangements with local private networks. PTBs have been prepared to enter joint ventures with non-PTB bodies (which have increasingly included Hong Kong companies). In effect, local PTBs and provincial governments have allowed FDI into China's mobile telecommunications networks.

Despite this, foreign investors are still officially barred from the telecommunications services sector. The MPT has continuously reiterated its position that China will not allow any individuals, organisations or companies outside the mainland to manage its public and private networks wire or wireless communications services.[6] In addition, network telecommunications operations appeared in the 'prohibited' list of the *Provisional Guidelines of Foreign Investment Projects*, which took effect on 27 July 1995, while FDI in equipment projects is to be 'encouraged'. Even though this latest edict would appear to have tightened up the regulatory framework, and hence precluded direct forms of FDI, in practice this has confirmed the strategy of firms to seek indirect forms of participation.

The position of the Chinese Government is driven by the reluctance of the MPT to share the lucrative domestic telecommunications market, as well as by China's leaders' concerns over sovereignty and security. However, it remains a grey area in Chinese administrative law whether the provincial PTBs and provincial governments do or do not have the authority to authorise FDI (Ure 1994: 188–9).

What cannot be refuted is that the involvement of local government and interest groups has increased the power of local PTBs. Increased financial and technical cooperation between the PTBs and local groups has led to the joint operation of new services. According to Tan (1994), PTBs will become independent local companies striving for maximum profits within their territories. Such a development may well speed up moves to split the MPT in two. In common with reforms in other countries, it would be expected that one part will regulate the industry, the other will provide services.

The slow liberalisation of telecommunications services in China can be contrasted with other East Asian economies and developing countries in general. Clearly, the existence of a capitalist system in other East Asian economies has facilitated liberalisation of telecommunications services in these countries. Telekom Malaysia faces competition from seven smaller competitors and, from January 1999, must allow equal access for all competitors to its network.[7] Singapore Telecom, the former State-owned operator in Singapore, was originally granted a monopoly for basic telephone services until 2007. However, the Government has now decided that in order to promote further growth in telecommunications services, Singapore Telecom will lose its monopoly in the year 2000.[8] Singapore Telecom will receive government compensation of S$1.5 billion, which the Singapore Government expects will be more than recouped from the economic gains as a result of early liberalisation. Liberalisation has also progressed, or is on the agenda, in Taiwan, Korea and Japan. Even in Vietnam, which is still nominally a communist country, two rival operators are emerging to challenge the dominance of Vietnam Posts and Telecommunications (VNPT), the state monopoly. The Vietnamese Government has hinted that foreign partners will be allowed to link up with VNPT's rivals, but has yet to formalise the extent of foreign participation. Despite this lack of clarity, one of VNPT's rivals is in talks with potential foreign partners.[9]

MARKET ENTRY MODES IN THE TELECOMMUNICATIONS INDUSTRY IN CHINA

International business theory suggests that initial entry by foreign firms into liberalising markets is most strongly related to market size, rather than to market growth (Clegg 1996). The initial choice of mode in terms of the foreign market servicing strategy (FMSS) is most influenced by the size of market, while switching from one mode to another is largely governed by the growth of the market.[10] As argued above, in the case of the Chinese economy, the size and strategic importance of the internal economy indicate a FMSS based on local production: if not FDI, then some alternative, collaborative, mode of participation.

In international business practice, a wide set of options is available for market entry and development. However, for service industries, and in particular for the telecommunications services sector, far fewer options are open, principally because of locational exigencies. In manufacturing industry, exporting is typically a practical method of foreign market servicing, especially in the early stages of market development, while in many services the exporting phase is often very short and of high cost. This results especially from the need for the temporary movement of factors of production, or customers between countries. However, in capital-intensive services such as telecommunications, there are additional special considerations. The infrastructural nature of the industry means that exporting as a phase of international market servicing does not, to all intents and purposes, exist. To use the terminology of Boddewyn et al. (1986), telecommunications services exemplify a 'location bound service', at least within the geographical area being served. For this same reason, Enderwick (1986) points out that service industries display a higher degree of geographical concentration than many other activities. This is largely because services, especially business services, naturally follow the location of client manufacturing activities. Equally, the demand for final services will also be strongly linked to household income. In the context of trade and location theory, the comparative advantage in production of most of the value-added in such activities lies within the market to be served. Internationalisation in the telecommunications industry therefore necessarily implies full-bodied local production, which will be concentrated in the centres of economic activity.

Given the locational characteristics of the industry, the next question is about the ownership of operations in the host country. In the light of the restrictions specific to the telecommunications operations sector identified in this chapter, the set of entry and development modes is reduced still further. The modes in evidence are that of representative office, joint venture, turnkey arrangements, and technical assistance agreements. These modes are actually complementary, in that the joint venture is a way of diluting the foreign element in local activity. The joint venture may accompany or precede the other methods of doing business. For example, the joint venture might construct a network, after which the operation of the network is carried out by a local Chinese operator drawing on consulting services from the foreign firm. In international business theory, representation via a local office is the minimum form of initial entry, typical when no substantial business at all is yet being supplied, but prospective to the growth of future business.

In China, the establishment of a representative office telegraphs to the government the foreign entrant's willingness to engage in more substantial business. It permits local information-gathering and the opportunity to influence liberalisation directly, and to engage in local discussion to the firm's competitive advantage. The foreign entrant may also have sufficient capitalisation to enable the provision of certain services under formal contract (e.g. network services such as e-mail). This can be viewed as a contractual joint venture. The most a representative office can legally offer in terms of business is consultancy and technical services. The supply of technical assistance can also be effected via a specific contract.

In a host market with unrestricted entry, the choice of international business mode is based on the minimisation of total cost, given the current or expected absolute size of the firm's market share. As the volume of business expands, theory suggests that the firm successively replaces lower commitment modes (with low fixed costs and high variable costs) with higher commitment ones (with high fixed and low variable costs) (Buckley and Casson 1981). In an environment of government-induced restrictions, the choice of mode reduces to a question of what is permitted. If the modes permitted allow foreign business to earn (or to anticipate) an adequate future profit, entry will be made. However, where the modal restrictions are binding, the firm is likely to enter at a lower level of commitment (or volume of trade) than in the absence of the restrictions. This argument is complicated slightly by the fact that the local customer or partner may have a considerable degree of market power in the host country, even to the extent of being a monopolist. This confers a degree of protection to the foreign supplier or partner, the net effect of which may be to increase the value of the local business. However, local market size in total would tend to be less than under competition.

Moreover, theory would suggest that the cultural differences between foreign firms and the host economy, and the regulatory and legal uncertainty in China, should strongly favour internalised forms of operation, in order to attenuate uncertainty. However, because direct services provision is not currently an option for incoming firms, a relationship-building form of entry mode is appropriate. Establishing such a local presence is not by any means a radical form of market entry, yet its importance, particularly in emerging markets, is understated in the mainstream international business literature.

The effect of the world-wide growth of telecommunications services for a country such as China is that, in the absence of adequate laws and regulations to prevent it, much of the most profitable activity within the economy might well be accounted for by foreign entrants. The position of the Chinese Government can be understood partly in terms of this perceived threat. The service-sector aspects of telecommunications services also bear strongly on internationalisation strategy. Research on the contrasts between manufacturing and service sector industries suggests that services are more prone to multinational production, principally because of the need for supply and demand to be in greater proximity in order to reduce costs. In the case of China's market, even for manufacturing firms, the absolute size of the domestic market is such that production within China is likely to be efficient relatively early in the process of internationalisation.

THE IMPLICATIONS FOR THE STRATEGIES OF FOREIGN TELECOMMUNICATIONS FIRMS IN CHINA

The standard international business literature suggests that firms have to take the foreign market environment as given, and therefore adjust their foreign market servicing strategy in the light of the conditions they face. In contrast, the political science literature places emphasis on the interplay between firms and local interest groups, and on the importance of firms' presence in target markets for the successful lobbying of government and government bodies to influence favourable outcomes. This aspect of the presence effect is an especially important consideration in markets where regulations or foreign investment laws are either absent, not implemented, or are in the process of being worked out. Indeed, it would otherwise be very difficult to explain the presence of multinational firms in a market where the existing official government position on foreign investment is prohibitive.

In practice, firms enter such environments when the potential rewards are substantial enough.[11] In this sense, uncertainty is not a given. The management of the foreign environment, and the associated mitigation of uncertainty and risk, are an integral part of the international strategy. Its role becomes all the more critical in the presence of potential market liberalisation and regulatory voids, as uncertainty over competitors' actions adds substantially to the firm's risk. It behoves any foreign investor at least to cultivate a close relationship with government and its representatives, in order to gain information on policy changes at first hand, and preferably prior to wider public announcement. The management of uncertainty by the firm can further extend to the level of seeking to influence the evolution of official positions, regulations and laws, either collectively or individually – in the hope of greater liberalisation.

World-wide, telecommunications services have customarily been subject to high degrees of state control (Kamall 1996). The effect of intervention and regulation in services has generally been an increased recourse to alternatives to FDI, such as international non-equity arrangements. The provisions for the handling of international telephone traffic that have traditionally existed between state telecommunications suppliers have reflected the historically high level of domestic protection. It is only relatively recently that it has become possible to entertain the existence of truly multinational, equity-based, supply in telecommunications which is integrated between countries and within firms.

The arguments for intervention and the regulation of both domestic and international services in general are founded on the notion of some form of alleged market imperfection or failure, often in respect of imperfect information over the quality and standard of supply. In the case of China, the issue is also a political one deriving, as noted earlier, from the strong preferences of the government. In a climate of actual or potential economic liberalisation, the incentives to enter telecommunications markets for relationship-building are especially acute.

The incidence of regulation in the context of the liberalising Chinese economy is a special case of the antagonism between the needs of the business community and economic development, and the preferences of the Chinese Government. The Chinese Government desires economic development, and therefore the inflow of foreign capital and technology. While the natural tendency of the telecommunications industry might be towards multinational production, this is clearly not entertainable in the normal way in China, both because of the desire to avoid excessive economic dependence and for political motives. Political and other non-economic arguments are invoked in justification of measures to limit foreign participation, in order that effective control remains within the grasp of the government, although hopefully without compromising the economic benefits of foreign participation. The vast size of the Chinese economy means that the bargaining power in this game is very much in the favour of the Chinese Government. A smaller host country would not enjoy such strategic advantages.

Because in any service sector there is a close correlation between the standard of the service and the underlying acceptability and reputation of the supplier, and because services are experience goods, the quality of supply can best be maintained through regulating the entry of firms into the industry. Acknowledging the importance of acceptability to the government, this argument applies with particular force to telecommunications services. In the absence of a coherent regulatory framework, the track record of firms as self-regulators assumes an overwhelming importance.

A corollary of this argument is that service providers operating under these conditions will experience extensive economies of scope. These economies are a function of the spread of a firm's activities rather than their scale. The classic sources of such economies in the service sector are those associated with a firm's large size: advantages of risk spreading and arbitrage; information about buyers and their wants that can be re-used to sell a number of products; assets having multiple uses in different activities. The reputation of the firm itself generates scope economies employed in the sale of a wide range of differentiated service products. In telecommunications provision this applies with particular force.

In the Western economies where liberalisation has progressed the furthest, the growth of multinational telecommunications service firms has been dramatic. The advantages conferred by the experience and reputation of the firm as a differentiated service provider at competitive rates have generated multinationals, partly as a solution to the problem of imperfect buyer information. Often this has been through joint ventures and strategic alliances, which speed up market entry when competitiveness is a function of an early presence. It is in service industries that the potential for the growth of multinational enterprise is the greatest.

The lessons for telecommunications firms seeking to enter the Chinese market is that they must put a premium on establishing a clear commitment. This commitment at the very least should be in the form of a representative office, but is best signalled by investment in some local production facilities. It is crucial to fix a reputation as a good citizen with the Chinese authorities, and to initiate the cultivation of *guanxi* – close personal connections or relations (see, for example, Child and Lu 1996: 4).

As has been argued, service sector industries tend to be among the most protected because, by their nature, they are most likely to satisfy candidacy for regulation. However, early entrants tend naturally to enjoy local market dominance and a key role in shaping future developments, which can work very much to their strategic advantage. Regulation in services is especially susceptible to lobbying by producers' interest groups. It is well known that the erection of non-tariff barriers to trade and investment can be disguised as the maintenance of standards.

Often, even in the West, there is a natural tendency for standards to be policed by existing suppliers, on the argument that they possess the necessary qualifications to judge and advise on the competence of potential entrants. However, even where the domestic suppliers' role is formally limited to the giving of advice, the evolution of regulations is always susceptible to lobbying. While telecommunications services firms may be entering the Chinese market via what might be described as alternative routes to FDI, there is every reason to believe that this strategy could lead to multinational operation in the longer term. Firms have every reason to play a long game, and to nurture mutually beneficial relations with Chinese Government interests

THE KEY EUROPEAN ENTRANTS IN THE CHINESE TELECOMMUNICATIONS INDUSTRY, AND THEIR LEADING FOREIGN RIVALS

Table 10.1 identifies the leading European entrants into the Chinese telecommunications equipment market and their rivals. For reasons already noted, the majority of foreign entrants are equipment manufacturers. The European manufacturers, Alcatel, Ericsson and Siemens have been as successful as their non-European rivals in entering the Chinese market. All the manufacturing companies have opted for joint ventures as the preferred mode of entry, but one non-European firm (Northern Telecom) has also chosen to supply additional services through formal contracts. An overview of the participants reveals that the most intense activity is underway in mobile and cellular telephony, fibre optic construction, and switching. The low cost of erecting cellular towers relative to fixed lines is recognised to be a crucial reason for the choice of this form of network in developing countries. This brings telephony to users who might otherwise not be covered so quickly, or at all. Despite the establishment of local manufacturing facilities, a great deal of telecommunications equipment is still imported. However, on the evidence of foreign firms' participation, the tendency must clearly be towards import substitution. This will meet the Chinese Government's priority of the inward transfer of technology and the need to reduce the demands on scarce foreign exchange.

Despite the official ban on the foreign operation of a public telecommunications network, there are a number of telecommunications services firms

Table 10.1 Key European entrants in Chinese telecommunications equipment manufacturing and construction operations, and main foreign rivals

	Date of entry where known	Mode of entry	Structure of venture	Chinese partner	Activity on entry	Any changes in activity since entry
European Firms						
Alcatel Alsthom-France (Shanghai Bell Telephone Equipment Manufacturing Co.)	1985	Joint venture through the acquisition of Belgium Bell in 1989 – Shanghai Bell	Belgium's Alcatel Bell (32%), MPT (60%) and Belgian government (8%) form the Shanghai Bell Telephone Equipment Manufacturing Co.	MPT, Beijing Telecom Administration	Sales and manufacture large switches, transmission equipment and telephone exchange used for public telephone networks	Telecom transmission, cable, business and rural communication systems and telecoms systems support. ATM network (experimental)
Ericsson-Sweden		Joint venture in Nov. 1993		MPT	Manufacture TACS base stations, switches and cellular mobile telephone handsets	AXE switches for public networks, mobile telephone systems and office switching systems
Siemens-Germany		Joint venture	40% of Beijing International Switching System Corp. (BISC)		Switching systems, PABXs, transmission equipment, radio handsets	

Table 10.1 (cont.)

	Date of entry where known	Mode of entry	Structure of venture	Chinese partner	Activity on entry	Any changes in activity since entry
Non European Firms						
Motorola Inc. US	1993	Joint venture			Mobile telephone (handset)	Cellular phones, paging systems, semi-conductors
Northern Telecom Ltd. Canada		Contract and joint venture	Tong Guang Nortel, Northern Telecom (55%) and China's Ministry of Electronics, through the China Tong Guang Electronics Corp., indirectly owns the balance	MPT, Ministry of Electronics	Switching equipment and software	PABXs, transmission lines, cellular phones
Champion Technology Holdings Ltd. Hong Kong	1991	Joint venture Chengdu mobile network	40% Champion Technology Holdings Ltd.	Local branch of the MPT and the PLA	Paging system	Cellular-phone network
Fujitsu-Japan	1982	Joint venture			SPCs	Switching systems, transmission equipment, communications software

with a presence in China. Table 10.2 suggests that non-European firms have been more successful than European firms in exploiting the loopholes in the vague regulatory framework. The immediate impression is that US firms have established an earlier and higher profile in entering the Chinese market than firms of other nationalities. However, it is necessary to have some grasp of the objectives of the firms concerned and of their strength of commitment to the market. In the years 1992 and 1993, many US telecommunications firms invested in China. Poor investment prospects in their home US market, exacerbated by domestic regulation and anti-trust law, provided an incentive to venture into foreign markets that appeared to promise greater growth. Furthermore, many US firms may have entered the Chinese market in order to boast a company presence there, with a view to bolstering company image, and not primarily for reasons of intrinsic interest in China. Indeed, in a number of cases the amounts invested were actually small, but were just sufficient to benefit the international reputation of the investing firms.

Despite the size and potential of the Chinese market, multinationals' investment in China is part of a global decision, and is evaluated on a comparative basis. After some two to three years, there is some evidence that certain US firms felt disappointed by the Chinese market. A case in point is Nynex, which withdrew senior management to redeploy them in more productive areas in the same region. Subsequent to further deregulation in the US market, it would appear that the relative attractiveness of China has waned, and US firms have actually expanded investment plans in their domestic market at the expense of investment plans outside the United States. Not surprisingly, reductions in commitment to China tend to go unannounced, on account of rivalry between international competitors. Bureaucratic barriers and restrictions on foreign investment have led some firms to reorientate towards the more mature economies or developing economies which do not pose these difficulties (Ingelbrecht 1995: 24). Even so, in the midst of this, it is possible to identify instances of unequivocal commitment to the Chinese market. For instance, AT&T opened its first corporate representative office in Beijing in October 1985, and now has a China Business Unit (AT&T China) – a fact which distinguishes it from other telecommunications firms, and which points to the importance of firm-specific advantages of size.

As regards other non-European firms, Singapore Telecom has signed a memorandum to form a joint venture with a local partner to finance the construction of a network in Shanghai. The network will be operated by Lian Tong under a cooperative agreement with Singapore Telecom's local partner. In return, Lian Tong will repay the joint venture's investment over a fixed period, and subsequently share a portion of future income with the joint venture (ibid.). In effect, Singapore Telecom earns revenue from the operation of a Chinese telecommunications network without owning a formal stake in the venture.

Table 10.2 Key European entrants in Chinese telecommunications services, and main foreign rivals

	Date of entry where known	Mode of entry	Structure of venture	Chinese partner	Activity on entry	Any changes in activity since entry
European Firms						
British Telecom UK	1995 Representative office in Beijing			MPT and PTBs	E-mail services	
France Télécom	1996			Lian Tong and Tianjin Communications Investment	Build network	
Deutsche Telekom	1996 Representative office in Beijing			China Telecom (directed by MPT)	Signed MoU to install and operate national and international network	
Non-European Firms						
AT&T US(a)	Oct. 1985 Representative office in Beijing	Joint venture		MPT and PTBs	Manufacture fibre-optic	Producing such items as optic-fibre cables and switching systems
Ameritech Telecommunications US	27 April 1995	Joint venture with China Communications System Co.	80% (Ameritech), 20% (Lian-Tong)	Lian Tong and China Communications System Co.	Build and operate GSM and fixed networks	
MCI US					Long-distance voice service	
Nynex US	1994	Joint venture-Ji Tong		Ministry of Electronics, Unicom	Network assistance	

Table 10.2 (cont.)

	Date of entry where known	Mode of entry	Structure of venture	Chinese partner	Activity on entry	Any changes in activity since entry
Sprint US(a)	1992			Telecom General Office of MPT, Lian Tong	Direct long-distance voice service	Connect US Internet through Sprintlink. Provide network connection
MTC Canada		Joint venture		PRC	Supply a cellular telephone network	
Hong Kong Telecom Hong Kong(C)	1988	Joint venture		MPT	Installed cable between Hong Kong and China, transmission facilities	Built networks
Singapore Telecom Singapore	1995	Joint venture Asia Pacific First Star Communications Technology	35% (Singapore) others: China's Ministry of Posts and Telecommunications and an investment group controlled by the Beijing Municipal government	MPT, Beijing Municipal government	Nationwide radio paging network	
Telstra-Australia	May 1995 – open an office in Beijing				Hoping to have a share in China's network operations	

Notes:
(a) Engaged in both manufacturing and service operations.
(b) This operation includes provisions governed by a signed memorandum.
(c) Hong Kong Telecom is a majority-owned foreign affiliate of Cable and Wireless (UK), in which the latter holds a 57.5 per cent equity share. However, it operates as a native Hong Kong firm, with a strategy of developing its own regional Asian hub.

While the US competition has tended to retreat from China, European firms – in particular Deutsche Telekom, France Telecom and British Telecom – can be seen to occupy a stronger position. These firms benefit from domestic monopoly or dominant market positions at home, and have substantial funds to invest abroad. It remains to be seen, however, whether European firms, like US firms before them, have invested only token amounts in China, and whether they will withdraw when full liberalisation in the EU telecommunications market occurs, scheduled for 1 January 1998.

CONCLUDING REMARKS

The inadequacy of the current legal and regulatory environment in China is largely the product of Chinese history and of the pace of economic change. Within a centrally planned system, control via internal directives is clearly sufficient. However, any departure from this economic model immediately means confusion. The presence of firms and interest groups with declining allegiance, or no allegiance whatsoever, to central planning demands a well-constructed regulatory framework. As there is currently no such framework, nor the prospect of one, a coalition of interested parties has emerged, including incoming firms, profit-seeking State bodies, and large customers. Foreign firms' entry strategies have adapted to encompass the placing of pressure on the authorities, in concert with those other groups who stand to gain from market liberalisation.

The regulations governing the entry strategies of foreign telecommunications services firms can be contrasted with those governing the choice of entry mode for banks (Chapter 11) and insurance companies (Chapter 12). While foreign operators are barred from offering telecommunications services, foreign banks are allowed to offer services to clients in China as long as they meet certain requirements. While only four foreign insurers have been granted licences to offer their services, many more have established representative offices in order to position themselves for eventual liberalisation. In many respects, this is similar to the strategy adopted by foreign telecommunications operators. However, it would appear that foreign telecommunications operators have been more adept at exploiting legal loopholes and pursuing indirect forms of FDI than their counterparts in the insurance industry.

The political uncertainty in the latter years of the Deng era was compounded by the uncertainty caused by the non-publication of a Telecommunications Law. Additionally, there are uncertainties over issues of authority, such as whether the provincial PTBs and the provincial governments have the power to authorise inward FDI in telecommunications. World-wide, the telecommunications industry is no stranger to uncertainty, because liberalised and competitive structures are by no means complete, even in the developed economies. At the same time, the industry is one of great opportunity because of the secular growth in the demand for communications. In China, strategic company decisions have to be made that position the firm appropriately both for the present closed market, and for the potential of a liberalised market in the future.

Unlike telecommunications liberalisation in most developed and developing countries, reform in China is being driven from the grass roots and from outside the MPT, not by central government decisions. Actors within China, such as other State bodies, large customers, as well as foreign firms, are challenging the current monopoly position of MPT. Instead of being transfixed by the current obstacles in China, foreign telecommunications firms have adapted their entry strategies. These firms' strategies have tended to be individualistic in nature rather than collective, in order to foster individual preferment. This is in good measure imposed by the need for close relations with those in authority in China. Only a limited number of firms can enjoy such close relationships, so collective representations are less appropriate and less effective.

The importance of proximity between supplier and customer is a distinctive feature of service sector activity. It is a standard consideration in the foreign market entry decision process, but becomes critical when government interests assume a crucial importance in local market preferences. Foreign firms that are potential service providers therefore pursue the maintenance of a good relationship with the MPT and local PTBs by offering advice or participating in joint ventures where possible.

Because the development goals of the Chinese Government can only be realised with the participation of foreign capital, ultimately some route must emerge through which foreign firms can enter the market in a substantial fashion which affords them the requisite control over the assets they allocate to the Chinese market. Those firms which see the importance of relationship building and are able to demonstrate commitment, most probably those with access to substantial finance, are in the best position to adopt the required long-term strategy.

NOTES

1 See Chapter 2 for further details on the *Provisional Guidelines on Foreign Investment Projects*.
2 An internal directive does not have any status within the legal system of China. However, the legal and political systems contrast markedly from those of Western countries, and such a directive is generally regarded as a provisional regulation or law.
3 See 'Telecom Rising Nationwide', *Beijing Review*, 36(9), March 1993: 1–7.
4 See 'New Alliances Fill Gaps', *Far Eastern Economic Review* 157(35), 1 September 1994: 48–9.
5 There are some seventeen partners in total in the joint venture. However, the three named Ministries are by far the dominant actors.
6 *China Daily*, 10 May 1993, cited in Tan (1994).
7 See the supplement on Malaysia, *Financial Times*, 18 July 1996.

8 See the supplement on Singapore, *Financial Times*, 2 July 1996.
9 See the supplement on Vietnam, *Financial Times*, 9 April 1996.
10 The underlying rationale for this is set out by Buckley and Casson (1981).
11 This is the concept of the compensating risk premium, familiar from the country risk analysis literature.

REFERENCES

Boddewyn, J., Halbrich, M. and Perry, A. (1986) 'Service Multinationals: Conceptualisation, Measurement and Theory', *Journal of International Business Studies*, 17(3): 41-57.

Buckley, P. and Casson, M. (1981) 'The Optimal Timing of a Foreign Direct Investment', *Economic Journal*, 91: 75-87.

Carver, A. (1996) 'Open and Secret Regulations and their Implication for Foreign Investment', in J. Child and Y. Lu (eds) *Management Issues in China*, Volume 2 *International Enterprises*, London: Routledge, pp.11–29.

Casson, M. (1982) 'Transaction Costs and the Theory of Multinational Enterprise', in A. Rugman (ed.) *New Theories of the Multinational Enterprise*, London: Croom Helm, pp.24–43.

Child, J. and Y. Lu (1996) 'China and the International Enterprise', in J. Child and Y. Lu (eds) *Management Issues in China*: Volume 2 *International Enterprises*, London: Routledge, pp.1–8.

Clegg, J. (1993) 'Investigating the Determinants of Service Sector Foreign Direct Investment', in H. Cox, J. Clegg and G. Letto-Gillies (eds) *The Growth of Global Business*, London: Routledge, pp.85–104.

Clegg. J. (1996) 'United States Foreign Direct Investment in the European Community: The Effects of Market Integration in Perspective', in F. Burton, M. Yamin, and S. Young (eds) *The Changing European Environment*, London: Macmillan, pp.189–206.

Clifford, M. (1994) 'A Question of Money', *Far Eastern Economic Review*, 157(14), 7 April: 47–48.

Economist Intelligence Unit (1993) 'Regional Infrastructure: Telecommunication in Guangdong Well Wired', *Business China*, 9 August: 3–4.

Enderwick, P. (1986) 'Service Sector Multinationals', Chapter 7 of Part 6 in M. Brooke and P. Buckley (eds) *Handbook of International Trade*, London: Kluwer, 6.7-01–6.7-18.

Ingelbrecht, N. (1995) 'Lian Tong Deal to Extend Singapore Role in China', *Communications Week International*, 147, 26 June: 3.

International Monetary Fund (1994) *International Financial Statistics Yearbook*, 47, Washington, DC: IMF.

Kamall, S. (1996) *Spicer's European Union Policy Briefings: Telecommunications*, London: Cartermill.

Kaye, L. (1992) 'Long March from Chaos', *Far Eastern Economic Review*, 155(22), 4 June: 54.

Tan, Z. (1994) 'Challenges to the MPT's Monopoly', *Telecommunications Policy*, 18(3): 174–81.

Ure, J. (1994) 'Telecommunications, with Chinese Characteristics', *Telecommunications Policy*, 18(3): 182-94.

Warwick, W. (1994) 'A Review of AT&T's Business History in China: The Memorandum of Understanding In Context', *Telecommunications Policy*, 18(3): 265–74.

Zhu, G. (1994) 'Telecom Development – the Chinese Way', *Intermedia*, 22(2): 17–19.

Zita, K. (1987) 'Modernizing China's Telecommunications', 1, London and Hong Kong: Economist Intelligence Unit/Business International.

11 The choice of market-servicing mode for European banks in China

Peter Chi-Ming Fu

INTRODUCTION

The banking sector in mainland China has undergone significant changes in recent years, and there have been numerous changes involving the regulatory framework. In particular, the potential contribution of foreign financial institutions to China's economic development has been recognised by the relaxation of restrictions in the *Regulations for the Administration of Foreign Investment Financial Institutions*[1] (hereafter the 'Regulations'), which were promulgated by the State Council in February 1994.

The adoption of these, and other related, regulations and laws[2] are necessary for the further development of the market economy in China. International trade and foreign investment are expected to grow and diversify in the future. The involvement of banks, especially those from developed countries, is needed to facilitate such activities. In addition to their main function as channellers of funds, the banks can also provide information on the domestic economy, its industries and on specific firms: information that is extremely welcome for customers who wish to trade with, or invest in, China. Moreover, the presence of foreign banks will promote competition, and provide models from which their Chinese counterparts can learn and hence improve efficiency in the longer term. In addition, the Chinese Government also believes that the reduction in the restrictions on the entry of foreign banks should lead to reciprocal access for Chinese banks in overseas markets.

Fu (1995) has identified that, in addition to the gradual relaxation of entry barriers and of restrictions on the scope of business in the recent legislation, a major reason for the increasing numbers of foreign banks which have sought to establish some form of physical presence within China has been the rapid growth of non-bank foreign direct investment. Foreign banks have to a great degree been 'client-following'. The aim of this chapter is to consider the choice of entry mode for foreign banks in China, and to illustrate the important factors by reference to the experience of European banks. The next section thus outlines the various ways in which banks can become involved in international operations, with particular reference paid to the various forms of 'multinational banking', i.e. activities carried out through banking establishments located in foreign centres (Pecchioli 1983: 51). This is followed by a review of the regulations regarding foreign financial institutions in China, which draws attention to the forms of multinational banking which are now permitted. Most studies of multinational banking treat these different forms of physical presence as one category (i.e. the internalised hierarchy). Here a model is put forward to explain the choice among the different forms, and the history of European involvement is assessed. Finally, consideration is given to the future form of European banks' involvement in China.

TYPES OF INTERNATIONAL INVOLVEMENT OF BANKS

The involvement of a bank in international operations can take place in a number of ways. The simplest way is through *correspondent banking* relationships. The banks involved agree to exchange deposits to provide for clearing cheques and to compensate each other for any other services rendered, usually by placing more deposits at the banks supplying correspondent services (Rose 1993: 47). At the international level, correspondent banking can be used to effect settlement, undertake exchange transactions, and provide information on the financial status of companies which are customers or prospective customers of a bank's clients. It is equivalent to the exporting activities of manufacturing firms. This approach is the *least costly* way of providing international services for banks' clients since it does not involve cross-border transfer of capital and other resources from home country, and no physical presence in another country is required. However, the opportunity for expansion is limited with this approach, because correspondent banks tend to favour their own interests rather than those of their counterparts. Furthermore, the inseparability[3] factor of banking services reduces the propensity for banks to engage in correspondent banking.

The alternative form of international involvement for banks is through the establishment of offices, or other types of physical presence overseas. For most types of financial services, some kind of physical presence is necessary to provide them adequately. Dunning (1993b: 273–75) found that the 'foreign presence index'[4] for US commercial banking/financial services, insurance, and investment banking (brokerage) firms was as high as 100 per cent, 78 per cent, and 84 per cent, respectively. A wide range of organisational forms are available to banks which plan to establish a presence in foreign countries (Khoury 1980: 89–105): the four major forms may be summarised as follows:

1 The *representative office* serves as point of contact for the provision of marketing information and the establishment of business connections. However, representative offices are not allowed to undertake any banking activities such as deposit-taking and lending. Foreign banks usually

adopt the representative office as an initial form of multinational banking, particularly for establishing a presence in developing countries.
2 *Subsidiaries/affiliates* are local institutions incorporated under host country law in which the bank holds a controlling/minority interest. They are separate legal entities from their parent bank and normally can conduct all the banking activities allowed to domestic banks of the host country.
3 *Foreign branches* are legal extensions of the parent bank, and are not locally incorporated companies. Creditors have claims on the assets of the parent bank. Foreign branches can usually offer the full range of banking services, including domestic deposit-taking and lending.
4 *Agencies* are also a legal extension of the parent bank from a foreign country. They can transfer and lend money, but cannot accept deposits from domestic sources. Trade financing and other commercial loans are their main services. Without access to funding from domestic deposits, agencies rely on funds transferred from their parent companies and related offices and funds borrowed in the interbank markets of the host country.

THE REGULATIONS REGARDING FOREIGN FINANCIAL INSTITUTIONS IN CHINA

After thirty years of isolation, foreign banking activities in China were reactivated in December 1979 when a representative office of the Export-Import Bank of Japan was established in Beijing. Since then, many foreign financial institutions have set up representative offices in Beijing, and later in other open cities. At the beginning of 1995, there were 393 representative offices of foreign financial institutions located in twenty cities in China.[5] According to the 1991 *PBOC Procedures for the Administration of the Establishment of Resident Representative Offices in China by Financial Institutions with Foreign Investment*,[6] a foreign representative office in China is limited to non-profit making activities such as consultancy, liaison, and market research.[7] It may not undertake profit-making activities on behalf of its Head Office or its branches.[8] Although representative offices do not directly engage in banking business, the regulations nevertheless empower PBOC and its branches to supervise, regulate and examine their work. The representative offices are required to submit an annual report on their activities during the previous year to PBOC, which has the right to inspect and examine documents held in their offices. Together with the restrictions on deposit-taking and lending services, most foreign commercial banks treat their representative offices as transitional structures while awaiting permission to establish branches in China.

In 1982, the Nam Yang Commercial Bank of Hong Kong established a branch in Shenzhen. On 2 April 1985, the State Council promulgated the *Regulations for the Administration of Foreign Investment Banks and Sino-Foreign Joint Venture Banks in Special Economic Zones* and, since then, foreign banks have been allowed to establish management set-ups[9] in the

Special Economic Zones (SEZs). On 8 September 1990, PBOC announced a directive on *Procedures for the Administration of Foreign Investment Financial Institutions and Sino-Foreign Joint Venture Financial Institutions in Shanghai*. Two years later, Shanghai took over Shenzhen's leading position in accommodating foreign financial institutions.

On 25 February 1994, the State Council promulgated the *Regulations for the Administration of Foreign Investment Financial Institutions*, which superseded the previous regulations for the SEZs and Shanghai. In the 'Regulations', five types of 'foreign investment financial institutions' are identified: branches of foreign banks; foreign investment banks; joint venture banks; foreign investment finance companies; and joint venture finance companies.[10]

According to the 'Regulations', foreign financial institutions wishing to establish either a branch, or a foreign investment bank, or a foreign investment finance company must have maintained a representative office in China for more than two years. Each party in a joint venture bank or finance company must be a financial institution, and the foreign party must have already established a representative office in China. In short, individual foreign financial institutions must have maintained at least one representative office in China before they can establish any form of management set-up in the country. This requirement highlights the cautious attitude of PBOC to the removal of the restrictions on foreign bank entry: two years' operation through a representative office may be regarded as a 'probation period' during which time PBOC is able to evaluate the 'conduct' of the foreign banks, before they are allowed to upgrade into branch operation. PBOC has also adopted a variety of other such 'probationary practices'. For example, foreign banks in China have traditionally had to follow a policy of one branch in one city. However, as from March 1996, this policy has been relaxed and they may now establish sub-branches in four cities (Shanghai, Tianjin, Guangzhou and Dalian), provided that they have been operating in China for at least three years, and that they have earned good profits in the last two years, and that they have had a monthly loan commitment of at least US$100m in the year preceding the year of application.[11]

Minimum capital and/or assets requirements are normally attached to the granting of the licence or authorisation for foreign bank entry in many countries,[12] in order to ensure that the foreign financial institutions are able to maintain a reasonable level of financial strength so as to carry on banking business in a sound and efficient manner. The minimum capital and assets requirements for the different types of foreign financial institutions in China are shown in Table 11.1. A registered capital requirement does not apply to branches of foreign banks, although there is a requirement that branches should hold RMB 100m in working capital. This figure is only one-third of the minimum registered capital required for a foreign investment or joint venture bank. However, a branch is not a separate legal entity, and the parent bank is legally liable for all of its debts in China.

Table 11.1 Capital and assets requirements for the different types of foreign financial institutions in China

Financial institution	Capital requirements	Assets requirements
Branch of a foreign bank	Working capital: Rmb 100m equivalent freely convertible currencies	Parent's assets totalling not less than US$20 bn
Foreign investment bank or joint venture bank	Registered capital (paid-up at least 50 per cent): Rmb 300m equivalent freely convertible currencies	Parent's assets totalling not less than US$10bn
Foreign investment or joint venture finance company	Registered capital (paid-up at least 50 per cent): Rmb 200m equivalent freely convertible currencies	Foreign party's assets totalling not less than US$10bn

Thus, protection against bankruptcy may be higher in branches, despite the lower capital requirement, as the parent bank acts as a guarantor and the working capital is typically in more liquid forms of assets.

Foreign-funded finance companies have a smaller capital requirement than foreign-funded banks, but are more restricted in the scope of their business: for example, finance companies are not permitted to undertake remittances or import/export clearings, and they can only accept foreign currencies deposits of at least US$100,000 with a term of at least three months. Foreign-funded banks are not subject to such limitations on minimum amount and maturity for deposit-taking business, although they are (like the finance companies) also prohibited at the current time from taking Renminbi deposits from local residents and enterprises. Since the beginning of 1997, a few foreign banks' (including the Hong Kong and Shanghai Banking Corporation) branch offices in the Pudong Development Area of Shanghai have been permitted to take Renminbi deposits on a trial basis. The branch office of the Sino-Europe joint venture (the International Bank of Paris and Shanghai) at Pudong has also recently been granted permission to offer Renminbi deposits with effect from September 1997.[13] If the restrictions on Renminbi business were to be relaxed in the future, the distinction between foreign-funded banks and finance companies in China would be similar to that in Hong Kong, where finance companies are referred to as deposit-taking companies (DTCs). Table 11.2 summarises the current scope of business for foreign-funded banks and finance companies in China.

Branches of foreign banks have traditionally been restricted to foreign currency business. As from March 1996, however, foreign-funded banks in Shanghai, Shenzhen, Jiangsu and Dalian have been permitted to act as designated foreign exchange banks (i.e. they can buy and sell foreign currencies against Renminbi) for foreign enterprises.[14] Furthermore, some joint venture banks (such as the Chinese Mercantile Bank and the Xiamen International Bank) are permitted to operate Renminbi business[15] in the

Table 11.2 Scope of business for foreign-funded banks and foreign-funded finance companies in China(a)

Scope of business	Foreign-funded bank	Foreign-funded finance company
Foreign exchange deposit	✓	✓(b)
Foreign exchange lending	✓	✓
Foreign exchange note discount	✓	✓
Approved foreign exchange investment	✓	✓
Foreign exchange remittances	✓	✗
Foreign exchange guarantee	✓	✓
Import and export clearing	✓	✗
Trading in foreign exchange for its own account and for clients	✓	✓
Acting as an agent for the exchange of foreign currencies and foreign exchange notes	✓	✗
Acting as an agent for foreign currency credit card payments	✓	✗
Custody and safe deposit box services	✓	✗
Credit investigation and advice	✓	✓
Foreign exchange trust	✗	✓
Approved domestic currency business and other foreign currency business	✓	✓

Notes:
(a) There are three types of foreign-funded bank: the foreign investment bank; the branch of a foreign bank; and the joint venture bank. There are two types of foreign-funded finance company: the foreign investment finance company; and the joint venture finance company.
(b) Each deposit must not be less than US$100,000, and must have a term of no less than three months.

same way as domestic banks. However, a major obstacle to the opening-up of Renminbi business at the retail level is the different profit tax rates levied on domestic and foreign-funded banks. At the end of 1996, the tax rates applied to foreign-funded, local joint-stock, and state-owned banks were 15 per cent, 33 per cent, and 55 per cent, respectively.[16] If the foreign-funded banks were allowed to compete unrestrictedly for Renminbi business with the domestic banks, it would be unfair to the latter. PBOC officials propose that a unified profits tax system is one of the prerequisites[17] for the further relaxation for Renminbi business.

Table 11.3 illustrates the growth of representative offices and management set-ups of foreign financial institutions (including insurance companies) since 1988. Between 1988 and 1995, the number of representative offices doubled from 202 to 426, while the number of management set-ups quadrupled from 32 to 129. Table 11.4 shows that the branch is the most prominent form of management set-up: the number of branches grew from 74 to 109 between 1993 and 1995, while the number of foreign investment banks only rose from three to five, and the number of joint venture banks remained stable at six.

Table 11.3 Growth of representative offices and management set-ups of foreign-funded financial institutions in China

Year	1988	1990	1992	1993	1994	1995
Representative offices	202	217	227	225	379	426
Management set-ups	32	38	85	90	116	129

Sources:
Y. C. Wong, 'The growth of Foreign Investment Financial Institutions', in P. K. Lau ed., *The Mega Trend of China's Economy 1995* (published in Chinese), Commercial Press (HK), p.193
List of Foreign Financial Institutions in China (up to the end of March, 1993), External Affairs Department, People's Bank of China (printed in Chinese)
Hong Kong Economic Journal, 25 January 1995, p.7. Data up to end of November 1994
Hong Kong Economic Journal, 9 August 1995, p.21. Data up to 10 July 1995

Table 11.4 Management set-ups of foreign-funded financial institutions in China

	Branches of foreign banks	Foreign investment banks	Joint venture banks	Foreign investment and joint venture finance companies	Branches of foreign insurance companies
1993	74	3	6	4	3
1995	109	5	6	5	4

Sources: *List of Foreign Financial Institutions in China* (up to the end of March, 1993), External Affairs Department, People's Bank of China (printed in Chinese)
Hong Kong Economic Journal, 9 August 1995, p.21. Data up to 10 July 1995

It should be noted that the total number of representative offices and management set-ups is not equivalent to the number of foreign financial institutions having a presence in China. The former is the total number of offices and branches of foreign-funded financial institutions (banks, financial companies, and insurance companies), incorporated either overseas or in the PRC. For example, the Standard Chartered Bank had seven branches and seven representative offices in different locations in China in 1993.

AN ECLECTIC MODEL FOR FOREIGN MARKET ENTRY MODE

As mentioned above, foreign financial institutions in China are restricted with regard to their initial entry mode to the establishment of representative offices, and it is only subsequently that they can upgrade their operations to some form of management set-up. It would thus be meaningless to analyse the determinants of their initial entry mode in China, since the representative office is the only permitted form. However, the determinants of their choice of post-entry market-servicing mode in the country (i.e. the decision on whether to maintain a representative office and/or to establish a different type of management set-up after the minimum residence requirement has been satisfied) deserves investigation. To achieve this objective, it is useful to adapt the framework used by Agarwal and Ramaswami (1992), and based on Dunning's eclectic model, for explaining the choice between exporting, licensing, joint venture, and sole venture (see Figure 11.1).

The entry mode behaviour of firms may be explained by the joint effects of three types of determinant factors: the ownership advantages of the firm, the location advantages of a market, and the internalisation advantages of integrating transactions within the firm. In their survey of ninety-seven US-funded multinational equipment leasing firms, Agarwal and Ramaswami (1992) analysed the choices of entry mode in three countries (the United Kingdom, Japan, and Brazil) according to the factors in Figure 11.1. Equipment leasing firms perform an important financial intermediary function, i.e. channelling funds from surplus units to deficit units, in a similar way to financial institutions. Indeed, equipment leasing can be regarded as financing (loans) secured with the equipment being leased. Furthermore, equipment leasing is typically demanded by corporate customers. Thus, equipment leasing is in many ways similar to the two most requested services provided by foreign financial institutions in China at the present time, namely, trade financing and project financing. Hence the above framework should thus apply well to the entry mode choices of foreign financial institutions. In the context of multinational banking, the exporting mode is equivalent to correspondent banking, licensing has no equivalent form, the joint venture has a direct counterpart in the joint venture bank, and the sole venture may be a wholly owned subsidiary form (i.e. a foreign-investment bank in the 'Regulations') or a branch.

Ownership advantages
Firm size
Multinational experience
Ability to develop differentiated products

Location advantages
Market potential
Investment risk

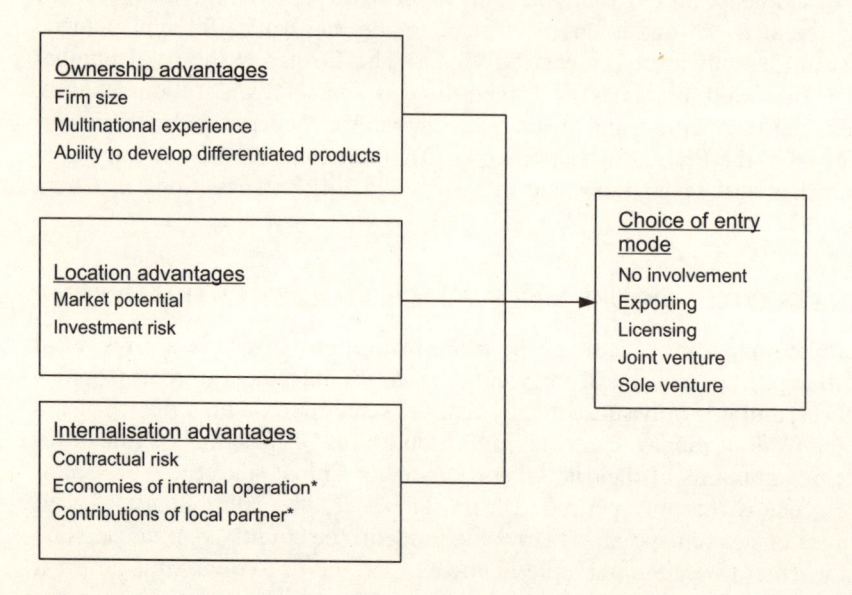

Internalisation advantages
Contractual risk
Economies of internal operation*
Contributions of local partner*

Choice of entry mode
No involvement
Exporting
Licensing
Joint venture
Sole venture

Figure 11.1 A schematic representation of entry choice factors
Source: Adapted from Agarwall and Ramaswami (1992)
Notes: * Added factor

Ownership advantages

The three most important ownership advantages which foreign financial institutions typically possess are size, multinational experience, and the ability to develop differentiated products. The size of a financial institution, the scope of its network, and its reputation (which is normally positively correlated with its size), can significantly affect its ability to secure funds at competitive prices (Dunning 1993b: 273). Size provides a cost-reducing advantage to financial institutions, and is expected to be positively correlated with the propensity of foreign financial institutions to enter China. In addition, large financial institutions have more resources and are more capable of absorbing risks because their assets are diversified. As a result, they are more able to select high control/high involvement modes such as branch. Furthermore, the assets and capital requirements for foreign banks' entry present significant barriers for smaller banks. For example, the US$20bn assets needed to establish a foreign branch is a stringent requirement which might be beyond the resources of many overseas banks which might like to enter the Chinese market.

As a result, the European banks with branches in China are big banks, though the same is also true of several of the banks with just representative offices. Tables 11.5, 11.6, and 11.7 provide details of the European banks in China according to the form of their multinational banking operation: branch and representative office; joint venture; representative office alone. The tables also provide two alternative measures of their size (i.e. their rankings by capital and by assets among the largest banks in the world). Although assets are often used as indicators of the size of firms, surveys on banks usually regard capital as a better measurement of strength. For example, the ranking in *The Banker* is based on tier-one capital, which includes common stock, disclosed reserves, and retained earnings.

Why should some large banks only have representative offices, but not branches, in China? There are three possible explanations. First, there are some banks (e.g. the Rabobank from the Netherlands) which have only set up their representative offices within the past two years, and are thus not yet eligible to establish a branch. Second, some banks may be eligible to upgrade to branch operation, but have adopted a corporate strategy of not running retail banking operations outside their home countries. Instead, such banks content themselves with the provision in China of mainly investment advising services, and such services can be provided adequately through a representative office. For example, the Swiss Bank Corporation has decided that its activities would be structured into four divisions comprising its core businesses (i.e. private banking and institutional asset management), investment banking, and in Switzerland alone, retail and commercial clients.[18] Third, there are other banks who have acquired an entry into the growing Chinese market through the purchase of majority

Table 11.5 European banks with branches and representative offices in China

Institution	Place of Incorporation	Branch	Representative office	Ranking by capital (a)	Assets in US$ (b)
Banque National de Paris	France	Shenzhen, Tianjin, Guangzhou	Beijing, Shanghai	19/33	325.3
Banque Indosuez	France	Shenzhen, Shanghai	Beijing, Guangzhou	127/114	87.4
Crédit Lyonnais	France	Shanghai, Xiamen, Tianjin	Beijing, Guangzhou, Shenzhen	38/41	339.4
Société Générale	France	Shenzhen, Tianjin, Guangzhou, Shanghai	Beijing	27/26	326.5
Deutsche Bank AG	Germany	Guangzhou	Beijing, Shanghai	6/13	503.4
Dresdner Bank	Germany	Shanghai, Shenzhen	Beijing	31/29	332.9
Banca Di Roma	Italy	Shanghai	Beijing	60/59	134.0
ABN AMRO Bank	Netherlands	Shanghai, Shenzhen	Beijing, Guangzhou, Tianjin	14/19	340.6
ING Bank	Netherlands	Shanghai, Shenzhen	Beijing, Shenyang	50/52	154.1
Banco Nacional Ultramarino S.A.	Portugal	Zhuhai		nil/nil	nil
Crédit Suisse	Switzerland	Shanghai	Beijing	13/15	358.7
Hongkong & Shanghai Banking Corp.	United Kingdom	Shenzhen, Shanghai, Xiamen, Qingdao, Tianjin, Beijing	Dalian, Guangzhou, Wuhan Chengdu	1/1	351.6
Standard Chartered Bank PLC	United Kingdom	Shenzhen, Shanghai, Tianjing, Haikou, Nanjing, Xiamen, Zhuhai	Beijing, Ningbo, Dalian, Guangzhou, Hangzhou, Qingdao, Nanning	118/87	60.4

Source: *List of Foreign Financial Institutions in China* (up to the end of March, 1993), External Affairs Department, People's Bank of China (printed in Chinese)
China Banking and Finance, Asia Law and Practice Ltd., Jan 93–Jan 96 issues, and *China Law and Practice*, Asia Law and Practice Ltd., Feb 96–June 96 issues

Notes:
(a) Ranking by 'The top 1000 world banks', *The Banker*, July 1996. Ranking by 'The world's top 200 banks', *Euromoney*, June 1996. Different rankings are due to different definitions of capital.
(b) *The Banker*, July 1996, pp. 143–93 or *Euromoney*, June 1996 if data is nil in the former.

Table 11.6 European banks with joint ventures in China

Institution	Foreign/domestic partners	Country of foreign partner	Head office
The International Bank of Paris and Shanghai	Banque Nationale de Paris/Industrial and Commercial Bank of China	France	Shanghai

Source: *List of Foreign Financial Institutions in China* (up to the end of March, 1993), External Affairs Department, People's Bank of China (printed in Chinese)

shares in other banks which already have active involvement in China. For example, in July 1996, Crédit Agricole bought 53 per cent of the shares in the Banque Indosuez, which had a strong franchise in equities, foreign exchange and corporate banking in Asia.[19] In particular, the Banque Indosuez has two branches and two representative offices at different strategic locations in China.

Firms with higher multinational experience may be expected to prefer investment modes of entry (Agarwal and Ramaswami 1992: 5). Erramilli and Rao (1990: 137) also noted that management's knowledge of foreign markets is positively correlated with the level and pace of the firm's resource commitments to these markets. Multinational experience reduces both uncertainty and the risk of international entry perceived by management. Hence, it is positively related with the resource commitment of foreign market-servicing modes. Thus the popularity of the branch as a form of management set-up for European financial institutions in China is partly due to the fact that most of the institutions are well experienced multinational banks and/or banks based in Hong Kong (and which thus have good market knowledge of China). Among the European banks which have branches in China (see Table 11.5), both the Hong Kong and Shanghai Bank and the Standard Chartered Bank established their presence in Shanghai in the nineteenth century, and their branches were still legally operative after 1949 (the year of establishment of the PRC Government). Other banks such as the Banque National de Paris (which set up a branch in China in 1860) and the Banque Indosuez also have a long history in China, withdrew after 1949 but returned in the 1980s. Their previous experience and connections with China enabled them to be members of the first batch of foreign banks entering China after the door was reopened in 1979. For the Banco Nacional Ultramarino S.A. of Portugal, its presence in Zhuhai can be explained by the proximity of Zhuhai to Macau – Portugal's colony for more than one hundred years.

Agarwal and Ramaswami (1992: 4) note that when a firm possesses the ability to develop differentiated products, it may run the risk of loss of long-term revenues if it shares this knowledge with host country firms. Thus, higher control market-servicing modes are often found for firms with higher

218 Peter Chi-Ming Fu

Table 11.7 European banks with representative offices in China

Institution	Place of incorporation	Representative office	Ranking by capital[a]	Assets in US$ b[b]
Östereichische Lander Bank	Austria	Beijing	nil/nil	nil
Generale Belgian Bank [e]	Belgium	Beijing, Shanghai	78/91	161.1
Krediet Bank N.V.	Belgium	Beijing, Shanghai	110/122	104.6
Unibank Denmark	Denmark	Beijing	nil/150[d]	41.8
Union Bank of Finland	Finland	Beijing	nil/nil	nil
Banque Paribas	France	Beijing, Shanghai, Guangzhou, Dalian	25/24	272.2
Compagnie Financière De Cic Et De L' Union Europeenne	France	Beijing	113/116 [d]	112.9
Caisse Nationale de Crédit Agricole	France	Beijing	2/10	386.4
Banque Française du Commerce Extérieur	France	Shanghai	nil/nil	nil
Bayerische Vereins Bank	Germany	Beijing	49/45 [d]	247.6
Commerzbank	Germany	Beijing	36/28	281.4
Westdeutsche Landesbank	Germany	Beijing, Shanghai	34/40	291.3
Banca Commerciale Italiana	Italy	Beijing, Shanghai	67/70	100.4
Banca Nazionale del Lavoro	Italy	Beijing, Shanghai	58/80	107.9
Banco Ambrosiano Veneto	Italy	Beijing	267/nil	34.1
CARIPLO	Italy	Beijing	43/51	117.6
Credit Italiano	Italy	Beijing	115/80	102.8
Istituto Bancario San Paolo Di Torino	Italy	Beijing	45/56	160.9
Monte Dei Paschi De Siena	Italy	Beijing	84/96	86.0
CMC Finance Company S.A.	Luxembourg	Beijing	nil/nil	nil
J.C.G. Bank Ltd.	Luxembourg	Beijing	nil/nil	nil
Den Norske Bank	Norway	Beijing	181/164	25.2
Rabobank Nederland[c]	Netherlands	Beijing	21/27	182.9
Bank of Foreign Trade of Russian Federation	Russia	Beijing	390/nil	4.9
Banco Español De Credito S.A.	Spain	Beijing	nil/177	42.1
Banco Exterior de España	Spain	Beijing	nil/nil	nil
Banco Santander	Spain	Beijing	55/46	135.6
Gotabanken	Sweden	Beijing, Shanghai	nil/nil	nil
Nordbanken	Sweden	Beijing	139/119	50.9
Skandinaviska Enskilda Banken	Sweden	Beijing	98/111	65.9
Svenska Handelsbanken	Sweden	Beijing	95/105	71.5
Gruppo Arca Nordest	Sweden	Beijing	nil/nil	nil
Swiss Bank Corporation (SBC)	Switzerland	Beijing, Shanghai	17/23	250.6
Union Bank of Switzerland	Switzerland	Beijing, Shanghai	3/8	336.2
ANZ Grindlays Bank	United Kingdom	Beijing	nil/nil	nil
Barclays Bank PLC	United Kingdom	Beijing, Shanghai	24/17	261.7
SG Warburg (purchased by SBC in 1995)	United Kingdom	Beijing	nil/nil	nil
Schroders Plc	United Kingdom	Shanghai	224/nil	18.1

Source: *List of Foreign Financial Institutions in China* (up to the end of March, 1993), External Affairs Department, People's Bank of China (printed in Chinese)
China Banking & Finance, Asia Law and Practice Ltd., Jan 93–Jan 96 issues, and *China Law and Practice*, Asia Law & Practice Ltd., Feb 96–June 96 issues
Notes:
(a) Ranking by 'The Top 1000 World Banks', *The Banker*, July 1996/ Ranking by 'The World's Top 200 Banks', *Euromoney*, June 1996. Different rankings are due to different definitions of capital.
(b) From *The Banker*, July 1996, Page 143–93 or *Euromoney*, June 1996 if data is nil in the former.
(c) *Hong Kong Economic Journal*, 15 November 1995, p.21.
(d) Not available on 'The world's top 200 banks' list. Writer determined their ranks according to the capital figures shown in the 'Biggest banks by country' list – a section also included in the survey.
(e) It was printed as 'Société Générale de Banque' in the *List of Foreign Institutions in China*. Writer checked and found that it should be Générale Belgian Bank.

levels of product differentiation. Sagari (1992) suggested that extensive product differentiation is a major source of competitive advantage of foreign banks over local banks. Due to the intangible nature of financial services, differentiation of banking products is not based upon visible product features and packaging but derives mainly from quality, which is normally evaluated on the basis of speed and reliability (i.e. the efficiency with which the transaction is effected). Walter (1985) has pointed out that the advantage of transactions efficiency might be very strong in countries characterized by poor financial practices such as slow decisions, high error rates, lack of clarity and tortuous bureaucracy. This observation is particularly applicable to the situation of China. For example, Standard Chartered Bank draws attention to its transactions efficiency in its booklet of *China Services*:

> The Standard Chartered Group has its headquarters in the City of London and provides a versatile range of banking, financial and related services through a network of offices in more than 60 countries. The advantage of such an international framework for the rapid progress of transactions is immense. Complex, multinational arrangements can be completed rapidly and efficiently.

The role of information in building competitive advantage for European banks in China is even more critical. 'Client-following' has been an important motive for the growth of multinational banking in China, and proprietary information on existing corporate customers and the industries they serve is an important input that helps to differentiate the services of one bank from those of others. According to Willem R C Pijpers, the General Manager of the ING Bank in Hong Kong, 'Overseas investors would trust their own banks before they would a foreign bank. In our position, we can keep them informed of the situation in China and also in Hong Kong since the two are in many ways inseparable' (Rogers 1994: 34).

Location advantages

The two most important factors favouring a local presence for foreign financial institutions are market potential and investment risk. The size and growth of a market have been found to be important determinants of foreign direct investment. Compared to non-investment modes of market-servicing, investment modes are expected to provide greater long-term profitability to a firm through the opportunity to achieve economies of scale and scope. Even if scale economies are not significant, a firm may still choose investment modes since they provide the firm with the opportunity to establish long-term market presence (Agarwal and Ramaswami 1992: 5–6). As a vast and growing economy, China provides attractive profit opportunities to foreign banks. The booming economy and growing foreign trade

Table 11.8 Country risk rankings for selected countries

Country	Rankings			Political risk (March 1997)
	March 1997	Sept 1995	Sept 1991	
Switzerland	10	1	8	25.00
Japan	13	6	1	24.65
Luxembourg	1	3	2	24.30
United Kingdom	4	9	4	24.02
Taiwan	19	16	12	20.99
Italy	25	24	21	20.49
Hong Kong	27	22	24	19.35
China	45	38	47	16.40
Poland	62	72	80	14.71
Philippines	54	53	75	14.57
Vietnam	73	69	—	11.73
Russia	91	142	108	8.09
Bulgaria	111	90	122	6.09
Nigeria	144	125	86	3.85
Cuba	175	177	118	1.55
Afghanistan	178	181	123	1.54
North Korea	179	179	—	1.25

Sources: *Euromoney*, September 1995, pp.307–10;
Euromoney, March 1997, pp.164–9

generate increased demand both for corporate banking services (e.g. infrastructure project financing, trade financing) and for consumer banking services (e.g. credit cards, deposits). Attracted by the high market potential, European banks are more willing to choose entry modes (such as branches and foreign investment banks) that secure integrated operations, even if they involve high resource commitments.

The higher the level of investment risk in the host country, the less likely are foreign financial institutions to favour entry modes with involve the commitment of resources. Investment risk reflects uncertainty over the continuation of present economic and political conditions, and of government policies which are critical to the survival and profitability of the multinational firm. Very often, investment risk arises from uncertainty about whether the host country government (or its successor) will arbitrarily change the 'rules of the game' so as to cause a loss or freezing of earnings and assets, even *in extremis* the loss of the entire foreign venture in the event of expropriation (Root 1994: 152). Agarwal and Ramaswami (1992) measure investment risk on the basis of managerial perceptions of the host government's policies toward conversion and repatriation of profits, expropriation of assets, and the stability of the political, social and economic conditions in the host country.

China's risk ratings have improved dramatically in recent years, and now compare favourably with many other developing economies (see Table 11.8), according to the *Euromoney* biannual poll of country risk. In the

March 1997 poll, China ranked forty-fifth (out of 179) countries for country risk,[20] and scored 16.4 (out of a maximum of 25) for political risk.[21] These rankings reflect the success of the economic reforms in China (Overholt 1993; de Keijzer 1992) together with the belief that unfavourable changes in the government's policy towards the conversion and repatriation of capital are not expected.

Internalisation advantages

The ownership advantages of the foreign financial institution establish its ability to compete effectively in the Chinese market, whist the improving locational advantages of that market increasingly favour investment-based modes of entry. But it is the internalisation variables which determine the form of entry mode, and here three determinants are of particular concern: contractual risk, economies of internal operations, and the potential contribution of local partners.

Firms will refrain from entering a country if the perceived risks of dissipation of knowledge and of deterioration of quality of services, and/or the costs of writing and enforcing contracts, are high. This is particularly critical for firms that have specialised knowledge, protection of which must be an important priority (Hill et al. 1990). On the other hand, the quasi-rents that can be earned from that knowledge will be enhanced if they enter a potential market.

At present, many of the legal requirements and practices of commercial banking[22] are new in China. Furthermore, communications technology and the financial infrastructure, although progressing, are still far below the standards of developed countries, or of the four Asian Tigers (Singapore, Hong Kong, Taiwan, and South Korea). The risks of deterioration of the quality of services and the costs of enforcing contracts are thus high in China. New entrants have to trade off the protection of proprietary knowledge against potential return. If they do decide to enter a new market, they will opt for a high control mode when the contractual risks are high.

Like other firms, a bank may enjoy cost savings through the horizontal and vertical integration of its operations. These economies of internal operation stem from efficiencies in marketing and account management, the availability and cost of funds transfers within the bank, larger and improved networks of market information and commercial intelligence (Gray and Gray 1981). As noted above, the crucial competitive advantages of European banks in China are proprietary information and transactions efficiency (speed and reliability). The latter is related to the operations and systems of the bank, and is determined by management know-how and communications technology, both of which are subject to economies of scale and scope when banks internalise their operations in new markets.

One of the major reasons cited by foreign banks in explaining their choice of wholly-owned branch instead of a joint venture is the associated enhanced flexibility in arranging resources (Ho 1995: 59). Such flexibility applies to funding, information and human resources, and is an advantage of internalised operations. The existence of economies of internal operation favour high-control modes (particularly branches) as forms of market-servicing mode for European banks in China.

Beamish (1988: 104) has emphasised the contribution of the local partner to a joint venture in terms of the provision of local knowledge of goods and factor markets, and suggested that successful partnerships economised on the information requirements of foreign investment and reduced uncertainty by pooling resources. In addition, a number of studies (Anderson and Coughlan 1987; Johanson and Vahlne 1977; Stopford and Wells 1972, cited by Kim and Hwang 1992) have shown that the greater the perceived distance between the home and host countries in terms of culture, economic systems, and business practices, the more likely it is that multinational firms will favour licensing or joint ventures rather than entry modes with high resource commitments. According to Kim and Hwang (1992: 36), this is because licensing and joint ventures enhance multinational firms' flexibility to withdraw from the host market should they be unable to adapt to the unfamiliar setting. As a result, joint ventures should in theory be prevalent as multinational firms expand to unfamiliar host countries.

EUROPEAN BANKS IN CHINA

The numbers of international licensing agreements and joint ventures have grown significantly in many industrial sectors in China since the adoption of the open-door policy. Yet the experience of European banks shows a complete absence of licensing agreements and only one joint venture (see Table 11.6) despite the potential contribution that local banks might make because of their knowledge of current business practice, the local economy, politics and culture. Why? As regards the first observation, the answer is simple. Financial services involve sophisticated skills, and are poor candidates for franchising (Root 1994: 135). Regarding joint ventures, the potential contribution of local partners is insignificant in comparison to the additional contractual risks involved. As noted above, most European banks currently operating in China are 'client-followers', whose objective is to serve corporate customers from their home countries who have invested, or who intend to invest, in China. To such customers, the local financial institutions in China are too inexperienced and cannot guarantee the standard of service required. In contrast, the European investors feel that European banks are more knowledgeable about their needs, particularly if they have already enjoyed previous positive experience of their services, and this would confirm their loyalty to these banks even in an unfamiliar environment. As a result, the branch is the most prominent form of management set-up for European financial institutions in China.

But why are branches favoured over wholly-owned subsidiaries? The explanation comes in three parts. First, the parent bank is subject to suit under its home country's law for any illegal action taken by its branch as the latter does not have its own juridical personality, and is also regulated by the host country's legal framework. Thus, a branch provides double protection to the customers, and this protection is very much valued by European non-bank multinational companies in China. Second, branches have less stringent lending limits than subsidiaries, since their limit is calculated on the basis of the reported capital of the parent bank. The financial backing of the parent permits the branch to make large loans to corporate borrowers (Khoury 1980: 99). Third, the working capital requirement for a branch of a foreign bank is Rmb 100m (equivalent freely convertible currencies) whereas the registered capital for a foreign-investment bank (wholly owned subsidiary) is Rmb 300m (equivalent freely convertible currencies). Hence, the capitalisation of a wholly owned subsidiary is much higher than that of a branch in China. For banks with total assets of over US$20bn (see Table 11.1), the branch form is thus more desirable.

CONCLUDING REMARKS

The aim of this chapter has been to apply the eclectic model of foreign market entry mode to explain the growth of branch operations of European banks in China. It has been argued that the perceived risks of the dissipation of proprietary knowledge, and of the deterioration of quality of services, and the costs of writing and enforcing contracts, have been significant disincentives to entry modes which require the participation of local financial institutions in China. Furthermore, the branch has been favoured over the wholly-owned subsidiary because its home country's legal protection is highly valued by target customers; the parent bank's financial backing increases its ability to make large loans; and it requires less capital infusion in China.

It is interesting to finish with two instances – neither of which involve European banks – where joint ventures have been the preferred form of entry mode for foreign banks. The first case illustrates that often not everything is as it might seem at first sight. It involves the Xiamen International Bank (established in 1985) whose two major shareholders are Min Xin Holdings Limited, and the Fujian Provincial branch of the Industrial and Commercial Bank of China. Min Xin was incorporated in Hong Kong in 1980, and is an investment holding company with subsidiaries and associates engaging in the areas of banking, financial services and insurance. Its operations mainly cover the areas of Fujian, Hong Kong, and Macau. However, its major shareholder is the Fujian Investment Company in China. In other words, the 'foreign' partner in the Xiamen International Bank is a company funded by Chinese capital. The Xiamen International

Bank should perhaps thus be considered as an outward investment from China, rather than as a Sino-foreign joint venture in China.

A similar situation exists for the Chinese Mercantile Bank, which was formed in 1993 by the Shenzhen branch of the Industrial and Commercial Bank of China, China Travel International Investment, and the Hong Kong Chinese Bank. Some 50 per cent of the shares in the Hong Kong Chinese Bank are held by the China Resources Group – a China-funded enterprise holding shares in a number of listed companies in Hong Kong. Both of these joint venture banks are permitted to operate Renminbi business: a core area of retail banking in China.

It has been noted at several points above that European banks have so far contented themselves with 'client-following' in China, and this is also true of many other Western banks. However, as the Chinese market develops further and the contractual risks diminish, and as European banks are emboldened to move into other forms of banking business (such as retail banking), so perhaps the advantages of collaboration with local partners through joint ventures will become more evident. The second case involves the China International Capital Corporation Limited which was established as a Sino-US joint venture in Beijing in 1995. The two major shareholders are the People's Construction Bank of China (PCBC) and the Morgan Stanley Group. The joint venture is an investment bank aimed at helping Chinese enterprises raise funds both locally and overseas, and at building a capital market in China, and is non-deposit taking. Both partners contribute critical inputs to the venture: Morgan Stanley provides expertise in investment banking and access to global capital markets, whereas PCBC provides local knowledge and ready access to large enterprises and local authorities in China. Perhaps this form of 'client-seeking' investment is the model for European banks in the future?

NOTES

1 *China Banking and Finance*, 18 April 1994: 5–10.
2 For example, the *Law of the People's Republic of China on the People's Bank of China*, passed in March 1995, which consolidated and endorsed the central bank functions of the People's Bank of China; the *Law of the People's Republic of China on Commercial Banks*, adopted in May 1995, which confirmed the commercialisation process of the specialised banks; the *Negotiable Instruments Law of the People's Republic of China*, passed in May 1995; the *Insurance Law of the People's Republic of China* came into effect in October 1995 (see Chapter 12 for further details); and the *Guarantee Law of the People's Republic of China*, passed in June 1995.
3 Moutinho (1991: 141–9) identifies 4 'I's as the characteristics of services: *Intangibility* – services do not consist of physical attributes which can be held, touched or seen before the purchase decision; *Inconsistency* – services quality varies because people who provide them have different capabilities and also vary in their job performance from day to day; *Inseparability* – services are supplied and consumed simultaneously (i.e. the consumer cannot be separated from the deliverer or the

setting in which the service occurs); and *Inventory* – services cannot be stored. The inventory cost of a service is the cost of reimbursing the person used to provide it.
4 The 'foreign presence index' of an industry measures sales of foreign affiliates as a proportion of exports plus sales of foreign affiliates.
5 These twenty cities were Beijing, Shanghai, Guangzhou, Shenzhen, Dalian, Qingdao, Tianjin, Fuzhou, Xiamen, Chengdu, Nanning, Zhuhai, Hangzhou, Wuhan, Quanzhou, Nantong, Ningbo, Kunming, Shenyang, and Chongqing.
6 These Procedures were promulgated on 15 June 1991 to repeal the *PBOC Procedures for the Administration of the Establishment of Representative Offices in China by Financial Institutions with Foreign or Overseas Chinese Investment*, issued on 1 February 1983.
7 In an interview, the Vice-President of Internationale Nederlander Group (ING) Bank, Mr. Nelson H F Chan, suggested that 85 per cent of the bank's offshore clients depended upon ING for advice and information on investment in China. See Rogers (1994).
8 *Banking and Finance*, 4(6) 22 July 1991: 6.
9 The term *management set-up* refers to more extensive forms of operation or presence of foreign funded financial institutions in China, such as branches, wholly owned subsidiaries, and joint ventures. This term is used in the *China Economic News*, 27, 17 July 1995.
10 A 'branch of foreign bank' is a banking office of a (parent) bank which is incorporated in a foreign country. It is an integrated part of the parent bank, and its creditors have claims on assets of the bank as a whole. A 'foreign investment bank' is a locally incorporated bank which is exclusively funded with foreign capital. The bank is a separate legal entity from the shareholding company. It is equivalent to a wholly owned subsidiary or sole venture. A 'joint venture bank' is a locally incorporated bank which is jointly owned by foreign financial institution(s) and Chinese financial institution(s). It is a separate legal entity from the holding parties, and is sometimes called a 'subsidiary' or an 'affiliate' (depending upon the level of ownership) of a foreign bank. A 'foreign investment finance company' is a locally incorporated finance company which is exclusively funded with foreign capital. It is a separate legal entity from the shareholding company. A 'joint venture finance company' is a locally incorporated finance company which is jointly owned by foreign financial institution(s) and Chinese financial institution(s). It is a separate legal entity from the holding parties.
11 *China Law and Practice*, 10(3), April 1996: 45.
12 For example, the Banking Ordinance of Hong Kong requires that the parent of a foreign applicant for a bank licence should have assets totalling not less than $US 16bn.
13 *Hong Kong Economic Journal*, 27 June 1997: 3
14 *China Law and Practice*, 10(3), April 1996: 6.
15 The 'bread-and-butter' business for local banks in China: it refers to conventional banking services (mainly deposit-taking and lending) for local residents and enterprises.
16 *Hong Kong Economic Journal*, 11 June 1996: 29.
17 Another prerequisite is the convertibility of Renminbi. It will be much more difficult to control the flow of foreign currencies and the exchange rate if foreign banks are allowed to engage in Renminbi business.
18 *The Banker*, July 1996: 118.
19 *Euromoney*, August 1996: 41.
20 The country risk assessment uses nine categories of scores with different weightings: economic data (25 per cent weighting); political risk (25 per cent); debt

indicators (10 per cent); debt in default or rescheduled (10 per cent); credit ratings (10 per cent); access to bank finance (5 per cent); access to short-term finance (5 per cent); access to international bond or syndicated loan markets (5 per cent); and discount on forfeiting (5 per cent). The highest score in each category receives the full mark; the lowest receives zero.
21 Political risk is defined as the risk of non-payment or non-servicing of payment for goods or services, loans, trade-related finance and dividends, and the non-repatriation of capital. It does not reflect the creditworthiness of individual parties in any country.
22 Before the banking reforms, most banks were State-owned banks which followed the government's administrative directions with regard to the determination of interest rates and the granting of loans.

REFERENCES

Abels, S. (1995), 'Soft Landing or Recession?', *Euromoney*, 317, September: 306–11.
Agarwal, S. and Ramaswami, S. (1992) 'Choice of Foreign Market Entry Mode: Impact of Ownership, Location and Internalization Factors', *Journal of International Business Studies*, 23(1): 1–27.
Anderson, E. and Coughlan, A. T. (1987) 'International Market Entry and Expansion via Independent or Integrated Channels of Distribution', *Journal of Marketing*, 51(1): 71–82.
Beamish, P. (1988) *Multinational Joint Ventures in Developing Countries*, London: Routledge.
Cho, K.R. (1985) *Multinational Banks: Their Identities and Determinants*, Michigan: Ann Arbor.
de Keijzer, A. (1992) *CHINA: Business Strategies for the '90s*, Berkeley: Pacific View Press.
Dipchand, C., Zhang, Y. and Ma, M. (1994) *The Chinese Financial System*, Westport, Conn: Greenwood Press.
Dunning, J. (1977) 'Trade, Location of Economic Activity and the Multinational Enterprise: A Search for an Eclectic Approach', in B. Ohlin, P. Hesselborn and P. Wijkman (eds) *The International Allocation of Economic Activity*, London: Macmillan, pp.395–418.
Dunning, J. (1993a) *Multinational Enterprises and the Global Economy*, London: Addison-Wesley.
Dunning, J. (1993b) *The Globalization of Business: The Challenge of the 1990s*, London: Routledge.
Erramilli, K. and Rao, C. (1990) 'Choice of Foreign Market Entry Modes by Service Firms: Role of Market Knowledge', *Management International Review*, 30(2): 135–50.
Fu, C. (1994) 'The Implications of Financial Reforms on Marketing Strategies of Banks in China', *Proceedings of the Tenth Annual Academic Conference of the China Marketing Association of Universities*, Hong Kong: Hong Kong Polytechnic University.
Fu, C. (1995) 'The Determinants of Growth of Multinational Banks in China', *Proceedings of Third International Conference on Global Business Environment and Strategy*, Hong Kong: City University of Hong Kong.
Gray, J. and Gray, H. (1981) 'The Multinational Bank: A Financial MNC?', *Journal of Banking and Finance*, 5(1), March: 33–63.
Grieves, R. (1986) 'Representative Offices with Very Little to Bank On', *Asian Business*, 22(12), December: 53–5.

Grubel, H. (1985) 'Multinational Banking', discussion paper no. 56, Singapore: Institute of Southeast Asian Studies, ASEAN Economic Research Unit.
Hill, C., Hwang, P. and Kim, W. (1990) 'An Eclectic Theory of the Choice of International Entry Mode', *Strategic Management Journal*, 11(2): 117–28.
Ho, C. (1995) 'Why Banks Go to China?: Explaining Multinational Banking Activities in the PRC', unpublished BABS Project Report, the City University of Hong Kong.
Johanson, J. and Vahlne, J.-E. (1977) 'The Internationalization Process of a Firm. A Model of Knowledge Development and Increasing Foreign Market Commitments', *Journal of International Business Studies*, 8(1): 23–32.
Khoury, S. (1980) *Dynamics of International Banking*, New York: Praeger Publishers.
Kim, W. and Hwang, P. (1992) 'Global Strategy and Multinationals' Entry Mode Choice', *Journal of International Business Studies*, 23(1): 29–54.
Lau, P. (ed.) (1995) *The Mega Trend of China's Economy 1995*, Hong Kong: Commercial Press (published in Chinese).
Leung, M. (1995) 'Banking Reform in the People's Republic of China and its Implications for Hong Kong as an International Banking Centre', in H. Davies (ed.) *China Business: Context and Issues*, Hong Kong: Longman Asia, pp.98–116.
Moutinho, L. (1991) 'Problem 9.1: The Four Is of Services', *Problems in Marketing: Analysis and Applications*, London: Paul Chapman Publishing.
Overholt, W. (1993) *China: The Next Economic Superpower*, London: Weidenfeld and Nicolson.
Pecchioli, R. (1983) *The Internationalization of Banking: The Policy Issues*, Paris: OECD.
People's Bank of China (1993) *List of Foreign Financial Institutions in China (up to the end of March 1993)*, Beijing: People's Bank of China.
Rogers, G. (1994) 'Banking on China – the Frontiers of Finance', *Hong Kong Business*, 13(145) July: 25–46.
Root, F. (1994) *Entry Strategies for International Markets*, rev. and expanded edn, Lexington, MA: Lexington Books.
Rose, P. (1993) *Commercial Bank Management*, Chicago: Irwin.
Sagari, S. (1992) 'United States Foreign Direct Investment in the Banking Industry', *Transnational Corporations*, 1(3), December: 93–123.
Stopford, J. M. and Wells Jr, L.T. (1972) *Managing the Multinational Enterprise*, New York: Basic Books.
Walter, I. (1985) *Barriers to Trade in Banking and Financial Services*, London: Trade Policy Research Centre.

12 The insurance industry in China
The experience of European, US and Japanese firms

Xiaohong Wu and Roger Strange

INTRODUCTION

'By any standard, the existing insurance industry in China is incompatible with China's fast social and economic development.'[1] This remark by the Deputy Director of the Department for the Supervision and Regulation of Foreign Financial Institutions at the People's Bank of China (PBOC) highlights the desperate need for the development and modernisation of the domestic insurance industry in China. The potential of the Chinese insurance market is enormous, and the world's leading insurance companies have indicated that they are only too eager to participate. Yet enthusiasm by the Chinese authorities for what the foreign insurers have to offer is tempered with caution. The Deputy Director again: 'Foreign insurers' skill and capacity will be necessary. But without an orderly point of entry, the impact on China's social and economic development could be disastrous' (Hadley 1995: 21). So the process of opening-up to foreign insurance companies has been slow and partial – with obvious parallels to the policies pursued a decade earlier regarding the opening-up of the country to foreign manufacturing investment.

In this chapter, we first consider the various modes through which insurance companies might enter foreign markets, and consider the choice between these modes from a theoretical perspective. The structure of the insurance industry in China is then briefly described, the potential growth of the market highlighted, and the development of the regulatory framework for foreign participation outlined. We then report the results of a questionnaire survey of foreign representative offices in China which throws light on their strategies for obtaining operating licences, their criteria for selecting Chinese partners for joint ventures, and their choice of location within the country. This survey reveals some interesting differences between European insurers and their US and Japanese counterparts. Finally, we speculate on the likely future development of the Chinese insurance industry, drawing upon the identified parallels with the development of the manufacturing sector.

CROSS-BORDER TRADE AND INTERNATIONAL INVESTMENT IN THE INSURANCE INDUSTRY

Insurance involves the transference of risk from individuals and organisations to specialist insurance companies who can use the laws of probability to spread risks efficiently. The end products of the industry may be divided into two broad categories: life insurance and non-life insurance. Life insurance involves payment to a beneficiary – usually a family member, business, or institution – in the event of the death of an individual. It is based on the pooling of a large number of independent individual risks, thereby reducing the overall risk. Non-life insurance (also known as property or casualty insurance) provides coverage for the insured against damage or destruction of his/her property, and against damage/destruction of other property and/or bodily harm caused by the negligence of the insured. In addition, reinsurance refers to the diversification of the risks accepted by individual insurers among other insurance companies. The reinsured company reduces its maximum possible loss either on an individual risk (facultative reinsurance) or on a large number of risks (automatic reinsurance) by ceding a portion of its liability to another insurance company (the reinsurer). Reinsurance enables an insurance company to expand its capacity, to stabilise its underwriting results, to finance its expanding volume of business, to secure catastrophe protection against shock losses, to withdraw from a line of business or geographical area, all within a relatively short time period.

International transactions in both direct insurance and reinsurance may be effected through arm's-length cross-frontier trade,[2] through non-equity agreements (e.g. franchise or management contracts) where the insurer/reinsurer appoints agents in foreign countries with binding powers to underwrite business on its behalf, or through foreign direct investment[3] (FDI) when the insurer/reinsurer establishes its own branch office or subsidiary in the foreign country. In order of increasing within-firm governance, the five[4] most common modes through which an insurance company can enter a foreign market are:

- establishment of a representative office;
- recruitment of a local management agent or broker;
- establishment of a branch office;
- establishment of a joint venture with an indigenous insurance company;
- establishment of a wholly owned subsidiary.

The representative office is the most common way for international insurance companies to establish an initial presence in a foreign market and, in some countries (e.g. China), it may be the only permissible way to enter that market. The main function of such an office is to collect information and to forward it to the Head Office, or one of the branches. It provides a combination of full management control with little resource commitment/risk (see Table 12.1). However, a representative office generally cannot

Table 12.1 International entry modes in the insurance industry

Major entry modes	Degree of control and integration	Degree of resource commitment/risk	Designation
Representative office	Full	Little	Full-control mode
Agent/broker	None/little	None/little	Shared-control mode
Joint venture	Some	Some	Shared-control mode
Branch/wholly-owned subsidiary	Full	Full	Full-control mode

Source: Adapted from Erramilli and Rau (1993)

conduct major insurance activities, and is usually given limited decision-making authority by the parent. It usually lacks economies of scale in its operations. And the normal range of insurance activities of the office is generally restricted by the host country government regulations. In some countries, such as China, representative offices are restricted to liaison-type activities of non-profit making functions.

The recruitment of a local management agent or broker facilitates a speedy entry into the foreign market, and may appeal to less-experienced companies. The agent/broker system also enables the insurance company to operate with low overheads, and the company may thus be more able to withstand a fall in premium income than one with a large branch organisation geared to obtaining business direct from the public. Other things being equal, the higher the proportion of fixed costs to total costs, the nearer a firm must operate to its planned capacity in order to cover total costs (Carter 1979). A number of differences exist between agency and brokerage. First, while an agent is in the employ of the insurer, a broker is employed by the insured. However, both agent and broker are remunerated by the insurer through the payment of commission on premiums handled and, moreover, a broker may perform certain duties on behalf of the insurer (e.g. issuing cover-notes and collecting premiums). Second, unlike an agent, a broker holds himself out to the public as possessing an expert knowledge of insurance business and the insurance market, and should have access to a representative range of insurers (ibid.).

Despite providing entry and operation flexibility, however, agency/brokerage has serious drawbacks. It gives the international insurance company very limited control and profits. Besides, the transactions cost involved in monitoring the performance of the general agencies can prove high, especially when the 'small-numbers bargaining' problem is present. In countries where insurance markets are underdeveloped, the range of agents/brokers available to the international insurance company is restricted and the agents/brokers generally become non-replaceable. Their tendency to behave opportunistically is reduced only through stringent negotiation and supervision of contractual relationships, and thereby greatly increase the transactions costs associated with this low-control mode. Agency/

brokerage, therefore, may not be a viable choice in countries where there are relatively few competent insurance entities. Under such circumstances, the international insurance company can significantly reduce its transactions costs by replacing external agents/brokers with its own employees, whose behaviour it can monitor and control more effectively (Dwyer and Oh 1988; Hennart 1989; Klein 1989). The agency/brokerage mode is thus usually a transitory entry mode for less experienced insurance companies. Companies with greater experience in entering foreign markets are less likely to use this entry mode (Schroath 1988; Huggins and Land 1996; LIMRA 1990; Gora 1991).

The joint venture is a partnership agreement in which two or more firms undertake a business project together, usually for a specific length of time. The benefits that can result from a joint venture include possible economies of scale, the reduction of total costs, and enhanced product differentiation. 'Ideally, the domestic company in a joint venture brings a brand name with local value as well as a distribution system'[5] (Meldrum 1996). Also, in a joint venture, the two parties share the risk involved in the alliance. In addition, a foreign insurer may face less stringent regulation upon entering the new market if it is paired with a company that is already doing business in that market. Moreover, the complementary functions of the local joint venture partner will typically help the multinational insurer to have a clear understanding of the local social, cultural, economic and political factors and to adapt policies, coverage and terminology to local needs (ibid.).

A joint venture, however, is not risk-free. There are additional costs attributable to shared decision-making and the coordination of partners, the lack of compatibility, as well as to partner-searching (Stopford and Wells 1972; Killing 1983; Harrigan 1985; Huggins and Land 1996). The companies may not be comparable in their objectives, their corporate philosophies and/or their cultural outlook, and they may lack mutual commitment. Carter (1979) has argued that firms may differ in their management objectives: some may seek long-term profit maximisation, others may only seek short-term profit maximisation; and some managements may have objectives other than profit. For example, they may seek to maximise either sales or market share, or perhaps to maximise the rate of growth of assets. Also, companies may find out later that they are partners in one arena and competitors elsewhere. In addition, a multinational insurance company operating in a joint venture may be frustrated that it is not in complete control of its own business. Moreover, it is a consensus among company executives that finding the right partner is a costly and time-consuming business (Schroath 1988). The costs of organising a joint venture can thus run high.

The international insurer has to weigh up the potential benefits against the potential drawbacks before entering into a joint venture. From the transactions cost viewpoint, a firm will attempt to form a joint venture *only if* perceived additional benefits outweigh expected the additional costs

(Beamish and Banks 1987). The international insurance company should thus abandon the joint venture mode of entry if the potential partner is complementary in functions but incompatible in objectives. For a joint venture to be viable:

> each party must have a strategic interest in the enterprise... It is essential that the long-term perspective be maintained. A joint venture should not be undertaken for a short-term gain. To succeed, a joint venture needs compatible corporate philosophies and cultural outlook and a mutual commitment.[6]

Amongst the various methods of entering a foreign market, the establishment of a branch office or subsidiary gives the head office the greatest control over its company's international activities. As a functional extension of the head office, branches have their policy and product decisions made and implemented primarily by home country personnel. In subsidiaries, the parent company typically maintains an oversight of activities, but is generally more concerned with global integration and the coordination of strategy.

The main difference between branches and subsidiaries is whether they are legal extensions of the parent company. A wholly-owned subsidiary (and a joint venture) is a local institution incorporated under host country law, and is a separate legal entity from its parent company. The parent company is thus not liable for the debts of its subsidiary in the host country. In contrast, as a legal extension of the head office, a branch is not a separate legal entity, and the parent company is liable for its debts. This legal difference has pros and cons attached. On the one hand, supported by the entire capital of the international insurance company, branches are often exempt from minimum capital requirements in the host country. In contrast, the establishment of a subsidiary usually requires a higher capitalisation than a branch of the same operational size. On the other hand, in some jurisdictions, the entire insurance company may come under the suit of local law for any act committed by its branches and offices. In contrast, insurance companies can isolate their head offices from host country laws by setting up subsidiaries.

Notwithstanding considerable management control, branch offices and subsidiaries are not without drawbacks. One of the major disadvantages is the high initial capital investment, and the reduced flexibility, i.e. high switching costs. Another major disadvantage is that they can be risky if the parent company is unfamiliar with ways of doing business in the host country (Waheed and Mathur 1995; Erramilli and Rao 1993). Knowing how to adapt to the needs of the host country is the key to successful global operations, especially for life insurance companies which depend on demand from the local populace rather than from MNEs.

For the foreign insurer, the choice of appropriate entry mode may be examined in the light of the familiar OLI (Ownership-Location-

Internalisation) framework, which has been extended to service industries by various authors (Dunning 1989; Enderwick 1989; Erramilli and Rao 1993). In brief, this suggests that the extent, pattern and growth of the international involvement of firms are determined by the interaction between the firm's ownership advantages, the location advantages of potential host countries, and the internalisation advantages of common governance of cross-border activities.

Ownership advantages

International insurance companies are typically capable of providing a better quality and a more extensive range of insurance policies at more competitive prices than local national insurers. These ownership advantages arise from a variety of factors.

The economies of scale and scope which are available to financial MNEs are well documented in the literature (Dunning 1989; Agarwal and Ramaswami 1992; Dunning 1993). Furthermore, as Peter Fu has already pointed out in Chapter 11, size and scope not only reduce costs but are also positively correlated with the propensity of financial institutions to enter foreign markets. On the one hand, large insurance companies with diversified assets are more able to absorb risks. On the other hand, the stringent asset and/or capital requirements imposed by many national governments mean that only large companies are eligible for entry.

The economies of scale of international insurance companies are reinforced by the organisation of the industry in which they operate. Many insurance companies operate internationally through pools, group or associations (Bickelhaupt and Bar-Niv 1983), such as, for example, the American Foreign Insurance Association (AFIA). An insurance pool writes business on behalf of its separate member-insurers, each of which shares a proportion of the insurance written by the pool. A second method of operation is through companies of a common insurance group of subsidiary companies. In fact, most of the major insurance companies have developed into composite groups transacting all classes of insurance business, so possessing the advantage of being able to offer the public a comprehensive insurance service. A third method of operation is an association, in which separate companies (rather than a pool or group) write insurance directly, but all share in losses and expenses. Examples of such associations are industrial Risk Insurers (IR) and the Factory Mutual Association (FMA).

Just as individuals and businesses buy insurance to protect themselves against loss by various perils, insurance companies likewise transfer insurance to reinsurers. Insurers have always sought to achieve the widest possible dispersion of risk. The major purpose of reinsurance is to share losses as widely as possible (Bickelhaupt and Bar-Niv 1983). Because of their world-wide reinsurance agreement, international insurance companies are able to spread further the risk of loss, to improve the stability of their underwriting results, and to achieve greater flexibility in the type and size of risks they are able to accept. In contrast, indigenous firms in underdeveloped insurance markets are disadvantaged in that they may not be able to obtain precisely the type of insurance cover they would like. For example, a new motor insurer may not be able to obtain quota share reinsurance, so restricting their rate of expansion and, on excess loss cover, it may be necessary for the company to carry higher retention limits than desired (Carter 1979). In addition, the indigenous firm may have to pay a larger proportion of its gross premium income for reinsurance than a large established international insurance company.

Although insurance is not a high-technology industry, it nevertheless demands a substantial degree of financial and marketing expertise. This expertise is more important in the provision of non-life insurance and reinsurance than in life insurance, and local companies may well not have the necessary skilled labour and technology.

The fact that they operate internationally helps create a prestigious corporate reputation for foreign insurers, and enables them to reap economic rents. Such a reputation advantage over indigenous firms is conducive to business development in that insurance buyers have 'accumulated preference for established insurers based on their reputation for financial strength, quality of service provided, etc.' (Carter 1979).

As a result of their economies of scale, international insurance companies are typically able to offer a wider range of services and products at more flexible terms, prices and conditions. This will include not only the devising of new forms of insurance to cater for new risks and the adapting of existing products to meet changing consumer requirements, but also the packaging of existing products in new ways to provide contracts which give wider cover at lower cost.

Because of their size and access to pools, etc., their easier access to international capital markets and world-wide reinsurance agreements, international insurance companies typically have larger underwriting capability for high risks which arise from natural hazards or from new, large-scale, technologically advanced industrial processes. Furthermore, from underwriting similar risks elsewhere in the world, they will have built up the technical competence to estimate possible loss frequencies and severity. This capabilities and competencies put them in a better position (relative to local insurers) to provide services for large MNEs investing in the local economy.

Even if international companies are no more efficient than their domestic competitors, they are often able to provide wider cover and/or additional ancillary services such as loss prevention and risk management. Furthermore, international insurance brokers may be able to provide competitive broking services by taking advantage of their privileged access to the international insurance/reinsurance network.

International insurance companies are able to offer a higher degree of security to policyholders due to their size, their larger capital bases, their ability to spread risks internationally, their easier access to international capital and reinsurance markets. And, last but not least, their international experience bestows the international insurance companies with greater knowledge of foreign markets, and reduces the risks and uncertainty of their investment environment.

Location advantages

Proximity between insurers and the markets in which they operate is needed for the protection of the integrity of the insurers' underwriting and the quality of their services. Speedy and efficient transfer of information between insurers and prospective clients is needed for risk assessment, tailoring insurance policies to the specific needs of clients, claims investigation, negotiation and settlement. This need for proximity, and for often instantaneous interaction between the insurer and the insured, has traditionally obliged insurers to have a physical presence in every country in which they wished to conduct business.

Recent developments in information technology have, however, opened up the possibility for some direct transactions of insurance business across borders without the need for a local presence. Through the use of computer-communications systems, these developments permit instantaneous, interactive, long-distance transactions and facilitate certain modes of international involvement. Three examples illustrate such facilitation. First, a locally-owned agency staffed by local nationals may be able to process information and transact business on the basis of guidelines provided by a foreign insurer. The agency may even retain control over operations to the extent that it has the option of placing business with the foreign insurer of its choice. Second, a locally-owned insurance company, which lacks the expertise and managerial skills to assess risks, might take advantage of the enhanced tradability of insurance products and license the required know-how from foreign companies (United Nations 1993). Third, locally-owned agencies or companies may place reinsurance directly with foreign insurers in return for the payment of a share of the premium income and a fee for the managerial services. Hitherto, the bulk of reinsurance business (especially in developing countries) has been transacted through large international brokers and specialist companies established in the local market.

However, the potentialities of information technology have not yet been substantially realised in the insurance industry.[7] There appears to be a general belief shared by insurance companies that a local presence remains essential for the effective development of business.[8] Indeed, it

> seems that, in the immediate future, FDI and TNC activities, will continue to be the most important form of delivering insurance services to foreign markets. In fact, their importance is likely to grow, precisely as a result of

the use of information technology because this technology considerably facilitates the success of these new and extended FDI-based groupings.

(United Nations 1993: 40)

The unbundling of functional tasks and their geographical dispersion have so far been very much confined to labour-intensive back office operations, such as data processing and claim processing, rather than the provision of insurance, which requires the expertise and managerial skills to assess risks. Moreover, the intra-company and inter-company networks which permit economies of common governance among geographically dispersed activities within a firm have been operated primarily to link insurers to tied agents/brokers or to link head office to branch offices, and this network-based linkage has been largely restricted to national markets with only a few companies using it internationally. And, even in these few cases, the application of the information technology has been used primarily to improve the efficiency of the existing business structure (normally incorporating extensive local presence) rather than to replace it with an alternative structure.

The insurance industry has thus lagged behind other service sectors in the widespread use of information technology. As the United Nations (1993) note, the choice between FDI and pure trade/licensing is largely governed by the nature of the transaction which is determined by the inherent characteristics and technological parameters of the service concerned. In the case of life insurance and some forms of health and personal accident cover, a local presence is demanded as close contact and trust between the insurers and the policyholders are of paramount importance. This is especially so when there is an insufficient local supply of suitable agents and telecommunications facilities/skilled labour offering products at competitive prices. Moreover, a local presence is often required for efficient transactions in the case of complex insurance products, such as the property or liability risks generated by large institutions. On the one hand, there are difficulties[9] in translating complex information requirements into electronic form, and these difficulties are compounded by the technical and legal differences between countries concerning electronic mail systems. Not only are international transactions hampered by the lack of a suitable telecommunications infrastructure providing competitive transmission costs in many developing countries, but the absence of clear case law contributes to uncertainty concerning the legal position of legal contracts concluded through electronic means. On the other hand, detailed scrutiny and risk assessment are needed to decide the precise structure and terms of cover for complex risks.

In contrast, the need for a local presence will generally be lower when risks are generally accepted and may be underwritten in reasonably standardised form by network-based trading and licensing agreements with local agents. Such risks are typically 'personal lines' in relation to property and liability held by private individuals. Here no detailed scrutiny or risk assessment is required because the liability on any one risk is small, and the number of homogeneous risks is sufficiently large to ensure that the application of probability will generate secure underwriting.

The idiosyncratic nature of the insurance business thus means that recent developments in telecommunications and information technology may only have a limited impact on the tradability of insurance products in the immediate future. A further factor favouring local presence is the plethora of government restrictions regarding cross-border trade and FDI in insurance (Carter and Dickinson 1977; Pfeffer 1978; Skipper 1987; Carter and Dickinson 1992). Many governments impose such restrictions in order to maintain national control of the insurance industry for a variety of reasons:

- to protect local consumers from loss in the event of insurance companies becoming insolvent or failing to provide an acceptable standard of services at a reasonable price;
- to foster a national insurance industry by protecting domestic insurers from foreign competition;
- to ease any strain on the balance of payments by avoiding the net long-term loss of foreign exchange arising from the purchase of insurance/reinsurance overseas and/or the remittance of funds by foreign-owned insurance companies;
- to retain the funds generated by insurance operations for investment through the local capital market;[10]
- to reduce, in the interest of national security, dependence on foreign insurance and/or reinsurance.

Cross-border trade in direct insurance has come under increasingly strict control by many governments, and the movement of premiums and claims payments have been increasingly circumvented by exchange-control restrictions (Carter and Dickinson 1992). In contrast, reinsurance has typically been subject to a much less prohibitive regime for two main reasons. On the one hand, reinsurance provides the means by which local insurers can gain access to the expertise and international capacity of the international market without the national government relinquishing control of the local industry. On the other hand, consumer protection is not so vital as most reinsurance takes place between sophisticated and well-informed companies. Thus, while many developing countries have increased their restrictions on trade/investment in direct insurance, there has been a growing demand for reinsurance so that indigenous insurers might compensate for their insufficient underwriting capacities.[11] The combined effect of a lesser need for proximity and more relaxed government regulations is that there is much less incentive for reinsurance companies to establish overseas offices/affiliates than direct insurance companies.

Internalisation advantages

The largest part of the value-adding activities of the insurance industry consists of the acquisition, interpretation and dissemination of information. As a service sector, the nature of the technology involved is 'soft'. 'Instead of involving primarily processes which can be patented and products which can be submitted to reverse engineering, many technologies typical of service industries are primarily skill and experience-intensive and require considerable organisation and management capabilities' (United Nations 1993: 89). The technology is thus intangible, idiosyncratic (tailored to the customer), skilled-labour intensive and, to a great extent, tacit and non-codified.

However, unlike many service sectors (e.g. hotels, restaurants, fast-food outlets, and car-rental companies) where performance requirements can be codified in a management contract or franchising agreement and hence may be easily transferred and monitored through a non-equity agreement, external quality control in the insurance industry is both more difficult and more expensive due to the nature of the business (United Nations 1989). Thus non-equity modes of market entry (e.g. intermediary brokers, agents) are typically only entertained as transitory steps to facilitate speedy market entry and the acquisition of local experience.

The transactions costs associated with market-based entry modes may well hinder the international insurance company from securing the full economic rent arising from its ownership advantages, and thus ensures that such companies will typically prefer equity-based modes of market entry. This leads to a choice between a wholly owned subsidiary and a joint venture with a local partner. The latter will typically be preferred if there is a need to reduce initial start-up costs, or a need to share the risks of providing insurance services, or a need to customise services to meet the requirements of local customers. The need to customise services 'often means that the ownership advantages of TNCs have to be combined with those of firms in the country in which the services are sold, if the economic rent of the former is to be maximised' (United Nations 1989: 98). In contrast, the wholly owned subsidiary will be favoured if there are high perceived risks of the deterioration of service quality or of the dissipation of proprietary knowledge, or if the costs of writing and enforcing suitable contracts are high, or where global strategic considerations warrant tight coordination across business units world-wide.

However, the choice of ownership structure may well be circumscribed by government regulations and/or requirements on local equity participation (see above). In particular, branches are often preferred to locally incorporated subsidiaries by host country governments because of the difference in legal liability and the implications for policyholder protection. Such requirements often force foreign insurers to adopt a 'second-best' entry mode (Carter and Dickinson 1977; Pfeffer 1978; Skipper 1987; United Nations 1993).

THE INSURANCE INDUSTRY IN CHINA

The People's Insurance Company of China (PICC) was established in 1949, after the foundation of the People's Republic. Subsequently, all other insurance companies in the PRC ceased to operate and, by 1956, PICC had a monopoly position. However, political upheaval and State planning both hindered the development of the domestic industry during the ensuing two decades: domestic insurance was suspended and business was limited to international cargo and aviation insurance.

The advent of economic reform in 1979 resuscitated the insurance industry in China. Domestic insurance was resumed in April 1979. As the sole insurance carrier in the whole of China, PICC enjoyed the strong and increasing demand for insurance services and showed great profitability through the 1980s. Figure 12.1 traces the underwriting and trading ratios[12] of PICC from 1980 onwards, and Figure 12.2 compares PICC's ratios with those for the non-life industries in the United States, Japan, and the United Kingdom. An additional factor contributing to PICC's impressive results was the annual capital injection by the Chinese Government into PICC's reserve fund, which enabled greater investment than would otherwise have been the case and hence improved underwriting and trading performance.

PICC's long-term monopoly was first broken by the establishment of the Xinjiang Agricultural Insurance Company in 1987, followed by the Pin An Insurance Company in 1988, and the China Pacific Insurance Company in 1991. Two regional insurers, Tian An and Da Zhong, were established in Shanghai in 1995, and PBOC awarded licences to a further two regional and three national insurance companies in early 1996. The two regional companies (Hua An based in Shenzhen, and Yong An based in Xian) both specialise in non-life insurance, as does one of the national companies (Hua Tai, based in Beijing). The other two national companies (Tai Kang and

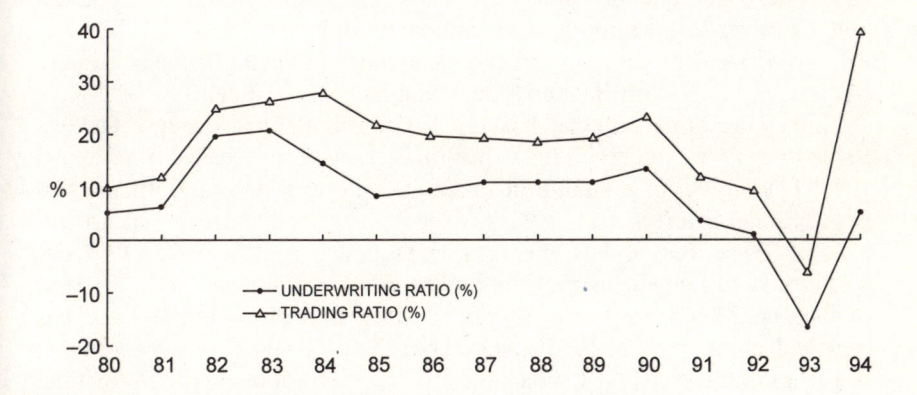

Figure 12.1 Underwriting and trading ratios of PICC, 1980–94
Source: Adapted from PICC Annual Report, 1993 and 1994

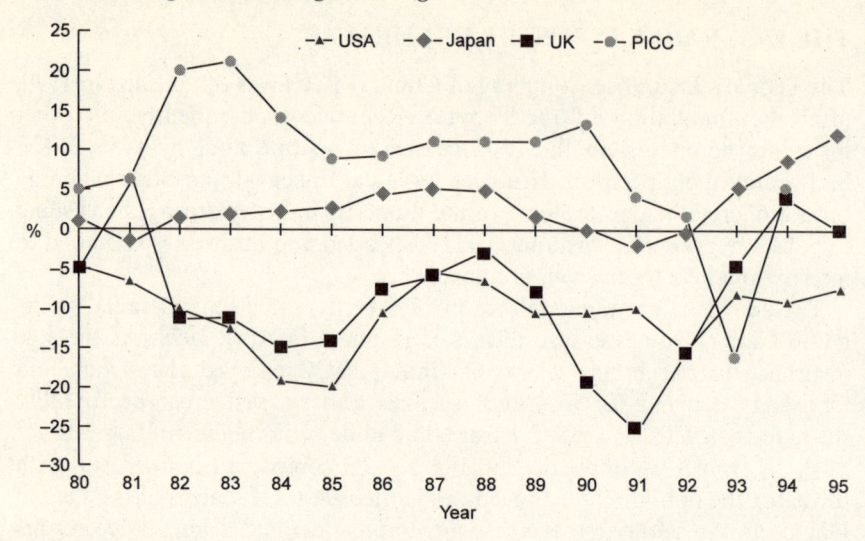

Figure 12.2 Underwriting ratio of PICC in comparison to that of USA, Japan, and UK markets (non-life), 1980–95
Source: *Sigma*, 1/95 Sedgwick, 12/1996); *Non-life Insurance in Japan Fact Book* (1995–1996) (The Marine and Fire Insurance Association of Japan, Inc, 1996); *Insurance Statistics Year Book* (1985–1995) (Association of British Insurers, 1996); *PICC Annual Report*, 1993 and 1994

Xin Hua) both specialise in life insurance, and are both based in Beijing. This increased competition is reflected in the sharp downward trend in PICC's performance since 1990. And, in accordance with the 1995 Insurance Law, PICC was transformed into the China Insurance Group in 1996, and three separate subsidiaries were established: PICC (Property); PICC (Life); and PICC (Reinsurance). There are currently thirty-six insurance companies operating in China (see Table 12.2), the fourteen companies noted above, seventeen regional companies (all joint ventures between PICC and local investors), and five companies involving foreign insurers (AIA twice, Tokio Marine and Fire, Manulife, Winterthur).

China's insurance industry has enjoyed substantial growth ever since its re-birth in 1979, and the annual insurance premium exceeded US$7bn in 1995. The growth in premium income has been most dramatic for the two new national insurers, China Pacific and Ping An, which recorded growth rates of 120 per cent and 270 per cent, respectively, over the period 1991–95. It is estimated that the market might well grow to Rmb200bn (US$24.1bn) by the year 2000, with projected annual increases in the region of 20–30 per cent and possibly more for life insurance. These dramatic projections are based upon the fact that China's insurance penetration[13] is far lower than most other countries, even developing countries. Thus insurance penetration in China was just 1.17 per cent of GNP in 1995, compared to 8–15 per cent in developed countries (see Figure 12.3). Insurance density[14] too is low in comparison with many other developing economies. Per capita insurance spending was a mere US$6.1 in China in 1995, compared to $39.1 in Mexico, $90.1 in Brazil, $146.5 in Chile, and $141.5 in Argentina. In Taiwan, South Korea and Japan, the comparable figures were US$678.5, US$1376, and US$5088 respectively.

Untapped demand, particularly for life insurance, is enormous. About half of China's urban residents (150m people) have bought some life insurance, but most of the rural residents – who account for 80 per cent of the population – remain unaware of its availability. However, this situation will gradually change as a result of increasing affluence, education, birth control, and other social changes. Furthermore:

- traditional superstitious fears of insuring against death are diminishing;
- the breakdown of extended families, and the increase of nuclear families, have necessitated people to plan for alternative sources of support, rather than solely relying on their children, in their retirement (Wu 1995);
- the reform of the social security system has accelerated the expansion of private long-term assurance services as the State's 'cradle to grave' provision is reduced. Labour regulations now require State-owned enterprises to purchase insurance for their employees from certified insurance companies. Private firms are also legally bound to insure their workers. 'Life insurance will have a wider and better development scope because China has decided to give full play to commercial insurance while developing social security' (EIU 1996).

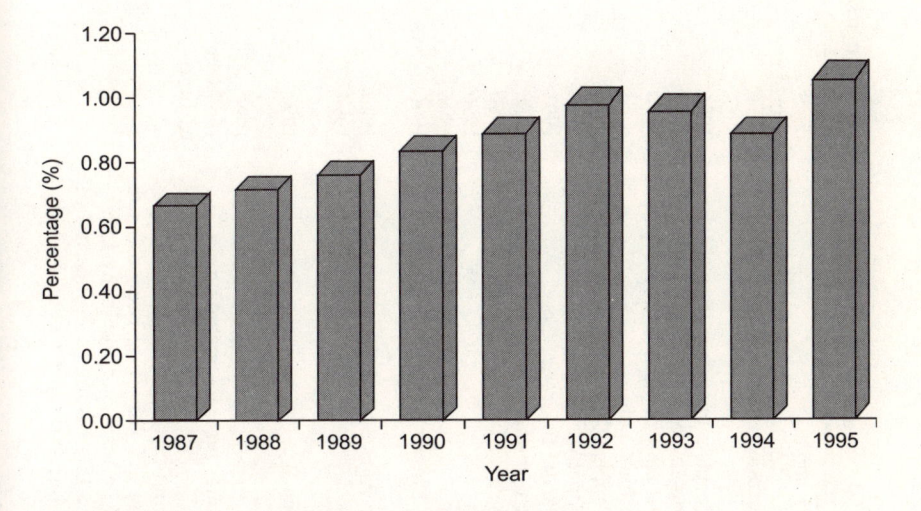

Figure 12.3 Insurance penetration in China, 1987–95
Sources: *Sigma*, various issues; National Statistics Bureau Report (*People's Daily*, overseas version, 5 March 1996)

Table 12.2 Major companies in China's insurance market

Company name	Year estab.	Nationality	Insurance type	Operational area	Corporate structure
China Insurance Group[a], including	1996	Chinese		National	State-owned holding company
The People's Insurance (Property) Company of China Ltd.	1996	Chinese	Property	National	Subsidiary
The People's Insurance (Life) Company of China Ltd.	1996	Chinese	Life	National	Subsidiary
The People's Insurance (Reinsurance) Company of China Ltd.	1996	Chinese	Reinsurance	National	Subsidiary
China Pacific Insurance Co.	1991	Chinese	Composite	National	Joint Stock
Ping An Insurance Company of China	1988	Chinese	Composite	National	Joint Stock
Tai Kang Life Insurance Company Ltd.	1996	Chinese	Life	National	Joint Stock
Xin Hua	1996	Chinese	Life	National	Joint Stock
Hua Tai	1996	Chinese	Property	National	Joint Stock
Yong A Property Insurance Company Ltd.	1996	Chinese	Property	Regional (Shaanxi)	Joint Stock
Xinjiang Agricultural Insurance Co.[b]	1986	Chinese	Agriculture	Regional (Xinjiang)	State-owned
Tian An	1994	Chinese	Property	Regional (Yangtze River Delta[c])	Joint Stock
Da Zhong	1995	Chinese	Property	Regional (Yangtze River Delta[c])	Joint Stock
Hua An Insurance Company Ltd.	1996	Chinese	Property	Regional (Guangdong)	Joint Stock
17 Regional Insurers, including	1986 (the earliest)	Chinese	Life	Regional (various)	JV between PICC and Local Companies
Sichun Life Insurance Company Ltd.				Sichun	
Changsha Life Insurance Company Ltd.				Changsha	
Dalian Life Insurance Company Ltd.				Dalian	
Shenyang Life Insurance Company Ltd.				Shenyang	
Xiamen Life Insurance Company Ltd.				Xiamen	

Table 12.2 (cont.)

Zhuhai Life Insurance Company Ltd.				Zhuhai	
Xiantan Life Insurance Company Ltd.				Xiantan	
Benxi Life Insurance Company Ltd.				Benxi	
Dandong Life Insurance Company Ltd.				Dandong	
Tianjin Life Insurance Company Ltd.				Tianjin	
Harbin Life Insurance Company Ltd.				Harbin	
Taiyuan Life Insurance Company Ltd.				Taiyuan	
Fuzhou Life Insurance Ltd.				Fuzhou	
Guangzhou Life Insurance Company Ltd.				Guangzhou	
Nanjing Life Insurance Company Ltd.				Nanjing	
Anshan Life Insurance Company Ltd.				Anshan	
Kunming Life Insurance Company Ltd.				Kunming	
American International Group (China) Ltd.	1992	American	Composite	Regional (Shanghai)	Foreign Branch Office
American International Group (China) Ltd.	1995	American	Composite	Regional (Guangzhou)	Foreign Branch Office
Tokio Fire & Marine (China) Ltd.	1994	Japanese	Property	Regional (Shanghai)	Foreign Branch Office
Winterthur Swiss Insurance (China) Ltd.	1997	Swiss	Property	Regional (Shanghai)	Foreign Branch Office
Zhong Hong Life Insurance Company[d]	1996	Sino-Canadian	Life	Regional (Shanghai)	JV with Sinochem[e]

Source: EIU (1996); Dongxiang Jiang (1997); Reactions (March, 1996); Insurance in China (monthly faxed newsletter), London: Reactions Publishing Group Ltd., various issues

Note: [a] The predecessor of the China Insurance Group is the People's Insurance Company of China (PICC) which was established in 1949. PICC was designated to replace all the other insurance companies from the last nationalist regime when the Chinese Communist Party claimed national power in 1949; [b] (Xinjiang Agricultural Insurance Co. is the only insurance company specialised in agricultural insurance in China, and its major client is the paramilitary frontier development unit – Xinjiang Production and Construction Corp; [c] Yangtze River delta include mainly Shanghai, Zhejiang province and Jiangsu province; [d] The Canadian partner is Manufacturer Life (Manulife) Insurance Company which has a controlling interest of 51% of the China joint venture; [e] Sinochem stands for China National Chemical Import & Export Corporation.

The regulatory framework for foreign participation

Legislation regarding representative offices dates back to the *Interim Regulations for Control of Resident Representative Offices of Foreign Enterprises in China*, which became effective on 30 October 1980. The regulations introduced a basic system for the approval and registration of representative offices which have, over time, been supplemented by many more detailed national and local regulations[15] on matters such as employment of staff, taxation of the office and its staff, foreign exchange control, continuing reporting requirements, use of company names and visas.

The 1980 *Interim Regulations* and the subsequent legislation have restricted the activities of representative offices, both in function and in location. The representative office is limited to liaison-type activities of a non-profit-making nature. Technically representative offices should not negotiate or sign contacts, engage in trading activities, or be directly involved in financing transactions.[16] Article 8 of the 1991 *PBOC Procedures for the Administration of the Establishment of Resident Representative Offices in China by Financial Institutions with Foreign Investment* stipulates that the work of a resident representative office of foreign financial (including insurance) institutions shall be limited to non-profit-making activities such as consultation, liaison and market investigation. The representative office is not allowed to engage in business operations on behalf of its parent company's head office agencies, including those in China. Although a certain level of trading or business activities in some industries have been tolerated by the Chinese authorities owing to the practical difficulties in delineating pure liaison-type activities and profit-making activities, such tolerance has certainly not been the case for the representative offices of foreign insurance companies and other financial institutions.[17] These foreign financial institutions have been subject to special rules and extra restrictive controls, and their business development in China has been severely circumscribed.

And special rules apply also to the location of representative offices of foreign financial institutions. The 1991 Procedures restrict their location to fourteen open cities. Moreover, the restrictive regulations regarding the operation of foreign financial institutions was also evident in the extra documents required for registration. In accordance with Article 4 of the 1986 *Provisional Regulations of Shanghai Municipality Concerning the Control of Representative Offices of Foreign Enterprises*, a banking, insurance, or stock exchange institution which desires to establish a resident representative office should, apart from submitting the documents and reference materials specified for other foreign institutions, submit at the same time an annual report on the accounts, liabilities, profits, and losses of the head offices of the enterprise, its contribution, and the composition of its Board of Directors.

Foreign equity participation in the Chinese insurance industry was totally banned under the 1985 *Provisional Regulations Governing the Administration of Insurance Enterprises*. In 1992, Shanghai was selected by the Chinese

Government as an experimental zone to test the impact of foreign participation, and American International Insurance (AIA)[18] became the first foreign insurer to be granted a licence to underwrite both life and non-life insurance. The so-called 'Shanghai Measures' were introduced to provide a legal framework for the supervision of foreign insurance companies, and these imposed strict entry requirements:

- three years' experience through a representative office in China;
- thirty consecutive years of experience in the insurance industry;
- total assets in excess of £5bn (US$7.94bn);
- corporate structure in the form of a joint venture or a branch office, but wholly owned subsidiaries not permitted.

A new *Insurance Law* came into effect on 1 October 1995. It was China's first ever unified Insurance Law, and 'a codification of internationally recognised insurance principles and the first attempt to create a comprehensive regulatory structure for China's burgeoning insurance industry' (Clifford Chance, 1995). Furthermore, the Law:

- created a national regulatory framework, requiring insurance companies to sustain a high level of liquidity, and clarifying the legal liabilities of companies which breached the laws and regulations;
- separated life insurance and non-life insurance, and commercial business and specialist non-commercial covers;
- contained clear definitions of core insurance concepts and a codification of the rights and liabilities of insurers and policyholders.

Foreign participation was only mentioned in the *Supplementary Provisions* of the new Law. Article 148 provides for the Law to apply to the establishment of an insurance company with an investment of foreign capital, and to the establishment within the PRC of branch offices of foreign insurance companies. The Shanghai Measures are acknowledged as the principal legal framework for the supervision and regulation of foreign insurance companies, even though various amendments have been introduced in accordance with the basic principles of the new Law. The main features of the current (early 1997) regulatory framework for foreign participation may thus be summarised as follows:

- stringent preconditions:[19] two years' experience through a representative office in China (as compared to the three years required under the Shanghai Measures; demonstrated financial prudence and a long history of conservative operation. It has been reported[20] that specific regulations will be enacted regarding the establishment of foreign insurance companies in China;
- a ban on wholly-owned subsidiaries in order to protect China from undercapitalised foreign insurers;
- limited number of possible locations: formerly only Shanghai, but extended to Guangzhou (the financial capital of South China) and its surrounding areas;

- the paramount importance of the goodwill of the Chinese authorities: applicants who satisfy the preconditions are not necessarily granted operating licences.

The rules for foreign entry were thus loosened somewhat by the *Supplementary Provisions*. American International Insurance Co. and American International Underwriter Co. established branch offices in Guangzhou in 1995 for the provision of life and non-life services respectively. According to PICC, China will open all its main cities to foreign insurers by the year 2000.[21]

Notwithstanding the above, there are still many discrepancies between the stipulations included in the new *Insurance Law* and those included in the Shanghai Measures.[22] These discrepancies have given rise to considerable confusion and uncertainty, and may well have been detrimental to the growth of foreign insurance business, as well as being incompatible with the major principles of the General Agreement on Trade in Services (GATS). It is not yet clear how, or indeed whether, these discrepancies will be removed. It should be borne in mind, however, that the *Insurance Law* was designed primarily to control the development of China's domestic insurance industry, rather than to encourage the openness of the industry even though it creates a more certain legal environment embracing international practice and thus prepares the conditions necessary for foreign participation.

Foreign participation in China's insurance industry

Despite its rapid growth, China's domestic insurance industry is still in its infancy and it suffers not only from a severe shortage of specialised labour but also from limited exposure to international practice and standards of service. As a result of their wide range of ownership advantages relative to indigenous companies, foreign insurers are faced with a range of enticing business opportunities:

- The provision of private retirement pensions has been encouraged by the Chinese authorities so as to free the State from the social welfare needs of a rapidly ageing population and enable it to target its limited resources to those in most need. But China lacks indigenous insurance companies with the experience to develop a private pension system, whereas foreign insurers/reinsurers would appear to be well placed to provide social welfare cover for those able to afford it.
- Foreign insurers/reinsurers are much better equipped to analyse and rate all sorts of exposures/liabilities related to construction, engineering and production associated with China's industrial expansion plans (Wu 1996). The Chinese companies have been finding that their knowledge and expertise have been stretched by the number and complexity of these risks. Thus, although Chinese non-life business volume increased by 65 per cent between 1992 and 1994, the profits of the Chinese insurance companies decreased by 18 per cent.

- Marketing skills are of particular importance for a country like China where the whole concept of insurance is new, and where policies are optional for much of the population. Given their long experience, foreign insurers have a clear advantage over their domestic competitors in pushing the concept of insurance and in developing the market.
- Foreign insurers also have a clear advantage with respect to risk management and loss prevention. Risk management is a relatively new practice in China. Most data available on natural hazards are related to the coastal areas, and there is very little information on seismic and climatic conditions in the inland provinces where many new factories and plants are now being established.
- The immaturity of the life insurance market, as evidenced by the low insurance density and penetration rates, reflects the fact that Chinese firms lack experience in selling life policies and in choosing suitable vehicles for long-term investments.
- The myriad new risks produced by China's economic development have challenged the capacity and expertise of China's domestic insurers. The insurance expertise and high capitalisation of foreign reinsurers are essential for the provision of sufficiently professional cover for rapid economic expansion.

The potential of China's insurance market, coupled with the relative lack of local expertise, have led to the world's leading insurance companies queuing up to start operations in China. The ban on cross-border trade, together with the technical features of the insurance business, have determined some form of local presence within the market. Given the high contractual risks involved in operating in China, one would expect foreign firms to have a strong preference for wholly owned subsidiaries as a mode of entry. Yet fear of foreign domination has led the authorities to thwart such desires, and the most common form of entry mode in the mid-1990s was the representative office

At the end of 1996, seventy-six foreign insurers (including insurance brokers) had opened about 160 representative offices in China (see Appendix C). The most favoured locations were Beijing (64 offices), Shanghai (46), Guangzhou (16), Shenzhen (16), Tianjin (8) and Dalian (6). Less than 3 per cent of the representative offices were located in other cities such as Xiamen, Shenyang and Chengdu. Some twenty-one of the seventy-six foreign insurers were American, fourteen were Japanese, twelve were British, and twelve were incorporated in other European countries (France, Germany, Netherlands, and Switzerland). The majority of these representative offices have been established since 1993.

The limitations of the representative office are such that many, if not all, of these foreign insurers are seeking operating licences to open branch offices and/or joint ventures. As noted above and summarised in Table 12.3, American International Insurance was the first foreign insurer to be granted an operating licence to open a branch office in China. The office

Table 12.3 Licensed foreign insurance companies in China

Venture Name	Foreign Partner	Chinese Partner	Country of Foreign Company	Business Type	Venture Type	Year Established	Location
American International Group China Ltd.[a]	American International Group	N/A	USA	Life and Non-life	Branch	1992	Shanghai
American International Group	American International Group	N/A	USA	Life and Non-life	Branch	1995	Guangzhou
Tokio Fire & Marine China Ltd.	Tokio Marine & Fire	N/A	Japan	Non-life	Branch	1994	Shanghai
Winterthur China Ltd.[b]	Winterthur Swiss Insurance Co.	N/A	Switzerland	Non-life	Branch	1997	Shanghai (Pudong)
Zhong Hong Life Insurance Co.[c]	Manulife (51%)	Sinochem	Canada	Life	Joint Venture	1996	Shanghai

Sources: 'Insurance in China' (Reactions Publishing Group Ltd., monthly faxed newsletter), various issues
Notes: (a) The first foreign insurer licensed to operate in China since 1949.
(b) The first European insurer licensed to operate in China since 1949.
(c) The first Sino-foreign insurance joint venture since 1949.

was opened in Shanghai in 1992, and was licensed to underwrite both life and non-life insurance. In September 1994, the Japanese company, Tokio Marine and Fire, was also authorised to establish a branch office to underwrite non-life insurance in Shanghai. AIA opened a second branch office in Guangzhou in October 1995 to underwrite both life and non-life insurance. The first joint venture was established in May 1996 when approval was granted for Manufacturers Life and Insurance Co. (Manulife) of Canada to set up a venture with China National Chemicals Import & Export Corporation (Sinochem): the venture started operation in Shanghai in late 1996. Following Manulife's example, the Swiss company Winterthur became the first European insurer licensed to operate in the Chinese market. Their Shanghai branch started to issue non-life insurance policies in January 1997.

RESULTS FROM THE QUESTIONNAIRE SURVEY

The influx of foreign insurers raises a number of interesting questions, to which answers were sought using a questionnaire survey:[23]

- what strategies had been adopted by foreign insurers in pursuit of the elusive operating licences?
- what criteria were used in the selection of Chinese partners in joint ventures?
- what were the criteria determining the choice of location within China; and which were the favoured locations on the basis of these criteria?

The survey was undertaken in July 1996. Questionnaires were distributed to ninety-five representative offices of foreign insurance companies in China, and forty-two valid responses were received (44 per cent response rate). These responses came from offices whose parent companies were European (18),[24] American (10), Japanese (12), Australian (1), and Canadian (1): 11 of the valid responses were from specialist life insurance companies; 14 from specialist non-life insurance companies; 10 from composite (i.e. life and non-life) insurers; 6 from insurance intermediaries; and 1 from a reinsurer: 18 of the offices were located in Beijing; 14 in Shanghai; 3 each in Guangzhou, Dalian and Shenzhen; and 1 in Tianjin.

The questionnaire involved two types of questions. The first type – used for eliciting views on location and selection criteria – required each respondent to score the importance of specific factors on a 5-point Likert-type scale. A score of 5 on this scale indicated that the factor was considered to be 'very important'; a score of 4 'quite important'; a score of 3 'important'; a score of 2 'of little importance'; and a score of 1 indicated 'of no importance'. The second type of question addressed the popularity of ten cities as locations for representative offices within China. Respondents were asked to score each city on each of the location factors using a 10-point scale. The distribution of data was found not to be normally distributed, so an appropriate non-parametric procedure was used for all statistical tests (i.e. the Kruskal-Wallis test as three populations were being compared).

Strategies to obtain operating licences

The award of a licence to establish a branch, a joint venture, or a wholly owned subsidiary – and hence to be able to engage in profit-making activities in the potentially lucrative Chinese market – is the aim of most foreign insurers. Notwithstanding the eligibility requirements set out in the Shanghai Measures and the *Supplementary Provisions*, approval is not automatic and 'winning over' the Chinese authorities requires rather more than demonstrable expertise and experience. As Roger Taylor, the Executive Deputy Chairman of Royal Sun Alliance, put it: 'It's politics – first, second, and third.'[25]

Our questionnaire survey thus sought views about the relative importance of a number of factors which might have a positive influence upon the authorities. These factors may be grouped as follows:

- corporate strategies which aid the development of the domestic insurance industry;
- the expertise and experience of the foreign insurer;
- 'political' strategies which foster good relations.

It has been noted above that the objective of the 1995 *Insurance Law* was to control the development of China's domestic insurance industry, rather than to encourage greater openness and/or competition. Furthermore, the reforms to the social security system, with the associated reduction in the State's provision of cradle-to-grave welfare, have led to particular demand for private life assurance services. It would thus seem wise for foreign insurers, in their pursuit of the coveted operating licences, to emphasise their potential contributions to the development of the domestic industry. This might be achieved through a clearly stated long-term commitment to the Chinese market or, more concretely, through investment in an insurance training and education programme. Or the foreign insurer might incorporate an explicit proposal to provide life insurance, given the importance attached to this by the authorities. The authorities also have a clear preference for the joint venture mode of entry, both to enhance the transfer of foreign know-how and to ensure some control over the activities of the foreign insurers. Hence an explicit strategy of forging a joint venture with a Chinese partner, notwithstanding any corporate preference for a wholly owned branch or subsidiary, might also be a successful strategy.

The expertise and experience of the foreign insurer may be captured under three headings. First, the length of time the foreign insurer has had links with China clearly testifies not only to experience and expertise, but also to commitment. Second, corporate expertise in life insurance may be particularly important given the requirements of the Chinese authorities. Third, the authorities' clear preference for foreign insurers of size and stature should be reflected in the weight accorded to financial prudence and corporate reputation.

The political dimension may be important at both the corporate and the governmental level. At the corporate level, *guanxi* has long been recognised as the lifeblood of the Chinese business community (Davies 1995; Bjorkman 1996; Roehrig 1994). 'Without *guanxi*, one simply can not get anything done. On the other hand, with *guanxi*, many things are possible' (Davies 1995). 'Companies possessing good *guanxi* with the right people are seen to enjoy an advantage over their rivals' (Bjorkman 1996). Thus the chances of being granted an operating licence might well depend upon maintaining good relations with PBOC. At the governmental level, it is expected that good relations between the foreign insurer's national government and the Chinese Government will also be important. It is widely believed (by the China executives of foreign insurers) that the Canadian insurer Manulife had, to a great extent, benefited from the fact that the Chinese authorities were reluctant to grant a licence to the German firm Allianz, following friction with the German Parliament over the issue of human rights. A coordinated approach involving active promotion by the foreign insurer's national government might also prove valuable, particularly in enabling potential entrants to leapfrog their competitors. Finally, given the politicisation of China's campaign for WTO admission, support for China's WTO membership campaign might also prove to be a fruitful strategy in the search for an operating license.

Table 12.4 provides a summary of the respondents' views on the relative importance of these eleven factors. The results confirm the expected importance of political considerations, with the promotion of good relations with PBOC and between the respective governments seen as crucial. At the other end of the scale come the factors related to the provision of life insurance. This probably reflects the fact that the development of all forms of insurance are required in China, even if life insurance is the type where the requirement is most urgent. The most surprising result is perhaps the low importance accorded to forging joint ventures with Chinese partners. Maybe, as Vanhonacker (1997) notes:

> What is more important than what the rule books say are the principles that underline the rules. China wants and needs its foreign investors to bring something of value to the table. My experience has shown time and time again that if they do, the form of investment is largely negotiable. That is why WFOEs are just as feasible as a way to enter the market of the Middle Kingdom as EJVs.

Table 12.4 Strategies to obtain operating licences, analysed by nationality of the foreign insurer

Strategy	Mean 40	European 18	US 10	Japan 12	Significance
Good relations with the PBOC	4.325	4.111	4.8	4.25	
Good relations between the foreign insurer's national government and the Chinese Government	4.175	4.111	4.5	4	
Clearly-stated long-term Commitment to Chinese market	4.025	4.167	4.1	3.75	
Financial prudence and corporate reputation	3.95	4	3.9	3.917	
Promotion by the foreign insurer's National Government	3.95	3.833	4.1	4	
Length of time foreign insurer has had links with China	3.625	3.778	3.3	3.667	
Investment in an insurance training and education programme	3.6	3.5	3.7	3.667	
Forging joint venture with Chinese partner	3.45	3.667	3.9	2.75	(a)
Support for China's WTO membership campaign	3.1	3	3.5	2.917	
Corporate expertise in life insurance	2.9	3.056	3.3	2.333	
Explicit proposal to provide life insurance	2.6	2.722	2.9	2.167	

Note: (a) denotes $p < 0.1$.

Kruskal-Wallis tests were also undertaken to see if there were any significant differences in the importance attached to the factors by the European, the US and the Japanese respondents in the sample. No such differences were found, except with regard to the importance of forging joint ventures with Chinese partners. Here the Japanese respondents gave significantly lower scores than their European and US counterparts, and this contributed to the low overall importance accorded to this strategy. This finding will be discussed further in the next section.

The selection of a Chinese partner for a joint venture

There is a shortage of empirical research on partner selection criteria both in service industries in general, and in the insurance industry in particular. What literature is available tends to draw on experiences from other industries, and highlights complementarity in function, and compatibility in objectives as the main bases for partner selection. On the one hand, a partner which can supply complementary skills or capabilities may be expected to help the firm obtain its strategic objectives (Tomlinson 1970; Berg and Friedman 1982; Killing 1983; Harrigan 1985; de Hoghton 1967; Franko 1971; Gullander 1976; Dymsza 1988). On the other hand, compatability between partners in terms of objectives, corporate philosophy, and mutual trust is clearly desirable (Awadzi 1987; Geringer 1988).

Geringer (1988, 1991) has differentiated various criteria as being either task-related (complementary) or partner-related (compatible). Task-related criteria are the operational skills and resources which a venture requires for its competitive success. Examples include patents or technical know-how, financial resources, experienced managerial personnel, and access to marketing and distribution systems. Partner-related criteria are those associated with the efficiency and effectiveness of partners' cooperation, including the partners' national or corporate culture, the degree of favourable past association between the partners, compatibility of and trust between partners' top management teams, and partners' organisational size or structure. Anderson and Paine (1975) assert that 'it is generally accepted that the perceptions of environmental and internal characteristics (rather than the 'objective' characteristics of the environment) are the important properties to consider in the strategy formulation process'. It may therefore be hypothesised that firms of different national origin (and different types of business) will put different weights upon different partner selection criteria.

Thus the questionnaire survey listed eleven criteria, grouped as below, as possible determinants of the selection of a Chinese partner:

- partner-related (compatibility) criteria;
- task-related (complementary) criteria;
- direction from the Chinese authorities.

As regards partner-related criteria, Schroath (1988) found that the biggest concern among international insurance companies about joint ventures was management control. The nature of the product and the desire to maintain acceptable levels of quality mean that foreign insurers are attracted by the willingness of the partner to accept foreign management control of the venture. Furthermore, given that trust between the two management teams has been identified as an important determinant of the success of joint ventures (Buckley and Casson 1988), a favourable past relationship would appear to be a sensible *a priori* criterion for partner selection.

A number of complementary criteria may be identified. The importance of the local knowledge and political clout of joint venture partners in the insurance industry has been highlighted by various authors (Schroath 1988; Huggins and Land 1996; LIMRA 1990; Gora 1991). Thus convenient access to partner's market network is likely to be an important complementary asset to fulfil the foreign firm's need to acquire country-specific knowledge of the customs of the Chinese insurance-buying public. In view of their different client bases, it is expected that life insurance and non-life insurance companies might have different perceptions of the importance of this criterion. It is expected that life insurance companies will attach more importance to this criterion, given that their primary clients are local Chinese residents, rather than multinational companies as is the case of the non-life insurance companies. In a similar vein, other criteria which might be suggested are the Chinese partner's facilities and resources, the partner's ability to offset risk, the partner's access to local financial markets, the partner's satisfactory location, and the partner's technological capacity and management resources. All such assets may be valued by the foreign insurer but, given the ownership advantages which foreign insurers are likely to enjoy (see above) relative to Chinese firms, it seems unlikely that such criteria will be of major importance. As regards political clout, the partner's contacts with central/local authorities are also expected to be an important criterion, given the need of political backing in such a heavily regulated and sensitive industry as the insurance industry in China.

Last but not least, the effects of government restrictions and guidance on the partner selection process must also be taken into account. In the opinion of one observer, PBOC will continue to be protective of the local insurance industry for the foreseeable future, and joint venture agreements will need to be reviewed and approved by PBOC with a paternalistic attitude towards local firms. A certain amount of 'interference' from the Chinese Government is to be expected in joint venture (JV) negotiations with local Chinese partners.[26] Zheng (1992) found that the selection process in China is sometimes circumscribed by the intervention of the central authorities in terms of the selection choice, partner availability and selection channels. Central government institutions tended to recommend enterprises under their own jurisdiction to foreign firms. Thus the final two criteria are the restrictions of PBOC or the Chinese Government and the guidance/persuasion of PBOC or the Chinese Government.

Table 12.5 provides a summary of the respondents' views on the relative importance of these eleven criteria. Four criteria have average scores in excess of four. Two of these relate directly to the direction of the Chinese authorities, and suggest that the choice of partner in the Chinese insurance industry is, in many instances, not really a choice but a requirement. This conclusion reinforces the impression, noted in the previous section, that good relations with the authorities are paramount in the pursuit of operating licences. A willingness of the partner to accept foreign management control of the venture was ranked equal first, and was particularly valued by the Japanese respondents. Some Chinese insurance company executives have little experience of the insurance industry in a capitalist sense, and may find it difficult to function in concert with the foreign partner's Westernised management and insurance principles.[27] Moreover, the local partner may also veto major decisions, such as amending the Articles of incorporation and increasing capital, which require unanimous approval. The other partner-related criterion, a favourable past relationship, also scored well.

Table 12.5 Selection criteria for joint venture partner, analysed by nationality of the foreign insurer

Criterion	Mean 32	European 16	US 8	Japan 8	Significance
Restriction of PBOC or the Chinese Government	4.442	4.25	4.375	4.25	
Willingness of the partner to accept foreign management control of the venture	4.442	4.186	4.125	4.375	
Partner's contacts with the central/local authorities	4.353	4.5	4.125	3.625	(b)
Guidance/persuasion of PBOC or Chinese Government	4.235	3.75	4.375	4.375	
Convenient accesses to partner's market network	3.588	3.875	3.75	2.75	(a)
Favourable past relationship	3.5	3.688	3	3.375	
Partner's facilities and resources (including labour and financial assets)	3.441	3.313	3.5	3.375	
Partner's ability to offset risk	3.412	3.188	2.75	3.625	
Partner's access to local financial markets	3.412	3.375	3.375	3.25	
Partner's satisfactory location	3	2.75	3.375	2.875	
Partner's technological capacity or management resource	2.941	2.813	2.75	3.125	

Notes: (a) denotes $p < 0.01$.
(b) denotes $p < 0.05$.

As regards the task-related criteria, the Chinese partner's contacts with the central/local authorities and convenient access to partner's market network were both deemed important, particularly by the European respondents. Indeed, the European and US respondents accorded significantly greater importance to these complementary assets than did the Japanese insurers. The reasons are perhaps twofold. First, the Japanese firms are probably more acquainted with the Chinese economy and culture than their Western counterparts, and thus have less need of local partners to build relationships with the authorities. Second, the Japanese insurers have, to a large extent, geared their operations to serving their existing client base of Japanese MNEs operating in China. Thus they have less use of local partner's market networks than do the European and US insurance companies. Such an explanation would be consistent with the low weight attached by Japanese insurers to forging joint ventures as a strategy for obtaining operating licences.

Political contacts and quick market access are capabilities which are difficult, if not impossible, for foreign insurers to obtain if they operate alone. In contrast, foreign insurers do not look to their Chinese partners to provide technological, managerial, and financial capabilities, hence the lower importance attached to these selection criteria. These findings are consistent with those of earlier studies on joint ventures in China, albeit for different industries (Shan 1991; Glaister and Wang 1993; Dong *et al.* 1997).

The choice of location

The selection of an appropriate location for a representative office[28] is determined by five broad groups of factors related to:

- market demand;
- competition;
- the availability of suitable inputs;
- operating costs;
- government influence.

In a country as vast as China and with such substantial regional variations in per capita income and even awareness of insurance, the state of the immediate local market takes on particular significance. We might therefore expect the locational decision to be affected by the current level of local market demand, by local market growth potential, by consumer risk awareness and the demand for insurance products, and by proximity to major clients. As regards this latter factor, it is important to note that several studies (Bickelhaupt and Bar-Niv 1983; Schroath 1988) have shown that insurance companies often feel compelled to follow their international clients in order to both win and retain business. Failure to do so may even result in domestic business being lost to competitors who are willing and able to provide the requisite services to the foreign subsidiaries. We might also expect the state of competition in the local market to be important, with relevant factors thus including proximity to major competitors supplying similar services, and the limited local provision of insurance services.

As regards the availability of suitable inputs, five factors may be identified: the availability and convenience of telecommunications facilities, the availability and convenience of travel facilities, the availability of specialised labour and financial service personnel, proximity to advisory services, and accessibility to the major financial markets of China. Operating costs are largely confined to manpower costs and office rental charges. And last, but certainly not least, government influence is likely to play a substantial role. Good relations with the PBOC might be ensured by locating the office near PBOC headquarters in Beijing or, alternatively, near one of the PBOC branches. And the government may also exert its influence rather more directly through guidance/persuasion or restrictions, through financial incentives, or through requirements to establish joint ventures. In the latter case, the location of the representation office might well be determined by the location of a suitable (future) joint venture partner.

Some nineteen factors which might impact upon the locational decisions of foreign insurers regarding their representative offices were thus identified. The survey results regarding the relative importance of these factors are shown in Table 12.6. The three most important factors were judged to be proximity to PBOC headquarters, local market growth potential, and proximity to major clients: all achieved mean scores markedly higher than the other factors. In general, the factors related to market demand and government influence scored well and appeared in the top half of the table, those related to the availability of inputs appeared in the middle of the table (but with mean scores less than three), while those related to competition and operating costs were judged to be of least importance. Manpower costs and office rental charges came bottom of the list of nineteen factors.

Comparisons of the mean scores returned by the 18 European (including the 12 UK) respondents with those of the 10 US and 12 Japanese respondents reveals significant differences for 6 of the factors. The Europeans and US respondents accorded significantly greater weight than the Japanese to local market growth potential, location of a suitable joint venture partner, and accessibility to the major financial markets in China. The Japanese respondents, on the other hand, attached significantly more importance than their European and US counterparts to proximity to major competitors supplying similar services, and proximity to advisory services. Both the Japanese and the European respondents attached great weight to proximity to major clients. Indeed, these three variables are all rated among the top four determinants of location choice by the Japanese respondents (together with proximity to PBOC headquarters).

These results suggest that the European and US insurers are more interested in the local market, while the Japanese are much more interested in

Table 12.6 Determinants of location choice, analysed by nationality of the foreign insurer

Factor	Mean	Europe 18	US 10	Japan 12	Significance
Proximity to PBOC headquarters	4	4.222	3.9	3.75	
Local market growth potential	3.825	4.167	3.9	3.25	(a)
Proximity to major clients	3.625	3.722	3.2	3.833	(b)
Government restriction	3.35	3.444	3.3	3.25	
Current local market demand	3.325	3.389	3.3	3.25	
Government guidance/persuasion	3.25	3.333	3.2	3.167	
Consumer risk awareness and demand for insurance products	3.25	3.278	3.4	3.083	
Accessibility to major financial markets in China	3.175	3.222	3.7	2.667	(a)
Availability and convenience of telecommunication facilities	3.175	3.056	3.6	3	
Proximity to PBOC branch	3.15	2.944	3.3	3.333	
Availability and convenience of travel facilities	2.975	2.944	3.2	2.833	
Availability of specialised labour and financial service	2.85	2.778	2.9	2.917	
Financial incentive	2.7	2.389	3.2	2.75	
Proximity to advisory services	2.65	2.444	2.2	3.333	(a)
Proximity to major competitors supplying similar services	2.625	2.333	2.2	3.4167	(a)
Location of a suitable joint venture partner	2.575	2.611	3.3	1.917	(b)
Limited local provision of insurance products	2.55	2.611	2.6	2.4167	
Manpower cost	2.275	2.278	2.3	2.25	
Office rental charge	2.2	2.222	2.1	2.25	

Notes: (a) denotes $p < 0.1$.
(b) denotes $p < 0.05$.

their established clients, at least at this initial stage of foreign participation in the China's insurance market. Apart from the political connections which are the common pursuit of insurers from all the three nationality groups, the Japanese insurers are distinctively motivated by 'client-following'. Furthermore, their significantly stronger propensity to locate in proximity to major competitors supplying similar services may well reflect a concentration of their corporate customers in China, or the 'follow-the-leader' behaviour that has characterised much Japanese FDI all over the world. In the same vein, it is interesting to note the much higher weight given to advisory services, perhaps indicating traditional Japanese concerns with the detail of their overseas ventures. In contrast, the Japanese pay very little attention to the location of a suitable joint venture partner in making their location decision. This research finding is echoed in the findings on partner selection, where the Japanese are found to be least interested in the complementary capabilities Chinese partners can provide in gaining quick local market entry.

As regards the favoured locations within China, the respondents were asked to provide scores on the basis of each of the nineteen factors for each of the following ten cities: Beijing, Chengdu, Dalian, Guangzhou, Shanghai, Shenyang, Shenzhen, Tianjin, Xiamen, and Xian. Shanghai was the preferred choice on the basis of fourteen of the factors: the exceptions were proximity to PBOC headquarters (Beijing), proximity to advisory services (Beijing), limited local provision of insurance products (Xian), manpower costs (Xian), and office rental charges (Xian).

An overall ranking of the relative desirability of each city (see Table 12.7) may be obtained by weighting the scores on each factor (on the 10-point scale) for each city by the relative importance (on the 5-point scale) accorded to that factor by each respondent. This overall ranking shows Shanghai to be the most favoured location, followed by Beijing, Guangzhou and Shenzhen. Tianjin and Dalian achieve rather lower overall ratings, but still score markedly higher than Xiamen, Chengdu, Shenyang, and Xian. No significant differences were found between the responses of the European, US and Japanese insurers, though some favouring of Dalian and Shanghai by the Japanese insurers is apparent.

CONCLUDING REMARKS

This chapter has outlined the development of the Chinese insurance industry up to the mid-1990s, and highlighted the enormous potential of the domestic market as a result of reforms in the social security system, the breakdown of extended families, and the diminution in superstitious fears regarding insuring against death. Together with the general rise in spending

Table 12.7 Favoured locations for representative offices, analysed by nationality of the foreign insurer

City	Mean 33	Europe 16	US 9	Japan 8	Significance
Shanghai	1.327	1.278	1.331	1.453	
Beijing	1.252	1.216	1.293	1.289	
Guangzhou	1.224	1.197	1.237	1.281	
Shenzhen	1.146	1.126	1.132	1.219	
Tianjin	1.002	1.01	0.984	1.008	
Dalian	1.000	0.993	0.922	1.133	
Xiamen	0.839	0.858	0.887	0.712	
Chengdu	0.762	0.806	0.736	0.679	
Shenyang	0.750	0.779	0.761	0.653	
Xian	0.700	0.736	0.719	0.572	

Note: The two responses from Canada and Australia were omitted from the analysis. The mean scores for each strategy are slightly different when these responses are included, and the ranking of strategies is also slightly different.

power in China, these developments present an enticing array of lucrative opportunities to international insurance companies blessed with expertise which is not yet possessed by their Chinese counterparts. Many European, US, and Japanese insurers are thus eager and willing to establish operations in China, but foreign participation is still strictly controlled by the Chinese authorities.

Licences to operate through branches or joint ventures are coveted by the foreign insurers, but approval by the Chinese authorities is far from automatic and must be earned. The chapter also reports the results of a questionnaire survey which sought responses *inter alia* on the strategies pursued by foreign insurers in pursuit of these licences, their criteria for the selection of Chinese partners in joint ventures, and their criteria in deciding where to locate within China. The importance of good relations with the Chinese authorities emerged strongly from the analysis of strategies, and the influence of the authorities was also felt in the selection of partners in joint ventures and in the choice of location.

Furthermore, some interesting differences were detected between the responses of the European insurers and their US and Japanese counterparts. It was found that Japanese insurers did not favour forging joint ventures as a strategy to win operating licences, and were less interested in the local partner's complementary skills than were their Western counterparts. This difference was echoed in the location choice, where the Japanese insurers were found to be more oriented to 'client-following' than the Europeans and Americans. In contrast, the European and US respondents were more local market-oriented. Furthermore, the Japanese 'client-following' market approach was evidenced by their favouring of Dalian and Shanghai, where much Japanese manufacturing investment is concentrated.

Although Winterthur has so far been the only European insurer to be granted an operating licence in China, many other European insurers have been actively involved in specialist education and training for the domestic insurance industry. One of the first foreign education initiatives was the Lloyds Scholarship set up in 1985. Eagle Star set up an examination centre in 1993, providing postgraduate tuition for the first Institute of Actuaries qualification in China. The Dutch insurer ING have sponsored an insurance and examination centre at Shanghai Jiao Tong University to provide training for medium and high-level managers in the local industry. And many more European companies (including Prudential, General Accident, Sun Alliance) have also been investing in insurance training (Maclean 1995). The potential benefits of such training are twofold. As noted above, such programmes are perceived by many foreign insurers as a good way to win over the Chinese authorities and secure an operating licence. And, if such a licence is eventually forthcoming, there is then a pool of ready-trained staff to employ.

In view of its rapid economic growth, the far-reaching social security reforms, and the sheer size of its population, China has the potential to become one of the world's largest insurance markets. Its full potential, however, cannot be realised unless major challenges are faced: the perfection of the legal framework; the acquisition of insurance know-how; and the raising of public awareness/understanding of insurance concepts. Foreign insurers can play a positive role in helping China to meet these challenges. In particular, they can assist with regard to the provision of technical expertise and risk management, the provision of complex cover demanded by foreign-funded enterprises, raising insurance awareness, the introduction of new, innovative products, assistance with the compilation of detailed insurance regulations; and help in the development of insurance training and the establishment of recognised insurance qualifications (Taylor 1996). By helping the development of China's insurance industry, foreign insurers will also help themselves by speeding up the opening process. The Chinese authorities have stated that the insurance market will open up fully for competition, but only when the domestic insurers can compete on an equal footing with the foreign insurers.

The pattern of liberalisation thus appears set to follow the gradualist approach witnessed in manufacturing: from SEZs and open cities to an all-round opening of the whole country; from joint ventures to a more liberal approach permitting wholly foreign-owned ventures; from centralised control of the allocation of operating licences to decentralised local autonomy; from strategically less important sectors to strategically important sectors. To provide but one example, there is a clear parallel between the requirement for foreign insurers to prove themselves through two years' operation of a representative office, and the requirement that foreign car manufacturers demonstrate their commitment through the establishment of parts etc. production.

NOTES

1 Remark by Mr Di Weiping, Deputy Director of the Department for the Supervision and Regulation of Foreign Financial Institutions at the People's Bank of China. See Hadley (1995: 19–23).
2 The insurer/reinsurer underwrites the insurance/reinsurance of risks located in foreign countries, and thus exports its services abroad. For a detailed discussion, see Carter and Dickinson (1992).
3 Also called establishment business.
4 Bickelhaupt and Bar-Niv (1983) list nine possible methods through which an insurance company can enter a foreign market., but the five noted here are the most common.
5 'Joint Ventures Hold Powerful Potential for Chinese Insurance Market,' *Reactions* (April 1996).
6 Ibid., *Reactions* (April 1996): 5.
7 One important exception is the handling of large commercial risks by international brokers.
8 See the conclusions drawn by the UN Transnational Corporations and Management Division from its survey of British insurance companies (United Nations 1993).

9   This is especially the case with the detailed terms and conditions of reinsurance contracts.
10 The time lag between the payment of premiums and the settlement of claims inevitably leads to the accumulation of funds over and above the capital subscribed by policyholders. This is especially the case for life insurance where the long-term nature of the product means that it may be a prime source of domestic savings.
11 A large volume of reinsurance trade also comes from captive insurance and reciprocal insurance. Captive insurance companies are formed by major industrial corporations to underwrite some of their own risks. One of the main reasons for forming a joint captive insurance company is that reinsurance may be obtained through the international reinsurance market at a more favourable premium and with higher limits of coverage: such companies are also responsible for a large part of cross-border direct insurance because of the premiums paid by MNEs and their foreign affiliates. Reciprocal insurance refers to reinsurance swaps between insurers: it takes place both between insurer groups, and between insurers and state-owned insurance companies of developing countries which wish to reduce the foreign-currency costs of acquiring foreign reinsurance.
12 The underwriting ratio is the profit or loss achieved by the insurer, calculated as premium income less the cost of claims and the insurers' expenses in connection with business. It is common for insurers to make underwriting losses, but these are usually offset by the investment income which accrues from the holding of premiums prior to their disbursement to meet claims. The insurer's overall trading result is then the underwriting profit/loss plus the investment income. The trading ratio is the trading result expressed as a percentage of premium income.
13 Total insurance premium as a percentage of GDP.
14 Per capita expenditure on insurance.
15 See, for example, the *Procedures for the Registration and Administration of Resident Representative Offices of Foreign Enterprises in China*, promulgated by the State Administration for Industry and Commerce, and effective from 15 March 1983; the *Provisional Regulations of Shanghai Municipality Concerning the Control of Representative Offices of Foreign Enterprises*, promulgated by the municipal government of Shanghai, and effective from 1 September 1986; and the *PBOC Procedures for the Administration of the Establishment of Resident Representative Offices in China by Financial Institutions with Foreign Investment*, promulgated on 15 June 1991. Article 6 of the 1991 Procedures stipulates that the Head Office of PBOC is responsible for the supervision, inspection and regulation of the resident representative offices stationed in Beijing, while its branches are authorised to exercise supervision, inspection and regulation of the local resident representative offices in other cities.
16 Article 3 of the 1983 Procedures stipulates that representative offices of foreign enterprises shall be understood as those engaging in non-direct-profit making operations.
17 According to the EIU (1997), foreign representative offices are increasingly able to get around the non-profit-making constraints by funnelling revenue generated in China back to overseas offices. Others carry out business in China but have their home country headquarters bill customers for China-related business.
18 A subsidiary of the American International Group.
19 As indicated by the Deputy Governor of PBOC, Mr Chen Yaoxian, at the China Summit on 14 November 1996.
20 *Insurance in China*, London: Reactions Publishing Group, December 1996.
21 See the 'World Insurance Report' in the *Financial Times*, 15 December 1995.

22 These discrepancies arise with regard to (a) the measures concerning the protection of policyholders from the insolvency of insurance companies or their failure to provide an acceptable standard of service at a reasonable price; (b) insurance business; (c) corporate form; (d) supervisory authority.
23 The questionnaire also sought information on the main problems encountered by foreign insurers in operating in China. These results are not reported here because of lack of space, but may be obtained from the authors. Also not reported here are the analyses of the questionnaire results by type of insurer.
24 Thirteen were British, three were Swiss, and one each were from Germany and the Netherlands.
25 From the Chairman's speech delivered by Mr Roger Taylor at the November 1996 London conference on 'China and India: the Insurance Potential', organised by the Reactions Publishing Group.
26 Speech by Dean T. Chiang of the Taiwanese law firm, Lee & Li, to the October 1996 conference on 'Strategic Issues 2000' in Kuala Lumpur.
27 Ibid.
28 Foreign insurance branches and Sino-foreign joint ventures are currently only permitted to operate in Shanghai and Guangzhou.

REFERENCES

Agarwal, S. and Ramaswami, S. (1992) 'Choice of Foreign Market Entry Mode: Impact of Ownership, Location and Internalization Factors', *Journal of International Business Studies*, 23(1): 1–27.
Anderson, C. and Paine, F. (1975) 'Managerial Perceptions and Strategic Behavior', *Academy of Management Journal*, 18(6), December: 811–23.
Association of British Insurers (1996) *Insurance Statistics Yearbook*, London: Association of British Insurers.
Awadzi, W. (1987) 'Determinants of Joint Venture Performance: A Study of International Joint Ventures in the United States', unpublished PhD thesis, Louisiana State University.
Beamish, P. and Banks, J. (1987) 'Equity Joint Ventures and the Theory of the Multinational Enterprise', *Journal of International Business Studies*, 19(2): 1–16.
Berg, S. and Friedman, P. (1980) 'Corporate Courtship and Successful Joint Ventures', *California Management Review*, 22(2): 85–91.
Bickelhaupt, D. and Bar-Niv, R. (1983) *International Insurance: Managing Risk in the World*, New York: Insurance Information Institute.
Bjorkman, J. (1996) 'Market Entry and Development in China', in J. Child and Y. Lu (eds) *Management Issues in China* Volume 2 *International Enterprises*, London: Routledge.
Buckley, P. and Casson, M. (1988) 'A Theory of Co-operation in International Business', *Management International Review*, 28: 19–38.
Buckley, P. and Casson, M. (1996) 'An Economic Model of International Joint Venture Strategy', *Journal of International Business Studies*, 27(5): 849–76.
Carter, R. (1979) *Economics and Insurance*, 2nd edition, Stockport: P.H. Press.
Carter, R. and Dickinson, G. (1992) *Obstacles to the Liberalisation of Trade in Insurance*, Thames Essay no. 58, London: Trade Policy Research Centre.
Carter, R. and Dickinson, G. (1977) *Barriers to Trade in Insurance and Reinsurance: A Conference Dossier*, Geneva: Association Internationale pour l'Etude d'Economie de l'Assurance.
Carver, A. (1996) 'Open and Secret Regulations and their Implications for Foreign Investment', in J. Child and Y. Lu (eds) *Management Issues in China* Volume 2 *International Enterprises*, London: Routledge.

Clifford Chance (1995) *The Insurance Law of the People's Republic of China: Introduction and Translation*, London: Clifford Chance.
Davies, H. (1995) 'Interpreting Guanxi: The Role of Personal Connections in a High Context Transactional Economy', in H. Davies (ed.) *China Business: Context and Issues*, Hong Kong: Longman Asia, pp.155–69.
de Hoghton, C. (1967) *Cross-channel Collaboration*, London: PEP.
Dong, H., Buckley, P. and Mirza, H. (1997) 'International Joint Ventures in China from a Managerial Perspective: A Comparison between Different Sources of Investment', in G. Chryssochoidis, C. Millar and J. Clegg (eds) *Internationalisation Strategies*, London: Macmillan, pp.171–91.
Dongxiang, J. (1997) *Insurance in China*, London: FT Financial.
Dubin, M. (1975) 'Foreign Acquisitions and Growth of Multinational Firms', unpublished PhD thesis, Harvard University.
Dunning, J. (1989) *Multinational Enterprises and the Growth of Services: Some Conceptual and Theoretical Issues*, New York: United Nations.
Dunning, J. (1993) 'The Globalization of Service Activities', in *The Globalization of Business: The Challenge of the 1990s*, London: Routledge, pp.242–443.
Dwyer, R. and Oh, S. (1988) 'A Transaction Cost Perspective on Vertical Contractual Structure and Inter-channel Competitive Strategies', *Journal of Marketing*, 52(2), April: 21–34.
Dymsza, W. (1988), 'Successes and Failures of Joint Ventures in Developing Countries: Lessons from Experience', in F. Contractor and P. Lorange (eds) *Corporate Strategies in International Business*, Lexington, Mass: Lexington Books, pp.403–24.
EIU (1996) 'Please, Please Me', *Business China*, 22 January, London: Economist Intelligence Unit, p.8.
EIU (1997) 'Representative Office', in *China Hand*, vol. 1, London: Economist Intelligence Unit, p.1.
Enderwick, P. (1989) *Multinational Service Firms*, London: Routledge.
Erramilli, K. and Rao, C. (1993) 'Service Firms' International Entry-mode Choice: A Modified Transaction-cost Analysis Approach', *Journal of Marketing*, 57(3), July: 19–38.
Franko, L. (1971) *Joint Venture Survival in Multinational Corporations*, New York: Praeger.
Geringer, J. (1988), *Joint Venture Partner Selection: Strategies for Developed Countries* New York: Quorum Books.
Geringer, J. (1991) 'Strategic Determinants of Partner Selection Criteria in International Joint Ventures', *Journal of International Business Studies*, first quarter, 22(1): 41–62.
Glaister, K. and Wang, Y. (1993) 'UK Joint Ventures in China: Motivation and Partner Selection', *Marketing Intelligence and Planning*, 11(2): 9–15.
Gora, J. (1991) *Strategic Alliances in the Life Insurance Industry*, Atlanta: Life Office Management Association Inc.
Gullander, S. (1976) 'Joint Ventures and Corporate Strategy', *Columbia Journal of World Business*, 11(1): 104–14.
Hadley, B. (1995) 'Dawn of a Market', in *Insurance in China*, London: Reactions Publishing Group Ltd.
Harrigan, K. (1985) *Strategies for Joint Venture Success*, Lexington, MA: Lexington, Publishers.
Hennart, J. (1989) 'Can the "New Forms of Investment" Substitute for the "Old Forms"? A Transaction Costs Perspective', *Journal of International Business Studies*, 20(2): 211–34.
Huggins, K. and Land, R. (1996) *Operations of Life and Health Insurance Companies*, Atlanta: Life Office Management Association Inc.

Killing, J. (1983) *Strategies for Joint Venture Success*, New York: Praeger.
Klein, S. (1989) "A Transaction Cost Explanation of Vertical Control in International Markets", *Journal of the Academy of Marketing Science*, 17(3), Summer: 253–60.
LIMRA (1990) *International Company Global Expansion*, Hartford, CT: Life Insurance Marketing and Research Association.
Lincoln National Corporation (1996) 'Joint Ventures Hold Powerful Potential for Chinese Insurance Market', *Reactions*, Supplement, April.
Maclean, N. (1995) 'Priorities for the European Business Community', speech to the Euro-China Business Forum, Brussels, 5 October.
Marine and Fire Insurance Association of Japan Inc. (1996) *Non-Life Insurance in Japan Fact Book (1995–1996)*, Tokyo: The Marine and Fire Insurance Association of Japan Inc.
Meldrum, S. (1996) *The Restructuring of China's Insurance Market. Sino-Foreign Joint Venture Opportunities in the Light of New Insurance Law*, mimeo, Lincoln National Corporation.
Pfeffer, I. (1978) 'Problems in International Insurance Markets', in J. Long (ed.) *Issues in Insurance*, vol. II, Malvern, Penn: American Institute for Property and Liability Underwriters.
PICC (1994) *PICC Annual Report*, Beijing: People's Insurance Company of China.
PICC (1995) *PICC Annual Report*, Beijing: People's Insurance Company of China.
Roehrig, M. (1994) *Foreign Joint Ventures in Contemporary China*, New York: St Martin's Press.
Schrouth, F. (1988) 'Mode of Foreign Market Entry: An Analysis of Property and Liability Insurance Industry'. *The Geneva Papers on Risk and Insurance*, 13(49): 361–76.
Schroath, F., Hu, M. and Chen, H. (1993) 'Country-of-Origin Effects of Foreign Investments in the People's Republic of China', *Journal of International Business Studies*, 24(2): 277–90.
Sedgwick Information Exchange Limited (1996) *Japan at a Glance*, 12/1996, London: Sedgwick Information Exchange Limited.
Shan, W. (1991) 'Environmental Risks and Joint Venture Sharing Arrangements', *Journal of International Business Studies*, 22(4): 555–78.
Shanghai Securities News, 12 October 1996.
Skipper, H. (1987) 'Protectionism in the Provision of International Insurance Services', *The Journal of Risk and Insurance*, 54(1): 55–85.
Stopford, J. and Wells, L. (1972) *Managing the Multinational Enterprise: Organization of the Firm and Ownership of the Subsidiaries*, New York: Basic Books.
Swiss Re (UK) (1995) 'The Performance of the Insurance Industry in International Comparison: A Risk-Adjusted Analysis', *Sigma*, Economic Studies no. 1/95, London: Swiss Reinsurance Company.
Taylor, R. (1996) 'Prospects for an Insurance Market in China', *International Insurance Report*, May: 9–11.
Tomlinson, J. (1970) *The Joint Venture Process in International Business: India and Pakistan*, Cambridge, MA: MIT Press.
United Nations, Centre on Transnational Corporations (1989) *Foreign Direct Investment and Transnational Corporations in Services*, New York: United Nations.
United Nations, Department of Social and Economic Development, Transnational Corporations and Management Division (1993) *Transnationalization of Service Industries*, New York: United Nations.
Vanhonacker, W. (1997) 'Entering China: An Unconventional Approach', *Harvard Business Review*, 75(2), March–April: 130–40.

Waheed, A. and Mathur, I. (1995) 'Wealth Effects of Foreign Expansion by U.S. Banks', *Journal of Marketing*, 19(5): 823–42.
'World Insurance Report', *Financial Times*, 15 December 1995.
Wu, X. (1995) 'On the Road to Regulation', *Reactions*, October: 57–61.
Wu, X. (1996) 'A Sense of Immaturity', *Reactions*, September: 48–52.
Zheng, J. (1992) 'Western Joint Ventures in China', unpublished PhD thesis, Reading University.

Section III

Future prospects and conclusions

13 Outward investment from China

Jim Slater

INTRODUCTION

Previous chapters of this book have dealt primarily with aspects of Sino-European trade, and with European investment into China, at the sectoral as well as at the aggregate level. To complete the range of economic interactions, this chapter attempts to assess the significance of China's own outward foreign direct investment (FDI): there are signs, confirmed by improvements in the quality of statistics, that what was regarded as a mere trickle has grown into something more forceful. China's liberalisation is a cautious process, and the slackening of restrictions on outward FDI shows an unprecedented willingness to explore the consequences of global exposure. The chapter concludes with a summary assessment of the strength of policy, and of the prospects for furthering this particular economic linkage between China and Europe.

CHINA'S POLICY ON OUTWARD INVESTMENT

Despite Europe's status as the world's largest magnet for FDI, Asian investors have seemed relatively immune to the attraction. The forces driving and attracting direct investment are well documented elsewhere, but a recent UNCTAD publication (UNCTAD-DITED 1997) specifically examined these factors in relation to Asian investment in Europe, and also posited courses of action, unilateral and bilateral, which would assist in the promotion of reciprocal investment. On the European side, impediments to and lubricants for FDI are generic, and apply as much to China as to other potential Asian investors. From China's perspective, there are problems relating to outward investment generally and obstacles particular to Europe.

Concerning the former, China's liberalisation from 1979 included relaxation of the restrictions surrounding outward direct investment (ODI). The intention was to encourage 'inward-oriented outward investment, geared towards domestic development' (Zhan 1995). Investment was to be controlled, and limited to those projects which related to security of access to scarce raw materials, the enhancement of trade and therefore access to foreign exchange, technology upgrading, and to the general promotion of trade links. The ensuing rapid growth of ODI brought problems. By no means all screened projects undertaken met the intended criteria or, indeed, ultimately were put through the screening and monitoring mechanism. The phenomenon of 'round-tripping' investment is one example of the abuse of the system, and there are other practices which have been undertaken with equally dubious intent. However, while the Chinese authorities clearly recognise the untoward consequences of liberalisation, there is unlikely to be an over-reaction, rather a tightening of the monitoring process which is likely to quieten ODI activity with minimal effect on *bona fide* projects. The following report[1] gives some indication of this attitude:

> Big changes in Chinese investment abroad are expected as the country winds up a three-year analysis of the sector and produces an expected package of reforms early next year, a senior trade official said. Wu Juren, deputy director-general of the policy and development department under the Ministry of Foreign Trade and Economic Co-operation (MOFTEC), said his department's campaign, begun in late 1993, to calculate how many projects China has really launched abroad is expected to be finished before the end of the year. Of all projects launched by domestic companies overseas, 4,933 involving a total investment of $5.54 billion have either earned MOFTEC's approval or have registered with Moftec. Because many companies have purposely avoided Moftec's supervision, it is impossible to know how many projects in all have been launched abroad, Wu said. 'We estimate that at least one-third of China-invested projects overseas failed to report to MOFTEC.' But such companies have not profited much from the deceit since immigration officials overseas often decline to confer visas to their staff on the premise that it is hard to distinguish the firms' employees from illegal immigrants, Wu said. 'We are working on a co-operative scheme with the countries concerned to end the chaos next year.' According to the proposed arrangement, Chinese people working abroad would be conferred licences to stay and work contingent upon their companies' production of credentials with the seal of MOFTEC, he said. MOFTEC will begin formal negotiations on the scheme as soon as it finishes consultation with the Ministry of Foreign Affairs. The proposed scheme will help China further its reform and opening and force companies reluctant to play by the rules to come back to the fold. China's history of launching trading houses overseas dates back to the founding of New China in 1949. The number of non-trading companies gradually increased after 1979 when the massive reform and opening drive started, he said. As far as MOFTEC can track, trading houses abroad totalled 3,006 with an overall investment of $3.52 billion at the end of June this year. Non-trading companies totalled 1,927 with an overall investment of $2 billion. Wu summarised the current situation of China's investment abroad as one of 'pros and

cons'. Most people laud capital inflow as an efficient means of utilising foreign capital but few people realise launching projects abroad also is a good use of foreign capital. He noted that natural resources development projects alleviate China's short supply of rich iron ore, timber and fishery resources; launching high-technology projects abroad gives China access to advanced international technologies. Manufacturing overseas also helps China sell more products abroad since it gives such companies natural access to the local market. As well, quota restrictions that block their parent companies at home have no binding force in the local market. And proximity to the local market helps them cut costs and lower prices, he said. Companies operating overseas also transfer advanced technology and information learned abroad back to China and in the end promote their parent companies globalization. 'But not all the 5,000 overseas companies have shown such promise,' Wu said. Some companies have been forcibly shut down for breaking local laws and most companies keep poor accounting records, creating trouble for the taxation departments of their resident countries. 'No specific figures are available but we estimate that a considerable part of overseas companies are losing money', he said.

Regarding Europe, obstacles confronting Chinese investors are mainly the same as those facing others from the Asian Newly Industrialising Economies (NIEs) and developing countries, but greater in degree. China's more recent international ties have been mainly with the United States: other NIEs have had links with, in particular, France, the Netherlands and the United Kingdom. The United States, Australia, and Canada are relatively homogeneous compared to Europe's cultural and linguistic diversity. The Chinese diaspora is more strongly represented in these countries, providing a progressive airlock for reducing cultural distance. Western Europe is also unattractive for natural resource-seeking, and land and labour costs are higher than in Eastern and Central Europe, and in Central Asia. However, the size of Western Europe's markets offers considerable long-term opportunities. One strategy, followed by some Korean companies, is investment in Central Europe because of proximity, costs and an optimistic view of the extension of the European Union.[2] To compete long-term in manufacturing, Chinese companies need to upgrade technology and perceived product quality. Inward investment, through partnership, joint venturing and other forms of alliance may improve export performance, but there are drawbacks relating mainly to common external trade barriers and the reluctance of firms investing in China to divulge strategic technologies. The absorption of Hong Kong (HK) into China provides a major opportunity for reducing cultural/psychological distance, or at least managing it, and for entrées into European businesses and markets. On balance, it is likely that, in the long term, China's interest in Europe is likely to increase rather than diminish and that alliances of some form will be the desired vehicle. In the short and medium term, it is likely that Chinese downstream, trade-supporting investment in Europe will continue, but at a rate well below the manufacturing and resource-seeking investment targeted to developing countries and the Republics of the former Soviet Union. In the longer term, ODI for technology acquisition and market access is likely to follow for the more successful Chinese firms in order to gain access to European markets. Globalisation has increased the speed of technology transfer, hence the more rapid growth rates of developing economies which have most recently achieved industrialisation. The long term regarding China, therefore, may be of shorter duration than the development stages of the Asian NIEs.

THE AGGREGATE PICTURE OF CHINA'S OUTWARD INVESTMENT

Until recently, little attention has been paid to China's ODI. This was mainly because of its apparent insignificance, but the growing disparity between statistics from different sources has alerted observers to this latest manifestation of Chinese liberalisation and globalisation. A small body of literature has appeared. Lardy (1994), noting the uncertainty concerning the accuracy of China's own figures, remarked upon the belief that cumulative Chinese investment in Hong Kong was in excess of US$10bn by 1993, and that World Bank estimates put the flow of Chinese ODI in 1992 alone at about US$4bn. Zhan (1995 especially, and 1990) has produced a detailed examination of China's ODI, showing the sectoral and geographical breakdown and discussing the behaviour, motives and policy implications of the transnationalisation of Chinese companies. More recently, Zhang and Van den Bulcke (1996) use the Investment Development Path (IDP) paradigm (Dunning 1981, 1986, 1993) to analyse changes in both inward and outward FDI. They conclude that the influence of government incentives, controls and policies has been central to kick-starting outward investment but that, increasingly, Chinese companies are seeking autonomously the benefits of internationalisation via the accepted motivators of capitalist companies (i.e. as a result of an appropriate combination of ownership, location, and internalisation advantages). McDermott and Huang (1996: 9) look deeper into the motivation of individual Chinese multinationals using qualitative/case methods. The five companies scrutinised, all State-owned, appeared to be profit-oriented, to be 'pursuing different types of international strategies to achieve their corporate objectives', while 'simultaneously serving well the national interest'. They also concluded that 'compared with Asia and North America, the EU has failed to attract much Chinese FDI and exports. This may change rapidly' (ibid.: 13).

The purpose of this section is to examine the nature, scale and trends of current Chinese outward investment, with special reference to Europe, and to attempt to assess future developments. Clearly, there are difficulties. As we shall see, Chinese direct investment in Europe is recent, and the scale is low and cannot be subjected to formal quantitative analysis. A case-by-case analysis might be preferred, but we do not have access to the strategic plans of individual corporations. Moreover, in the early stages of outward investment, intangibles such as cultural distance are felt by many authors to be important factors in the choice of investment destination, but have largely resisted quantitative analysis (see, for example, Yi and Slater 1995). Nevertheless, while Chinese companies currently operate in a rather special environment, there may be no reason to expect them to behave in a manner significantly different from other MNEs in seeking to take advantage of increasing globalisation, if and when they are subjected to less government restriction.

The phenomenon of historically low levels of economic activity followed by rapid growth and development as has been experienced elsewhere in Pacific Asia, suggests quantitative analysis may have little predictive value. Further, an even more fundamental problem lies in the quality of available statistical data. China's own published figures for ODI are based upon a method of collection which considerably underestimates flows. It is probably for this reason that China's ODI has received such little attention. The official Chinese figures are gathered by the MOFTEC. IMF figures,[3] collected in association with the State Administration of Foreign Exchange Control of China (SAFE), indicate volume orders of greater magnitude.[4] Table 13.1 provides aggregate data on China's ODI from these two sources for the years between 1985 and 1995.

Table 13.1 shows the erratic nature of the flows (typical of most FDI flow data), a major shift in magnitude from 1991/92, and the huge discrepancies between the MOFTEC and the IMF/SAFE data: the former giving little clue to any dramatic upward shift in 1991. It should be added that China's inward investment has increased so much over the period, that the ratio of outward to inward investment has *decreased* (see Table 13.2).

Table 13.1 China's outward direct investment 1985–95 (US $m)

	1985	1986	1987	1988	1989	1990	1991	1992	1993	1994	1995
IMF/SAFE	629	450	645	850	780	830	913	4000	4400	2000	3467
MOFTEC	47	33	410	75	236	77	362	196	120	81	

Source: IMF International Financial Statistics Almanac of China's Foreign Economic Relations and Trade

Table 13.2 Ratio of outward to inward investment for China, 1985–94 (outward investment as % of inward investment)

	1985	1986	1987	1988	1989	1990	1991	1992	1993	1994
IMF/SAFE	38	24	28	27	23	24	21	36	16	6
MOFTEC[a]	2.4	1.5	15.5	2.0	6.3	2.1	7.8	1.7		0.04

Source: IMF International Financial Statistics Almanac of China's Foreign Economic Relations and Trade
Note: (a) Based on aggregate inward FDI.

The trend in the quantity of China's ODI has clearly been upward, if uneven. The magnitude of ODI put China among the leading investors from developing countries in the mid-1990s, as well as being the largest recipient (40 per cent of the total in 1995) in the same category. Viewing China retrospectively as including Hong Kong would, however, change the picture considerably. Evidently the aggregate figures need to be broken down and analysed qualitatively in order to obtain a more accurate focus on China's 'real' outward investment and, for the purpose of this chapter, on the European connection.

It is well known that most of China's outward investment has been directed towards 'Greater China', particularly Hong Kong. Of this, a significant proportion has been a means of recycling funds back into China, either through 'round-tripping' – a means of concealing the original source of funds as to take advantage of concessions and incentives designed to encourage inward foreign investment – or through 'reverse investment', a means of generating funds otherwise difficult to obtain for domestic investment. For example, the purchase and successful development of a HK company may be used to raise capital from the HK money markets through listing, flotation or even loans. The extent of this is difficult to estimate. Harrold and Lall (1993) arrive at a figure at 25 per cent, but their approach fails to distinguish between the two methods for 'recycling' funds. As Zhan (1995) points out, there is a difference between reverse investment and round-tripping in that the former represents capital accumulation via a genuine increase in economic activity and wealth generation, rather than a mere diversion of capital. Either way, as policies aimed at phasing out the particular privileges accorded to foreign firms take effect, the incentives for round-tripping are likely to diminish. Hong Kong acts as a springboard for China's outward trade and investment and, in the reverse direction, as a stepping stone for inward investors and traders. Deducting China's investment into Hong Kong from its outward aggregates, and deducting Hong Kong's investment into China (80 per cent of the total HK FDI in 1995) from *its* outward aggregate, would go some way to providing clearer signs of the inward and outward investment patterns of the 'enlarged' China. However, this is not easily done: the published MOFTEC figures do give a breakdown of investment by destination, but as we have already seen, are of dubious accuracy. IMF data exist, but are not published, and access to them is beyond the resources of this writer. Estimates of the geographical breakdown of China's outward investment flows are provided by Zhan (1995) (see Figure 13.1).

Figure 13.1 indicates that only about one-third of China's outward investment has extended beyond the cultural and geographical proximity of Asia–Pacific. Of this third, about half has been absorbed by North America and about one-quarter by Oceania, of which Australia has been the main recipient with additional substantial investment in Papua New Guinea. Africa apart, Western Europe received the smallest of the regional investment tranches.

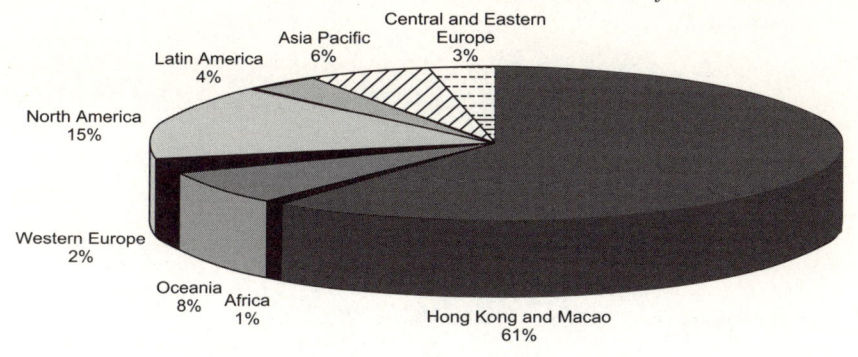

Figure 13.1 Geographical distribution of China's outward direct investment, 1979–94 (%)
Source: Zhan (1995): author's estimates based on various sources

Figures 13.2 and 13.3 show a breakdown based on MOFTEC data taken from Zhang and Van Den Bulcke (1996). These MOFTEC figures show a very different picture. This is mainly because, not only do they under-report actual ODI, but also they exclude or, at least, do not contain information on a number of categories of capital movements (e.g. in the financial services sector). The 'non-trade' figures relate mainly to manufacturing and natural resources investments, the 'total' figures to these plus only certain trade-related investments. Even so, while it is reasonable to surmise that most of the investment in Hong Kong and Macau is in services, the MOFTEC figures still seem severely to underestimate the importance of the manufacturing sector. Zhan (1995) estimates that 22 per cent of China's outflows in manufacturing over the period were destined for Hong Kong – a considerably higher proportion than the 9 per cent MOFTEC estimate –

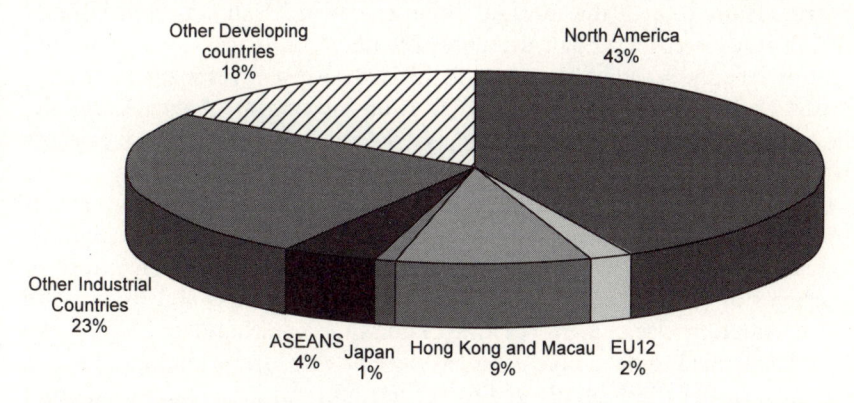

Figure 13.2 Geographical distribution of China's 'non-trade' outward direct investment, 1979–92 (%)
Source: MOFTEC (1984–1993), taken from Zhang and Van Den Bulcke (1996)

276 *Jim Slater*

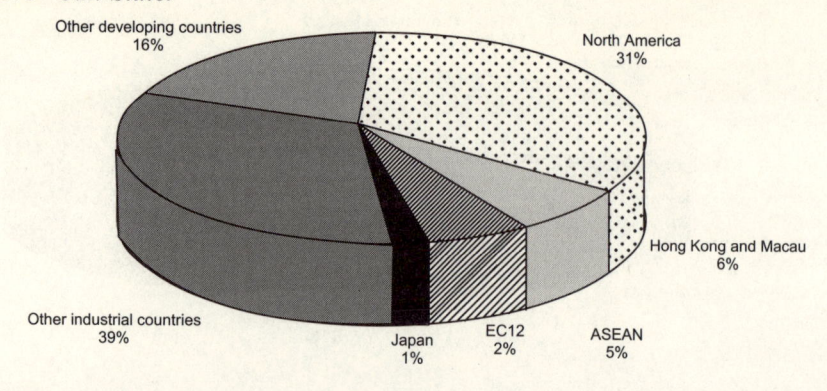

Figure 13.3 Geographical distribution of China's 'total' outward direct investment, 1979–92 (%)
Source: MOFTEC (1984–1993), taken from Zhang and Van Den Bulcke (1996)

Pie chart segments: Other developing countries 16%; North America 31%; Hong Kong and Macau 6%; ASEAN 5%; EC12 2%; Japan 1%; Other industrial countries 39%.

making China the second largest contributor to Hong Kong's FDI stock in manufacturing. However, while all of these inconsistencies suggest that the publicly available data should be treated with extreme caution, both sets differ little in their estimates of the proportion of China's outward FDI in Europe. For the period 1979-94, Zhan (1995) estimates 2 per cent to Western Europe and 3 per cent to Eastern Europe. The MOFTEC figures suggest 2 per cent to the twelve Member States of the European Community (EC12) for 1979-92.

Zhan also gives estimates of the sectoral breakdown of China's outward FDI (see Figure 13.4). Again there is a major discrepancy compared with the MOFTEC figures. As mentioned above, the latter relate primarily to the non-trade sector, and according to Zhang and Van Den Bulcke (1996), 'nearly 86 per cent of the total of Chinese outward FDI was concentrated in non-trade sectors'. Zhan estimates 39 per cent to manufacturing and natural resources, suggesting that China's outward investment is characterised by a dominance of trade-supporting investment. Almost certainly, the major source of the discrepancy is the omission of financial services from the MOFTEC figures.

Geographically, ODI in services is the most widespread, and comprises primarily trade-supporting, banking and financial services including, increasingly, insurance. Natural resource investment, based upon perceived shortages of certain raw materials (e.g. oil, timber, metals and fishery) are concentrated in Oceania, North and Latin America. Manufacturing investment has tended to be in product areas of relatively low technological input, and has primarily been motivated by the need for market proximity in order to circumvent trade barriers. Clearly, China's abundant factor endowments in land and labour generate little in the way of push factors to stimulate outward investment. Rather, as has been observed elsewhere (e.g. Zhan

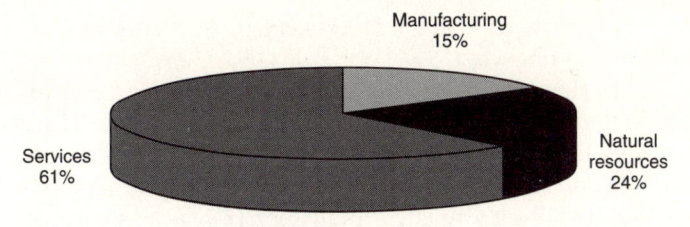

Figure 13.4 Sectoral distribution of China's outward direct investment, 1980–94 (%)
Source: Zhan (1995): author's estimates based on various sources

1995), relative prices *within* China have motivated shifts in industrial location following the 'flying geese' movements observed across borders in the whole of the Asia–Pacific Region. That is, investment is moving from the more developed (coastal) provinces to the less developed, inland provinces: flying ducks? However, there are a number of cases of successful and unsuccessful Chinese ventures into technology upgrading through ODI, mainly in the United States. Of some notoriety was the proposed acquisition of Mamco Manufacturing Company by China National Aero-Technology Import and Export Corporation, which was blocked by the Committee on Foreign Investment in the United States on national security grounds (Graham and Krugman 1991). However, there are a number of success stories where technological upgrading has been less ambitious and less sensitive: for example, Shougang Corporation's acquisition of Masta Engineering Co., a leading US designer and manufacturer of hot rolling mills and other heavy metallurgical plant. Whilst a great deal of China's ODI is linked to overseas ethnic Chinese, this and other cases indicate that the motivation, ability and institutional arrangements are in place to facilitate and encourage further bona fide transnationalisation. Presumably, the difficulties associated with such ventures (e.g. cultural distance, institutional differences, and adjustment difficulties to market-oriented economies) will diminish with experience and, perhaps most important, as China's stock of human capital improves qualitatively through internationalisation and exposure to advanced technologies.

CHINA'S INVESTMENT ACTIVITY IN EUROPE

As regards Europe, Figure 13.1 shows that Chinese cumulative investment in Eastern Europe was greater than that in Western Europe between 1979 and 1994. Sectorally, there is greater evidence of manufacturing activities of the export-replacing type in Central and Eastern Europe. Most Western European activity seems to be in services (e.g. banking and insurance in the United Kingdom, Luxembourg and Germany). Schultz (1995) estimates that about two-thirds of China's investment in Germany in 1992 was in services, excluding finance.

Other figures (UNCTAD-DITED, 1996) indicate an increase in Chinese ODI stock in the European Union, from 2 per cent in 1980 to 11 per cent in 1992 (see Table 13.3). China was second only to Indonesia in the proportion of its own ODI stock in the European Union. This would represent a total of about US$110m of an estimated total stock (using the same measure) of US$1bn. Using Zhan's (1995) estimate of 2 per cent based on a total stock at 1994 of US$16bn, a figure of about US$300m emerges (and about $450m in Central and Eastern Europe). It would be tempting to conclude that there has been a considerable absolute increase in Chinese investment in Western Europe, but the figures do stem from different sources.

The OECD is another source of relevant data (OECD 1995). The information is sparse, but where it exists and where Chinese investment is non-zero or is not held back for confidentiality reasons, is summarised in Table 13.4. The reporting problems are evident. Stock figures are given only for France, Germany and Italy, amounting to approximately US$100m by 1992. Aggregate figures for the EU(12) are not provided. The same problem exists with the European Union's own figures (EUROSTAT 1995).

In Central and Eastern Europe, China is a more conspicuous investor. Table 13.5 shows the investment stock to be primarily in the Russian Federation, but with significant representation in Estonia, Hungary, Latvia, Lithuania and Poland. The total is in excess of US$200m. It is likely that much of the stock in the Russian Federation and elsewhere in Eastern Europe is associated with State-owned enterprises established before the break-up of the Soviet Union. Interestingly, non-Japanese FDI in this region is high compared with Japanese FDI, a reversal of the picture in Western Europe.

Table 13.3 Outward investment by developing Asian countries in the European Union, 1980 and 1992 (as % of total outward investment)

	1980	1992
China	2	11
NIEs	2	4
Hong Kong	1	3
Korea	30	7
Singapore	3	7
Taiwan	—	2
ASEAN 4	—	20
Indonesia	1	49
Malaysia	—	—
Philippines	—	3
Thailand	3	5

Source: UNCTAD

Table 13.4 Inward investment flows and stocks from China to Europe, by country, 1984–93

	1984	1985	1986	1987	1988	1989	1990	1991	1992	1993
Belgium-Luxembourg (m BFr)										
Flows	—	—	—	4	37	1	121	355	71	421
France (m FFr)										
Flows	1	124	1	0	0	0	3	5	−219	9
Stock						106	99	182	383	
Germany (m DM)										
Flows	1	—	−1	2	3	−22	−10	—	−1	17
Stock	3	16	25	22	40	53	64	71	98	108
Italy ('000 m lire)										
Flows										−1
Stock								1	1	1
Spain (m ptas)										
Flows								36	323	263
Sweden (m krone)										
Flows						1	—	—	2	—
UK (£m)										
Flows	—	—	—	—	20	6	−7	1	−8	14

Source: OECD (1995)

Table 13.5 Cumulative FDI in Central and Eastern European countries in which China is a principal investor (US$m)

Country	FDI	Year
Russian Federation	164	to 1994
Poland	25	to 1994
Hungary	6	to 1993
Estonia	2	to 1993
Latvia	0.5	to 1994

Source: UNCTAD-DITED (1996)

OUTWARD INVESTMENT IN HUMAN CAPITAL

Given the historical leanings of China towards the United States, and the post-Nixon *rapprochement*, it is not surprising that a good deal of China's interest in both human and physical capital investment has been in that country. There is some evidence that China's overseas investment in human capital is becoming more intense, certainly since 1980. Table 13.6 shows the number of students studying abroad, based on official Chinese data. Table 13.7 shows the number of Chinese students studying in three Anglophone countries, based on Western data. From 1989 onwards, the total number of Chinese students studying in the United Kingdom, Australia and Canada has been fairly steady at about 50,000 per year. The only notable change has been a shift away from Australia in favour of the USA. This plateau

Table 13.6 Numbers of Chinese students studying overseas, 1976–94

Year	Students studying overseas
1976	277
1977	220
1978	860
1979	1,777
1980	2,124
1981	2,922
1982	2,326
1983	2,633
1984	3,073
1985	4,888
1986	4,676
1987	4,703
1988	3,786
1989	3,329
1990	2,950
1991	2,900
1992	6,540
1993	10,742
1994	19,000

Source: China Statistical Yearbook 1996

Table 13.7 Numbers of Chinese students studying in three Anglophone countries (USA, UK, Australia), 1988–94

Year	Australia	UK	USA	Total
1988/89	528	1,500	29,040	31,068
1989/90	15,568	1,600	33,390	50,558
1990/91	10,393	1,600	39,600	51,593
1991/92	5,287	1,644	42,940	49,871
1992/93	4,565	1,702	45,130	51,397
1993/94	4,534	1,757	44,381	50,672

Source: British Council, Education Counselling Services (1994)

seems to have followed a steady rise from about 1984. This may or may not be a direct reflection of Chinese policy: on the other hand, it may be an indirect reflection through aid and other external funding relationships. In China there seems to have been a shift away from central funding and selection, to funding and selection by municipalities and enterprises, whether state or private.

Again, there are major discrepancies between the Chinese and Western figures, and these are in the same direction as those reported for the ODI figures. The Western figures are for three countries only, and yet, for 1993, show eight times more students studying in these countries alone than for the outgoing world total according to Chinese figures. UNESCO (1995) figures for 1990-92 indicate approximately 3 per cent of Chinese students in tertiary education are studying abroad. This compares with 32 per cent of Hong Kong, 38 per cent of Malaysian, and 25 per cent of Singaporean students. Students studying abroad are, of course, only a part of the Chinese population gaining overseas experience: many others travel for business and diplomatic reasons. The trend in the number of exit visas issued would thus provide an alternative, perhaps better, indicator of overseas exposure and, one suspects, would show a steep upward trend in recent years. However, the point is that over the decade, at least in absolute terms, a substantial number of the citizens of the PRC have been exposed to external ideas, cultures and technologies.

THE POTENTIAL ADVANTAGES TO EUROPE OF CHINESE DIRECT INVESTMENT

Economy-wide, the benefits of inward investment to a largely post-industrial Western Europe are well recognised, and have been encouraged within the European Union by a variety of incentive measures emanating from Brussels as well as from the individual Member States. These may well prove attractive as Chinese multinationals become more sophisticated but the shock effect of anti-dumping measures, if imposed, may provoke a more dramatic shift in attitude. However, if Chinese investment in Europe is to be other than the greenfield, wholly-owned venture type, what are the benefits to European organisations of joint venturing? From many firms' perspectives, inward investment is likely to be seen as a competitive threat. However, there are also opportunities. The principal, short-term, one is an injection of capital to facilitate modernisation and R&D. Even small and medium-sized enterprises (SMEs) can benefit from alliances with their Asian counterparts. There are, for example, many cash-rich Taiwanese engineering SMEs seeking alliances with counterparts in Europe in order to upgrade their technology and willing to seek jointly market penetration in existing and new markets. However, PRC investment into Europe is likely to be spearheaded by large TNCs. Some of these are already operating in a manner similar to Korean *chaebols*. On the assumption that the globalisation of Chinese business is likely to continue and develop, European firms with some strategic vision should at least consider capitalising on opportunities.

> Asian firms have developed alternative methods of production and human resource management in industries ranging from high technology ones such as electronics to traditional ones such as shipbuilding... The Japanese example is well-established, but innovations in other firms should not be dismissed... The sheer diversity of Asian firms means that their investments in Europe could contribute to the local business community through an influx of new ideas and ways of doing things.
>
> (UNCTAD-DITED 1996)

Clearly, these benefits can only be realised through active collaboration.

European–Asian networks of firms based on complementary technologies and skills could form a viable and competitive basis for a firmer economic link in the Asia–Europe parts of the Triad. Joint products in nearby countries, especially in Central and Eastern Europe and in south Mediterranean rim economies could benefit considerably from the pooling of resources.

The preceding quotations refer to the benefits of joint ventures between European and Asian companies in general. What then might be the *specific* benefits to European companies of joint venturing with Chinese companies outside China? It is well documented that European joint ventures in China are fraught with difficulties arising from the cultural and legislative aspects of doing business there. If more Chinese companies have a stake in Europe or in third markets with European partners, then perhaps these frictions may lessen. However, to end on a cliché, the benefits of collaboration with Chinese outward investors might be grounded more firmly through research with those Western firms already engaged in such partnerships.

NOTES

1 *China Daily*, 28 July–3 August 1996.
2 The various Europe Agreements, concluded by the European Union with several Eastern European countries, are relevant in this regard. See Chapter 3 for further details.
3 Available from 1985 in IMF *International Financial Statistics*.
4 For a summary of the technical details of both methods of collection, see Zhan (1995: 72).

REFERENCES

British Council, Education Counselling Services (1994) *Overseas Student Statistics 1993/94*, London: British Council.
Dunning, J. (1981) 'Explaining the International Direct Investment Position of Countries: Towards a Dynamic or Development Approach', *Weltwirtschaftliches Archiv*, 117(1): 30–64.
Dunning, J. (1986) 'The Investment Development Cycle and Third World Multinationals', in K. Khan (ed.) *Multinationals of the South: New Actors in the International Economy*, London: Frances Pinter.
Dunning, J. (1993) *Multinational Enterprises and the Global Economy*, London: Addison Wesley.
EUROSTAT (1995) *European Direct Investment 1984–93*, Brussels: Statistical Office of the European Communities.
Graham, E. and Krugman, P. (1991) *Foreign Direct Investment in the United States*, Washington, DC: Institute for International Economics.
Harrold, P. and Lall, R. (1993) 'China: Reform and Development in 1992–93', World Bank Discussion Paper, no. 215, Washington, DC: World Bank.
International Monetary Fund, *International Financial Statistics*, (various issues), Washington, DC: IMF.

International Monetary Fund, *Balance of Payments Statistics Yearbook*, (various issues), Washington, DC: IMF.
Lardy, N. (1994) *China in the World Economy*, Washington, DC: Institute for International Economics.
McDermott, M. and Huang, C. (1996) 'Industrial State-Owned Multinationals from China: the Embryonic Years, 1985–92', *Asia Pacific Business Review*, 3(1): 1–15.
Ministry of Foreign Trade and Economic Co-operation (1993) *Almanac of China's Foreign Economic Relations and Trade 1993/94*, Hong Kong: China Resources Advertising Co. Ltd.
Ministry of Foreign Trade and Economic Cooperation (1994) *Almanac of China's Foreign Economic Relations and Trade 1994/95*, Hong Kong: China Resources Advertising Co. Ltd.
Organisation for Economic Co-operation and Development (1995) *International Direct Investment Statistics Yearbook*, Paris: OECD.
Schultz, S. (1995) 'East Asian Investment in Europe and Germany', *Deutsches Institut für Wirtschaftsforschung, Beiträge zur Strukturforschung*, 160, Berlin.
State Statistical Bureau of the People's Republic of China (1996) *China Statistical Yearbook 1996*, Beijing: China National Economy Publishing House.
UNCTAD-DITED (1996) *Sharing Asia's Dynamism: Asian Direct Investment in the European Union*, United Nations: New York and Geneva.
UNCTAD-DTCI (1995, 1996) *World Investment Report*, Geneva: United Nations.
UN-CTNC (1992) *World Investment Directory*, Vol. 1 *Asia and the Pacific*, New York: United Nations.
UNESCO (1995) *Statistical Yearbook*, Paris: UNESCO.
Yi, Z. and Slater, J. (1995) 'National Culture Characteristics as a Determinant of FDI', Working Paper 95/04, Department of Commerce, University of Birmingham.
Zhan, J. (1990) 'China's Outward Investment: Policies and Practices', *Intertrade*, 8(3): 42–7.
Zhan, J. (1995) 'Transnationalization and Outward Investment: The Case of Chinese Firms', *Transnational Corporations*, 4(3): 67–100.
Zhang, H-Y. and Van den Bulcke, D. (1996) 'China: Rapid Changes in the Investment Development Path', in J. Dunning and R. Narula (eds) *Foreign Direct Investment and Governments: Catalysts for Economic Restructuring*, London: Routledge, pp.380–422.

14 Conclusions

An assessment of the strengths of the current and the future economic relationships between China and Europe

Jim Slater

INTRODUCTION

In his introduction to this book, Roger Strange poses three questions. How important is China as an economic partner for Europe? How important is Europe as an economic partner for China? How is the bilateral relationship likely to evolve? This short conclusion aims to highlight the analytical contributions in the volume, particularly with respect to the first two questions, and to speculate about the third, given the economic and political trends also documented.

THE CURRENT ECONOMIC RELATIONSHIP

Taken at face value, the aggregate statistics, either from domestic or international sources, appear to indicate that China–Europe trade and investment flows are relatively unimportant. North America, ASEAN, the Asian NIEs and Japan each account for higher proportions than the European Union in most categories. Using unadjusted and easily available figures, a fairly dismal picture appears of the EU interest in China. In 1995, China's share of total EU imports was about 4 per cent (2 per cent in manufactures), and only 2-3 per cent of EU exports were destined for China. EU direct investment in China represents about 4-5 per cent of the total stock of foreign direct investment (FDI) in China, but this amount is an insignificant proportion of the total EU stock of outward FDI. From China's perspective, however, the European Union is rather more important: the European Union accounted for 12.3 per cent of China's exports in 1995, and provided 14.4 per cent of her imports. About 2 per cent of China's stock of outward direct investment seems to reside in the European Union (with a further 3 per cent in the Central and Eastern European countries), accounting for a negligible proportion of total FDI into the European Union. In terms of trade and investment, therefore, it would appear that the Sino-European bilateral relationship should be more apparent to China than to Europe.

However, as suggested by many of the chapters in this book, the aggregate figures conceal a great deal and are, ultimately, historical summaries.

Furthermore, the Sino-European bilateral relationship is also clouded by a number of special features:

- Hong Kong's entrepôt role, masking a considerable proportion of China's international trade with Europe and elsewhere;
- Reverse investment and round-tripping of Chinese funds, again primarily via Hong Kong;
- Routing of both inward and outward FDI through Hong Kong;
- Inaccuracies in the collection and reporting of data;
- The importance of technology imports through contracts;
- The continuing selective progressive liberalisation of China's trade and investment policies;
- Major differences in the sectoral composition of current trade and investment in both directions between China and her economic partners.

Briefly, the first chapters in this book indicate that a re-drafting of statistical boundaries amplifies considerably the significance of China's international economic relations, and that Europe's role is more important than the brief summary of convention-based figures quoted above would suggest. The industry studies which follow show opportunities for European companies which may develop as the liberalisation process continues.

THE FUTURE ECONOMIC RELATIONSHIP

It is abundantly clear, however, that these opportunities for European business will be allowed to develop only if the Chinese authorities permit. There is probably less political risk of the cataclysmic variety than of international political relations inhibiting or damaging business links. Whilst businesses are undoubtedly capable of self-inflicted damage through an insensitive approach to China operations, the major political issues in China's opening-up constitute hazards likely to be present into the foreseeable future. Much will depend upon the extent to which political antipathies translate into sanctions which effect real harm. China is extremely sensitive about external pressure over what its leaders consider internal issues, particularly human rights and the status of Taiwan. Trade sanctions are likely to provoke selective retaliation, and the EU's current concern with dumping could generate setbacks for some businesses. In Chapters 1 and 3, Roger Strange has highlighted many of these uncertainties and has plotted a reasonably optimistic path for international negotiations. China's foreign economic policy, on balance, probably provides more opportunities than threats for European business.

Dependence is not an objective of opening-up, rather, it is an outcome to be avoided. Comparative advantage notwithstanding, as more strategic and sensitive commercial and industrial sectors are exposed to outside involvement, it is likely that this will be undertaken on a collective portfolio basis.

That is, in no important sector will China want all her 'eggs laid in one foreign basket'. The examples of the telecommunications, automotive, and financial services industries described in earlier chapters suggest that European companies may have not only the expertise, but also the tacit approval, if not blessing, of the Chinese authorities to share some of the potential of these enormous markets, perhaps even in preference to their counterparts from other industrial powers. In the domestic markets, economies of scale and other sources of competitive advantage may be considered less important than a measured divide-and-rule policy. Indigenisation of new industries and protection through transition of existing State-owned enterprises, and other forms of Chinese enterprise, are likely to be prime concerns.

In the short and medium term, therefore, the prospects for European businesses in their China dealings look promising. Despite an unhappy historical relationship with Europe, particularly with Britain, fears of an excessive accretion of economic power by Japanese and American MNEs may place limits on Chinese acceptance of efficiency as the sole criterion for market access. This is not to accuse European firms of uncompetitiveness. Rather, it is to suggest that European firms may have opportunities in sectors (e.g. automobiles) where they are not globally dominant and, conversely, that their access may also be restricted where they do have clear competitive advantage. By and large, European companies may have some political advantage, particularly if they keep their noses clean and may be doubly advantaged in some sectors, but are no more likely to be granted exclusivity than their rivals.

The long term is, by definition, even more speculative. The more painful China's transition to a market economy, the more interventionist is likely to be industrial policy. An important feature is likely to be the globalisation of China's industries. Chinese MNEs are beginning to develop, and to be accorded new freedoms to manage their own affairs provided the results are seen to be harmonious with the development of the home economy and the social cohesion of the Chinese nation. If national confidence builds alongside successful growth of these MNEs, then there could be further opportunities for relaxation of controls on outside participation in China's domestic economy. As pointed out in Chapter 13, participation in this stage of the development path by European firms in terms of collaboration and partnership with these putative MNEs in their activities outside China may generate both new capabilities relevant to the China market and unanticipated opportunities for ventures in third markets.

Finally, many of the sectoral opportunities discussed in this book are already being cultivated by large, internationally oriented companies. Europe is much better represented than the aggregate statistics would suggest, and is well placed in the newly liberalising sectors. Trade and investment in more technologically advanced products are above the global average. This asymmetry seems to be to Europe's advantage, in the sense of heightening the EU's importance to China. As ever, links are spearheaded by the larger companies, with possible attendant benefits for the suppliers of components and trade-supporting services. What of the prospects for European small and medium exterprises (SMEs)? Current EU industrial policy is promoting networking, particularly among small firms, although largely in terms of local survival. In Chapter 9, Howard Davies reported, using the watch industry as an example, on the implied complacency and 'rabbit-in-the-headlights' reaction to the glare of environmental change which this kind of industrial organisation may engender. Little attention has been paid to networking which may benefit smaller companies which are geographically, culturally and developmentally distant. Much of the benefit claimed for networking in Europe relies upon examples of parochial *atelier* districts which have achieved some international success, albeit with limited technological or market development. However, there are many SMEs within Europe with capabilities in technological development, for example in product and process engineering, who might form alliances with their counterparts in China to mutual profit. Raising awareness of these opportunities, and assisting in the reduction of information and transactions costs, might be an aspect of industrial policy which could be investigated by the relevant Directorate in Brussels. It may of course be argued *a priori* that only the key players in the global commodity and supply chains have the clout and knowledge to foster such collaboration among their suppliers. The question is perhaps open but this author is unconvinced that unassisted market activity will substantially extend Sino-European co-operation at SME level, notwithstanding reduced information costs through, for example, the Internet.

Gordon Robinson and Ian Stones (Chapter 7) make a simple point about the vast potential of China's markets: if car consumption attains European levels, then required annual production would equal current *global* production plus 35 per cent. Roger Strange (Chapter 1) quotes 1994 World Bank figures ranking China as seventh in the world economy. Barring political regression, all signs point to rapid and sustainable growth rates into the twenty-first century. Whatever the debates about China's ascendance, there are major opportunities now and in the future for European businesses. Although it is likely that much of China's own trade and investment will be directed towards nearer partners and developing countries, China's domestic market, European and third markets offer considerable potential for joint venturing. The ongoing series of Asia–Europe Meetings (ASEM) recognise at a political level the underlying economic trends and the need to develop enabling policies to promote cooperation at the business level. With such a synchronisation of green lights, the road is open for a considerable increase in two-way traffic between China and Europe.

Appendices

Appendix A

Table A1 Calculation of EU exports to China, 1978–95 (US$m)

Year	Reported EU exports to China (a)	EU re-exports to China through Hong Kong (b)	Estimated HK margin on EU goods re-exported through Hong Kong to China	Adjusted value of EU goods re-exported through HK to China	Total EU exports
1978	1979	4	0	4	1983
1979	3010	26	3	24	3034
1980	2478	42	4	38	2516
1981	2217	81	8	73	2290
1982	2105	85	9	77	2182
1983	2574	132	13	119	2693
1984	2929	262	26	236	3165
1985	5482	511	51	460	5942
1986	6403	452	45	407	6810
1987	6429	591	59	532	6961
1988	6771	967	97	870	7641
1989	6901	1062	109	952	7853
1990	6701	1115	126	989	7690
1991	6942	1613	150	1463	8405
1992	8651	2337	217	2120	10771
1993	13264	3706	289	3417	16681
1994	14645	4251	242	4009	18654
1995	16981	4851	243	4608	21589

Sources for exchange rates: *Hong Kong Review of Overseas Trade* (1977–1990)
Annual Review of Hong Kong External Trade (1991–1995)

Notes:
(a) IMF, *Direction of Trade Statistics Yearbook*.
(b) Census and Statistics Department, Hong Kong (HKCSD).

Table A2 Calculation of EU imports from China, 1978–95 (US$m)

Year	Reported EU imports from China (a)	China re-exports to EU through Hong Kong (b)	Estimated margin on Chinese goods re-exported to EU	Adjusted value of Chinese goods re-exported through HK to the EU	Estimated value of direct Chinese exports to EU	Adjusted value of EU imports from China
1978	1289	55	6	49	1234	1284
1979	1984	103	10	93	1881	1974
1980	2753	156	16	141	2597	2737
1981	2583	202	20	182	2381	2563
1982	2437	164	16	148	2273	2421
1983	2485	172	17	155	2313	2468
1984	2638	240	24	216	2398	2614
1985	2971	405	41	365	2566	2930
1986	4105	711	71	640	3394	4034
1987	5946	1679	168	1511	4267	5778
1988	7718	3050	305	2745	4668	7413
1989	9159	4623	532	4091	4536	8627
1990	12312	7196	1252	5944	5116	11060
1991	16917	9995	2049	7946	6922	14868
1992	19454	12362	2831	9534	7092	16623
1993	21403	14438	3768	10669	6965	17635
1994	25051	15436	3844	11592	9615	21207
1995	32450	17828	4457	13371	14622	27993

Sources for exchange rates: As for Table A1
Notes:
(a) *Direction of Trade Statistics Yearbook*.
(b) Census and Statistics Department, Hong Kong (HKCSD).

Table A3 Adjusted bilateral trade balances for selected EU Member States with China, 1978–95 (US$m)

Year	Bel-Lux	Italy	UK	Ireland	Den	Spain	Neth	France	Germany	EU(12)	EU(15)
1978	+161	−10	−36	−5	−24	−2	+11	−26	+631	+699	+778
1979	+54	−115	+170	−6	−21	−5	+8	+14	+970	+1060	+1157
1980	−75	−178	+50	−10	−18	−53	−121	−157	+356	−222	−141
1981	−49	−57	−90	−12	−26	−34	−41	−222	+273	−273	−280
1982	+68	−205	−136	−8	+77	+15	−121	−87	+179	−239	−227
1983	+104	−135	−79	−10	−30	+29	−37	+42	+353	+225	+287
1984	+142	+48	+104	−11	−25	+82	+16	−80	+264	+551	+703
1985	+169	+297	+236	−4	0	+355	+82	+352	+1496	+3012	+3314
1986	+168	+407	+431	−16	−59	+97	−31	+15	+1757	+2776	+3068
1987	+90	+173	+213	−16	−42	+7	−109	−170	+1081	+1183	+1366
1988	+162	+53	+195	−32	−156	−115	−101	−370	+678	+228	+268
1989	+155	−208	+155	−43	−180	−260	−147	0	−162	−774	−931
1990	+156	−576	+243	−69	−160	−371	−379	−560	−1580	−3370	−3490
1991	+316	−597	−46	−97	−284	−675	−521	−1193	−3273	−6463	−6658
1992	+279	−650	+21	−112	−295	−1091	−200	−1514	−2168	−5853	−6071
1993	+601	+749	+469	−253	−270	−398	−548	−1306	+71	−954	−989
1994	+396	+262	+231	−187	−294	−625	−826	−939	−572	−2554	−2419
1995	−699	+193	−2860	−197	−247	−608	−1043	−306	−471	−6404	−5553

Sources: As for Table A1.
Note:
EU(12) refers to the twelve Member States prior to 1995. EU(15) refers to the fifteen Member States from 1995 – i.e. including Austria, Finland and Sweden.

Appendix B
The definition of high-technology, medium-technology, and low-technology trade according to the standard international trade classification (Rev.3)

HIGH-TECHNOLOGY

SITC Heading

- 54   Medicinal and pharmaceutical products
- 713 Internal combustion piston engines, and parts thereof, nes
- 714 Engines and motors, non-electric (other than those of groups 712, 713 and 718); parts, nes of these engines and motors
- 716 Rotating electric plant and parts thereof, nes
- 718 Other power generating machinery and parts thereof, nes
- 75   Office machines and automatic data processing machines
- 76   Telecommunications and sound recording and reproducing apparatus and equipment
- 771 Electric power machinery (other than rotating electric plant of group 716), and parts thereof
- 774 Electro-diagnostic apparatus for medical, surgical, dental or veterinary sciences and radiological apparatus
- 78   Road vehicles (including air-cushion vehicles)
- 791 Railway vehicles (including hovertrains) and associated equipment
- 792 Aircraft and associated equipment; spacecraft (including satellites) and spacecraft launch vehicles; and parts thereof
- 87   Professional, scientific and controlling instruments and apparatus, nes
- 88   Photographic apparatus, equipment and supplies and optical goods, nes; watches and clocks
- 891 Arms and ammunition
- 898 Musical instruments and parts and accessories thereof; records, tapes and other sound or similar recordings (excluding goods of groups 763 and 883)

MEDIUM-TECHNOLOGY

SITC Heading

- 51 Organic chemicals
- 52 Inorganic chemicals
- 53 Dyeing, tanning and colouring materials
- 55 Essential oils and resinoids and perfume materials; toilet, polishing and cleansing preparations
- 57 Plastics in primary forms
- 58 Plastics in non-primary forms
- 59 Chemical materials and products nes
- 62 Rubber manufactures nes
- 69 Manufactures of metals nes
- 711 Steam or other vapour generating boilers, super-heated water boilers, and auxiliary plant for use therewith; and parts thereof
- 712 Steam turbines and other vapour turbines, and parts thereof, nes
- 721 Agricultural machinery (excluding tractors) and parts thereof
- 722 Tractors (other than those of items 744 14 and 744 15)
- 723 Civil engineering and contractors' plant and equipment
- 724 Textile and leather machinery, and parts thereof, nes
- 725 Paper mill and pulp mill machinery, paper cutting machines and other machinery for the manufacture of paper articles; parts thereof
- 726 Printing and bookbinding machinery, and parts thereof
- 727 Food-processing machines (excluding domestic)
- 728 Other machinery and equipment specialised for particular industries, and parts thereof, nes
- 73 Metalworking machinery
- 74 General industrial machinery and equipment, nes, and machine parts, nes
- 772 Electrical apparatus for switching or protecting electrical circuits or for making connections to or in electrical circuits
- 773 Equipment for distributing electricity, nes
- 775 Household type, electrical and non-electrical equipment, nes
- 776 'Electrical parts and components'
- 778 Electrical machinery and apparatus, nes
- 793 Ships, boats (including hovercraft) and associated equipment
- 81 Prefabricated buildings; sanitary, plumbing, heating and lighting fixtures and fittings, nes
- 897 Jewellery, goldsmiths' and silversmiths' wares, and other articles of precious or semi-precious materials, nes

LOW-TECHNOLOGY

All other SITC headings.

Appendix C

Table C1 Representative offices and branches of foreign insurance companies in China

Institute	Place of incorporation	Representative office/branch	Year/month of establishment	Trading history with China
Aetna International	USA	Beijing	1992	
Aetna International	USA	Shanghai	1993	
Aetna International	USA	Shenzhen	1995	
Aetna International	USA	Guangzhou	1996	
Alexander & Alexander	USA	Beijing	1995	
Alexander & Alexander	USA	Shanghai	1995	
Allianz AG	Germany	Beijing,	1993	
Allianz AG	Germany	Shanghai	1994	
Allianz AG	Germany	Guangzhou	1994	
American International Group	USA	Beijing		1920s
American International Group	USA	Shanghai (branch),	Sept. 1992	1920s
American International Group	USA	Guangzhou (branch)	Oct. 1995	1920s
American International Group	USA	Shenzhen		1920s
American International Group	USA	Shekou		1920s
American Reinsurance Company	USA	Beijing	Nov. 1994	
American Reinsurance Company	USA	Shanghai	1995	
American Reinsurance Company	USA	Shenzhen	1996	
Aon Corporation	USA	Beijing	Jan. 1996	
Asahi Mutual Life Insurance Company	Japan	Shenzhen	July 1995	
Asia Insurance		Shenzhen		
Assicurazioni Generali	Italy	Beijing	1996	
Assurance Générales de France International (AGF)	France	Shanghai	Nov. 1995	
Axa Corp.	France	Beijing		
China-American Insurance		Beijing		

Appendices 297

Table C1 (cont.)

Institute	Place of incorporation	Representative office/branch	Year/month of establishment	Trading history with China
Chiyoda Fire & Marine Insurance Company	Japan	Beijing		
Chiyoda Fire & Marine Insurance Company	Japan	Shanghai	April 1994	
Chiyoda Fire & Marine Insurance Company	Japan	Tianjin	1996	
Chiyoda Mutual Life	Japan	Beijing		
Chiyoda Mutual Life	Japan	Shanghai		
Chiyoda Mutual Life	Japan	Tianjin		
Chubb (Federal Insurance Company)	USA	Beijing	April 1994	
Chubb (Federal Insurance Company)	USA	Shanghai	Sept. 1995	
Chubb (Federal Insurance Company)	USA	Shenzhen	Nov. 1995	
CIGNA International	USA	Beijing	March 1994	
CIGNA International	USA	Shanghai (Pudong)	Aug. 1995	
CIGNA International	USA	Guangzhou	1997	
CIGNA International	USA	Shenzhen	pending	
Colonial Mutual	Australia	Shanghai	May 1995	1990s
Colonial Mutual	Australia	Beijing	1990s	
Commercial Union	UK	Beijing	May 1994	1863
Commercial Union	UK	Guangzhou	August 1995	1863
Commercial Union	UK	Shanghai	June 1996	1863
Continental Insurance	USA	Beijing		
DAI-ICHI Mutual Life	Japan	Beijing		
Eagle Star	UK	Beijing	1908	
Eagle Star	UK	Shanghai	Oct. 1992	1908
Fuji Fire & Marine Insurance Company	Japan	Shanghai	April 1995	
Gan SA	France	Beijing	Aug. 1994	
General Accident	UK	Beijing	March 1994	1908
General Accident	UK	Shanghai	April 1995	1908
General Accident	UK	Guangzhou	1997	1908
Gerling Konzern Allgemeine Versicherungs AG	Germany	Beijing	Nov. 1995	
Great Eastern Life	Singapore	Shanghai	1997	
Guardian Royal Exchange	UK	Beijing	1996	
GUI JANG Insurance	HK	Beijing	June, 1993	
Hyundai Insurance Company	South Korea	Beijing		
Internationale Nederlanden Group	Netherlands	Beijing	1993	1886
Internationale Nederlanden Group	Netherlands	Shanghai	May, 1993	1886
Internationale Nederlanden Group	Netherlands	Guangzhou	Nov. 1994	1886
Internationale Nederlanden Group	Netherlands	Shenzhen		1886
Internationale Nederlanden Group	Netherlands	Shenyang	1995	1886
Internationale Nederlanden Group	Netherlands	Dalian		1886

298 *Appendices*

Table C1 (cont.)

Institute	Place of incorporation	Representative office/branch	Year/month of establishment	Trading history with China
ITT Hartford Insurance	USA	Xiamen	April 1995	
John Hancock Mutual Life Insurance Company	USA	Beijing	1994	
John Hancock Mutual Life Insurance Company	USA	Shanghai	Oct. 1995	
John Hancock Mutual Life Insurance Company	USA	Tianjin	Oct. 1995	
Koa Fire & Marine Insurance Company	Japan	Beijing		
Koa Fire & Marine Insurance Company	Japan	Shanghai	Feb. 1995	
Kyoritsu Ltd	Japan	Shanghai	Oct. 1995	
Lincoln National Corporation	USA	Beijing	Jan. 1994	
Lincoln National Corporation	USA	Shanghai	Sept. 1995	
Lincoln National Corporation	USA	Guangzhou	May 1996	
London Insurance Group	Canada	Beijing	May 1994	
Lucky Insurance Group	South Korea	Tianjin	Feb. 1995	
Lucky Insurance Group	South Korea	Shanghai	pending	
Lucky Insurance Group	South Korea	Beijing	pending	
M Thai Insurance Ltd.	Thailand	Shanghai		
Manulife Financial	Canada	Beijing	1992	1893
Manulife Financial	Canada	Shenzhen	1993	1893
Manulife Financial	Canada	Shanghai	1994 (rep. office); May 1996 (JV)	1893
Manulife Financial	Canada	Chengdu	Nov. 1994	1893
Manulife Financial	Canada	Guangzhou	1995	1893
Meiji Mutual Life Insurance Company	Japan	Beijing	July 1995	
Metropolitan Life Insurance	USA	Beijing	1997	
Minet Asia	UK	Shanghai		
Ming An Insurance Company Ltd.	HK	Shanghai		
Ming An Insurance Company Ltd.	HK	Shenzhen		
Ming An Insurance Company Ltd.	HK	Shekou		
Mitsui Marine & Fire Insurance Company	Japan	Beijing	1981	
Mitsui Marine & Fire Insurance Company	Japan	Dalain	1993	
Mitsui Marine & Fire Insurance Company	Japan	Shanghai	1993	
Mitsui Marine & Fire Insurance Company	Japan	Shenzhen	1994	
Mitsui Marine & Fire Insurance Company	Japan	Guangzhou	Feb. 1996	
Mitsui Marine & Fire Insurance Company	Japan	Tianjin,	Nov. 1995	
National Mutual Asia	Australia	Beijing	Nov. 1993	

Appendices 299

Table C1 (cont.)

Institute	Place of incorporation	Representative office/branch	Year/month of establishment	Trading history with China
National Mutual Asia	Australia	Guangzhou	March 1995	
National Mutual Asia	Australia	Shanghai	1995	
National Mutual Asia	Australia	Chengdu	pending	
National Mutual Asia	Australia	Wuhan	pending	
National Mutual Asia	Australia	Dalian	pending	
New York Life Insurance	USA	Shanghai	1994	
New York Life Insurance	USA	Guangzhou	1996	
Nichido Fire & Marine	Japan	Beijing		
Nippon Life Insurance Company	Japan	Beijing	1987	
Nippon Life Insurance Company	Japan	Shanghai	1994	
NTUC Income Co-operative Insurance Company	Singapore	Beijing	1995	
Principal Mutual Life Insurance Company	USA	Beijing	June 1995	
Prudential Corporation Plc.	UK	Beijing		
Prudential Corporation Plc.	UK	Guangzhou	Nov. 1994	
Prudential Corporation Plc.	UK	Shanghai	Nov. 1994	
Prudential Insurance Company of America	USA	Shanghai	June 1995	
Royal & Sun Alliance	UK	Beijing	1992 (Sun Alliance) Sept. 1995 (Royal Insurance)	
Royal & Sun Alliance	UK	Dalian	April 1994	
Royal & Sun Alliance	UK	Shanghai	1995	
Samsung Fire & Marine Insurance Company	South Korea	Beijing	April 1995	
Samsung Life Insurance Company	South Korea	Beijing	April 1995	
Sangyong Insurance Company	South Korea		pending	
Standard Life	UK	Shanghai	1996	
Sumitomo Marine & Fire Insurance Company	Japan	Beijing	Sept. 1982	
Sumitomo Marine & Fire Insurance Company	Japan	Guangzhou	Sept. 1993	
Sumitomo Marine & Fire Insurance Company	Japan	Shanghai	Nov. 1993	
Sumitomo Marine & Fire Insurance Company	Japan	Dalian	Dec. 1993	
Sumitomo Marine & Fire Insurance Company	Japan	Shenzhen	Nov. 1994	
Sun Life Insurance Company	Canada	Beijing	May 1995	1930s
Sun Life Insurance Company	Canada	Shanghai	August 1995	1930s
Swiss Life Insurance and Pension Company	Switzerland	Beijing	August 1995	
Swiss Reinsurance	Switzerland	Beijing	1996	

Table C1 (cont.)

Institute	Place of incorporation	Representative office/branch	Year/month of establishment	Trading history with China
Swiss Reinsurance	Switzerland	Shanghai	1996	
Toho Life Insurance	Japan	Beijing		
Tokio Marine & Fire Insurance Company	Japan	Beijing	July 1980	
Tokio Marine & Fire Insurance Company	Japan	Shanghai (branch)	Jan. 1993 (rep.office); Sept. 1994 (branch)	
Tokio Marine & Fire Insurance Company	Japan	Guangzhou	June 1993	
Tokio Marine & Fire Insurance Company	Japan	Dalian	Dec. 1993	
Tokio Marine & Fire Insurance Company	Japan	Shenzhen	Jan. 1994	
Tokio Marine & Fire Insurance Company	Japan	Tianjin	Feb. 1996	
Tokio Marine & Fire Insurance Company	Japan	Nanjing	1997	
Top Glory Insurance Co.	HK	Beijing	1996	
Transamerica Occidental Life Insurance Co.	USA	Beijing	1993	
Transamerica Occidental Life Insurance Co.	USA	Tianjin	1995	
Transamerica Occidental Life Insurance Co.	USA	Shanghai	1996	
Travelers/Smith Barney	Beijing			
Union Des Assurance De Paris (UAP)	France	Beijing	Feb. 1995	
Unipol	Italy	Beijing	1996	
Winterthur Swiss Insurance Company	Switzerland	Beijing	March 1994	1970s
Winterthur Swiss Insurance Company	Switzerland	Tianjin	July 1994	1970s
Winterthur Swiss Insurance Company	Switzerland	Shanghai	March 1995 (rep. office); Jan. 1997 (branch, non-life)	1970s
Winterthur Swiss Insurance Company	Switzerland	Guangzhou	1996	1970s
Yasuda Fire & Marine Insurance Company	Japan	Beijing	1981	
Yasuda Fire & Marine Insurance Company	Japan	Dalian	1993	
Yasuda Fire & Marine Insurance Company	Japan	Shenzhen	1993	
Yasuda Fire & Marine Insurance Company	Japan	Shanghai	1994	
Yasuda Mutual Life Insurance Company	Japan	Beijing	Sept. 1995	
Zurich Insurance	Switzerland	Beijing	1980	

Sources: Compiled from various sources, including *Insurance in China* (monthly faxed newsletter), London: Reactions Publishing Group Ltd; 'Representation in China', *Asia and Pacific Insurance Newsletter* (November 1995): 205–10

Table C2 Representative offices and branches of foreign insurance brokers in China

Institute	Place of incorporation	Representative office/branch	Year/month of establishment	Trading history with China
Aon Corp.	USA	Beijing		
Bain Clarkson	UK	Beijing	1986	
Houlder Insurance Far East	USA	Beijing	pending	
Houlder Insurance Far East	USA	Shanghai	pending	
Inchcape	UK	Beijing	1987	
Inchcape	UK	Shanghai		
Jardine CMG Life	UK	Beijing		
Jardine CMG Life	UK	Shanghai		
Johnson & Higgins	USA	Beijing	1995	
Johnson & Higgins	USA	Shanghai	1996	
Marsh & Mclennan	USA	Beijing	April 1994	
Marsh & Mclennan	USA	Shanghai	1996	
Sedgwick	UK	Beijing	1981 (rep. office); 1993 (branch)	1970s
Sedgwick	UK	Shanghai	1994	1970s
Sedgwick	UK	Shenzhen		1970s
Willis Corroon	UK	Beijing	1994	1926
Willis Corroon	UK	Shanghai	1994	1926

Sources: Compiled from various sources, including *Insurance in China* (monthly faxed newsletter), London: Reactions Publishing Group Ltd; 'Representation in China', *Asia & Pacific Insurance Newsletter* (November 1995): 205–10.

Index

ABN AMRO Bank 216
Afghanistan 82, 85, 94, 220
Africa 83, 84, 89, 92, 275
African, Caribbean and Pacific countries 62
Agarwal, S. 213, 214, 217, 219, 220, 233
agent/broker 230, 231
Agnelli 135
Al-Ali, S. 98
Albania 63, 65, 74
Alcatel 191, 198, 199
American Foreign Insurance Association 233
American International Group 243
American International Insurance 240, 245, 246, 247, 248
American International Underwriter Co. 246
Ameritech Telecommunications (United States) 202
Amin, A. 167
Anderson, E. 222
Anderson, C. 252
Anderson, P. 173
Anshan Life Insurance Company Ltd 243
anti-dumping proceedings 70–3
Argentina 71, 241
Ariff, M. 83
Armenia 88
Ash, R. 30, 102
Asia 2, 7, 64, 272; East 8; South 92; Southeast 29, 54
Asia Commercial 182, 183, 184
Asia Pacific 3, 14, 15, 273, 274, 275, 277
Asia Pacific Economic Cooperation 34, 81, 84, 87–90, 92, 93
Asia-Europe Meeting (ASEM) 92, 287
Asian Development Bank 86, 87

Association of Southeast Asian Nations 81, 82, 84, 93, 94, 284; Free Trade Area 84, 85, 88; Growth Area 87; Industrial Projects Program (AIP) 83; outward investment from China 275, 276; regionalism 83, 88, 89, 90, 91, 92; summit 85
AT&T 191, 201, 202
automotive industry 131–46; components supply industry 140–1; development 133–5; European Union operations in China 141–5; industry policy in 1990s 136–8; operational and investment environment 138–9; post-Mao period 135–6
Automotive Industry Enterprises Policy 137
Australasia 7
Australia 14, 70, 203, 249, 271, 274, 279, 280; see also Closer Economic Relations
Austria 8, 28, 70, 116, 218
Awadzi, W. 252
Azerbaijan 82, 94

Banca Di Roma 216
Banco Nacional Ultramarino S.A. 216, 217
Bandai 154, 156, 161
Bangladesh 82, 83, 94
Bank of China 50, 142
Banks, J. 232
Banque Indosuez 216, 217
Banque National de Paris 216, 217
Bar-Niv, R. 233, 255
Barnard, C. 169
Barnett, A.D. 100
Barry-Jones, R. 156
Barshefsky, C. 34

Bayer 141
Beamish, P. 222, 232
Beccatini, G. 167
Beijing 56, 60, 93; insurance industry 239, 240, 247, 249, 258; International Switching System Corporation 199; Municipal government 203; Telecom Administration 199
Beijing Jeep Corporation 136, 142, 143
Beijing Matsushita 110
Belarus 91
Belgium 28, 110, 218, 279; technology intensiveness of trade with China 116, 119–21, 123, 125–6
Belussi, F. 167
Benxi Life Insurance Company Ltd 243
Berg, S. 252
Berliet 134
Best, M. 167
Bhutan 82, 83, 94
Bickelhaupt, D. 233, 255
Bjorkman, J. 250
Bloomfield, G. 134
BMW/Rover 143
Boddewyn, J. 194
Bolivia 65
Bond, M. 180
Bosch 140
Bosnia-Herzegovina 65
Brazil 64, 71, 110, 214, 241
British Telecom 202, 204
Brittan, Sir L. 144
Brose 141
Brunei 82, 87, 94
Brusco, S. 174
Buckley, P. 195, 253
Bulgaria 7, 8, 63, 64, 74, 220
Burma *see* Myanmar

Cambodia 87, 88, 90
Canada: insurance industry 243, 248, 249, 250; outward investment from China 271, 279; technology intensiveness of trade with China 116, 119–21, 123, 125–6; telecommunications services 200, 203
Canada–United States Free Trade Area 84
Carney, M. 170, 177, 178, 181
Carter, R. 230, 231, 234, 237, 238
Carver, A. 188
Casson, M. 195, 253

Castells, M. 167
Central America 7
Central and Eastern Europe 7, 75, 134, 284; outward investment from China 271, 275, 276, 277, 278, 282
chaebols 281
Champion Technology Holdings Ltd (Hong Kong) 200
Chan, H. 54
Chandler, A.D. 109, 168, 169
Changchun 134, 136, 137, 140
Changsha Life Insurance Company Ltd 242
Chapuis, A. 172
Chen, C. 52, 54
Chen, J. 2, 114–28
Chen Zutao 135
Chengdu 247, 258
Child, J. 138, 197
Chile 241
China Business Unit 201
China Communications System Co. 202
China Foreign Exchange Trade Network (Shanghai) 51
China Insurance Group 240, 242
China International Capital Corporation Limited 224
China National Aero-Technology Import and Export Corporation 277
China National Chemicals Import and Export Corporation 248
China Pacific Insurance Company 239, 240, 242
China Resources Group 224
China Schindler 109, 110
China Telecom 202
China Travel International Investment 224
Chinese Customs Administration 22, 25; *see also* General Administration of Customs
Chinese family businesses 178, 182
Chinese Mercantile Bank 211, 224
Chinese Taipei 35–6
Christopherson, S. 167
Chrysler 136, 142, 143
Citroen 143
Civil War 1948–9 (China) 150
Clegg, J. 4, 188–206
Clifford Chance 245
Clifford, M. 190, 191
Closer Economic Relations 84
Cohen, W.M. 103

Colombia 65
commodity chains in international organisation of production 148–9
Common Agricultural Policy 64
Common Customs Tariff 65
Commonwealth of Independent States 89, 93
Commonwealth Preference System 150
Connecteurs Cinch 141
Conroy, R. 9, 101, 102, 107
consumption tax 54
correspondent banking 208
Costa Rica 65
Coughlan, A. 222
Council of Ministers 147
Crédit Agricole 217
Crédit Lyonnais (France) 216
Crédit Suisse 216
Crevoisier, O. 174
Croatia 65
Cuba 220
Cultural Revolution 60, 100, 135
Czech Republic 7, 8, 63, 64, 74

Da Zhong insurance company 239, 242
Dahlman, C. 102
Daihatsu 136
Dailywin 184
Dalian 210, 211, 247, 249, 258, 259; Life Insurance Company Ltd 242
Dana 139
Dandong Life Insurance Company Ltd 243
Davies, H. 2, 4, 27, 98–111, 166–85, 250, 287
de Bruijn, E. 134, 142
de Hoghton, C. 252
de Keijzer, A. 221
Delphi 141
Deng Xiaoping 27, 98, 135
Denmark 28, 155, 158, 218
Department of Trade and Industry 159
deposit-taking companies 211
Deutsche Bank AG 216
Deutsche Telekom 202, 204
Dicken, P. 133
Dickinson, G. 237, 238
Dong, H. 255
Dongguan 20
Dosi, G. 171, 174
Dresdner Bank (Germany) 216
Drucker, P. 133
Dunning, J. 106, 208, 214, 215, 233, 272

Dwyer, R. 231
Dymsza, W. 252

Eagle Star 259
East Asian Economic Caucus 81, 84, 87–8, 90, 93
ECIA 141
Economic Cooperation Organization 81, 82, 84, 88, 89, 90, 92, 93, 94; Almaty Outline Plan 1993 85; Quetta Plan of Action 1993 85
Economic and Technological Development Zones 47, 55
Economic and Trade Commission (or Bureau) 49
Ecuador 65
Egana 182, 183
El Salvador 65
Enderwick, P. 194, 233
Ericsson 198, 199
Erramilli, K. 217, 230, 232, 233
Ertl 154
Estonia 65, 74, 278, 279
Essen European Council 59
Europe 1, 2, 7; Agreements 8; foreign direct investment 30; Industrial Revolution 103; insurance industry 5, 228, 249, 259; joint ventures and insurance industry 255; location choice and insurance industry 256, 257, 258; operating licences in insurance industry 251, 252; outward investment from China 269, 271–8, 281, 282; policy reform 57; regionalism 81, 82, 83, 84, 90; Supplies 184; technology transfer 99, 100, 104, 108, 111; *see also* European; market-servicing mode
European Commission 3, 159, 160, 161
European Community 8; Generalised System of Preferences 64; and Hong Kong 13; outward investment from China 276; textile agreements 67, 68, 69; Tiananmen Square 73; *see also* European Union
European Council 3, 161
European Court of Justice 147, 159, 161
European Free Trade Area 62
European Union 3, 8, 9, 10, 21–6; anti-dumping proceedings 70, 72; foreign direct investment 29, 53, 54;

foreign trade system reform 49;
Generalised System of Preferences 65,
66; and Hong Kong 14, 18; outward
investment from China 272, 281;
policy reform 56; re-export trade 15,
16, 17, 19; regionalism 89, 92, 93, 94,
95; technology intensiveness of trade
with China 115, 116, 119–21, 123,
124, 125–6; textile agreements 69;
trade policy in 1990s 74, 75; World
Trade Organization 34, 35, 36; toy
manufacture 163; *see also* European
Union trade policy; Regulation
(EEC)
European Union trade policy 59–80;
anti-dumping proceedings 70–3;
Generalised System of
Preferences 63–6; official relations
establishment 59–61; textile
agreements 66–9; Tiananmen
Square 73; Trade
Agreement 1978 61–3; Trade and
Economic Cooperation
Agreement 1985 69; trade policy in
mid 1990s 73–6
Export–Import Bank of Japan 209

Factory Mutual Association 233
Federation of Hong Kong
Industries 150
Ferdinand, P. 115
Ferguson, C. 168
Fiat 132
Finland 8, 28, 116, 218
Fisher-Price 154
Five-Year Plans 101, 142; Sixth
(1981–6) 136; Seventh (1986–90) 136,
190
flexible production networks *see* watch
industry in Switzerland and Hong
Kong/China
Florida, R. 168
Foray, D. 167
Ford 132, 141, 142
foreign branches 209
foreign direct investment 1, 2, 4, 7, 8,
10, 26–32, 45, 284, 285; foreign trade
system reform 50; insurance
industry 229, 235, 236, 237, 257;
outward investment from China 269,
272, 273, 276, 278; policy reform 56,
57; technology transfer 106–8, 109,
110; telecommunications services 188,

192, 193, 196, 198, 204; Tiananmen
Square 73; World Trade
Organization 35
Foreign Exchange Adjustment (swap)
Centres 50, 51
foreign exchange rate system, reform
of 50–1
foreign investment enterprises 10, 31–2;
foreign exchange rate system
reform 51; foreign trade system
reform 48, 49, 50; taxation system
reform 54–5, 56
Foreign Investment in the United States
Committee 277
foreign market servicing strategy 193
Foreign Trade Corporation 46, 47, 49
Foreign Trade and Economic
Commission (or Bureau) 48
foreign trade and investment 45–58;
foreign direct investment regime
reform 51–4; foreign exchange rate
system reform 50–1; foreign trade
system reform 45–50; taxation system
reform 54–6
Foreign Trade Law 1994 47, 48
former Soviet Union 2, 7; automotive
industry 131, 134; banking 218, 220;
and European Union trade policy
in 1990s 74; Generalised System of
Preferences 65; outward investment
from China 272, 278, 279;
regionalism 84, 85, 88, 89, 90, 91;
technology intensiveness of trade with
China 116; technology transfer 100,
101; Trade Agreement 1978 63
Foster, M.J. 1, 45–58
France 14, 24; automotive
industry 135, 136, 139; banking 216,
217, 218; foreign direct
investment 29; insurance
industry 247; outward investment
from China 271, 278, 279; technology
intensiveness of trade with China 116,
118, 119–21, 123, 125–6; technology
transfer 105, 106; Télécom 202, 204;
telecommunications services 199, 202,
204; toy manufacture 158
Franko, L. 252
Friedman, P. 252
Fu, C. 207–26
Fu, P. 5, 233
Fujian 223
Fujitsu (Japan) 200

Fuzhou Life Insurance Company Ltd 243

Gabriel, P. 103
Gabus, A. 174
Gang of Four 101
General Accident 259
General Administration of Customs 21, 117
General Agreement on Tariffs and Trade 10, 34; Article XXIV 89; Contracting Parties 32; foreign trade system reform 47; Generalised System of Preferences 63; regionalism 81, 92, 93; textile agreements 66; toy manufacture 159; Working Party on China's Status as a Contracting Party 32–3; *see also* Uruguay Round; World Trade Organization
General Agreement on Trade in Services 246
General Motors 132, 141, 142
Generalised System of Preferences 23, 63–6, 67, 74, 76
Georgia 88
Gereffi, G. 148, 154, 168
Geringer, J. 252
Germany 7, 14, 24, 25; automotive industry 139, 140, 143, 145; banking 216, 218; European Union trade policy in 1990s 74; flexible production networks 182, 183; foreign direct investment 28, 29; insurance industry 247, 250; outward investment from China 277–8, 279; regionalism 91; technology intensiveness of trade with China 116, 118, 119–21, 123, 125–6; technology transfer 105, 106, 110; telecommunications services 199, 202, 204; toy manufacture 149, 151–2, 156, 158, 160, 161, 162; Trade Agreement 1978 63
GKN 141
Glaister, K. 255
Glasmeier, A. 171, 172, 174, 179, 181
Gora, J. 231, 253
Graafsma, F. 72
Graham, E. 277
Gray, H. 221
Gray, J. 221
Greater Mekong Subregion 2, 87, 92

Great Leap Forward (1958–60) 100, 134
Greece 28, 158
Grimwade, N. 67
Gross Domestic Product 8, 46, 118
growth triangles *see* sub-regional economic zones
Guatemala 65
Guangdong Province 12, 16, 20; flexible production networks 167; foreign direct investment 28; regionalism 86; technology transfer 101
Guangzhou 136, 140, 210; insurance industry 245, 246, 247, 248, 249, 258; Life Insurance Company Ltd 243
guanxi 250
Gulf Cooperation Council 84
Gullander, S. 252

Hadley, B. 228
Hainan Island 136
Hainan Province 55
Hall, P. 167
Hamel, G. 170
Harbin Life Insurance Company Ltd 243
Harrigan, K. 231, 252
Harrison, B. 168, 172, 178
Harrold, P. 33, 45–6, 122, 274
Harwit, E. 134, 135, 136, 142
Hasbro 154, 155, 161
Hayek, F. 169
Hayek, N. 176
Hella 141
Hendryx, S. 102
Hennart, J. 231
High Technology Development Zone 55
Hill, C. 221
Hishida, M. 135
Ho, C. 222
Ho, S. 2, 100
Hodgetts, R. 132
Honduras 65
Hong Kong 2, 3, 4, 9–10, 10–18, 36, 37, 285; anti-dumping proceedings 70, 71, 72; banking 211, 217, 219, 220, 221, 223, 224; Basic Law 56; Chinese Bank 224; European Union/China trade 21, 22, 24, 25; foreign direct investment 27, 28, 29, 30, 52, 53; Generalised System of Preferences 64, 65; outward investment from China 271, 272, 274, 275, 276, 278,

281; policy reforms 45; processing and assembly arrangements 20; Productivity Council 181; Quality Assurance Agency 181; re-export trade 123–6; regionalism 86, 88; and Shanghai Banking Corporation 211, 216, 217; technology intensiveness of trade with China 114–23, 127; technology transfer 101, 102, 108, 109, 110, 111; Telecom 203; telecommunications services 192, 200, 203; Trade Development Council 159; Watch and Clock Technology Centre 181; watch industry 173, 176–84; toy manufacture 149, 150, 151–2, 153, 154, 155, 162
Hopkins, T. 168
Hu, X. 72
Hua An Insurance Company Ltd 239, 242
Hua Tai insurance company 239, 242
Huang, C. 272
Huang, F. 101
Hubei Province 134
Huenemann, R. 2, 100
Huggins, K. 231, 253
Huizhou 136
human capital 279–81
Hungary 7, 8, 278; European Union trade policy in 1990s 74; Generalised System of Preferences 64; outward investment from China 279; Trade Agreement 1978 63
Hussain, A. 31
Hwang, K. 180
Hwang, P. 222

Iceland 180
Illbruck 141
Imada, P. 83, 85
Imai, S. 17, 115
Import/Export Chamber of Commerce 49
Income Tax Law for Enterprises with Foreign Investment and Foreign Enterprises 54
India 70, 71, 72, 82, 83, 85, 88, 94, 183
Indonesia 13, 14; Association of Southeast Asian Nations 82, 94; foreign direct investment 30; outward investment from China 278; re-exports of China origin 15;

regionalism 83, 86, 87, 91; technology intensiveness of trade with China 122
Industrial and Commercial Bank of China 217, 223, 224
industrial and commercial consolidated tax 54
Industrial Risk Insurers 233
ING Bank (Netherlands) 216
Ingelbrecht, N. 201
Institute of Actuaries 259
insurance industry: European, US and Japanese firms 228–62; cross-border trade and international investment 229–38; foreign participation 246–8; internalisation advantages 238; joint ventures and Chinese partners 252–5; location advantages 235–7; location choice 255–8; operating licences, strategies to obtain 249–52; ownership advantages 233–5; questionnaire survey results 248–58; regulatory framework for foreign participation 244–6
Insurance Law 1995 240, 245, 246, 249
Interim Regulations for Control of Resident Representative Office of Foreign Enterprises of China 1980 244
internalisation advantages 214, 221–2, 238
International Bank of Paris and Shanghai 211, 217
International Monetary Fund 21, 25, 51, 117, 273, 274
international political economy 147, 156–7, 159, 162, 163
intra-Association of Southeast Asian Nations tariffs 85
Investment Development Path 272
Iran 82, 84, 94
Ireland 28
Ishiro, K. 140–1
Islam, S. 75
Italy: automotive industry 135; banking 216, 218, 220; flexible production networks 167, 174; foreign direct investment 28, 29; outward investment from China 278, 279; technology intensiveness of trade with China 116, 118, 119–21, 123, 125–6; technology transfer 105, 106; toy manufacture 151–2, 158

ITT 141
Iveco 143, 144

Japan 1, 2, 3, 7, 59, 284, 286;
  anti-dumping proceedings 70, 71, 72;
  automotive industry 131, 132, 145;
  automotive industry post-Mao 135;
  banking 214, 220; components supply
    in automotive industry 141;
  development of automotive
    industry 133; European operations in
    automotive industry 142, 143;
  European Union trade policy 60;
  European Union/China trade 26;
  flexible production networks 172,
    177–83; foreign direct investment 28,
    29, 30; and Hong Kong 13, 14, 16, 18;
  insurance industry 5, 228, 239–41, 243,
    247–9, 259; joint ventures in insurance
    industry 254, 255; location choice in
    insurance industry 256, 257, 258;
  operating licences in insurance
    industry 251, 252; operational and
    investment environment in automotive
    industry 139; outward investment
    from China 275, 276, 278, 281;
  regionalism 87, 88, 91, 93, 94;
  technology intensiveness of trade with
    China 114–16, 118–27; technology
    transfer 99, 100, 104, 105, 106, 108,
    110; telecommunications services 193,
    200; World Trade Organization 34, 35;
  toy manufacture 151–2, 154, 161, 162
Jaquet, E. 172
JC Penney 155
Jia, X. 134, 142
Jiangsu 211
Jilin 53
Johanson, J. 222
Joint Committee 61, 64
joint ventures 110, 138, 141, 143, 230,
    231–2; and Chinese partners 252–5;
  insurance industry 253; technology
  transfer 107, 109

K-mart 155
Kamall, S. 4, 188–206
Kampuchea 65
Kapur, H. 60–1, 62, 64, 67
Kazakhstan 82, 90, 91, 92, 94
Kenney, M. 168
key capabilities *see* watch industry in
  Switzerland and Hong Kong/China

Khoury, S. 208, 223
Killing, J. 231, 252
Kim, W. 222
Kinmen 35
Klein, S. 231
Kögel 141
Kohari, S. 29, 115
Kohli, S. 184
Koito Manufacturing 141
Korea: outward investment from
  China 271, 278, 281; re-exports
  destined for China 17;
  regionalism 87, 88, 91; technology
  intensiveness of trade with China 114,
  116, 119–26; telecommunications
  services 193; *see also* North; South
Korzeniewicz, M. 148, 168
Krugman, P. 120, 277
Kueh, Y. 30, 102
Kunming Life Insurance Company
  Ltd 243
Kyrgyzstan 82, 90, 91, 94

Latin America 64, 83, 89, 275, 276
Latvia 65, 74, 278, 279
Labinal 141
Lall, R. 274
Lall, S. 99
Lan, P. 103
Lan, Z. 68
Land, R. 231, 253
Landes, D.S. 171
Laos 65, 87, 88, 93
Lardy, N. 18, 24, 26, 120, 272
Lau, C.K. 167
Lau, P. 213
Lazerson, M. 168
learning-by-doing 100, 109
Lee, J. 27
Lego 155, 156
Leonard-Barton, D. 170, 173, 175
Leung, H. 102
Leung, W.-S.M. 4, 188–206
Levinthal, D.A. 103
Lian Tong and Tianjin Communications
  Investment 202
Lian Tong (Unicom) 192, 201, 203
licensing agreements 103, 104
Light Industry Department 138
Lithuania 65, 74, 278
Liu, Y.-C. 37
Lloyds Scholarship 259
location advantages 214, 219–21, 235–7

location choice 255–8
Lomé Convention 62, 64
Lorenz, D. 86
Lower Yangtze zone 87
Lu, Y. 197
Lucas 141
Luxembourg 28, 218, 220; outward investment from China 277, 279; technology intensiveness of trade with China 116, 119–21, 123, 125–6

Mathur, J. 232
Matsu 35
Mattel 155, 161
Macau 223; foreign direct investment 28, 52; outward investment from China 275, 276; regionalism 86, 88
McDermott, M. 272
Macedonia 65
Maclean, N. 259
Macneil, I. 169
Maillat, D. 173, 175
Malaysia: Association of Southeast Asian Nations 82, 94; flexible production networks 177, 183; foreign direct investment 30; outward investment from China 278, 281; regionalism 83, 85, 86, 87, 91; technology intensiveness of trade with China 122; Telekom 193
Maldives 82, 83, 94
Mamco Manufacturing Company 277
MAN 144
Manufacturers Life Insurance Co. (Manulife of Canada) 240, 248
Mao Zedong 59, 61
market entry models 193–5
market-servicing mode for European banks 207–26; eclectic model for foreign market entry mode 213–22; international involvement, types of 208–9; internalisation advantages 221–2; location advantages 219–21; ownership advantages 215–19; regulations regarding foreign financial institutions 209–13
Marshall, A. 167
Masta Engineering Company 277
MCI US 202
Mediterranean countries 62, 64, 84, 282
Meldrum, S. 231

Mercedes Benz 137, 143, 144
Mexico 70, 84, 241
Middle East 64
Min Xin Holdings Limited 223
Ministry of Economic Affairs 30
Ministry of Electronics 192, 200, 202
Ministry of Foreign Affairs 270
Ministry of Foreign Economic Relations and Trade 46, 73, 105; see also Ministry of Foreign Trade and Economic Cooperation
Ministry of Foreign Trade and Economic Cooperation 47–9, 50, 270, 276; foreign direct investment reform 53; outward investment from China 273, 274, 275; Quota Licence Affairs Bureau 49; see also Ministry of Foreign Economic Relations and Trade
Ministry of Machine-Building Industry 138
Ministry of Post and Telecommunications 189–90, 191, 192, 193, 199, 200, 202, 203, 205
Ministry of Power 192
Ministry of Railways 192
Ministry of Trade 163
Mischief Reef 91
Motorola 191, 200
Mongolia 63, 74, 87, 88, 91, 92
Moore, W. 180
Morgan Stanley Group 224
most favoured nations 35, 61, 83, 85, 93
MTC Canada 203
Multi-Fibre Agreement 7, 63, 64, 66, 67, 68; 1 (1974–7) 66, 67; 2 (1978–81) 67; 3 (1982–6) 67, 68; 4 (1986–91) 67, 68
multilateralism 81
multinational enterprises 106, 148, 156, 273, 286; insurance industry 232, 233, 234, 255
Myanmar (Burma) 65, 87, 88, 91

Nam Yang Commercial Bank of Hong Kong 209
Nanjing 134; Life Insurance Company Ltd 243
Nepal 82, 83, 90, 94
Netherlands 14, 24; banking 215, 216, 218; foreign direct investment 28; insurance industry 247, 259; outward investment from China 271;

Netherlands (*cont.*)
  technology intensiveness of trade with China 116, 119–21, 123, 125–6; toy manufacture 158
New International Division of Labour 148
Newton, J. 3, 147–64
New Zealand *see* Closer Economic Relations
newly industrialising economies 83, 115, 271, 272, 284
Nicaragua 65
Nigeria 220
Nippondenso 141
Nissan 142
Nisseibo 141
Nixon, R. 60
NKO 141
North America 2, 3, 7, 90, 132, 284; outward investment from China 272, 274, 275, 276; *see also* Canada; United States
North American Free Trading Area 84
North Korea 16, 63, 74, 89, 220
Northern Growth Triangle 87
Northern Telecom 191, 198, 200
Norway 26, 70, 71, 72, 218
Nynex 201, 202

Oceania 274, 275
Oh, S. 231
open-door policy 1, 2, 11, 24, 131
operating licences 249–52
Organisation for Economic Cooperation and Development 102, 121, 278
original equipment manufacturing 149, 151, 182
outward investment 269–82, 284; activity in Europe 277–9; aggregate picture 272–7; human capital 279–81; policy 269–72; potential advantages to Europe 281–2
outward processing 10, 13, 20–1
Overholt, W. 221
own brand manufacturing 149
ownership advantages 214, 215–19, 233–5
Ownership-Location-Internalisation framework 232–3

Paine, F. 252
Pakistan 82, 83, 84, 85, 89, 94
Panama 65

Panda Motors (Huizhou) 136
Papua New Guinea 274
Park, J. 51, 53
PBOC Procedures for the Administration of the Establishment of Resident Representative Offices in China by Financial Institutions with Foreign Investment 266, 305
Pearl River Delta 2, 29, 86, 87, 152, 153
Pecchioli, R. 208
Penghu 35
People's Bank of China 5, 51; banking 209, 210, 212; insurance industry 228, 239, 244, 250, 251, 253, 254, 256, 257, 258
People's Construction Bank of China 224
People's Insurance Company of China 239, 240, 246
Perkins 143
Peru 65
Peugeot 136, 138, 143
Peugeot-Citroen 132
Pfeffer, I. 237, 238
Philippines 82, 83, 87, 220; Association of Southeast Asian Nations 94; outward investment from China 278; regionalism 91
Pijpers, W.R.C. 219
Pilkington 110, 141
Ping An Insurance Company 239, 240, 242
Piore, M. 168
People's Liberation Army 200
Plettac 141
Poland 7, 8, 35, 278; automotive industry 134; banking 220; European Union trade policy in 1990s 74; Generalised System of Preferences 64; outward investment from China 279; Trade Agreement 1978 63
Pomfret, R. 2, 3, 81–96
Porter, M. 167, 173, 178
Portugal 8, 28, 158, 216, 217
post and telecommunications bureaux 189–90, 192, 202, 204, 205
Powell, W. 167
Prahalad, C. 170
Preferential Tariffs Protocol 84
preferential trading arrangement scheme 83, 84, 85
Prime, P. 51, 53

processing and assembly
  arrangements 18–21
Provisional Regulations of Shanghai
  Municipality concerning the Control
  of Representative Offices of Foreign
  Enterprises 1985 244
Provisional Regulations Governing the
  Administration of Insurance
  Enterprises 1986 244
Prudential 259
PSA suppliers 140, 143
Pu, Z. 53
Pudong Development Area of
  Shanghai 51, 55, 211

Rabobank (Netherlands) 215, 218
Ramaswami, S. 213, 214, 217, 219, 220,
  233
Rao, C. 217, 230, 232, 233
Redding, S.G. 178
Redmond, J. 68
regionalisation 81, 86
regionalism in Asia 2, 81–96; extreme
  scenario 88–9; likely scenario 89–90;
  options 90–2; pre 1990s 83–4;
  revival 84–5; sub-regional economic
  zones 85–8
Regulation (EEC) No.519/94 74
Regulation (EEC) No.958/93 75
Regulation (EEC) No.2532/78 62, 63
Regulation (EEC) No.3030/93 75
Regulation (EEC) No.3286/80 63
Regulation (EEC) No.3420/83 63, 74
Regulation (EEC) No.1765/82 74
Regulation (EEC) No.1766/82 62, 74
Regulations for the Administration of
  Foreign Investment Banks and Sino-
  Foreign Joint Venture Banks in
  Shanghai 267
Regulations for the Administration of
  Foreign Investment Banks and Sino-
  Foreign Joint Venture Banks in
  Special Economic Zones 267
Regulations for the Administration of
  Foreign Investment Financial
  Institutions 263, 267
Renault 143, 144
Renminbi deposits 51, 211, 212, 224
representative office 208–9, 229–30
Riedel, J. 149–50
Robbins, K. 167
Robinson, G. 3, 131–46, 287
Robock, S. 98

Roehrig, M. 250
Rogers, G. 219
Romania 7, 8, 63, 64, 78
Root, F. 220, 222
Rootes, Lord 133
Rose, P. 208
round-tripping 30
Ruggiero, R. 36
Rugman, A. 132

Stones, I. 3, 131–46, 287
Stopford, J.M. 222, 231
Storper, M. 167, 168, 172, 178
Sabel, C. 168
Sagari, S. 219
Saiag 141
Salais, R. 168
Saxenian, A. 167, 168
Scania 144
Schrouth, F. 231, 253, 255
Schultz, S. 277–8
Science, Technology and Industry of
  National Defence Commission 48
Scoville, W. 103
Shan, W. 255
Shanghai 37, 136, 140; automotive
  industry 134, 141, 143; banking 210,
  211; Bell Telephone Equipment
  Manufacturing Co. 110, 199;
  Belling 110; -EK Chor 109, 110;
  insurance industry 245, 247, 248, 249,
  258, 259; Jiao Tong University 259;
  regionalism 86; Tractor Factory 142;
  Volkswagen 109, 110, 136, 140, 143;
  Yaohua 110; *see also* Pudong area
Shanghai Measures 245, 246, 249
Shenyang 136, 247, 258; Life Insurance
  Company Ltd 242
Shenzhen 20, 51, 211; banking 224;
  insurance industry 239, 247, 249, 258;
  Konka 110; Special Economic
  Zones 86
Shougang Corporation 277
Shutt, J. 168
Sichun Life Insurance Company
  Ltd 242
Siemens 140, 198, 199
Singapore 13, 14, 183; Association of
  Southeast Asian Nations 82, 94;
  banking 221; foreign direct
  investment 28, 30; Generalised
  System of Preferences 64, 65;
  outward investment from China 278,

312   Index

Singapore (*cont'*.)
   281; re-exports of China origin 15;
   regionalism 84, 85; technology
   intensiveness of trade with China 116,
   119–26; Telecom 203;
   telecommunications services 193, 201,
   203
Singapore–Johor–Riau (Sijori) zone 86,
   87
Single European Market 8, 84, 157, 160
Sino-British Joint Declaration
   (December 1984) 36
Sit, V. 179
Skipper, H. 237, 238
Slater, J. 5, 269–82, 284–7
Slovak Republic 8
Slovenia 65
small and medium-sized enterprises 281,
   287
Soames, C. 60–1
Société Générale (France) 216
Sogefi 141
South Africa 70, 71, 72
South America 7, 8
South Asian Association for Regional
   Cooperation 81–5, 88–90, 92–4
South Korea 10; anti-dumping
   proceedings 70, 71, 72; automotive
   industry 131, 133, 135, 143;
   banking 221; foreign direct
   investment 28; Generalised System of
   Preferences 64, 65; insurance
   industry 241; regionalism 91;
   technology intensiveness of trade with
   China 118
South Pacific Forum 84
Spain 8, 24; anti-dumping
   proceedings 70, 72; banking 218;
   foreign direct investment 28, 29;
   outward investment from China 279;
   technology transfer 105, 106; toy
   manufacture 158, 160–1, 162
Special Administrative Region of
   China 36
Special Economic Zones 47, 55, 56;
   banking 209–10; insurance
   industry 260; Shenzhen 4
Spratley Islands 91
Sprint (US) 203
Sri Lanka 70, 82, 83, 94
State Administration of Foreign
   Exchange Control of China 51,
   273

State Administration for Industry and
   Commerce 53
State Commission for Economics and
   Trade 49
State Council 18, 47, 48; banking 207,
   209, 210; foreign direct investment
   reform 52, 53; taxation system
   reform 54, 55; technology
   transfer 101; telecommunications
   services 188, 190
State Economic and Trade
   Commission 48
State Planning Commission 48, 49, 50,
   138
State Planning Committee 138
State Science and Technology
   Commission 48, 50
State-Owned Enterprises 139
Standard Chartered Bank 213, 216, 217,
   219
Standard International Trade
   Classification 18, 117
Stelux 182, 183, 184
Stewart, S. 103
Steyr 143, 144
Strange, R. 1, 2, 5, 7–40, 59–80, 114–28,
   132, 228–62, 284, 285
Strange, S. 156, 157, 159
sub-regional economic zones 85–8, 91
subsidiaries/affiliates 209
Sumatra 87
Summit of the Americas 93
Sun Alliance 259
Sung, Y.-W. 10, 16, 26, 30, 32
Supplementary Provisions
   (insurance) 246, 249
Sweden 8, 28, 116, 199, 218, 279
Switzerland 4, 9; ASUAG (holding
   company) 172, 176; banking 216,
   218, 220; EBAUCHE S.A.
   (trust) 171; Electronics and
   Microtechnological Centre 174;
   European Union/China trade 26;
   foreign direct investment 28, 29;
   insurance industry 243, 247, 248; Jura
   Arc region 166, 167, 173, 175;
   regionalism 83; Société Suisse de
   Microélectronique et d'Horlogerie
   (SMH) 176; Statut de
   l'Horlogerie 172; SWATCH 176,
   180, 184; Swiss Bank
   Corporation 215; technology
   intensiveness of trade with China 116;

technology transfer 110; Union de Branches Annexes de l'Horlogerie (UBAH) 171; Watch Federation 171; watch industry 168, 171–6, 178, 179, 181, 182, 184

T&N 141
Tai Kan insurance company 239
Taikang Life Insurance Company 242
Taiwan 10, 183, 285; anti-dumping proceedings 71, 72; automotive industry 135, 141; banking 220, 221; Customs Territory 35; European Union trade policy 60, 61; foreign direct investment 28, 29, 30, 52–3; and Hong Kong 13, 14, 16, 18; insurance industry 241; outward investment from China 278, 281; re-export trade 15, 16, 17, 19; regionalism 88, 89, 90, 91; technology intensiveness of trade with China 114, 116, 118–26; technology transfer 108; telecommunications services 193; World Trade Organization 34, 36
Taiyuan Life Insurance Company Ltd 243
Tajikistan 82, 94
Takayama, Y. 131, 136
Tan, G. 83
Tan, R. 87
Tan, Z. 190, 192
Tang, M. 87
taxation system, reform of 54–6
Taylor, R. 249, 260
technology: appropriate/ inappropriate 99; contractual/ internalised 107; embodiment: hardware/software 99, 100, 101, 103; explicit/codified 99, 104; high/low 99, 102; *see also* technology intensiveness of trade with China; technology transfer
technology intensiveness of trade 114–28; main trading partners 115–20; re-export trade through Hong Kong 123–6; technology composition of trade 121–3
technology transfer, Europe's role in 98–111; through contracts 103–6; through foreign direct investment 106–8; defining 'technology' and 'technology transfer' 98–100; experience 100–3; qualitative considerations 109–10
Teece, D. 99
Telecommunications Law 191, 204
telecommunications services 188–206; foreign firms, implications for strategies of 195–8; history 189–90; key European entrants and leading rivals 198–204; market entry models 193–5; modernisation, emerging liberalised environment and foreign participation 190–3
Telstra-Australia 203
Temic 141
Tenneco 141
textile agreements 66–9
Textiles Department 138
Thailand: anti-dumping proceedings 71, 72, 183; Association of Southeast Asian Nations 82, 94; automotive industry 145; foreign direct investment 28, 30; Greater Bangkok zone 87; outward investment from China 278; regionalism 83, 85, 86, 87, 92, 93; technology transfer 109, 110
Thant, M. 86
Tian An insurance company 239, 242
Tiananmen Square 73, 105
Tianjin 136, 210, 247, 249, 258; Life Insurance Company Ltd 243
Timex 184
Tokico 141
Tokio Fire & Marine 240, 243, 248
Tomlinson, J. 252
Tomy 154
Tong Guang Electronics Corporation 200
Tooze, R. 156
Toy Manufacturers of Europe 147, 156, 159, 160, 161, 162
Toyota 132, 135, 136, 142
Toys R Us 155
Tracy, N. 29–30
Trade Agreement 1978 1, 23, 61–3, 64, 67, 69
Trade and Economic Cooperation Agreement 1985 61, 69
trade policy and bargaining models 160–1
transnational corporations 235, 238, 281
Treaty of Amity and Cooperation 88

Treaty on European Union 8
Triad 54, 282
TRW 141
Tse, L. 3, 147–64
Tsui, E. 150–2
Tumen River Area Development Project 2, 87, 91, 92
Turkey 71, 72, 82, 84, 89, 91, 94
Turkmenistan 82, 94
turnkey arrangements 100, 103
Tushman, M. 173
Tyco Toys Inc 154, 161

Ukraine 91
Unicom 202
United Kingdom 14, 24, 286; automotive industry 133; banking 214, 216, 218, 220; foreign
United Kingdom (*cont.*)
  direct investment 28, 29, 53–4; insurance industry 239, 240, 247, 256; outward investment from China 271, 277, 279, 280; technology intensiveness of trade with China 116, 118, 119–21, 123, 125–6; technology transfer 105, 106, 110; telecommunications services 190, 202, 204; toy manufacture 147, 150–2, 156, 158–62
United Nations 10, 109, 117, 236; Conference on Trade and Development 63, 269; Development Programme 87; Economic and Social Commission for Asia and the Pacific 87
United States 1, 2, 3, 59, 103, 286; anti-dumping proceedings 70, 71, 72; automotive industry 131, 132, 135, 141, 143, 145; banking 208, 214, 224; European Union trade policy 60; European Union/China trade 24, 26; flexible production networks 167, 168, 171, 172, 184; foreign direct investment 28, 29, 30, 53, 54; and Hong Kong 13, 14, 16, 18; insurance industry 5, 228, 239–40, 243, 247–9, 259; joint ventures in insurance industry 255; location choice in insurance industry 256, 257, 258; Office of Technology Assessment 99; operating licences in insurance industry 251, 252; outward investment from China 271, 277, 279, 280; re-export trade 14, 15, 16, 17, 19;

regionalism 91, 94; technology intensiveness of trade with China 114–27; technology transfer 99, 104, 105, 106, 108; telecommunications services 200, 201, 202–3, 204; United Nations embargo 177; World Trade Organization 34, 35, 36; toy manu-facture 149, 150, 151–2, 154, 155, 156, 161, 162; *see also* insurance industry
Ure, J. 190, 191, 192
Uruguay 71
Uruguay Round 7, 8, 33, 35, 64, 67, 81
Uzbekistan 82, 94

Vahlne, J.-E. 222
Valeo 141
value-added tax 54
Van den Bulcke, D. 272, 275–6
Vanhonacker, W. 251
Varity 141
Vermulst, E. 72
Vietnam 74, 90, 91; Association of Southeast Asian Nations 82, 94; banking 220; regionalism 87, 91; telecommunications services 193; Trade Agreement 1978 63
Volkswagen 132, 133, 137, 138, 141, 142, 144; *see also* Shanghai
Volvo 143, 144

watch industry in Switzerland and Hong Kong/China 166–85; capabilities and adaptation mechanisms 170–1; flexible production networks as model for economic development 167–8; Hong Kong/China: 'merchant-manufacturing' and its limits 176–84; production networks, adaptive efficacy of 168–70; Switzerland: commitment to precision and its limits 171–6
Watkins, D. 72
WABCO 141
Waheed, A. 232
Wakabayashi, M. 17, 29, 115
Walker 141
Wall, D. 81
Wallerstein, I. 168
Walmart 155
Walter, I. 219
Wang, L. 2, 114–28

Wang, Y. 255
Warwick, W. 190, 191
Wells Jr, L.T. 222, 231
Westphal, L. 102
Whitla, P. 2, 98–111
Whitley, R. 178
Whittington, R. 168
wholly foreign-owned enterprises 50, 107, 251
wholly-owned subsidiary 230, 232
Williamson, O. 168, 169, 170, 176, 180
Winterthur China Ltd 240, 248
Winterthur Swiss Insurance Ltd 243
Wolff, A. 99
Wong, S.-L. 179
Wong, Y.C. 213
World Bank 73, 272, 287
World Trade Organization 2, 7, 10, 32–6; Agreement on Textiles and Clothing 67, 69; automotive industry 139, 141; China Working Party 34; European Union trade policy in 1990s 73, 74, 75; flexible production networks 181; foreign direct investment 31; foreign trade system reform 47; insurance industry 250, 251; policy reform 56, 57; Protocol on Accession 36, 74; regionalism 81, 85, 89, 90, 91, 93, 94–5; toy manufacture 162; *see also* General Agreement on Tariffs and Trade
Wu, J. 270–1
Wu, X. 5, 228–62
Wu Yi, Madam (Minister of Foreign Trade) 48, 160
Wu Zhenquan 105
Wuhan 136, 140

Xiamen 247, 258; International Bank 211, 223–4; Life Insurance Company Ltd 242
Xian 239, 258
Xi'an Janssen 110
Xiantan Life Insurance Company Ltd 243
Xin Hua insurance company 239–40, 242
Xinjiang 92; Agricultural Insurance Company 239, 242; Tianshan 110

Yahuda, M. 141
Yanbian autonomous prefecture 92
Yi, Z. 273
Yong An Property Insurance Company Ltd 239, 242
Young, S. 103
Yue, X. 61, 62–3, 68–9, 73
Yugoslavia 70, 71, 72
Yukawa, T. 132, 138
Yunnan Province 87, 92, 93

ZF 140
Zhan, J. 269, 272, 274, 275, 276, 277, 278
Zhang, H.-Y. 272, 275–6
Zhao Ziyang 98
Zheng, J. 253
Zhong Hong Life Insurance Company 243, 248
Zhou Enlai 61
Zhu, G. 190
Zhuang, J. 31
Zhuhai 86; Life Insurance Company Ltd 243
Zita, K. 190
Zodoria, D. 100